# Cer Europe

## Quality camping & caravanning sites

**Alan Rogers**

2008

INSPECTED CAMPSITES & SELECTED

Compiled by: Alan Rogers Guides Ltd

Designed by: Paul Effenberg, Vine Design Ltd

Maps created by Customised Mapping (01769 540044) contain background data provided by GisDATA Ltd
Maps are © Alan Rogers Guides and GisDATA Ltd 2008

© Alan Rogers Guides Ltd 2008

Published by: Alan Rogers Guides Ltd,
Spelmonden Old Oast, Goudhurst, Kent TN17 1HE
www.alanrogers.com  Tel: 01580 214000

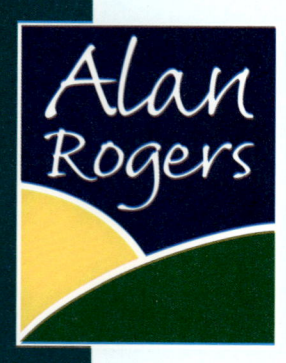

British Library Cataloguing-in-Publication Data:
A catalogue record for this book is available from the British Library.

ISBN-13  978-1-906215-04-0

Printed in Great Britain by J H Haynes & Co Ltd

While every effort is taken to ensure the accuracy of the information given in this book, no liability can be accepted by the authors or publishers for any loss, damage or injury caused by errors in, or omissions from, the information given.

All rights reserved. No part of this publication may be reproduced, stored in a retrieval system or transmitted, in any form or by any means, electronic, mechanical, photocopying, recording or otherwise, without prior permission in writing from the publishers.

# Contents

- **4** Introduction
- **6** How To Use This Guide
- **10** Alan Rogers Awards
- **13** Introduction to Central Europe

- **14** Greece
- **34** Croatia
- **64** Slovenia
- **78** Romania
- **84** Hungary
- **106** Slovakia

- **114** Czech Republic
- **136** Poland
- **151** Lithuania
- **158** Latvia
- **165** Estonia
- **171** Journey to Russia

- **177** Travelling in Europe
- **182** Open All Year, Dogs
- **189** Reports by Readers
- **191** Maps

- **201** Town and Village Index
- **203** Index by Campsite Number
- **205** Index by Country and Campsite Name
- **207** Questionnaire

# the Alan Rogers approach

**Welcome to the 2008 Edition**

Last year we celebrated the publication of the fortieth editions of the Alan Rogers Guides. Since Alan Rogers published the first campsite guide that bore his name, the range has expanded to six titles covering 27 countries. What's more, Alan Rogers Guides are now firmly established in the Netherlands too.

In 2004 the European Union welcomed ten new members and the resulting publicity has lead to an increased interest in visiting the fascinatng and welcoming countries of Central Europe. Several European guides list camping and caravanning sites in these countries but very little information is available in English and none providing impartially written, detailed reports on campsites that have been individually inspected and selected. Once again, we hope you enjoy some happy and safe travels – and some pleasurable 'armchair touring' in the meantime!

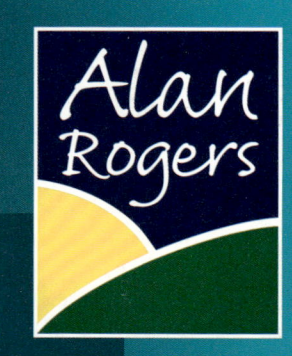

## A question of quality

The criteria we use when inspecting and selecting sites are numerous, but the most important by far is the question of good quality. People want different things from their choice of campsite so we try to include a range of campsite 'styles' to cater for a wide variety of preferences: from those seeking a small peaceful campsite in the heart of the countryside, to visitors looking for an 'all singing, all dancing' site in a popular seaside resort. Those with more specific interests, such as sporting facilities, cultural events or historical attractions, are also catered for.

The size of the site, whether it's part of a chain or privately owned, makes no difference in terms of it being required to meet our exacting standards in respect of its quality and it being 'fit for purpose'. In other words, irrespective of the size of the site, or the number of facilities it offers, we consider and evaluate the welcome, the pitches, the sanitary facilities, the cleanliness, the general maintenance and even the location.

> "…the campsites included in this book have been chosen entirely on merit, and no payment of any sort is made by them for their inclusion."
>
> Alan Rogers, 1968

**INSPECTED & SELECTED SINCE 1968**

# Welcome to the 2008 Edition

**INSPECTED CAMPSITES & SELECTED**

### Expert opinions

We rely on our dedicated team of Site Assessors, all of whom are experienced campers, caravanners or motorcaravanners, to visit and recommend sites. Each year they travel some 100,000 miles around Europe inspecting new campsites for the guide and re-inspecting the existing ones. Our thanks are due to them for their enthusiastic efforts, their diligence and integrity.

We also appreciate the feedback we receive from many of our readers and we always make a point of following up complaints, suggestions or recommendations for possible new sites. Of course we get a few grumbles too – but it really is a few, and those we do receive usually relate to overcrowding or to poor maintenance during the peak school holiday period. Please bear in mind that, although we are interested to hear about any complaints, we have no contractual relationship with the campsites featured in our guides and are therefore not in a position to intervene in any dispute between a reader and a campsite.

HIGHLY RESPECTED BY SITE OWNERS AND READERS ALIKE, THERE IS NO BETTER GUIDE WHEN IT COMES TO FORMING AN INDEPENDENT VIEW OF A CAMPSITE'S QUALITY. WHEN YOU NEED TO BE CONFIDENT IN YOUR CHOICE OF CAMPSITE, YOU NEED THE ALAN ROGERS GUIDE.

- ☑ Sites only included on merit
- ☑ Sites cannot pay to be included
- ☑ Independently inspected, rigorously assessed
- ☑ Impartial reviews
- ☑ Over 40 years of expertise

### Independent and honest

Whilst the content and scope of the Alan Rogers guides have expanded considerably since the early editions, our selection of campsites still employs exactly the same philosophy and criteria as defined by Alan Rogers in 1968.

### 'telling it how it is'

Firstly, and most importantly, our selection is based entirely on our own rigorous and independent inspection and selection process. Campsites cannot buy their way into our guides – indeed the extensive Site Report which is written by us, not by the site owner, is provided free of charge so we are free to say what we think and to provide an honest, 'warts and all' description. This is written in plain English and without the use of confusing icons or symbols.

5

Written in plain English, our guides are exceptionally easy to use, although a few words of explanation may be helpful. This guide is divided firstly by country, subsequently (in the case of larger countries) by region. For a particular area the town index at the back provides more direct access.

## The Site Reports – *Example of an entry*

### Site Number Site name
Postal Address (including county)
Telephone number. Email address

A description of the site in which we try to give an idea of its general features – its size, its situation, its strengths and its weaknesses. This section should provide a picture of the site itself with reference to the facilities that are provided and if they impact on its appearance or character. We include details on pitch numbers, electricity (with amperage), hardstandings etc. in this section as pitch design, planning and terracing affects the site's overall appearance. Similarly we include reference to pitches used for caravan holiday homes, chalets, and the like. Importantly at the end of this column we indicate if there are any restrictions, e.g. no tents, no children, naturist sites.

**Country**

### Facilities
Lists more specific information on the site's facilities and amenities and, where available, the dates when these facilities are open (if not for the whole season). Off site: here we give distances to various local amenities, for example, local shops, the nearest beach, plus our featured activities (bicycle hire, fishing, horse riding, boat launching). Where we have space we list suggestions for activities and local tourist attractions.

**Open:** Site opening dates.

### Directions
Separated from the main text in order that they may be read and assimilated more easily by a navigator en-route. Bear in mind that road improvement schemes can result in road numbers being altered.

GPS: references are provided as we obtain them for satellite navigation systems (in degrees and minutes).

### Charges 2008

## Indexes
Our three indexes allow you to find sites by country, site number and name, by country and site name (alphabetically) or by the town or village where the site is situated.

## Campsite Maps
The maps of each country are designed to show the country in relation to others and will help you to identify the approximate position of each campsite. The colour of the campsite number indicates whether it is open all year or not. You will certainly need more detailed maps and we have found the Michelin atlas to be particularly useful.

## Facilities
### Toilet blocks
We assume that toilet blocks will be equipped with a reasonable amount of British style WCs, washbasins with hot and cold water and hot showers with dividers or curtains, and will have all necessary shelves, hooks, plugs and mirrors. We also assume that there will be an identified chemical toilet disposal point, and that the campsite will provide water and waste water drainage points and bin areas. If not the case, we comment. We do mention certain features that some readers find important: washbasins in cubicles, facilities for babies, facilities for those with disabilities and motorcaravan service points. Readers with disabilities are advised to contact the site of their choice to ensure that facilities are appropriate to their needs.

### Shop
Basic or fully supplied, and opening dates.

### Bars, restaurants, takeaway facilities and entertainment
We try hard to supply opening and closing dates (if other than the campsite opening dates) and to identify if there are discos or other entertainment.

### Children's play areas
Fenced and with safety surface (e.g. sand, bark or pea-gravel).

### Swimming pools
If particularly special, we cover in detail in our main campsite description but reference is always included under our Facilities listings. Opening dates, charges and levels of supervision are provided where we have been notified.

### Leisure facilities
For example, playing fields, bicycle hire, organised activities and entertainment.

### Dogs
If dogs are not accepted or restrictions apply, we state it here. Check the quick reference list at the back of the guide.

### Off site
This briefly covers leisure facilities, tourist attractions, restaurants etc. nearby.

## Charges
These are the latest provided to us by the sites. In those few cases where 2007 or 2008 prices are not given, we try to give a general guide. We normally use the local currency but some campsites outside the Euro zone are happy to accept Euros and where this is the case we quote charges in this currency.

## Reservations
Necessary for high season (roughly mid-July to mid-August) in popular holiday areas (ie beach resorts). Contact the campsite(s) of your choice direct using the contact details shown in the site reports.

### Telephone numbers
The numbers given assume you are actually IN the country concerned. If you are phoning from the UK remember that a first '0' is usually disregarded and replaced by the appropriate country code. For the latest details you should refer to an up-to-date telephone directory.

## Opening dates
Are those advised to us during the early autumn of the previous year – sites can, and sometimes do, alter these dates before the start of the following season, often for good reasons. If you intend to visit shortly after a published opening date, or shortly before the closing date, it is wise to check that it will actually be open at the time required. Similarly some parks operate a restricted service during the low season, only opening some of their facilities (e.g. swimming pools) during the main season; where we know about this, and have the relevant dates, we indicate it – again if you are at all doubtful it is wise to check.

## Using the Alan Rogers Guides

Some site owners are very laid back when it comes to opening and closing dates. They may not be fully ready by their stated opening dates – grass and hedges may not all be cut or perhaps only limited sanitary facilities open. At the end of the season they also tend to close down some facilities and generally wind down prior to the closing date. Bear this in mind if you are travelling early or late in the season – it is worth phoning ahead.

The Camping Cheque low season touring system goes some way to addressing this in that participating campsites are encouraged to have all key facilities open and running by the opening date and to remain fully operational until the closing date.

**WHETHER YOU'RE AN 'OLD HAND' IN TERMS OF CAMPING AND CARAVANNING OR ARE CONTEMPLATING YOUR FIRST TRIP, A REGULAR READER OF OUR GUIDES OR A NEW 'CONVERT', WE WISH YOU WELL IN YOUR TRAVELS AND HOPE WE HAVE BEEN ABLE TO HELP IN SOME WAY.**

**WE ARE, OF COURSE, ALSO OUT AND ABOUT OURSELVES, VISITING SITES, TALKING TO OWNERS AND READERS, AND GENERALLY CHECKING ON STANDARDS AND NEW DEVELOPMENTS.**

We wish all our readers thoroughly enjoyable Camping and Caravanning in 2008 – favoured by good weather of course!

**THE ALAN ROGERS TEAM**

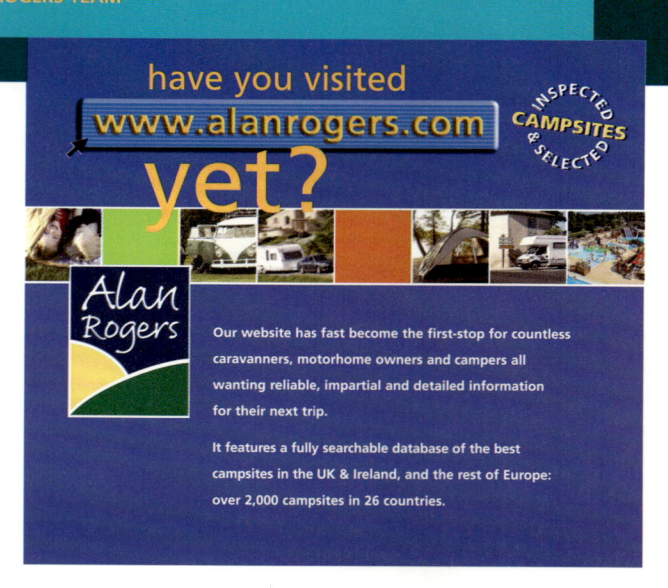

---

have you visited
**www.alanrogers.com**
yet?

INSPECTED CAMPSITES & SELECTED

Alan Rogers

Our website has fast become the first-stop for countless caravanners, motorhome owners and campers all wanting reliable, impartial and detailed information for their next trip.

It features a fully searchable database of the best campsites in the UK & Ireland, and the rest of Europe: over 2,000 campsites in 26 countries.

# Countries

Countries of Central Europe

- Estonia
- Latvia
- Lithuania
- Poland
- Czech Republic
- Slovakia
- Romania
- Hungary
- Slovenia
- Croatia
- Greece

# the Alan Rogers awards

In 2004 we introduced the first ever Alan Rogers Campsite Awards.

Before making our awards, we carefully consider more than 2000 campsites featured in our guides, taking into account comments from our site assessors, our head office team and, of course, our readers.

Our award winners come from the four corners of Europe, from southern Portugal to the Czech Republic, and this year we are making awards to campsites in 14 different countries.

Needless to say, it's an extremely difficult task to choose our eventual winners, but we believe that we have identified a number of campsites with truly outstanding characteristics.

In each case, we have selected an outright winner, along with two highly commended runners-up.

Listed below are full details of each of our award categories and our winners for 2007.

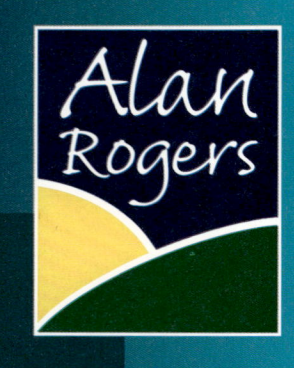

### Alan Rogers Progress Award 2007

This award reflects the hard work and commitment undertaken by particular site owners to improve and upgrade their site.

**WINNER**

| AU0060 | Natterersee, Austria |

**RUNNERS-UP**

| BE0712 | Ile de Faigneul, Belgium |
| DE3672 | Elbsee, Germany |

### Alan Rogers Welcome Award 2007

This award takes account of sites offering a particularly friendly welcome and maintaining a friendly ambience throughout reader's holidays.

**WINNER**

| FR24090 | Soleil Plage, France |

**RUNNERS-UP**

| IR9610 | Mannix Point, Ireland |
| UK4640 | Goosewood, England |

### Alan Rogers Active Holiday Award 2007

This award reflects sites in outstanding locations which are ideally suited for active holidays, notably walking or cycling, but which could extend to include such activities as winter sports or water sports

**WINNER**

| DK2170 | Klim Strand, Denmark |

**RUNNERS-UP**

| FR09060 | Pre Lombard, France |
| DE3450 | Munstertal, Germany |

### Alan Rogers Motorhome Award 2007

Motorhome sales are increasing and this award acknowledges sites which, in our opinion, have made outstanding efforts to welcome motorhome clients.

**WINNER**

| PO8210 | Campismo Albufeira, Portugal |

**RUNNERS-UP**

| IR9650 | Woodlands Park, Ireland |
| FR29180 | Les Embruns, France |

## Alan Rogers 4 Seasons Award 2007

This award is made to outstanding sites with extended opening dates and which welcome clients to a uniformly high standard throughout the year.

### WINNER

| CH9575 | Eienwaldi, Switzerland |
|---|---|

### RUNNERS-UP

| AU0440 | Schluga, Austria |
|---|---|
| IT6814 | Flaminio, Italy |

## Alan Rogers Seaside Award 2007

This award is made for sites which we feel are outstandingly suitable for a really excellent seaside holiday.

### WINNER

| ES8030 | Nautic Almata, Spain |
|---|---|

### RUNNERS-UP

| FR85210 | Les Ecureuils, France |
|---|---|
| IT6036 | Ca Pasquali, Italy |

## Alan Rogers Country Award 2007

This award contrasts with our former award and acknowledges sites which are attractively located in delightful, rural locations.

### WINNER

| UK1020 | Oakdown, England |
|---|---|

### RUNNERS-UP

| CZ4896 | Camping Country, Czech Republic |
|---|---|
| NL5980 | De Roos, Netherlands |

## Alan Rogers Rented Accommodation Award 2007

Given the increasing importance of rented accommodation on many campsites, we feel that it is important to acknowledge sites which have made a particular effort in creating a high quality 'rented accommodation' park.

### WINNER

| ES8480 | Sanguli, Spain |
|---|---|

### RUNNERS-UP

| NL5575 | Scheldeoord, Netherlands |
|---|---|
| CR6736 | Valdaliso, Croatia |

## Alan Rogers Unique Site Award 2007

This award acknowledges sites with unique, outstanding features – something which simply cannot be found elsewhere and which is an important attraction of the site.

### WINNER

| FR78040 | Huttopia Rambouillet, France |
|---|---|

### RUNNERS-UP

| FR80070 | Ferme des Aulnes, France |
|---|---|
| UK1590 | Exe Valley, England |

## Alan Rogers Family Site Award 2007

Many sites claim to be child friendly but this award acknowledges the sites we feel to be the very best in this respect.

### WINNER

| NL5985 | Beerze Bulten, Netherlands |
|---|---|

### RUNNERS-UP

| UK0170 | Trevella, England |
|---|---|
| ES8540 | Torre del Sol, Spain |
| IT6014 | Villaggio Turistico Internazionale, Italy |

## Alan Rogers Readers' Award 2007

In 2005 we introduced a new award, which we believe to be the most important, our Readers' Award. We simply invited our readers (by means of an on-line poll at www.alanrogers.com) to nominate the site they enjoyed most. The outright winner for 2007 is:

### WINNER

| ES8530 | Playa Montroig Resort, Spain |
|---|---|

## Alan Rogers Special Award 2007

A special award is made to acknowledge sites which we feel have overcome a very significant setback, and have, not only returned to their former condition, but has added extra amenities and can therefore be fairly considered to be even better than before. In 2007 we acknowledged two campsites, which have undergone major problems and have made highly impressive recoveries.

| CH9510 | Aareg, Switzerland |
|---|---|
| IT6845 | San Nicola, Italy |

# Need a **low cost ferry?**

Do you have a caravan, motorhome or trailer and want the best deal on your cross-Channel ferry? Then visit www.ferries4campers.co.uk for the lowest prices for campers and caravanners from major ferry operators. Now there's no need to 'go round the houses' for numerous quotes – all the best deals are in one place.

**It couldn't be simpler** - just click, choose a ferry and book...

## www.ferries4campers.co.uk

- Special deals for caravans and motorhomes
- View routes and compare prices
- Book online at any time of day
- Secure payment guaranteed
- Fully searchable by route and operator
- Instant real-time availability provided

## ferries4campers.co.uk

**norfolk**line DOVER - DUNKERQUE FERRIES | P&O Ferries | EURO TUNNEL | SEAFRANCE DOVER - CALAIS FERRIES | Brittany Ferries | Condor ferries

## Introduction to Central Europe

May 2004 saw the accession of ten new countries into the European Union, eight of which are featured in this guide. Romania and Bulgaria joined the EU in January 2007 and we are pleased to feature a selection of Romanian campsites. We have plans to visit Bulgaria in the future.

We continue to be impressed by the overall quality improvements of many campsites in these countries, and have been struck by the numbers of campers, caravanners and motorcaravanners venturing into this 'New Europe'.

Croatia, of course, is outside the EU, but we feel that this guide would be incomplete without its inclusion, given the quality of many campsites and their interest as destinations.

We wish you well on your travels and hope that this guide will help you discover some fine campsites in regions with real appeal.

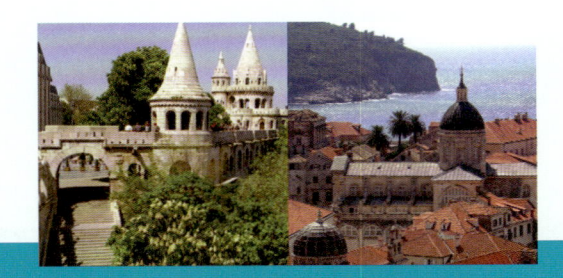

We would like to thank the Audiovisual Library of the European Commisssion and the various National Tourist Offices for making photographs available for this guide.

# Greece

**MAP 1**

The country's coastline offers huge variety – sheltered bays and coves, golden stretches of sand with dunes, pebbly beaches, coastal caves with steep rocks and volcanic black sand and coastal wetlands.

Stretching from the Balkans in the north to the south Aegean, Greece shares borders with Albania, Macedonia, Bulgaria and Turkey.

It is above all a mountainous country – the Pindus range forms the backbone of mainland Greece, extending through central Greece into the Peloponnese and Crete. The majority of islands throughout the Aegean are, in fact, the mountain peaks of the now submerged landmass of Aegeis, which was once the link between mainland Greece and Asia Minor. Mount Olympus in the north of the country, known from Greek mythology as the abode of the gods, is the highest mountain (2,917 m).

Six thousand islands are scattered in the Aegean and Ionian Seas, a unique phenomenon on the continent of Europe; of these islands, only 227 are inhabited.

After a seven-year dictatorship in Greece, a referendum was held in 1974 and the system of government changed from a constitutional monarchy to a Presidential Parliamentary Democracy; Greece has been a member of the EU since 1981.

**Population**
10.9 million

**Capital**
Athens with a population of 3.2 million.

**Climate**
Greece has a Mediterranean climate with plenty of sunshine, mild temperatures and a limited amount of rainfall. In summer the dry hot days are cooled by seasonal winds called the meltemi, while mountainous regions have generally lower temperatures. The winters are mild in lowland areas, yet, the mountains are usually snow-covered.

**Language**
Greek, but most of the people connected to tourism and the younger generations currently practice English and sometimes German, Italian or French.

**Currency**
Euro

**Time**
GMT + 2 (GMT + 3 from last Sunday in March to last Sunday in October).

**Telephone**
The country code for Greece is 00 30. Mobile telephone coverage is generally good in most parts of the country except for certain areas: mountains and on some small islands.

# Greece

GREECE IS, OF COURSE, THE LAND OF ANCIENT LEGENDS, SITES AND TREASURES, AND IS THE HOME OF THE OLYMPIC GAMES, BUT PRESENT-DAY GREECE OFFERS MUCH MORE – FASCINATING NATURAL GEOGRAPHY, A 16,000 KILOMETRE HOLIDAY COASTLINE OF ISLANDS AND BEACHES, AND A WARM AND VARIED MODERN CULTURE.

## Public Holidays

New Year's Day 1 Jan; Epiphany 6 Jan; Shrove Monday Orth. Easter; Independence Day 25 Mar; Easter: Good Friday, Easter Sunday and Easter Monday (Orthodox); Labour Day 1 May; Whit Sunday and Monday (Orthodox); Assumption Day 15 Aug; Ochi Day (National Fest) 28 Oct; Christmas 25/26 Dec.

## Motoring

Speed limits are 100-120 km/h on highways unless otherwise posted; 50 km/h in residential areas unless otherwise marked. An international driver's license is required. Road signs are written in Greek and repeated phonetically in English. Drive on the right. Passing on the right side is strictly prohibited. Drivers and passengers must wear safety belts. Take special care when crossing unguarded level railway crossings. Road tolls exist on two highways in Greece, one leading to Northern Greece and the other to the Peloponnese. Greece has one of the highest rates of traffic fatalities in Europe. Visitors must be prepared to drive defensively and observe caution as pedestrians.

## Tourist Office

Greek National Tourism Organisation
4 Conduit Street, London, W1S 2DJ
Tel: 020 7495 9300 (Enquiries & Information)
Fax: 020 7287 1369
Email: info@gnto.co.uk
Internet: http://www.gnto.co.uk/

## British Embassy

1 Ploutarchou Street, 106 75 Athens
Tel: (30) 210 727 2600

## Places of interest

*Acropolis*: dominating Athens, the Acropolis is one of the archetypal images of Western civilisation.

*Firá:* the island capital of Firá is one of several villages that teeter at the edge of Thíra's caldera cliff (Santorini).

*Olympia*: one of the most important sites of antiquity, dedicated to the father of the gods, Zeus. Olympia is the birthplace of the Olympic games.

*Delphi:* in ancient times considered to be the centre of the known world, the place where heaven and earth met. This was the place on earth where man was closest to the gods.

## Cuisine of the region

*Souvlakia:* Grilled lamb on skewers.

*Yiouvetsi*: Lamb casserole with pasta and cheese.

*Dolmadakia me rizi:* Grapevine leaves stuffed with rice and herbs, then boiled.

*Keftedes:* Meatballs made from minced beef or veal and usually served as an appetiser.

*Amygdalota:* From the island of Hydra, and made from an almond and semolina dough shaped into a pear shape and baked.

*Baklava*: Sweet, spiced pastries with syrup covering.

# Greece

## GR8000 Camping Batis

40 Klm Kavala, Thessalonika Old Road, GR-65500 Kavala (E.Macedonia & Thrace)
Tel: 2510 24 3975. Email: info@batis-sa.gr

This site is ideally suited, both for those travelling to and from the Turkish border at Ipsala/Kipi and also for those wishing to explore the north of Greece. This refurbished, modern site also offers good low season camping opportunities and is likely to be very busy with families in the high season. Pitches are small and well shaded by tall trees. Istanbul is an easy day's drive away, even allowing for the border formalities and visas for entry into Turkey are swiftly obtained for € 15 ($20; they will not accept Turkish Lira or Sterling). Indeed, you can enjoy a wonderful stay in Istanbul without leaving Europe since you don't enter Asia until you cross the Sultan Mehmet toll bridge. A trip into Kavala (€ 5 by taxi) is well worth it, as is a meal at the Panos Zafira restaurant on the quayside.

### Facilities
Two excellent toilet blocks (refurbished in 2006) include good showers, WCs and washbasins. Sinks for dishwashing and clothes washing. Facilities for emptying chemical toilet. Restaurant with terrace. Bar and a managed beach. Paddling pool (1/6-1/9). Play area. English is spoken. Off site: Kavala and the Northern Greek coast.

**Open:** All year.

### Directions
From Central Greece leave the motorway at first exit for Kavala. Drive towards the town and site is on the right on an incline after a right hand bend. Driving from the Turkish border exit motorway at first Kavala exit and follow the old road into the town centre. Then follow the promenade out of town to site on the left after 4 km. GPS: N40:54.550 E24:22.400

### Charges 2007
Per unit incl. 2 persons        € 12,50 - € 20,50
No credit cards.

Check real time availability and at-the-gate prices...
www.alanrogers.com

## GR8120 Camping Poseidon Beach

Platamon-Pieria, GR-60065 Neos Panteleimonas (Central Macedonia)
Tel: **235 204 1654**

This site is located in a rural area at the foot of Mount Olympus, just off the motorway which follows the coast from Thessalonica to Athens. The area is known for its golden beaches and, as its name suggests, this campsite enjoys direct access. The 250 pitches are on level ground shaded by mature trees and a variety of shrubs and all have 16A electricity. There is a good restaurant, which is open for most of the season. The site is also close to the 10th century castle of Platamon, which is the principal attraction of the area. There may be some noise from the nearby railway and motorway.

### Facilities

Two modern and one refurbished sanitary blocks with mainly British style WCs (one Turkish toilet per block), open washbasins and controllable showers. Chemical disposal. Laundry sinks, washing machines and dryers. Covered dishwashing area. Shop, bar and restaurant (all May - Sept). Fishing.

**Open:** 1 March - 31 October.

### Directions

From E75 Thessaloniki - Athens motorway (toll road) turn left signed Neos Panteleimonas. Cross over railway bridge and turn left onto coastal road. In 500 m. turn right at campsite sign next to Camping Heraklia. Site is on right in 300 m. GPS: N40:00.778 E22:35.430

### Charges guide

| | |
|---|---|
| Per person | € 4,40 - € 5,00 |
| child (2-9 yrs) | € 2,35 - € 3,00 |
| pitch incl. car | € 5,90 - € 7,70 |
| electricity | € 3,40 |

## GR8125 Camping Comitsa

GR-63075 Nea Roda (Central Macedonia)
Tel: **237 703 1577**. Email: **info@camping-comitsa.gr**

Mount Athos is a Holy mountain to the Greeks and at 2,030 m. it is the highest point of Halkidiki's most easterly peninsula. Camping Comitsa is a modern site of the 'all singing, all dancing' variety (Greek style). It has 110 pitches, of which 45 are for tourers, although most will not be suitable for vehicles over 2.6 m. high because of the screens that provide much needed shade. In fact, if your outfit is over 2.8 m. look elsewhere. Having said that, if your vehicle is low enough the site offers excellent facilities in a fascinating location.

### Facilities

Two excellent toilet blocks include showers, WCs and washbasins. Two kitchens include sinks, electric hobs and fridges. Laundry with washing machine. Facilities for emptying chemical toilet. Well stocked shop. Bar. Restaurant. Club/TV room. Sandy beach in sheltered cove. Tents, rooms, bamboo huts and caravans to rent. Dogs are not accepted. Off site: Agio Oros, Ouranopoli (for boat trips) and Trypiti for the ferry to Amoliani.

**Open:** 1 May - 30 September.

### Directions

Site is 4.8 km. south of N Roda on Agio Oros on a road that is not shown on any map we could find. Driving south from Lerissos go through N Roda and at the football field (look for the floodlights) turn left and take the first right. The road bears left down to the coast. At the beach turn right and after 200 m. fork right and follow the unpaved road for 3.9 km. to the site. GPS: N40:22.552 E23:57.953

### Charges 2007

| | |
|---|---|
| Per unit incl. 2 persons | € 20,00 - € 25,00 |

## GR8130 Camping Delphini

GR-63075 Lerissos (Central Macedonia)
Tel: **237 702 2208**. Email: **info@campingdelphini.gr**

Just 27 km. south of the birthplace of Aristotle is the small town of Lerissos, on the peninsula of Agio Oros, famous for Mount Athos and the Byzantine monasteries. Camping Delphini offers a simple, quiet campsite with 70 pitches which are all for touring units, in a neat, wooded area. The dense trees provide ample shade, so there are none of those horizontal screens found on many Greek campsites. The restaurant and bar provide simple Greek meals and a place to chat to the locals in the cool shade of the terrace or under a parasol.

### Facilities

The toilet block includes showers, WCs (some Turkish) and washbasins. Kitchen with sinks, electric hobs and fridges. Laundry with washing machines. Facilities for emptying chemical toilet. Bar and simple restaurant. Off site: Agio Oros, Beach 200 m. Boat trips, watersports and parachute jumps.

**Open:** 1 May - 30 September.

### Directions

Camping Delphini is just 2 km. south of Lerissos on the main Agio Oros coast road.
GPS: N40:23.385 E23:53.590

### Charges guide

| | |
|---|---|
| Per person | € 3,54 |
| child | € 1,95 |
| pitch incl. electricity | € 5,16 - € 6,20 |

Check real time availability and at-the-gate prices...
www.alanrogers.com

## GR8135 Camping Kouyoni

GR-63100 Gerakini (Central Macedonia)
Tel: 237 105 2226. Email: kouyoni@acn.gr

The busy motorway south of Thessaloniki clearly shows the popularity of Halkidiki and this coastal area. Camping Kouyoni provides a site that is popular with local Greeks, who have had static caravans here for many years, and also has flats that are available to rent. With a total of 86 pitches only 40 are available for touring units and only a few of these are suitable for motorcaravans and larger caravans. There is limited space for car parking and this further restricts access. The pitches are more earth than grass and when we visited a thunderstorm quickly turned the pitch into mud.

### Facilities
Two excellent toilet blocks include showers, WCs and washbasins. Kitchen includes sinks, barbecues and fridges. Laundry with washing machines. Facilities for emptying chemical toilet. Small shop. Pool bar and restaurant. Swimming and paddling pools. Sandy beach. Off site: Mount Athos and Sithonia.

**Open:** 1 May - 30 September.

### Directions
Gerakini is about 80 km. south of Thessaloniki on the main road to Sithonia. You can either turn off to the village and beach and go east towards the site or stay on the main road and turn right just before a petrol station (well signed) to the site.

### Charges 2007
Per unit incl. 2 persons € 18,00 - € 20,90

## GR8140 Lacara Camping

Akti Koutloumoussi, GR-63088 Nikiti (Central Macedonia)
Tel: 210 894 2091. Email: info@lecara-camp.gr

This site had been described to us as having two bubbling springs and a stream flowing through it into a small marsh. It also has 10 km. of forest roads and paths in private woodland. It sounds idyllic, but please note the first sentence – this means mosquitoes and that is verified by the small shop's stock of citronella candles of every size and description and sprays to suit everyone. The 150 pitches that are suitable for caravans (out of a total of 250) are small and set among trees leading down to a sandy beach. Pitches are marked by low wooden rails and the buildings are basic. It rather reminded us of a 1960s scout camp and here all the toilets are Greek style (that's the same as Turkish).

### Facilities
Six basic toilet blocks include showers, WCs (Turkish style) and washbasins. Kitchens include sinks for dishwashing. Laundry with washing machine. Facilities for emptying chemical toilet. Beach bar. Small shop. Restaurant. Sandy beach. Bamboo huts and wooden bungalows to rent. Tennis. Off site: Sithonia and Mount Athos.

**Open:** 1 May - 30 September.

### Directions
Although the postal address is Nikiti the site is some considerable way south. Take the east coast road of Sithonia and site is 16 km. south of Vourvourou.
GPS: N40:10.237 E23:51.211

### Charges guide
| | |
|---|---|
| Per person | € 5,00 - € 6,00 |
| child (2-9 yrs) | € 3,00 - € 3,50 |
| pitch incl. electricity | € 11,80 - € 13,30 |

## GR8145 Camping Areti

GR-63081 Neos Marmaras (Central Macedonia)
Tel: 237 507 1430. Email: info@camping-areti.gr

If you imagine Greek campsites as being set immediately behind a small sandy beach in a quiet cove with pitches amongst the pine and olive trees which stretch along way back to the small coast road; then you have found your ideal site. Camping Areti is conveniently located just off the beaten track on the peninsula of Sithonia. It has 130 pitches, all for tourers (no static caravans are allowed). The olive groves at the rear provide hidden parking spaces for caravans and boats that can be brought to the site when the owner is present.

### Facilities
Three excellent toilet blocks include showers, WCs and washbasins. Kitchen with sinks, electric hobs and fridges. Laundry with washing machines. Facilities for emptying chemical toilet. Small shop and restaurant. Sandy beach. Bungalows to rent. Fishing, sailing and swimming. Off site: Riding nearby. Sithonia, Mount Athos and the nearby Spalathronissia islands.

**Open:** 1 May - 31 October.

### Directions
Although the postal address is Neos Marmaras the site is 12 km. south. So stay on the main coast road, go past the casino resort at Porto Carras and 5 km. further on turn right towards the site (signed). Then turn right again and go down to the coast where you must turn left and go for about 1.5 km. Turn right into site access road. Reception is about 700 m.
GPS: N40:01.451 E23:48.957

### Charges 2007
| | |
|---|---|
| Per person | € 8,10 - € 9,00 |
| pitch incl. electricity | € 13,90 - € 15,00 |

No credit cards.

Check real time availability and at-the-gate prices...
www.alanrogers.com

# Greece

### GR8150 Camping Isa
GR-63072 Tristinika (Central Macedonia)
Tel: 237 505 1235

Sithonia is the middle of three peninsulas on Halkidiki and is a popular Greek tourist destination with a good motorway south from Thessaloniki to Neos Moudania. Camping Isa is one of the larger sites on Sithonia and therefore has more facilities than many smaller sites. Behind a good sandy beach and amongst mainly olive and willow trees, the 250 pitches are clearly marked and some have high screens to offer some shade. Only the two front rows have sea views. Many people visit the area to see Mount Athos and the monasteries on Agio Oros, the third peninsula.

#### Facilities
Three toilet blocks include showers, WCs and washbasins. Sinks for dishwashing. Laundry with washing machines and ironing boards. Facilities for emptying chemical toilet. Motorcaravan service point. Beach bar. Shop. Restaurant. Sandy beach. Fishing, boating and swimming. No dogs are allowed. Off site: Mount Athos.

Open: 1 May - 30 September.

#### Directions
Camping Isa is on the Sithonia peninsula. You should follow the main coast road some 18 km. south of Neos Marmaras. A right hand turn is well signed and the site is 700 m. down this smaller road.
GPS: N39:59.759 E23:52.901

#### Charges guide
Per unit incl. 2 persons and electricity € 24,50 - € 26,25

### GR8220 Camping Valtos
Valtos Beach, GR-48060 Parga (Epirus)
Tel: 268 403 1287. Email: info@campingvaltos.gr

Valtos Camping lies two kilometres from the picturesque village of Parga and just 100 metres from the lively sandy beach at Valtos. This is a friendly, unpretentious site with a good range of amenities, including a shop, bar and restaurant. The 92 touring pitches here are of various sizes, all with electrical connections (16A). There is little grass but adequate shade is supplied by mulberry, lemon and olive trees. Access to the site is quite narrow and owners of larger motorhomes will need to be careful. A 20 minute walk uphill to Parga castle gives magnificent views of the harbour and surrounding countryside.

#### Facilities
Two toilet blocks – one modern and one refurbished. Washing machine. Motorcaravan service point. Shop, bar, takeaway food and restaurant (all May - Sept). Caravans for rent. Off site: Beach 60 m. Water taxi to Parga beach. Bicycle hire 2 km. Sailing, fishing and boat launching 60 m. Boat trips to the Ionian islands. Walking trails.

Open: 1 May - 30 September.

#### Directions
From Igoumenitsa head south towards Preveza (E55). Turn right to Parga and continue on the coastal road towards Anthousa. Site is signed to the right at the end of Valtos beach road.
GPS: N39:17.133 E20:23.390

#### Charges guide
| | |
|---|---|
| Per person | € 4,50 - € 5,00 |
| child | € 2,50 - € 3,00 |
| pitch incl. car and electricity | € 9,50 - € 11,50 |

### GR8225 Camping Enjoy-Lichnos
Lichnos, GR-48060 Parga (Epirus)
Tel: 268 403 1171. Email: holidays@enjoy-lichnos.net

This is a quiet campsite located at the base of a steep and winding road with attractive views of the Ionian Sea and the coastlines towards Preveza and Parga. The site has been created on a steep incline with terraced pitches which tend to be on the small side. The ground levels out in front of the beach and pitches here have sea views. In all there are electricity connections for around 100 pitches and further space for about 300 tents under the shade of the 500 year old olive trees. The sandy beach is the site's main attraction and various water-based activities are available.

#### Facilities
Unisex toilet blocks in 'portacabin' style unit are situated on each terrace with washbasins (cold water only) and showers. Two further sanitary blocks one of which has wheelchair access. Laundry area with one washing machine and ironing facilities. Covered dishwashing area. Chemical disposal point. Shop. Bar and beach bar. Restaurant with discount for campsite visitors and children's menu. English is spoken. Off site: Parga, ruins of Nekromanteio, island of Lefkada.

Open: 1 May - 31 October.

#### Directions
From Igoumenitsa head south (E55) towards Preveza. At sign for Parga turn right and follow road for 7 km. At Lichnos village turn left at Lichnos Camping and Apartments. Campsite entrance is 500 m. down steep slope (use low gears).
GPS: N39:16.903 E20:26.037

#### Charges 2007
| | |
|---|---|
| Per person | € 5,20 - € 5,50 |
| child | € 3,00 - € 3,50 |
| pitch incl. car | € 7,20 - € 10,30 |
| electricity | € 4,00 |

Check real time availability and at-the-gate prices...
www.alanrogers.com

# Greece

## GR8235 Camping Kalami Beach

Plataria, GR-46100 Igoumenitsa (Epirus)
Tel: 266 507 1211

A warm welcome awaits you on your arrival at Camping Kalami Beach. This family run site is ideally situated 8 kilometres from the ferry port of Igoumenitsa, where it is possible to take cruises to several islands and to Italy. The site is very well cared for with an attractive floral display around the reception building. There are 75 pitches of varying sizes with 10A electricity. Although the site is quite steep in places, the pitches themselves are level and well drained and those at the front of the site above the beach have panoramic views across the sea and to the mountains of Corfu. A flight of steps leads down to the beach and the crystal clear waters of the Ionian sea which are perfect for swimming. The site owners can arrange water skiing with a local company for those interested in more active water sports.

### Facilities

One sanitary block with British style WCs, washbasins and showers. Second block has showers and washbasins in cabins. Chemical disposal point. Laundry room with sinks and washing machines and dryer (token operated). Dishwashing area inside. Shop. Bar and restaurant, takeaway. Beach at site.

**Open:** 1 March - 31 October.

### Directions

From Igoumenitsa head south on the E55 towards Preveza. In 8 km. site is on right, well signed. Entrance is 300 m. down a steep narrow lane. GPS: N39:28.427 E20:14.449

### Charges 2007

| | |
|---|---|
| Per person | € 5,50 |
| child (4-10 yrs) | € 2,80 |
| pitch incl. car | € 6,50 - € 9,50 |
| electricity | € 3,80 |

Discounts available for low season and stays over ten nights in high season.
No credit cards.

## GR8255 Camping Vrachos Kastraki

Kastraki, GR-42200 Kalambaka (Thessaly)
Tel: 243 202 2293. Email: kastraki@meteoracamping.gr

The region of Meteora is named after the impressive rock formations which rise out to the plain of Thessaly and which now have ancient monasteries clinging to their summits. Camping Vrachos Kastraki is ideally placed to visit this unusual landscape as it is situated in a valley surrounded by mountains and the huge natural sculptures. There are around 260 pitches, many quite small and suitable only for tents. Electricity is said to be available for all but in some cases cables would have to cross roads. Individual pitches are not marked and there is a policy of pitch where you like. There is plenty of shade from mature almonds, acacias and poplars. There is a warm welcome from the Tsourvakas family on arrival, which immediately helps the visitor unwind after the journey through the mountain passes. The site owners can advise on the numerous places of interest to visit. For the adventurous visitor, rock climbing, abseiling, canoeing and mountain biking can be organised from the site. Those less actively inclined can relax and enjoy the sunshine and the view from beside the pool. The restaurant, which is open all year, is very good value. The site also provides a covered barbecue area and excellent cooking facilities with three designated picnic areas.

### Facilities

Two modern sanitary blocks provide British style WCs and open washbasins. Chemical disposal point. Laundry room with sinks and washing machines. Covered dishwashing area. Cooking facilities with picnic areas. Shop. Bar, restaurant and snack bar. Outdoor swimming pool (1/4-31/10). Play area. Off site: Climbing, trekking, abseiling, mountain biking, rafting.

**Open:** All year.

### Directions

The Igoumenitsa - Ioannina new motorway was only partly open when we visited. Some sections of the route are steep and winding on small narrow roads. At Ioannina take the E92 to Trikala in an easterly direction – steep, winding and very slow moving. At Kalambaka turn left towards Kastraki. In 1.5 km. campsite entrance is on left. Campsite is well signed along the route. GPS: N39:42.791 E21:36.917

### Charges guide

| | |
|---|---|
| Per person | € 5,00 |
| child (4-10 yrs) | € 3,00 |
| pitch incl. car | € 2,00 - € 4,00 |
| electricity | € 3,00 |

Check real time availability and at-the-gate prices...
www.alanrogers.com

## GR8280 Camping Sikia

GR-38500 Kato Gatzea (Thessaly)
Tel: 242 302 2279. Email: info@camping-sikia.gr

Camping Sikia is an attractive, well maintained site enthusiastically run by the Pandelfi family. The site offers 80 pitches of varying sizes all with 16A electricity. They are arranged on terraces and may become quite dusty during the dry season, but most are well shaded by olive trees. There are superb views from some pitches – the sea to the south and the mountains to the north. There are also 17 apartments to rent. The calm sea and golden beaches of the Pagasitikos Gulf make this a perfect spot for family holidays. The site is just 100 m. from a sand and shingle beach on the edge of a rocky bay which is ideal for swimming and snorkelling. At weekends it is possible to take the train up into the Mount Pelion to explore the picturesque villages of the region. Once the summer residence of the gods of Olympus, Pelion now welcomes hikers, mountain bikers and climbers. Facilites for the disabled have been improved.

### Facilities

Two modern and one refurbished sanitary blocks with British style WCs, open washbasins and pre-set showers. Facilities for disabled visitors are planned. Chemical disposal point. Laundry area with sinks, washing machines and ironing facilities. Covered dishwashing area with free hot water. Shop. Bar. TV room. Internet corner. Restaurant. Communal barbecue areas (barbecues not allowed on pitch). Volleyball and basketball. Fishing. Dogs are not allowed on the beach. Off site: Bicycle hire 1 km. Riding 2 km. Sailing 2 km. Pelion steam railway, boat trips to Skiathos.

**Open:** 1 April - 31 October.

### Directions

Follow E75 south towards Lamia, turn left at sign for Volos onto E92. Follow coastal road towards Argalasti for 18 km. Site is off the coastal road on the right at Kato Gatzea immediately past Camping Hellas. GPS: N39:18.616 E23:06.587

### Charges 2008

| | |
|---|---|
| Per person | € 5,50 - € 6,50 |
| child (12-16 yrs) | € 4,00 - € 5,00 |
| child (4-12 yrs) | € 3,00 - € 4,00 |
| pitch incl. car | € 7,50 - € 8,50 |
| electricity | € 3,80 |

## GR8285 Camping Hellas International

GR-38500 Kato Gatzea (Thessaly)
Tel: 242 302 2267. Email: camping-hellas@argo.net.gr

There is a warm welcome from the English speaking brother and sister team who own and run Camping Hellas. The campsite has been in the family since the sixties, when tourists first asked if they could camp overnight and use the facilities of the taverna. It is in a beautiful setting in a 500 year old olive grove, right next to the beach and the calm blue waters of the Pagasitikos gulf. Everything is kept spotlessly clean and the owners have many plans for further improvements. There are around 100 pitches all with 16A electricity. Pitch sizes vary and some parts are more level than others, but shade is plentiful thanks to the olive trees. The restaurant is a traditional Greek taverna serving local sea food and there is also a bar conveniently located next to the beach. The surrounding area has plenty to explore including the picturesque villages of Mount Pelion or the island of Skiathos. At weekends a steam train departs from the nearby village of Ano Lechonia on a journey through spectacular mountain scenery.

### Facilities

One modern and one old sanitary block, both very clean with British style toilets and open washbasins. Very good facilities for disabled visitors. Laundry room with sinks and washing machines, ironing facilities. Dishwashing sinks. Shop has essentials from 15 April, fully stocked from May. Bar. TV room. Restaurant (from April). Boat launching. Dogs are not allowed on the beach. Off site: Fishing 5 km. Sailing 5 km. Riding 18 km. Bicycle hire 18 km. Pelion steam railway, boat trips to Skiathos.

**Open:** 15 March - 31 October.

### Directions

From the north follow the E75 towards Lamia. Turn left at sign for Volos onto E92. Follow coastal road south towards Argalasti for 18 km. Site is off coastal road on right at Kato Gatzea.
GPS: N39:18.650 E23:06.546

### Charges guide

| | |
|---|---|
| Per person | € 5,00 - € 6,00 |
| child (12-16 yrs) | € 4,00 - € 5,00 |
| child (4-11 yrs) | € 3,00 - € 3,50 |
| pitch incl. car | € 6,30 - € 8,30 |
| electricity | € 3,60 |

## GR8300 Camping Dounis Beach

GR-30020 Antirrio (Western Greece)

Tel: **263 403 1565**. Email: **campdounis@yahoo.gr**

At Antirrio the coast comes closest to the Peloponnese. A regular car ferry operated here – it still does today but most of the traffic uses the modern toll bridge to Rio, across the 'little Dardanelles' on the southern shore. There is little more to Antirrio than the bridge and ferry, although beside the harbour, guarding the Gulf of Corinth, stands the originally Frankish and Venetian Kastro Roumelis. Camping Dounis Beach is 1.5 km. away and offers 90 grass pitches all with electricity. A family run site, it is very popular with Greek families who come here every July and August for the beach and the fishing.

### Facilities

Two toilet blocks include showers, WCs and washbasins. Sinks for dishwashing and laundry. Facilities for emptying chemical toilet. Small shop and small restaurant (1/7-15/8). Barbecues are not permitted.
Off site: Nafpactos and further afield, Patras.

**Open:** 1 May - 30 November.

### Directions

From the new Rio - Antirrio toll bridge, site is 1.5 km. from the slip road towards Nafpactos. It is on the right on a left hand bend. Coming from Nafpactos, site is 1.5 km. before Antirrio village and the bridge which can be seen for miles.
GPS: N38:20.508 E21:46.240

### Charges 2008

| | |
|---|---:|
| Per person | € 10,00 |
| child | € 4,00 |
| pitch incl. car | € 10,00 - € 7,30 |
| electricity | € 4,00 |

No credit cards.

## GR8320 Camping Olympia

Olympia, GR-27065 Pyrgos (Western Greece)

Tel: **262 402 2745**

This small, basic site has 73 pitches, of which only 30 are for caravans or motorcaravans, and it is likely to be the first site you find as you enter Olympia. A narrow circular road climbs around the site and access is restricted by low overgrown trees. Tents can pitch amongst the orange trees in the centre. All touring pitches have 10A electricity. Being on the same level as the village centre and just a short walk away, it is well located for visiting all the sights, including the Olympic Museum and the site of Ancient Olympia.

### Facilities

The old toilet block is clean and serviceable. Sinks for dishwashing. Facilities for emptying chemical toilet. Bar and restaurant open only in the high season. Swimming pool. Off site: Ancient Olympia.

**Open:** All year.

### Directions

From the new main road turn towards the town of Olympia and site is on the right before the main built up area.

### Charges guide

| | |
|---|---:|
| Per unit incl. 2 persons | € 17,00 |

## GR8325 Camping Fournia Beach

Kastro, GR-27050 Killinis (Western Greece)

Tel: **262 309 5095**. Email: **fournia-beach@acn.gr**

The village of Kastros and the Chlemoutsi castle that towers above it can be seen for miles across the flat landscape towards the coast. Camping Fournia Beach is owned by the four Lefkaditis brothers and their wives have ensured that this new site is awash with flowering shrubs. The site offers 90 first class pitches and modern facilities, and the bar and restaurant sit in a landscaped area high above the beach with spectacular views across the sea to Zakinthos. Steps to the beach provide private access to the sandy cove below. The brothers plan to install a swimming pool.

### Facilities

Two modern toilet blocks include showers, WCs and washbasins and good facilities for disabled visitors. Laundry with washing machines, sinks and hot water. Kitchen with hobs, fridge and freezer. Shop. Restaurant and bar overlooking the sea and the island of Zakinthos. Accommodation for rent. Off site: Chlemoutsi castle.

**Open:** 1 April - 30 October.

### Directions

Travel 61 km. south of Patras on the main road to Pyrgos. At traffic lights, turn west signed Killinis and Zakinthos. Site is well signed from here, 15 km. and past village of Kastros. Descend towards the thermal springs and go straight ahead on a left hand hairpin bend towards the beach.

### Charges 2007

| | |
|---|---:|
| Per unit incl. 2 persons and electricity | € 16,50 - € 19,85 |

# Greece

## GR8330 Camping Ionion Beach

Glifa, GR-27050 Vartholomino Ilias (Western Greece)

Tel: 262 309 6395. Email: ioniongr@otenet.gr

This is a well kept site in a beautiful location by the Ionian Sea, created from former farmland by the Fligos family. Much has changed since they welcomed their first guests in 1982, when they still left plenty of space for growing potatoes. Now it is a modern site with a large pool and a paddling pool and two blocks of apartments to rent. Separated by a variety of trees and oleander bushes, there are 235 pitches with 16A electricity and of between 80 and 100 sq.m. Those at the front of the site have a view over the sea and the island of Zakynthos. The campsite has its own beach bar for snacks and exotic cocktails and there is also a restaurant, which has no set menu but serves Greek specialities prepared by Mrs Fligos. Motorcaravanners should be aware that public transport in the area is poor, but it is possible to arrange car or motorcycle hire at the site.

### Facilities

Two modern sanitary blocks with British style WCs and showers with washbasins in cabins. Motorcaravan service point. Turkish style chemical disposal point. Laundry room with sinks and washing machine. Covered dishwashing area. Shop, bar, restaurant (15/4-15/11). Internet access in bar. Swimming pool and paddling pool (15/4-15/11). Caution is advised as there are no depth markings in the pool. Play area. Off site: Ferries to Zakynthos from Kilini, ancient city of Olympia, Frankish fortress of Chlemoutsi.

Open: All year.

### Directions

From Patra head south on E55 towards Pyrgos. At sign for Vartholomio, turn right in town centre turn right at sign for Glyfa and Ionion Beach. In 15 km. campsite sign is on right. For those coming from the north of Greece, the there is a toll for the Korinthian gulf bridge toll (€ 15,50 each way when we visited). GPS: N37:50.197 E21:08.028

### Charges 2007

| | |
|---|---|
| Per person | € 5,50 - € 6,00 |
| child (5-12 yrs) | € 3,50 - € 4,00 |
| pitch incl. car | € 7,00 - € 13,00 |
| electricity | € 3,60 |

Discounts available for long stays.

## GR8335 Camping Diana

GR-27065 Olympia (Western Greece)

Tel: 262 422 314

Camping Diana has 40 pitches, but 15 are under dense tree cover and are only suitable for tents. The remaining 25 are off a sloping concrete road in small open areas and pitch size will be small at best. Each has a 10A electricity supply nearby. When we visited the site was quite busy and it could get overstretched at times. One visitor told us that noise from the clubs in town was a little intrusive but overall they felt it was a good site. That confirmed our view and despite being old it offered a pleasant stay close to the wonders of both modern and ancient Olympia.

### Facilities

The single toilet block is old, but clean. Facilities for emptying chemical toilet. Washing machine. Very small shop. Swimming pool. Off site: Ancient Olympia.

Open: 1 May - 30 September.

### Directions

Site is to the west of the town, about 200 m. from the centre. Go through the town and past the station, then turn right. At the back of the town signs up the hill lead to the site.

### Charges 2007

| | |
|---|---|
| Per person | € 7,00 |
| child | € 5,00 |
| pitch | € 7,00 - € 8,00 |
| electricity | € 5,00 |

www.alanrogers.com

All campsites are inspected & selected by Alan Rogers.

Just Click and Go!

INSPECTED CAMPSITES & SELECTED

Check real time availability and at-the-gate prices...

www.alanrogers.com

# Greece

### GR8340 Camping Alphios

GR-27065 Olympia (Western Greece)
Tel: **262 402 2951**. Email: **alphios@otenet.gr**

High above ancient and modern Olympia, this site enjoys spectacular views, both across the adjoining countryside and to the coast at Pyrgos. It provides 97 pitches of which 40 are for touring units. They all have 16A electricity and many have high reed screens that provide shade. Olympia is a popular tourist destination with dozens of coaches each day bringing tourists from around the world to this small town and the adjoining archaeological sites. However, the area also offers opportunities for walking and cycling amidst some wonderful scenery and this site provides a good base for excursions to the surrounding northern Peloponnese countryside.

**Facilities**

Two toilet blocks include showers, WCs and washbasins. Two kitchens with sinks for dishwashing, electric hobs and fridges. Laundry with washing machines. Small shop. Bar and restaurant. Swimming pool. Off site: Ancient Olympia. Town centre within walking distance.

**Open:** 1 April - 15 October.

**Directions**

Site is located at a height of 400 m. to the west of the town, about 1.5 km. from the centre. Go through the town and past the station. Turn right, then at back of the town follow signs up the hill to the site.

**Charges guide**

| | |
|---|---|
| Per person | € 6,00 |
| child | € 3,50 |
| pitch incl. electricity | € 9,60 - € 10,10 |

### GR8470 Camping Rovies

GR-34200 Rovies (Central Greece)
Tel: **222 707 1120**. Email: **info@campingevia.com**

When we visited, this site had only just reopened for business after renovation and redecoration and cleaning was well in hand. On the western coast of Evia, this site provides 150 average size pitches, of which 40 are used by static caravans. Served by a central spine road, they are all directly behind the pebble beach and most, despite the trees, flowering shrubs and screens, have views to the sea. Diving clubs are beginning to use the site as a result of the many diving opportunities that this coast offers and it is also popular with Greek families in high season.

**Facilities**

The toilet block includes showers, WCs and washbasins. Two kitchens with sinks for dishwashing, electric hobs for cooking and fridges. Chemical disposal. Small shop and restaurant (1/7-31/8). Fishing.

**Open:** 1 April - 30 October.

**Directions**

Site is 16 km. south of Loutra Aidipsou on the island of Evia, about 4 km. north of the village of Rovies. GPS: N38:50.162 E23:11.267

**Charges 2007**

| | |
|---|---|
| Per person | € 5,00 - € 6,00 |
| child | € 3,50 - € 4,50 |
| pitch incl. car | € 7,50 - € 13,50 |
| electricity | € 4,00 |

### GR8475 Camping Pefki

GR-34200 Pefki (Central Greece)
Tel: **222 604 1121**

Evia, the second largest Greek Island, offers dramatic scenery and the north end of the island provides an opportunity to get away from the crowds of Attica. It also offers an alternative route between Athens and Thessaloniki and avoids the boring motorway route towards Lamia. Camping Pefki is an older site, just across the beach road from the sea and small beach. There are 85 small pitches and 14 rooms to rent. All the pitches are under screens and the site is covered with trees and flowering shrubs, and serviced by a narrow, winding road. All together, this restricts access for large units.

**Facilities**

Three toilet blocks include facilities for disabled visitors. Two kitchens include sinks for dishwashing, gas hobs and fridges. Laundry with washing machine. Chemical disposal. Small shop. Rooms to rent. Off site: Evia, Loutra Aidipsou (for the hot spring) and the Agiokampos ferry.

**Open:** 1 June - 30 August.

**Directions**

The main road runs from Loutra Aidipsou to Agriovotano at the northern tip of Evia. About 11 km. west of Agriovotano turn towards Pefki and at the beach turn right. Site is 1.5 km. along this road on the right. GPS: N39:01.173 E23:13.563

**Charges guide**

| | |
|---|---|
| Per person | € 4,00 - € 5,00 |
| child (4-10 yrs) | € 2,20 - € 3,00 |
| pitch | € 6,50 - € 8,30 |
| electricity | € 3,00 |

Check real time availability and at-the-gate prices...
www.alanrogers.com

## GR8520 Camping Delphi

GR-33054 Delphi (Central Greece)
Tel: 226 508 2209. Email: info@delphicamping.com

Delphi Camping enjoys a stunning location in a conservation area on the slopes of Mount Parnassus, just 4 kilometres from ancient Delphi. There are some truly outstanding views over valleys of olive groves across to the Gulf of Corinth. The site's 80 pitches all offer electrical connections (6A) and some benefit from the great views. This is a well managed and well equipped site with an attractive pool and a friendly bar featuring an exhibition of paintings by Avyeris Kanatas, a former owner of the site. The prevailing ambience here is geared towards a peaceful, relaxing stay.

### Facilities

Two toilet blocks – one modern and one refurbished. Facilities for disabled visitors. Washing machine. Motorcaravan service point. Shop, bar, takeaway food and restaurant (all April - Oct). Swimming pool. Tennis. Play area. Off site: Bus stop opposite site entrance with regular service to Delphi, Athens and other places of interest. Beach 13 km. Walking trails (for example to Chrisso 3 km).

**Open:** 1 April - 20 October.

### Directions

From Delphi take the road towards Itea. Just after a bridge, 4 km. from Delphi, turn right towards Chrisso. Site is 500 m. on the right.
GPS: N38:28.712 E22:28.484

### Charges 2007

| | |
|---|---|
| Per person | € 5,90 - € 6,40 |
| child (4-10 yrs) | € 3,70 - € 4,30 |
| pitch incl. car | € 7,30 - € 8,10 |
| electricity | € 3,90 |

## GR8525 Chrissa Camping

Chrisso, GR-33054 Delphi (Central Greece)
Tel: 226 508 2050. Email: info@chrissacamping.gr

This well kept site is located close to Delphi which was once sacred to the god Apollo and is now the setting for some of the most important monuments of ancient Greek civilisation. The site's situation on a hill ensures stunning views across a vast olive grove to the Gulf of Corinth beyond. There are 60 pitches with electricity connections (16A). They are mainly arranged on terraces as the site is quite steep, which means that everyone can enjoy the views. As the site is in a conservation area, mobile homes are not permitted but there are some round wooden cabins to rent which blend in very well with the natural environment.

### Facilities

Modern toilet block with British style WCs, open washbasins and controllable showers. Plastic seats available in showers. Motorhome service point. Chemical disposal point. Laundry room with sinks, washing machine and dryer. Dishwashing room. Shop (1/4-30/10). Bar, restaurant and takeaway (weekends only in winter). Outdoor pool and paddling pool. Barbecues are not allowed. Internet point. Off site: Beach 10 km. Skiing 18 km. Delphi.

**Open:** All year.

### Directions

From Patra head west on E65 (48) towards Itea. Continue towards Delphi and 6 km. from Delphi, Chrisso is signed on the right. Site is directly opposite, clearly signed and entrance is 300 m. down a narrow lane. GPS: N38:28.346 E22:27.549

### Charges 2008

| | |
|---|---|
| Per person | € 5,50 - € 6,50 |
| child (4-10 yrs) | € 3,50 - € 4,00 |
| pitch incl. car | € 8,00 - € 9,00 |
| electricity | € 4,00 |

Camping Cheques accepted.

## GR8450 Camping Milos

GR-34008 Eretria (Attica)
Tel: 222 906 0420. Email: info@camping-in-evia.gr

The island of Evia could easily be mistaken for part of the mainland now that it is connected to Attica by two bridges and several ferries. It is, however, the second largest Greek Island, Crete being that much bigger. Camping Milos is on the coast just over a mile north of Eretria and provides 64 pitches. 40 pitches provide space for tents, caravans and motorhomes, all under screens of varying height. So inevitably there is limited space for each group, although there should be no problem in low season.

### Facilities

Two toilet blocks are old and not particularly clean. Facilities for disabled visitors. Two kitchens with sinks for dishwashing, gas hobs and fridges. Laundry with washing machines. Chemical disposal. Small shop. Bar/restaurant (1/7-30/8, weekends only 1-30/9). Off site: Evia.

**Open:** 1 April - 30 September.

### Directions

From Chalkida follow signs for Eretria or South Evia down the coastal road. Site is on the right before Eretria, 20 km. south of Chalkida. From the ferry (Oropos - Eretria) leave the dock, go through the town and join the main road north to site on the left after 2 km. GPS: N38:23.465 E23:46.505

### Charges 2007

| | |
|---|---|
| Per person | € 5,30 - € 5,90 |
| child (4-10 yrs) | € 2,90 - € 3,30 |

# Greece

## GR8560 Camping Ramnous
174 Poseidon Avenue, GR-19007 Marathonas (Attica)
Tel: 294 552 44. Email: ramnous@otenet.gr

Famous for the battle that created a world famous race, Marathon needs little introduction. The regular bus service to Athens takes 90 minutes which is not much faster than today's Olympic athletes. However, this site with its 110 pitches is alongside a great sandy beach and is about 6 km. from the village, near the large new town of Nea Makri. Whilst there are sites nearer to Athens, Camping Ramnous has the benefit of its beach location and peace and quiet that is difficult to find near the bustling Greek capital.

### Facilities
Two toilet blocks include showers, WCs and washbasins. Sinks for dishwashing and hobs for cooking. Chemical disposal. Shop, bar and restaurant (1/6-1/9). Water playground for children. Sandy beach with water slide. Off site: Athens 41 km.

**Open:** All year.

### Directions
Heading north out of Nea Makri, site is well signed but turn right towards Schinos and then right again at traffic lights. Just past the Olympic rowing centre turn right towards the site which is on the left.

### Charges guide
| | |
|---|---|
| Per person | € 6,00 - € 6,50 |
| child | € 4,50 |
| pitch incl. electricity | € 12,00 - € 16,00 |

## GR8565 Camping Kokkino Limanaki
GR-19009 Rafina (Attica)
Tel: 229 403 1604. Email: travelnet@otenet.gr

This site is an ideal base for visiting the famous ancient sites of Athens as it lies just 20 minutes away from the Acropolis. The site is located 100 m. above sea level, but also has access to the beach below. There are 100 pitches of various sizes on partly sloping ground some of which have views over the Aegean sea and nearby islands. All pitches have 16A electricity. The single sanitary block has unisex showers and may be stretched at busy times. A torch would be useful at night. The site has its own bar and restaurant with sea views from the terrace.

### Facilities
Single toilet block with open style washbasins and unisex showers. Dishwashing sinks, washing machine and ironing board. Fridges for hire. Chemical disposal. Bar and restaurant. Takeaway (July and August). Off site: Fishing 1 km. Boat launching 4.5 km. Beach 200 m.

**Open:** 1 May - 30 September.

### Directions
Travelling south on E75 towards Athens turn right onto slip road signed Varibobi. At traffic lights turn left and follow signs to Nea Makri. Enter town and follow signs to Rafina; 1.6 km. after leaving Nea Makri at traffic lights turn left (signed Kokkino Limanaki) and follow signs to site.
GPS: N38:01.899 E24:00.095

### Charges guide
| | |
|---|---|
| Per person | € 5,90 - € 6,50 |
| child | € 4,30 |
| pitch incl. electricity | € 8,60 - € 10,00 |

## GR8580 Camping Bacchus
GR-19500 Sounio (Attica)
Tel: 229 203 9262. Email: linosclub@grmail.com

Camping Bacchus is a small but welcoming site in a remote area. Just 12 of its 55 pitches are available for tourers with the rest taken up by mobile homes and caravans to rent. The site is on partly sloping ground with shade provided by pine trees. It is 100 metres from a sandy beach, where there are great views out over the Aegean Sea and its islands. The campsite shop opens all year but stock is rather limited. There is also a bar (all year) and restaurant (May to October). The temple of Poseidon is only 4.5 km. along the coastal road. It is best experienced at sunset when the sea glows fiery red.

### Facilities
Three old sanitary blocks with British style WCs, washbasins with cold water only, two also have controllable showers. Coin operated washing machine, sinks, open air dishwashing. Chemical disposal point. Shop. Bar. Restaurant (May – Oct). Internet access. Communal area for barbecues. Play area. Off site: Sailing, fishing 100 m. Temple of Poseidon at Sounio, ferry service to Aegean islands from Lavrio.

**Open:** All year.

### Directions
From Athens travelling south take the R89 (partly new motorway) towards Markopoulo. Continue south on R89 signed Sounio. At Lavrio campsite signs 4 km. Site is on left.
GPS: N37:40.596 E24:02.880

### Charges 2007
| | |
|---|---|
| Per person | € 7,00 |
| child (4-10 yrs) | € 4,00 |
| pitch incl. electricity | € 9,50 - € 11,00 |
| car | € 3,50 |

Check real time availability and at-the-gate prices...
www.alanrogers.com

## GR8590 Camping Athens

198-200 Leoforos Athinon, GR-12136 Athens (Attica)
Tel: 210 581 4114. Email: info@athenscamping.com.gr

Camping Athens is an 'all year' site, located to the west of the city and convenient for visiting Athens. The site prides itself on friendly Greek hospitality and offers 66 touring pitches most of which have 16A electricity connections. The pitches are of a reasonable size and are generally well shaded. Smaller pitches are available for tents. The two toilet blocks are of modern design and seemed well maintained when we visited. There is a bus stop opposite the site entrance with a frequent service to the city centre, 7 km. away (tickets are for sale in reception). There are no mobile homes here.

### Facilities

Two modern toilet blocks. Washing machines. Shop. Bar. Takeaway food and restaurant. All amenities are available late April - late October. Excursions can be arranged. Barbecues and open fires are strictly forbidden. Off site: Bus stop opposite site entrance with frequent service to city centre or metro station.

**Open:** All year.

### Directions

From the north (Thessaloniki) take E75 signed Athina Pireas, then the E94 west (towards Korinthos, second exit). Site is on the right after 2 km. and is well signed. From the south (Peloponissos) take the E94 towards Athina - Pirea. Continue towards Athens. Site is 4 km. after Dafni monastery. Keep to the right hand lane and make a U-turn in about 800 m. GPS: N38:00.533 E23:40.326

### Charges 2008

| | |
|---|---|
| Per person | € 8,00 |
| child | € 4,00 |
| pitch incl. car | € 9,00 - € 12,00 |
| electricity | € 4,00 |

### ATHENS CAMPING

Open all year around, is situated only 7 km from the center of Athens, connected with an excellent organised bus service, provides all necessary and high quality facilities and services for a comfortable and unforgetable stay.

198 - 200 Athinon Ave. - 121 36 Athens, Greece - Tel. 210 581 4114 - Fax 210 582 0353
E-mail: info@campingathens.com.gr - www.campingathens.com.gr

## GR8595 Camping Nea Kifissia

Potamou 60 & Dimitsanas, Adames, GR-14564 Nea Kifissia (Attica)
Tel: 210 620 5646

Many visitors to Greece will want to spend some time in Athens, the capital. Camping Nea Kifissia offers one of the best opportunities to do that, being in a quiet location with easy access. A small site, run personally by the Komianidou family, there are 66 level pitches, some with shade, in well kept grounds. A regular bus service runs to the Kifissia metro station for fast and regular transport to all the sights. The Acropolis, Parthenon and the Porch of Caryatids are essential viewing, as are the many museums. Athens' shops and the flea market near Monastiraki also have much to offer. Others will not want to miss the famous Greek National Guards who mount the guard in front of the Tomb of the Unknown Soldier in Plateia Syntagmatos.

### Facilities

A centrally positioned toilet block includes showers, WCs and washbasins. Chemical disposal. Washing machine. Bar and coffee shop (1/6-20/9). Swimming pool (1/6-20/9). Communal barbecue area. English spoken in reception. Off site: Athens 16 km. (45 minutes by bus/metro).

**Open:** All year.

### Directions

From Athens - Thessaloniki motorway take New Kifissia exit. Coming from Athens, turn sharp left down Ermionis and turn right into Dimitsanas to site. From the north take same exit and then almost a U-turn along small road that runs parallel to the motorway. Site is well signed but turn left down Aigiou to site. GPS: N38:06.002 E23:47.500

### Charges guide

| | |
|---|---|
| Per person | € 7,00 |
| child | € 4,00 |
| pitch incl. electricity | € 12,00 - € 15,00 |

## Greece

### GR8605 Camping Alkioni
Alkioni Holidays A.E, GR-20300 Schinos (Peloponnese)
Tel: 274 405 7294. Email: campingalkioni@yahoo.gr

If you are going to travel this distance, then you need to be assured the drive was worth it. At the end of May, when we arrived here the site was not open. In fact the new tarmac road through the site was just being laid. Major refurbishment was also nearing completion with the four good toilet blocks that will serve the 200 pitches just needing the finishing touches. The new bar, restaurant and shop were almost complete. The site slopes down to the small shingle beach along the new winding road and the level, flat pitches are on terraces at various levels.

#### Facilities
Four refurbished toilet blocks include showers, WCs and washbasins. Sinks for dishwashing. Electric hobs for cooking. Facilities for emptying chemical toilet. Restaurant. Bar. Small shop. Off site: Small beach. Loutraki 36 km.

**Open:** 1 June - 31 December.

#### Directions
Leave Athens - Corinth motorway at Loutraki exit and shortly afterwards bear right and continue to and through Loutraki. Ahead is a mountain peak (1,032 m.) – you have to climb around this to site. Entering Perachora fork right to Pisia and Schinos. Go through Pisia and descend towards Schinos and coast. Turn left at start of the village to small square where U-turn towards Strava.

#### Charges 2007
| | |
|---|---|
| Per person | € 4,10 - € 4,70 |
| child | € 2,30 - € 2,90 |
| pitch incl. electricity | € 10,40 - € 11,80 |

No credit cards.

---

### GR8615 Camping Blue Dolphin
Lecheon, GR-20011 Corinth (Peloponnese)
Tel: 274 102 5766. Email: skouspos@camping-blue-dolphin.gr

Camping Blue Dolphin is a site that needs some modernisation but offers good opportunities to visit the northern Peloponnes and, in particular, Corinth and the canal. With 74 pitches (50 for touring) the site is well used by many European touring clubs. Most pitches have low reed screens which limit their use for high vehicles, but a few can accommodate units up to 3.2 metres. The owners offer a variety of tourist opportunities with coach trips and the chance to sail through the famous canal.

#### Facilities
The toilet block includes showers, WCs and washbasins. Sinks for dishwashing. Chemical disposal. Washing machines. Small shop. Bar and restaurant with limited menu. Shingle beach on the Gulf of Corinth. Off site: Corinth Canal.

**Open:** 1 April - 20 October.

#### Directions
Coming from Athens on the motorway take Loutraki exit and bear left over the canal. Continue along the old Corinth - Patras road for 6 km. and site is well signed on the right. From Patras use ancient Corinth exit and turn left towards Lecheon beach. Site signed.

#### Charges 2007
| | |
|---|---|
| Per unit incl. 2 persons | € 19,00 - € 23,00 |
| incl. electricity | € 18,22 - € 26,90 |

---

### GR8625 Camping Bekas
Gialasi, GR-21052 Ancient Epidavros (Peloponnese)
Tel: 275 309 9930. Email: info@bekas.gr

Just 60 kilometres south of Corinth you will find the town of Ancient Epidavros, and just south of that is Camping Bekas. With 150 pitches (120 for touring) set amongst the trees you will find shade and a quiet atmosphere. Arranged along a small sand and shingle beach, the site offers opportunities for swimming, sailing and fishing. The Argolid region of the Peloponnese has much to offer the inquisitive tourist. About 12 kilometres south is the sanctuary of Asclepios.

#### Facilities
Three toilet blocks include the usual facilities including two shower rooms for disabled visitors. Laundry with washing machine. Shop. Bar. Restaurant (15/5-15/9). Internet access. TV room. Sand and shingle beach. Apartments to rent. Off site: Theatre of Epidavros 12 km.

**Open:** 1 April - 20 October.

#### Directions
To avoid driving right through the town of Ancient Epidavros take the southern exit towards the town. Turn inland here down a slip road, then turn under the main road above towards the town. On entering the town turn right towards Gialasi and site is about 1.6 km. on the left. GPS: N37:37.076 E23:09.475

#### Charges 2007
| | |
|---|---|
| Per person | € 5,00 - € 5,50 |
| pitch incl. electricity | € 10,00 - € 15,00 |

---

Check real time availability and at-the-gate prices...
www.alanrogers.com

## GR8635 Camping New Triton

Plaka Drepano, GR-21060 Nafplio (Peloponnese)

Tel: 275 209 2128

What do we look for in a good campsite in Greece? Given the excellent Greek weather, the answer is probably a good, flat pitch with some shade, excellent toilets and showers that are spotlessly clean, a small shop and proximity to a beach and local tavernas. Well, here you have it all! Under the control of the owners, Mr & Mrs George Christopoulous, this is an exceptional site with 40 good size touring pitches under high screens, just across the road from Drepano beach. Local tavernas are within strolling distance and the town's shops are about a mile away.

### Facilities

Excellent refurbished toilet blocks include showers, WCs and washbasins. Baby bath. Facilities for disabled visitors. Chemical disposal. Laundry with washing machines and ironing board. Electric hobs for cooking. Fridge and freezer available. Small shop (1/6-30/9). Off site: Drepano beach, local tavernas and bars. Assini.

**Open:** 1 April - 30 October.

### Directions

From Nafplio follow the main road west and then turn right towards Drepano. In the town follow the signs Plaka Drepano and turn left towards the coast. At the beach turn right and site is just ahead.

### Charges guide

| | |
|---|---|
| Per person | € 6,00 - € 7,00 |
| child | € 3,00 - € 6,00 |
| pitch incl. car and electricity | € 9,00 - € 11,00 |

## GR8640 Camping Kastraki

Assini, GR-21100 Nafplio (Peloponnese)

Tel: 275 205 9386. Email: sgkamania@kastrakicamping.gr

Ancient Assini, where Camping Kastraki is located, inspired the Nobel Prize winning poet, George Seferis, to write one of his most beautiful poems. This alone attracts the more romantic traveller to head for this wonderful coast. Others attracted by the magic of the shores of the Argolid will not be disappointed. Nearby Nafplio was the Capital of the newly formed Greek state from 1828 to 1834 when this role passed to Athens. Camping Kastraki, run personally by the owner, George Karmaniolas, offers 200 good pitches set amongst eucalyptus and pine trees trees that border a narrow shingle beach.

### Facilities

Refurbished toilet block includes showers, WCs and washbasins. Facilities for disabled visitors. Sinks for dishwashing. Gas hobs for cooking. Chemical toilet emptying point and motorcaravan service point. Washing machines. Small shop, bar and restaurant during high season. Flats to rent nearby. Slipway for small boats. Off site: Nafplio and Ancient Assini.

**Open:** 1 April - 20 October.

### Directions

From Nafplio, head towards Tolo and go through the modern town of Assini. Shortly before Tolo, site is well signed on the left. From Drepano head towards Tolo and turn left at T-junction to site on the left. GPS: N37:31.680 E22:52.572

### Charges 2007

| | |
|---|---|
| Per person | € 7,20 - € 8,00 |
| child (4-10 yrs) | € 4,30 - € 4,80 |
| pitch incl. car | € 10,70 - € 14,80 |
| electricity | € 3,50 |

## GR8685 Camping Gythion Bay

GR-23200 Gythion (Peloponnese)

Tel: 273 302 2522. Email: info@gythiocamping.gr

Camping Gythion Bay has 71 unmarked pitches set amongst orange, fig, olive and pine trees and all with electricity. Some trees limit access but the owner Mr Zafirakos is dealing with this to improve the site. Indeed he has also been busy refurbishing the toilets, showers and other facilities. With a good beach alongside the site, there are good opportunities for windsurfing and storage for boards is available. This is a good starting point for excursions to the Caves of Diros and for wider exploration of Lakonia and especially Inner and Outer Mani and Sparta.

### Facilities

Four toilet blocks include the usual facilities and facilities for disabled visitors. Sinks for dishwashing. Laundry with washing machines. Chemical disposal. Small shop (1/5-30/9). Bar (1/5-30/9). Restaurant (10/6-17/9). Windsurfing and limited boat launching. Small beach. Play area. Off site: Gythio 4 km.

**Open:** All year.

### Directions

Site is about 4 km. south of the fishing port of Gythio on the road to Aeropoli. It is between two petrol stations on the left and has a wide entrance. GPS: N36:43.725 E22:32.746

### Charges 2007

| | |
|---|---|
| Per person | € 5,00 - € 5,50 |
| child | free - € 3,50 |
| pitch incl. car | € 7,10 - € 11,30 |
| electricity | € 3,60 |

Check real time availability and at-the-gate prices...
www.alanrogers.com

# Greece

## GR8690 Camping Anemomilos
GR-24006 Finikounda (Peloponnese)
Tel: 272 307 1120

Having found this exceptional site, we are not sure we really want to encourage too many people to come here. We came to stay one night to inspect the site and stayed much longer enjoying the beautiful sandy beach, turquoise sea and the quayside fish restaurants in the nearby village. Many German campers come here for the windsurfing, sailing and beach life generally. The site offers 80 level pitches with good shade and great views. The small picturesque village, just a few minutes walk away, is at the back of the bay.

### Facilities
Two excellent toilet blocks includes showers, WCs and washbasins. Facilities for disabled visitors. Chemical disposal. Laundry with washing machines and ironing boards. Two kitchens with sinks, electric hobs for cooking, fridges and ice machines. Bar and small shop (1/5-31/10). Beach. Off site: Restaurant opposite. Riding. Finikounda and the Inouse Islands. Tractor rides around the local villages!

**Open:** 1 March - 31 November.

### Directions
Site is just 5 minutes walk from the centre of Finikounda. From the village head west and turn left at the end of the wide pavement. The site is 300 m. ahead.

### Charges guide
| | |
|---|---|
| Per person | € 4,50 - € 5,00 |
| child (5-12 yrs) | € 2,50 - € 3,00 |
| pitch | € 5,50 - € 7,00 |
| electricity | € 3,00 |

## GR8695 Camping Finikes
GR-24006 Finikounda (Peloponnese)
Tel: 272 302 8524. Email: camping-finikes@otenet.gr

This brand new site offers 80 level pitches with good shade and great views. It also has 12 bungalows to rent. Some pitches have high reed screens that give good protection from the blazing Greek sun and the turquoise sea is great for swimming, windsurfing and sailing. The site is at the western corner of Finikounda Bay and has direct access to the sandy beach. As you would expect from a new site the facilities are excellent and in low season, when there are 18 or less campers, each camper is given the keys to a WC and shower for their own personal facilities.

### Facilities
The excellent toilet block includes showers, WCs and washbasins. Facilities for disabled visitors. Kitchen includes sinks, electric hobs and fridges. Laundry. Facilities for emptying chemical toilet. Bar, small shop and restaurant. Accommodation to rent. Off site: Finikounda and the Inouse Islands.

**Open:** All year.

### Directions
Site is 2 km. from the centre of Finikounda. From the village head west and turn left into the site. GPS: N36:48.169 E21:46.863

### Charges 2007
| | |
|---|---|
| Per person | € 4,50 - € 5,00 |
| child (4-12 yrs) | € 3,00 - € 3,50 |
| pitch incl. car | € 5,50 - € 8,10 |
| electricity | € 3,00 |

No credit cards.

## GR8700 Camping Erodios
Koroni, Gialova, GR-24001 Pylos (Peloponnese)
Tel: 272 302 8240. Email: erodioss@otenet.gr

This brand new site sets a standard not seen anywhere else in Greece! The owner, Efthinios Panourgias, has given great thought to what is needed and then provided it to the highest possible standard in an environmentally friendly way. He is constantly on the site ensuring these high standards are maintained and already has plans for further improvements to the site. The 90 pitches have high reed screens to provide shade which is most welcome given the high temperatures even in the low season. There is direct access to a sandy beach and the glorious turquoise sea in a sheltered bay north of the busy town of Pylos.

### Facilities
Three excellent toilet blocks include showers, WCs and washbasins. Facilities for disabled visitors. Two kitchens include sinks, electric hobs and fridges. Laundry. Facilities for emptying chemical toilet. Motorcaravan service points. Very good shop. Bar/café with Internet. Excellent restaurant. Bicycle, car and motorbike rental. Barbecue. Play area for under 5s. Eight bungalows for rent.
Off site: Pylos.

**Open:** 25 March - 31 October.

### Directions
From Pylos head north on the main road and fork left towards Gialova. Once in the village turn left, signed to site and Golden Beach. Site is on the left in 700 m. From Gargaliari head south towards Pylos and in the village of Gialova turn right towards the site. GPS: N36:57.028 E21:42.030

### Charges 2007
| | |
|---|---|
| Per person | € 5,00 - € 6,00 |
| child | € 3,00 |
| pitch incl. electricity | € 9,00 - € 14,00 |

Check real time availability and at-the-gate prices...
www.alanrogers.com

# Greece

## GR8370 Camping Dionysus

Dassia, Kerkyra, GR-49100 Corfu (Ionian Islands)
Tel: 266 109 1417. Email: laskari7@otenet.gr

The Ionian island of Corfu is known by most as a popular tourist destination but perhaps not considered by many for camping. The hourly ferry from Igoumenitsa, takes 90 minutes to cross to Kerkyra and cost us only € 48 for our 7 m. motorcaravan and € 5.80 for each passenger each way. Ferries from Italian ports now stop here en-route to either Igoumenitsa or Patras so it is possible to break your journey to mainland Greece. The north of the island now has some good campsites and Dionysus is amongst them, with its 107 pitches of which 55 are suitable for touring units.

### Facilities

Two excellent toilet blocks include showers, WCs and washbasins. Sinks for dishwashing. Washing machine. Facilities for emptying chemical toilets. Bar, small shop and restaurant. Swimming pool. Off site: Beach 600 m. Kerkyra 9 km.

**Open:** 1 April - 15 October (depending on the weather).

### Directions

Most people will arrive in Corfu on one of the many ferries from either Igoumenista or one of the Italian ports. So, from the ferry terminal turn right initially signed Paleokastritsa. After 8 km. turn right at traffic lights signed Dassia. Site is on the right after 1 km. GPS: N39:39.413 E19:50.704

### Charges 2008

| | |
|---|---|
| Per person | € 4,80 - € 5,40 |
| child | € 2,60 - € 3,30 |
| pitch | € 9,90 - € 13,60 |

## GR8375 Camping Karda Beach

Dassia, P.O. Box 225, GR-49100 Corfu (Ionian Islands)
Tel: 266 109 3595. Email: campco@otenet.gr

The popular holiday island of Corfu offers many sporting and leisure activities and access to it is easy, and comparatively cheap, via one of the many ferries from either Igoumenitsa or one of the Italian ports serving the Greek mainland. Camping Karda Beach offers a quiet low season site with excellent facilities, close to the beach and the island's main town, Kerkyra. It also offers a popular high season site for families and those looking for good weather, good beaches and lots of activities close at hand. It has 127 good grassy pitches (70 for touring units), under tall trees, all clearly marked with flowering shrubs and with 16A electricity and water on each pitch.

### Facilities

Three excellent toilet blocks includes showers, WCs and washbasins. Facilities for disabled visitors. Fridges. Laundry. Facilities for emptying chemical toilet. Bar, small shop and restaurant (open all day). Swimming pool with sunbeds. Internet access. Billiards. Table football and table tennis. Children's playground and pool. Bungalows to rent. Off site: Beach 50 m. Kerkyra 12 km. Dassia 1-2 km.

**Open:** 20 April - 30 October.

### Directions

From the ferry terminal turn right initially signed Paleokastritsa. After 8 km. turn right at traffic lights signed Dassia. Go through Dassia and site is on the right after 1 km. just after a right hand bend. GPS: N39:39.146 E19:50.449

### Charges 2007

| | |
|---|---|
| Per person | € 5,80 - € 6,30 |
| child (4-10 yrs) | € 3,30 - € 3,50 |
| pitch incl. car and electricity | € 11,00 - € 14,70 |

## GR8385 Camping Paleokastritsa

Paleokastritsa, GR-49083 Corfu (Ionian Islands)
Tel: 266 304 1204

Paleokastritsa is a very popular holiday resort on Corfu and this may mean there is some traffic noise at this small, simple campsite. The village, as it once was, has one of the best beaches on the island and this is now shared by many hotels and rented apartments. The small harbour just 2 km. further down the hill is also very popular and being a dead end is a turning place for coaches and buses. For those looking for a quiet, low season campsite, this may be ideal. Apart from the basics, it has nothing to offer but that is perhaps one of its beauties.

### Facilities

Two clean toilet blocks include showers, WCs and washbasins. Sinks for dishwashing and laundry. Facilities for emptying chemical toilets. Off site: Beach 500 m. down steps.

**Open:** 1 May - 30 September.

### Directions

It could not be easier to find this site. As you enter Paleokastritsa it is on the right just as the built up area begins. GPS: N39:40.586 E19:40.517

### Charges guide

| | |
|---|---|
| Per person | € 4,20 - € 4,80 |
| child (4-10 yrs) | € 2,30 - € 2,90 |
| pitch incl. car | € 5,40 - € 7,00 |
| electricity | € 3,00 |

Check real time availability and at-the-gate prices...
www.alanrogers.com

### GR8420 Camping Poros Beach

Poros, GR-31100 Lefkada (Ionian Islands)
Tel: 264 509 5452. Email: irene@porosbeach.com.gr

Poros is at the southern end of the island of Lefkada and this site is at the end of a steep, winding and narrow lane (3 km. long and 10 hairpin bends). The owners have made a massive, recent investment in building new flats for rent at the top of the site where reception, the shop, pool and bar/restaurant are located. However, this has been at the expense of the campsite some 40 m. lower down at beach level. There are 53 pitches, all for touring units, set amongst olive and pine trees. It is impossible to use the site's internal road for vehicles so having stopped at reception you continue down the hill to a second entrance. A stony beach is just across the road and the small bay has a taverna and bar.

#### Facilities
The sanitary block is old and in need of investment, but it is acceptable. British and Turkish WCs. Facilities for disabled visitors but used as the cleaner's cupboard. Sinks for dishwashing. Chemical disposal. Small shop, bar and restaurant at the higher level. Swimming pool (15/6-16/9). Communal barbecue area. Off site: Stony beach.

**Open:** 1 May - 30 September.

#### Directions
From Lefkada take main road south towards and through Nidri. After climbing long hill, turn left, signed Poros. After 2 km. fork right down a narrow winding lane towards the site (3 km. long and 10 hairpin bends – meeting oncoming traffic is a bit of a problem! GPS: N38:38.501 E20:41.759

#### Charges guide
| | |
|---|---:|
| Per person | € 5,00 - € 7,00 |
| child | € 2,50 - € 4,00 |
| pitch | € 7,00 - € 10,50 |
| electricity | € 5,00 |

### GR8425 Camping Kariotes Beach

Kariotes, GR-31100 Lefkada (Ionian Islands)
Tel: 264 507 1103. Email: campkar@otenet.gr

The island of Lefkada is one of the few Ionian islands that you can access without using a ferry. This campsite is 500 m. from the beach on the main road south (slight traffic noise). There are 50 pitches amongst tall olive trees, but only about 15 places are suitable for caravans or motorhomes. A small, simple restaurant is opened on demand, so speak early to one of the Livitsanou family if you want to eat there. Kariotes village has a small mini-market and three tavernas in a square about 300 m. from the site. To reach the island, you will probably go through the tunnel and then cross the unique bridge – if the klaxon goes it is worth parking and watch the bridge go into action to allow access for boats. Lefkada town is large and probably you could find just about everything there but the rest of the island is rural and quiet.

#### Facilities
Two toilet blocks include the usual facilities. Sinks for dishwashing. Chemical disposal. Bar and restaurant subject to demand. Swimming pool (1/6-30/9). Off site: Village 300 m. Beach 500 m.

**Open:** 15 April - 10 October.

#### Directions
Lefkada is 100 km. south of Igoumenista, approached via Preveza. Follow signs for Aktio, through the tunnel (toll € 5 for motorcaravan) and then follow signs for Lefkada to the town by crossing the bridge. At the end of the causeway turn left and head around the bay (towards marina), then follow signs for Nidri. Just past Lidl, enter village of Kariotes and site is 300 m. on the right. Don't go down the slip road but turn right into the vehicle entrance. GPS: N38:48.258 E20:42.849

#### Charges guide
| | |
|---|---:|
| Per person | € 5,50 - € 6,00 |
| child | € 3,00 - € 3,50 |
| pitch incl. car | € 6,00 - € 8,50 |
| electricity | € 3,20 |

## Travelling to Greece

One of our site assessors, Dave Church, undertook a lengthy motorcaravan journey through Central Europe and into Greece, returning via Italy. Dave has made the following notes which we hope will be helpful for those planning to venture to Greece. Our thanks to Dave for his report.

### The route

Those visiting Greece for the first time will experience a warm and genuine welcome especially in the north where the British tourer is a still a relative rarity since the Balkans war.

The route into Greece travelling through Czech Republic, Hungary, Serbia and Macedonia is not as convoluted as certain rumours have led to believe. The main motorway is E75, a toll road and a vignette is required for Hungary, Serbia and Macedonia before entering Greece. Road surfaces are often poor and potholes are not unusual! Vigilance is required at all times.

Although these countries are not members of the European Union, the euro is readily accepted. Don't forget to inform your insurance company of your planned route and insist on a Green Card or you will incur extra insurance cover costs before entry is allowed. It's essential to carry all necessary vehicle documents.

From Italy there are three principal ferry ports: Venice, Ancona and Brindisi. Some ferry operators offer 'On board camping' with electrical hook-ups, showers and toilets. Passengers are allowed to sleep in their own caravans or motorcaravans. Pets are also accepted.

### Driving in Greece

Once in Greece major roads are of generally good quality. Many major roads charge tolls. Secondary roads inevitably are of poorer quality and a more careful approach is advised! Greek driving can be erratic. We found overtaking on both sides quite common, and there can be a rather cavalier approach to traffic signals. Unfortunately, Greece has one of Europe's highest incidence of road fatalities in Europe. Police patrol are common and random checks appear to be the norm. Mobile phones should not be used when driving. In the event of breakdown, two warning triangles are required, one should be placed 100 m. behind the vehicle and one much closer. Fuel prices are amongst the cheapest in Europe, and most petrol stations, particularly on motorways, accept credit cards. In more isolated areas, cash may be required.

### Camping in Greece

- Camping gas cylinders are readily available from many supermarkets and campsites. Some campsites even offer a refill facility, to be accepted at your own risk!
- Mobile phone coverage is good but their use can be expensive. Our standard rate was 95p per minute. It's worth considering purchasing a phone card. At either € 3 or € 5, this is probably the most cost effective method.
- It is essential to obtain the new European Health Insurance Card (formerly E111). Medical treatment is free upon presentation of this card. For minor ailments local pharmacies (Formakio) are available to dispense certain drugs and medicines without prescription. Doctors' surgeries and hospitals are generally efficient, but can be crowded in larger towns.
- Most campsites we visited were family run, well maintained with good facilities. Pitches are generally fairly small and safety distances are virtually non existent. Some sites provide a limited number of large pitches. In any event, it's worth checking before pitching. In remote areas facilities may be more basic, but quite acceptable. Camping Card International (CCI) is accepted on most campsites, although some will insist on retaining your passport. For longer stays (28 days or more) reduced rates are often available.
- Electrical amperage is generally between 6-10 amps. However, you will need to provide a CEE connector from the site supply.
- Most sites accept pets free of charge. Pets are accepted in Greece under the new 'Pet Passport Plan' providing all documents and vaccinations are up to date. You can obtain more information at the DEFRA website: www.defra.gov.uk.

Eating out in tavernas is invariably cheap, with a reasonable menu selection. Tipping is at your discretion. Visitors to Athens are highly recommended to use public transport which is cheap and reliable. Tickets for both the bus and underground system can be obtained from campsites or designated shops. Ferry services are, of course, popular and plentiful. Some may require advance booking. It's worth trawling the internet or maybe visiting the many travel agents to obtain the best prices.

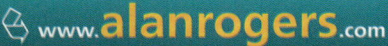

Check real time availability and at-the-gate prices...
www.alanrogers.com

# Croatia

**MAP 2**

With its warm seas, crystal-clear waters and over one thousand islands to explore, Croatia is an ideal place to try scuba diving. Diving centres can be found at the larger resorts.

The heart-shaped peninsula of Istria, located in the north, is among the most developed tourist regions in Croatia. Here you can visit the preserved Roman amphitheatre in Pula, the beautiful town of Rovinj with its cobbled streets and wooded hills, and the resort of Umag, well-known for its recreational activities, most notably tennis. Islands are studded all around the coast, making it ideal for sailing and diving enthusiasts. Istria also has the highest concentration of campsites.

Further south, in the province of Dalmatia, Split is the largest city on the Adriatic coast and home to the impressive Diolectian's Palace. From here the islands of Brac, Hvar, Vis and Korcula, renowned for their lively fishing villages and pristine beaches, are easily accessible by ferry. The old walled city of Dubrovnik is 150 km south. At over 2 km. long and 25 m. high, with 16 towers, a walk along the city walls affords spectacular views.

**Population**
4.5 million

**Capital**
Zagreb

**Climate**
Predominantly warm and hot in summer with temperatures of up to 40°C.

**Language**
Croatian, but English and German are widely spoken.

**Currency**
Kuna

**Telephone**
The country code is 00 385

**Banks**
Mon-Fri 08.00 - 19.00

**Shops**
Mainly Mon-Sat 08.00-20.00, although some close on Monday and Sundays.

# Croatia

CROATIA HAS THROWN OFF OLD COMMUNIST ATTITUDES AND BLOSSOMED INTO A LIVELY AND FRIENDLY PLACE TO VISIT. A COUNTRY STEEPED IN HISTORY, IT BOASTS SOME OF THE FINEST ROMAN RUINS IN EUROPE AND YOU'LL FIND PLENTY OF TRADITIONAL COASTAL TOWNS, CLUSTERS OF TINY ISLANDS AND MEDIAEVAL VILLAGES TO EXPLORE.

## Public Holidays

New Year's Day; Epiphany 6 Jan; Good Friday; Easter Monday; Labour Day 1 May; Parliament Day 30 May; Day of Anti-Fascist Victory 22 June; Statehood Day 25 june; Thanksgiving Day 5 Aug; Assumption 15 Aug; Independence Day 8 Oct; All Saints 1 Nov; Christmas 25, 26 Dec.

## Motoring

Croatia is proceeding with a vast road improvement programme. There are still some roads which leave a lot to be desired but things have improved dramatically. Roads along the coast can become heavily congested in summer and queues are possible at border crossings. Drive carefully especially at night - roads are usually unlit and have sharp bends. Tolls: some motorways, bridges and tunnels. Cars towing a caravan or trailer must carry two warning triangles. It is illegal to overtake military convoys.

## Tourist Office

Croatian National Tourist Office
2 The Lanchesters,
162-164 Fulham Palace Road
London W6 9ER
Tel: 0208 563 7979  Fax: 0208 563 2616
Email: info@cnto.freeserve.co.uk
Internet: www.croatia.hr

## British Embassy

Ivana Lucica 4, Zagreb
Tel: (385)(1) 6009 100

## Places of interest

*Dubrovnik:* particularly appealing is the old town Stari Grad, with marble-paved squares and steep cobbled streets.

*Risnjak and Paklencia National Parks:* both have excellent areas for hiking, the latter has excellent rock climbing opportunities.

*Rovinj:* an active fishing port, an excellent collection of marine life can be found at the aquarium.

*Split:* Diocletian's Palace, Maritime Museum.

*Zagreb:* the capital of Croatia, with a whole host of museums.

## Cuisine of the region

*Brodet:* mixed fish stewed with rice

*Burek:* a layered pie made with meat or cheese

*Cesnjovka:* garlic sausage

*Kulen:* paprika-flavoured salami

*Manistra od bobica:* beans and fresh maize soup

*Piroska:* cheese doughnut

*Struki:* baked cheese dumpling

Virtually every region produces its own varieties of wine.

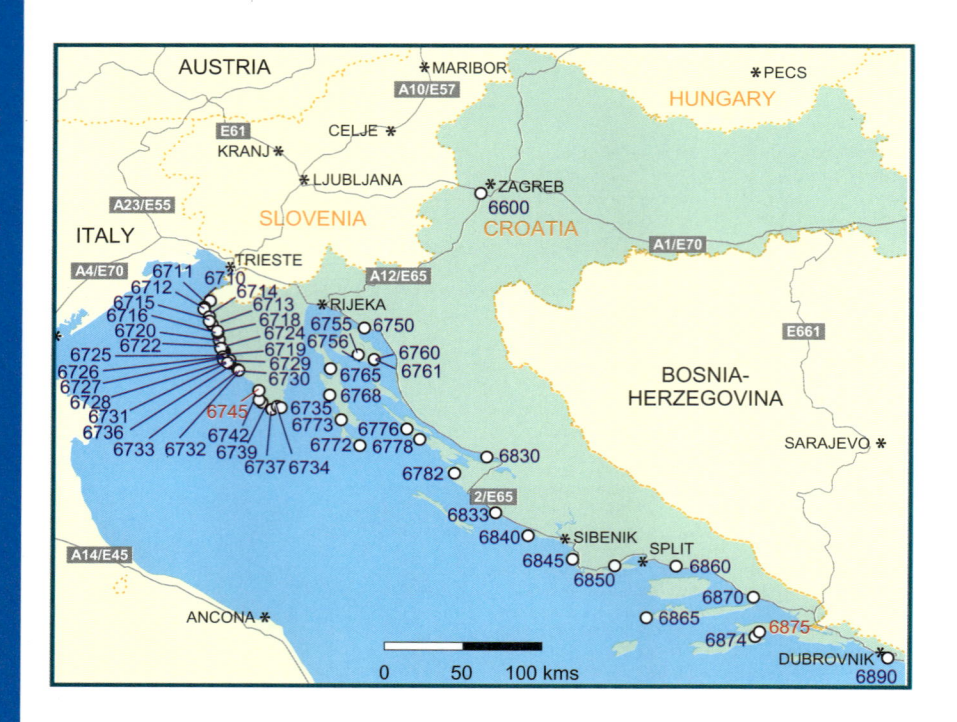

### CR6710 Naturist Camping Kanegra

Kanegra bb, HR-52470 Umag (Istria)

Tel: 052 709 000. Email: camp.kanegra@istraturist.hr

Sitting as it does, almost on the Slovenian border, this could be said to be the first and last campsite in Croatia and it is part of the Istraturist group. The smart air conditioned reception sets the tone for this very pleasant naturist site which is located alongside the large Kanegra bungalow complex, and campers are able to share its comprehensive facilities. The site occupies a five hectare strip of coast winding between the imposing 120 metre rock face of an ancient quarry and the clear sea. It is directly across the bay from the town of Portoroz (Port of Roses) which is Slovenia's major seaside resort and is a pleasant backdrop from Kanegra. The site has an open aspect with very little shade and sparkling clear waters off the rocky beach which runs its total length. A sensible safe area is roped off for swimmers. There are 190 level pitches on sandy soil with sparse grass (90 of which are seasonal), they vary in size (80-100 sq.m) and are marked out and numbered, with electricity (10A; Europlugs). This is a pleasant naturist site with a calming family atmosphere and pleasant places to eat. The restaurant and buffet bar enjoy fine sea views and there is an animation programme for all age groups. Unusually for naturist sites, there is no objection to single men. Its proximity to Slovenia (Portoroz 13 km. around the bay) makes it a possible base for visiting some of this country's delights as well as those of Croatia.

#### Facilities

Two well equipped toilet blocks with washing up and laundry sinks are kept very clean. Free washing machine. Beach showers. There are no facilities for disabled campers here. Motorcaravan service point. Supermarket. Library. Two bars, three snack bars and two restaurants, all open until late. Nightly 'Tropic' disco in the adjacent bungalow complex but reportedly this doesn't disturb the campsite. Playground in beach area. Use of all sporting facilities in the bungalow park. Many watersports. Off site: Riding 3 km. Boat launching 1 km. Fishing. Tennis in Umag.

**Open:** 21 April - 30 September.

#### Directions

From Koper in the north just over the Italian border, follow signs to Umag however turn north towards Kanegra 5 km. before Umag. If approaching from the south, after Umag follow the main coast road north towards Savudrija (do not turn off towards this town) and then Kanegra.
GPS: N45:28.782 E13:34.260

#### Charges 2007

| | |
|---|---|
| Per person | € 3,50 - € 6,00 |
| child (5-11 yrs) | € 2,00 - € 3,50 |
| pitch incl. electricity | € 7,00 - € 15,00 |
| dog | € 2,00 - € 3,00 |

For stays less than 3 nights in high season add 10%.

## CR6711 Autocamp Pineta

Istarska bb, HR-52475 Savudrija (Istria)

Tel: 052 709 550. Email: camp.pineta@istraturist.hr

One of the older sites at the western end of Istria, it is part of the Istraturist Group and has been greatly improved over the last few years. Pineta is a medium sized site of 17 hectares, getting its name from being set amongst a forest of fully mature pine trees around two sides of a coastal bay. Split by the main beach access road, the reception area is separate from the camping area which has a security entrance by the shop. This is a site for those who prefer cooler situations as the dense pines provide abundant shade. Those who like the peaceful life will enjoy this site. There are 460 pitches of which 160 are occupied on a long stay basis. Pitches are numbered and are 80-120 sq.m. all having access to electricity (10A). Sea bathing is easy from the site and sunbathing areas are on the rocks the whole length of the site. Fishing is possible (with permit). Some pitches are sited a long walking distance from the sanitary blocks, but there are pleasant views on the way.

### Facilities

Toilet blocks have been refurbished to a high standard. Hot and cold showers (plus showers for dogs). Mostly British style WCs and a few Turkish style. Excellent facilities for disabled campers. Dishwashing and laundry sinks. Fresh water at toilet blocks only apart from 'blue coded' pitches. Drive over motorcaravan service point. Supermarket. Six bars, three restaurants and a snack bar, all open long hours with reasonable prices. Tennis. Fishing (subject to permit). Barbecues on communal areas only. Activities centre. Evening music. Off site: Gas is available in local garage 500 m. from the site entrance. Riding 3 km. Golf 3 km.

**Open:** 21 April - 30 September.

### Directions

From Trieste - Koper (Capodistra) - Umag road look for Savundrija signs. Site is 6 km. north of Umag.

### Charges 2007

| | |
|---|---|
| Per person | € 3,50 - € 6,00 |
| child (5-11 yrs) | € 2,00 - € 3,50 |
| pitch incl. electricity | € 6,00 - € 12,20 |

For stays less than 3 nights in high season add 10%.

## CR6712 Camping Stella Maris

Savudrijska cesta bb, HR-52470 Umag (Istria)

Tel: 052 710 900. Email: camp.stella.maris@istraturist.hr

This extremely large, sprawling site of 4.5 hectares is split by the Umag - Savudrija road. The camping site is to the east and reception and the amazing Sol Stella Maris leisure complex, where the Croatian open tennis tournament is held (amongst other competitions), is to the west. Located some 2 km. from the centre of Umag, the site comprises some 575 pitches of which 60 are seasonal and 20 are for tour operators. They are arranged in rows on gently sloping ground, some are shaded. Campers select their pitches all of which have electricity (10A). Many improvements over the last few years have made a huge impact on the standard of camping here. The site's real strength is its attachment to the leisure complex, with numerous facilities available to campers. There are two swimming pools (one sea water) and a very pretty pebble beach area where sun loungers may be hired for € 1 per day. There is a huge entertainment area and the choice of seven restaurants and bars including a cocktail bar and buffet bar with great sea views at night. Boats may be launched or hired at the marina and bikes hired for some challenging tours of the area.

### Facilities

Three sanitary blocks of a very high standard. Hot water throughout. Excellent facilities for disabled visitors. Dishwashing and laundry sinks. Large supermarket (07.00-22.00 hrs opposite reception). Huge range of restaurants, bars and snack bars. International Tennis centre. Water sports. Fishing (permit required from Umag). Animation programme for children. Communal barbecue areas. Off site: Land train every 15 minutes into Umag and a local bus service to towns further along the coast. Excursions organised. Golf 25 km. Riding 1 km.

**Open:** 21 April - 30 September.

### Directions

Site is 2.5 km. north of Umag. On entering Umag look for signs on the main coast road to all campsites and follow the Stella Maris signs.

### Charges 2007

| | |
|---|---|
| Per person | € 3,50 - € 6,80 |
| child (5-11 yrs) | € 2,00 - € 4,00 |
| pitch | € 8,00 - € 15,00 |

For stays less than 3 nights in high season add 10%.

## CR6713 Camping Mareda

Mareda, HR-52466 Novigrad (Istria)

Tel: 052 755 291. Email: camping@laguna-novigrad.hr

Camping Mareda is about 4 km. from Novigrad, a small and picturesque coastal town. It is surrounded by a wood of oak trees, which stretches as far as the coast, and many acres of vineyards. Mareda is on hilly ground with 800 sloping grass and gravel pitches, most with shade from mature trees and some with views of the sea. There are 410 pitches for touring units, all with 16A electricity and 28 with electricity, water and drainage. Some are marked and numbered on two areas near the sea, the others are for free camping in other areas of the site where it may be difficult to find space in high season. This site is an ideal base for day trips to Novigrad, Pula or Rovinj or for sailing, diving and swimming in the Adriatic. In high season the site organises masked balls, live music with dancing and 'The Blue Night of Mareda'. There is a private beach, partly rocky, partly concrete, with a pier for fishing and which creates a safe area for swimming.

### Facilities

Four modern toilet blocks with British and Turkish style toilets, open plan washbasins and hot showers. Child-size toilets and basins. Laundry with sinks and washing machine. Dishwashing under cover. Supermarket. Coffee bar and normal bar with terrace. Restaurant. Tennis. Fishing. Boats, kayaks, canoes and pedaloes for hire. Games hall with video games. Organised entertainment. Off site: Historic towns of Pula, Novigrad and Rovinj are close.

**Open:** 1 April - 30 September.

### Directions

In Novigrad follow site signs for 4 km. north and then left to the site. GPS: N45:20.618 E13:32.889

### Charges 2007

| | |
|---|---|
| Per person | € 3,40 - € 5,90 |
| child (5-10 yrs) | free - € 3,50 |
| pitch | € 2,80 - € 9,90 |
| electricity | € 2,20 - € 3,00 |
| dog | € 3,00 - € 4,50 |

---

## CR6714 Camping Finida

Finida bb, HR-52470 Umag (Istria)

Tel: 725950. Email: camp.finida@istraturist.hr

Finida is part of the Istraturist group and is a contrast to other sites in the area in that it is a small and unassuming with a rustic Croatian feel on just 3.3 hectares. Many improvements have been made over the last few years. The beach runs the length of the site. It is heavily wooded affording abundant shade. Large motorcaravans will be tested in reaching some areas of the site due to narrow roads and leaning trees. There are 280 marked pitches (90-100 sq.m), all with 10A electricity (Europlugs), 103 also have water and TV connection. The lack of a swimming pool is not a problem as the site is alongside the sea with pleasant large flat rocks and a stony beach for sunbathing. There is a large choice of watersports with pedaloes for hire, surfing (in the right weather) and there is a resident diving club where lessons can be purchased. A delightful restaurant has a patio looking over the sea and the views at night are very special. Finida will appeal to those who prefer the cosiness of a smaller site.

### Facilities

Three new toilet blocks contain mostly British style WCs and a few Turkish style with all modern facilities. New facilities for disabled campers. Dishwashing and laundry sinks (hot and cold water). Motorcaravan service point (a bit tight to drive onto). Small but well stocked supermarket. Bar, snack bar and restaurant (08.00 - midnight). Washing machines. Table tennis and minigolf. Fishing (subject to permit). Boats may be moored off the beach. Pedalos. Bicycle hire. Communal barbecue areas. Off site: Five buses per day into Umag and Novigrad. Golf 10 km. Riding 3 km.

**Open:** 21 April - 30 September.

### Directions

Site is on the right off the Umag - Norigrad, 4 km. south of Umag.

### Charges 2007

| | |
|---|---|
| Per person | € 3,50 - € 6,00 |
| child (5-11 yrs) | € 2,00 - € 3,50 |
| pitch incl. electricity | € 7,00 - € 15,00 |
| dog | € 2,00 - € 3,00 |

Check real time availability and at-the-gate prices...
www.alanrogers.com

## CR6715 Camping Park Umag

Karigador bb, HR-52466 Novigrad (Istria)

Tel: 052 725 040. Email: camp.park.umag@istraturist.hr

This extremely large site is very well planned in that just 50% of the 127 hectares is used for the pitches, thus leading to lots of open space around the pitch area. It is the largest of the Istraturist group of sites. The very long curved beach is of rock and shingle with grassy sunbathing areas. There are many watersports on offer and a new swimming pool complex has four pools, cascades and fountains. Of the 1,800 pitches, 1,440 of varying sizes, all with 10A electricity, are for tourers and there are 350 seasonal pitches. Some pitches have shade. Several of the restaurant/bars offer excellent views over the sea and are most attractive for a romantic dinner. The site is very popular with the Dutch and a friendly and happy atmosphere is prevalent even in the busiest times. Some noise is transmitted from the road alongside the site and there is a late night disco which may disturb some campers (choose your pitch carefully). The ancient towns of Umag and Novigrad are close and served by buses for those who wish to explore their fascinating past. The supporting entertainment and other events including sports facilities, combined with good value for money make this a great choice for your camping holiday.

### Facilities

There are 10 toilet blocks which include 2 bathrooms with deep tubs. Two blocks have children's WCs and there are facilities for disabled campers. The site has plans to update these facilities. Dishwashing and laundry sinks. Fresh water and waste water points only at toilet blocks. Drive over motorcaravan service point. Range of shops and supermarket. Bars, snack bars and restaurant (musical entertainment some evenings) all open early morning to midnight (one until the small hours). Tennis. Fishing (permit from Umag). Football, minigolf, table tennis. Watersports. Swimming pool complex. Off site: Riding near. Bus service to Umag and Novigrad.

**Open:** 20 April - 30 September.

### Directions

Site is located on the Umag - Novigrad road approx. 6 km. south of Umag. Look for large signs.

### Charges 2007

| | |
|---|---|
| Per person | € 3,80 - € 7,00 |
| child (5-11 yrs) | € 2,00 - € 4,50 |
| pitch incl. electricity | € 8,60 - € 17,50 |
| dog | € 2,00 - € 3,20 |

For stays less than 3 nights in high season add 10%.

## CR6716 Camping Laterna

Lanterna, HR-52440 Porec (Istria)

Tel: 052 404 500. Email: laterna@valamar.com

This is one of the largest sites in Croatia with an amazing selection of activities and high standards and is part of the Camping on the Adriatic group. Reception is buzzing in high season as around 10,000 guests are on site. Set in 90 hectares with over 3 kilometres of beach, there are 3,000 pitches of which 2,600 are for touring units. Facilities at Lanterna are impressive with the whole operation running smoothly for the campers. The land is sloping in parts and terraced in others. There is a large pool and pretty bay with rocky beaches and buoyed safety areas. Some of the marked and numbered pitches are shaded and arranged to take advantage of the topography. Pitches are 60-120 sq.m with some superb locations right on the sea, although these tend to be taken first so it is advisable to book ahead. Some of the better pitches are in a 'reserved booking' area. Terracing has improved the view in many areas. Electrical connections are 10A. Many activities and quality entertainment for all are available both on and off site – you are spoilt for choice here, including a vast choice of places to eat. Prices tend to be higher than other sites in the area but you get value for money with the supporting facilities.

### Facilities

The 14 sanitary blocks (many refurbished in 2007) are clean and good quality. Children's facilities and baby care areas, some Turkish style WCs, hot showers with some blocks providing facilities for disabled people. Three supermarkets sell most everyday requirements. Fresh fish shop. Four restaurants, bars and snack bars and fast food outlets. Adult's pool and two children's swimming pools. Sand-pit and play areas, with animation for all in high season. Tennis. Table tennis. Bicycle hire. Watersports. Boats for rent. Minigolf. Riding. Dogs are restricted to a certain area. Internet café. Jetty and ramp for boats. Off site: Nearest large supermarket in Novigrad, 9 km. An hourly bus service runs from the reception area. Fishing. Riding 500 m.

**Open:** 1 April - 15 October.

### Directions

The turn to Laterna is well signed off the Novigrad to Porec road about 8 km. south of Novigrad. Continue for about 2 km. down the turn off road towards the coast and the campsite is difficult to miss on the right hand side.

### Charges 2007

| | |
|---|---|
| Per person | € 3,85 - € 6,60 |
| child (4-10 yrs) | free - € 4,65 |
| pitch incl. electricity | € 6,60 - € 12,25 |
| with water | € 8,35 - € 14,95 |

Prices for pitches by the sea are higher.

*Check real time availability and at-the-gate prices...*

www.alanrogers.com

## CR6720 Naturist Centre Ulika

Cervar, HR-52440 Porec (Istria)

Tel: 052 436 325. Email: mail@plavalaguna.hr

One of the many naturist campsites in Croatia, Ulika is run by the same concern as Zelena Laguna (CR6722) and Bijela Uvala (CR6724) and offers similar facilities. The site is well located, occupying a small peninsula of some 15 hectares. This means that there is only a short walk to the sea from anywhere on the site. The ground is mostly gently sloping with a covering of rough grass and there are 388 pitches with electricity connections. One side of the site is shaded with mature trees but the other side is almost devoid of shade and could become very hot. There are many activities on site (see below) and an excellent swimming pool. The reception office opens 24 hours for help and information. Single men are not accepted. All in all, this is a pleasant, uncomplicated site which is well situated, well managed and peaceful.

### Facilities

Six toilet blocks provide mostly British style WCs, washbasins (half with hot water) and showers (around a third with controllable hot water). Facilities for disabled visitors. Dishwashing and laundry sinks (half with hot water). Laundry. Motorcaravan service point. Supermarket (seven days per week). Restaurant, pizzeria and snacks. Bicycle hire. Swimming pool. Fishing. Tennis. Table tennis. Minigolf. Water sports - water skiing, windsurfing, etc. Volleyball. Boating - marina on site. Off site: Bicycle hire 3 km. Riding 15 km. Porec the nearest town is 6 km. (a must to visit) with a regular bus service running from site reception.

**Open:** 19 March - 7 October.

### Directions

Site is approx. 3 km. off the main Novigrad - Porec road, signed in village of Cevar.
GPS: N45:15.424 E13:35.027

### Charges 2007

| | |
|---|---|
| Per person | € 3,80 - € 7,00 |
| child (4-10 yrs) | free - € 4,90 |
| pitch | € 5,60 - € 13,20 |
| electricity | € 2,30 - € 3,20 |
| dog | € 3,10 - € 5,60 |

## CR6722 Autokamp Zelena Laguna

HR-52440 Porec (Istria)

Tel: 052 410 101. Email: mail@plavalaguna.hr

A busy medium sized site (by Croatian standards), Zelena Laguna (green lagoon) is very popular with families and boat owners. Part of the Plava Laguna Leisure group that has eight other campsites and seven hotels in the vicinity, it is long established and is improved and modernised each year as finances permit. The 1,100 pitches (540 for touring units) are a mixture of level, moderately sloping and terraced ground and range in size from 40-120 sq.m. Slopes will be encountered on the site with a quite steep hill leading to the highest point allowing impressive views over the sea. Access to the pitches is by hard surfaced roads and shingle tracks which generally allow adequate space to manoeuvre. There are plenty of electrical hook-ups (10A). 42 super pitches are very popular and in other areas there are many water points. Like all others in the area, Zelena Laguna can get very crowded in late June, July and August and as it can get very hot in high summer (40°C), the pitches nearest the sea and therefore the sea breezes, are recommended (book ahead). The sea runs along two sides of the site and has mostly rocky beaches with Blue Flag status into which paved sunbathing areas have been inserted. At one end of the beach is an impressive marina where visitors may park their yachts. Approximately 25% of the beach area is reserved for naturists. There are many attractions to amuse you here or ample opportunity to just relax as it is quite peaceful.

### Facilities

The sanitary blocks are good and some have been refurbished. The washbasins have hot water and there are free hot controllable showers in all blocks. Toilets are mostly British style and there are facilities for disabled campers. Supermarket and mini-market. Several restaurants and snack bars. Swimming pool. Sub-aqua diving (with instruction). Tennis (instruction available). Five-a-side football. Bicycle hire. Boat hire (motor and sailing). Boat launching. Beach volleyball. Riding. Aerobics. Animation programme for the family. Off site: Small market and parade of shops selling beach wares, souvenirs etc. immediately outside site. Regular bus service and also a small 'land train' known as the 'Bumble Zug' from the adjacent hotel complex into the centre of Porec (alternatively it is 15 minutes drive but parking tends to be somewhat chaotic) but for the adventurous a water taxi to Porec harbour. Supermarkets in Porec (4 km). Fishing 5 km. (permit required). Riding 300 m.

**Open:** 19 March - 7 October.

### Directions

Site is between the coast road and the sea with turning 2 km. from Porec towards Vrsar. It is very well signed and is part of a large multiple hotel complex.

### Charges 2007

| | |
|---|---|
| Per person | € 3,80 - € 7,00 |
| child (4-9 yrs) | free - € 4,90 |
| pitch | € 5,60 - € 13,20 |
| electricity | € 2,30 - € 3,20 |
| dog | € 3,10 - € 5,60 |

## CR6724 Camping Bijela Uvala

Bijela Uvala, Zelena Laguna, HR-52440 Porec (Istria)
Tel: 052 410 551. Email: mail@plavalaguna.hr

Bijela Uvala is part of the Plava Laguna Leisure group and is a large friendly campsite with an extensive range of facilities. The direct sea access makes the site very popular in high season. The topography of the site is undulating and the gravelled or grassy pitches are divided into zones which vary considerably. As the coastline winds along the site, the rocky and intermittently paved sea access increases with boat launching facilities, beach volleyball and various eateries dispersed along it. The 2000 pitches, 1476 for touring, are compact and due to the terrain some have excellent sea views and breezes, however as usual these are the most sought after so book early. They range from 60-120 sq.m. and all have electricity, 400 also have water connections. Some are formal with hedging, some are terraced and most have good shade from established trees or wooded areas. There are also very informal areas where unmarked pitches are on generally uneven ground. The smaller of the two pools is in a busy complex adjacent to the sea which includes a large entertainment area and a family style restaurant. There are many sporting facilities and fairground style amusements (some at extra cost). The adjoining campsite Zelena Laguna is owned by the same organisation and access to its beach (including a naturist section) and facilities is via a gate between the sites or along the beach. A large sports complex is also within walking distance. This site is very similar to Camping Zelena Laguna but with fewer permanent pitches.

### Facilities

Eight sanitary blocks are clean and well equipped with mainly British style WCs. Free hot showers and hot water for dishwashing and laundry. Washing machines. Facilities for disabled visitors. Motorcaravan service point. Gas. Fridge boxes. Two restaurants, three fast food cafés, two bars and a bakery. Large well equipped supermarket and mini-market. Two swimming pool complexes, one with a medium size pool and the other a larger lagoon style with fountains. Tennis. Playground. Amusements. TV room. Animation centre. Off site: Zelena Laguna campsite facilities. Sports complex 100 m. Naturist beach 25 m.

**Open:** 19 March - 7 October.

### Directions

The site adjoins Zelena Laguna. From the main Porec to Vrsar coast road turn off towards coast and the town of Zelena Laguna 4 km. south of Porec and follow campsite signs.

### Charges 2007

| | |
|---|---|
| Per person | € 3,80 - € 7,00 |
| child (4-9 yrs) | free - € 4,90 |
| pitch | € 5,60 - € 13,20 |
| electricity | € 2,30 - € 3,20 |
| dog | € 3,10 - € 5,60 |

---

# POREČ   Istria   CROATIA

## PLAVA LAGUNA
### SPECIAL OFFERS 2008:

- CHILDREN GO FREE
  ✓ 0-3,99 years for the whole season
  ✓ 4-9,99 years for the low season

- DISCOUNTS
  ✓ for the low season
  ✓ 10 % extra discount for longer, continuous stays in low season
  ✓ discounts for members of the Laguna Club, CCI, autoclubs and naturist association

### Attractive services for a great holiday:
✓ sport & animation
✓ sea beach with sunbathing terraces (Blue Flag recognition)
✓ pools
✓ comfortable waterhouses
✓ parcelled pitches
✓ boat mooring
✓ restaurants

PLAVA LAGUNA – HR Poreč, R. Končara 12
Tel. +385/52/410-102; Fax +385/52/451-044
reservations@plavalaguna.hr
www.plavalaguna.hr

Camping ★★★★ ZELENA LAGUNA: An extraordinary experience amidst nature BIJELA UVALA: Family holiday campsite with 2 pools, NATURIST CENTER ULIKA: Naturist centre with new mobilehomes, CAMPING PUNTICA ★★ Green and quiet

# Croatia

## CR6726 Naturist Camping Istra

Grgeti 35, HR-52452 Funtana (Istria)
Tel: 052 445123. Email: istra@riviera.hr

Located in the tiny and picturesque village of Funtana, this peaceful site is part of the Camping on the Adriatic group. Istra has a fine array of facilities and, although there is no pool, it is surrounded by sparkling sea water on three sides. The formally marked pitches ring the peninsula and some are directly at the waters edge giving great views of the island off to the South (early booking is advised). The usual ban regarding single men and men only groups applies. Additionally motorcycles, although not banned, are not welcome. There are 1000 pitches on site with 745 for tourists, most with ample shade and varying in size from about 60-120 sq.m. The ground is undulating and some areas have been cut into low terraces. There is 10A electricity and water points scattered around the site. Two large, informal and central zones have sloping pitches, some with water and electricity. The pretty town of Vrsar has many points of interest and two small supermarkets. This is a very pleasant site with a peaceful air and eminently suitable for those who just want to relax in the sun.

### Facilities

Five old and five new sanitary buildings provide toilets, washbasins, showers (hot and cold), hair dryers and some facilities for disabled campers. Washing up and laundry sinks, some with hot water. Laundry facilities. Small supermarket. Restaurant and bars. Shop. Play areas. Entertainment for children in high season. Miniclub. Organised sport. Minigolf. Tennis. Massage. WiFi near reception. Off site: Fishing. Riding 1 km. Shops and restaurants in Funtana short walk from the gate. Serious shopping is Porec, some 7 km. away with a regular bus service from the village.

**Open:** 1 April - 8 October.

### Directions

Site is signed off the Porec - Vrsar road about 6 km. south of Porec in the village of Funtana. Access for large units could be difficult when turning off the main road from the direction of Porec, If this looks as if it might be difficult, go past the signed turning and turn around in the night club car park a few metres further on. The problem is less when approaching from Vrsar.

### Charges 2007

| | |
|---|---|
| Per person | € 3,35 - € 5,80 |
| child (4-10 yrs) | free - € 3,90 |
| pitch incl. electricity | € 5,70 - € 13,10 |
| with full services | € 8,25 - € 14,10 |
| dog | € 3,35 - € 4,75 |

Prices for pitches by the sea are higher.

## CR6727 Camping Valkanela

Valkanela, HR-52450 Vrsar (Istria)
Tel: 052 445 216. Email: valkanela@maistra.hr

Camping Valkanela is located in a beautiful green bay, right on the Adriatic Sea, between the villages of Vrsar and Funtana. It offers 1200 pitches, all with 6A electricity. Pitches near the beach are numbered, have shade from mature trees and are slightly sloping towards the sea. Those towards the back of the site are on open fields without much shade and are not marked or numbered. Most numbered pitches have water points close by, but the back pitches have to go to the toilet blocks for water. Unfortunately the number of pitches has increased dramatically over the years, many are occupied by seasonal campers and statics of every description, and parts of the site resemble a shanty town. Access roads are gravel. For those who like activity, Valkanela has four gravel tennis courts, beach volleyball and opportunities for diving, water skiing and boat rental. There is a little marina for mooring small boats and a long rock and pebble private beach, with some grass lawns for sunbathing. It is a short stroll to the surrounding villages with their bars, restaurants and shops. There may be some noise nuisance from the disco outside the entrance and compared to most the site looks overcrowded and depressing.

### Facilities

Fifteen toilet blocks of varying styles and ages provide toilets, open style washbasins and controllable hot showers. Child-size toilets, basins and showers. Bathroom (free). Facilities for disabled visitors. Laundry with sinks and washing machines. Dishwashing under cover. Two supermarkets. Souvenir shops and newspaper kiosk. Bars and restaurants with dance floor and stage. Patisserie. Tennis. Minigolf. Fishing. Bicycle hire. Games room. Marina with boat launching. Boat and pedalo hire. Disco outside entrance. Daily animation programme for children up to 12 yrs. Excursions organised. Off site: Riding 2 km.

**Open:** 7 April - 30 September.

### Directions

Follow campsite signs from Vrsar.
GPS: N45:09.913 E13:36.434

### Charges 2007

| | |
|---|---|
| Per person | € 4,20 - € 6,40 |
| child (5-11 yrs) | free - € 3,60 |
| pitch incl. electricity | € 6,40 - € 14,90 |
| dog | € 2,50 - € 6,00 |

Check real time availability and at-the-gate prices...
www.alanrogers.com

### CR6725 **Camping Porto Sole**
Porto Sole, HR-52450 Vrsar (Istria)
Tel: **052 441 198**. Email: **portosole@maistra.hr**

Located near the pretty town of Vrsar and its charming marina, Porto Sole is a large campsite with 800 pitches and is part of the Maistra Group. The pitches vary; some are in the open with semi shade and are fairly flat, others are under a heavy canopy of pines on undulating land. There is some terracing near the small number of water frontage pitches. The site could be described as almost a clover leaf shape with one area for rental accommodation and natural woods, another for sporting facilities and the other two for pitches. There is a large water frontage and two tiny bays provide delightful sheltered rocky swimming areas. In peak season the site is buzzing with activity and the hub of the site is the pools, disco and shopping arcade area where there is also a pub and both formal and informal eating areas. The food available is varied but simple with a tiny terrace restaurant by the water.

#### Facilities
Five completely renovated toilet blocks have mostly British style WCs and are clean and well maintained. The low numbers of showers (common to most Croatian sites) result in long queues. Facilities for disabled visitors and children. Washing machines and dryers. Dishwashing and laundry (cold water). Large well stocked supermarket (1/5-15/9). Small shopping mall. Pub. Pizzeria. Formal and informal restaurants. Swimming pools (1/5-29/9). Play area (alongside beach). Boules. Tennis. Table tennis. Minigolf. Massage studio. Disco. Animation in season. Mini Club. Scuba diving courses. Boat launching.
Off site: Marina, sailing 1 km. Vrsar 2 km. Riding 3 km.

**Open:** 7 April - 29 September.

#### Directions
Follow signs towards Vrsar and take turn towards Koversada, then follow campsite signs.

#### Charges 2007
| | |
|---|---|
| Per person | € 4,60 - € 6,50 |
| child (5-12 yrs) | free - € 4,20 |
| pitch | € 6,40 - € 12,80 |
| dog | € 3,10 - € 5,30 |

Camping Cheques accepted.

## CR6729 Naturist Camping Koversada

Koversada, HR-52450 Vrsar (Istria)

Tel: 052 441 378. Email: koversada-camp@maistra.hr

According to history, the first naturist on Koversada was the famous adventurer Casanova. Today Koversada is an enclosed holiday park for naturists with bungalows, 1,700 pitches (1438 for tourers, all with 6/8A electricity), a shopping centre and its own island. The main attraction of this site is the Koversada island, connected to the mainland by a small bridge. It is only suitable for tents, but has a restaurant and two toilet blocks. Between the island and the mainland is an enclosed, shallow section of water for swimming and, on the other side of the bridge, an area for mooring small boats. The pitches are of average size on grass and gravel ground and slightly sloping. Pitches on the mainland are numbered and partly terraced under mature pine and olive trees. Pitching on the island is haphazard, but there is also shade from mature trees. The bottom row of pitches on the mainland has views over the island and the sea. The site is surrounded by a long beach, part sand, part paved.

### Facilities

Seventeen toilet blocks provide British and Turkish style toilets, washbasins and controllable hot showers. Child-size toilets and basins. Family bathroom (free). Facilities for disabled visitors. Dishwashing under cover. Laundry service. Supermarket. Kiosks with newspapers and tobacco. Several bars and restaurants. Playing field. Tennis. Minigolf. Fishing. Boats, surf boards, canoes and kayaks for hire. Paragliding. 'Tweety club' for children. Live music. Sports tournaments. Off site: Riding 2 km.

**Open:** 15 April - 30 September.

### Directions

Site is just south from Vrsar. From Vrsar, follow site signs. GPS: N45:08.573 E13:36.316

### Charges 2007

| | |
|---|---|
| Per person | € 4,70 - € 6,60 |
| child (7-11 yrs) | free - € 3,30 |
| child (12-18 yrs) | € 3,20 - € 4,50 |
| pitch | € 6,20 - € 15,00 |
| dog | € 3,10 - € 5,30 |

Camping Cheques accepted.

---

**Naturist park Koversada Vrsar** — Istria, Green Mediterranean, Croatia

New seaside lots! Children's clubs and playgrounds! ONLINE BOOKING

A Mediterranean paradise in a superb natural setting; the gentle climate and clean seas have made this a favourite summer holiday destination for many generations of naturists.

tel: +385 (0)52 441 278 / fax: 441 761 / koversada-camp@maistra.hr    www.maistra.hr    maistra

---

## CR6718 Naturist Camping Solaris

Lanterna bb, HR-52440 Porec (Istria)

Tel: 052 465 110. Email: camping-porec@valamar.com

This naturist site has a most pleasant feel and when we visited in high season there were lots of happy people having fun. A pretty cove and lots of beach frontage with cool pitches under trees makes the site very attractive. 500 of the 1,330 pitches are available to tourists, with 600 long stay units. There are 80 fully serviced pitches (100 m. sq) available on a first-come, first-served basis, an ample supply of electricity hook-ups and plentiful water points. As this is a naturist site, single men and groups consisting of men only are prohibited and there are restrictions on photography. There is a small, but very pleasant pool close to the restaurant which has a lifeguard (clothing is not allowed in the pool). For those who embrace the naturist regime or want to give it a try, this is a pleasant, quiet site with above average facilities in an area of outstanding natural beauty.

### Facilities

Thirteen excellent, fully equipped toilet blocks (four upgraded in 2007) provide toilets, washbasins and showers (hot and cold). Some blocks have facilities for disabled visitors. Washing machines and ironing facilities. Restaurants and fast food. Supermarkets. Swimming pool. Tennis. Bicycle hire. Riding. Play areas. Entertainment. Off site: Excursions. Riding and fishing 500 m.

**Open:** 1 April - 7 October.

### Directions

Site is 3 km. off the Novigrad - Porec road about 8 km. south of Novigrad and is well signed. Camping Lanterna is also down this road so signs for this camp may be followed also.

### Charges 2007

| | |
|---|---|
| Per person | € 3,50 - € 5,95 |
| child (4-10 yrs) | free - € 4,20 |
| pitch incl. electricity | € 5,90 - € 12,85 |

---

Check real time availability and at-the-gate prices...

www.alanrogers.com

## CR6733 Camping Vestar
HR-52210 Rovinj (Istria)
Tel: 052 800 250. Email: crs@maistra.hr

Camping Vestar, just 5 km. from the historic harbour town of Rovinj, is one of the rare sites in Croatia with a partly sandy beach. Right behind the beach is a large area, attractively landscaped with young trees and shrubs, with grass for sunbathing. The site has 750 large pitches, of which 600 are for tourers, all with 16A electricity (the rest being taken by seasonal units and 14 pitches for tour operators). It is largely wooded with good shade and from the bottom row of pitches there are views of the sea. Pitching is on two separate fields, one for free camping, the other with numbered pitches. The pitches at the beach are in a half circle around the shallow bay, making it safe for children to swim. Vestar has a small marina and a jetty for mooring small boats and excursions to the islands are arranged. There is a miniclub and live music with dancing at one of the two bar/restaurants in the evenings. The restaurants all have terraces, one covered with vines to protect you from the hot sun.

### Facilities
Five modern and one refurbished toilet block with mainly Turkish style toilets and some British style, open washbasins and controllable hot showers. Child-size basins. Family bathroom. Facilities for disabled people. Laundry service. Fridge box hire. Motorcaravan services. Shop. Two bar/restaurants. New large swimming pool. Playground. Tennis. Fishing. Boat hire. Miniclub (5-11 yrs). Excursions. Off site: Riding 2 km. Rovinj 5 km.

**Open:** 1 May - 1 October.

### Directions
Follow site signs from Rovinj.
GPS: N45:03.259 E13:41.141

### Charges 2007
| | |
|---|---|
| Per person | € 4,10 - € 7,90 |
| child (7-11 yrs) | free - € 4,90 |

Croatia

## CR6719 Camping Puntica

Rade Koncara 12, Funtana, HR-52449 Porec (Istria)
Tel: 052 445 720. Email: ac.puntica@plavalaguna.hr

Puntica is a small, unassuming and old-fashioned campsite in a superb location. Everything is modest here and, if small is your thing, you will love it. There are 250 pitches, with 104 for tourers. Some of the flat, variably sized pitches (80-120$^2$m) are shaded amongst trees which could test larger units but the waterside pitches are wonderful. Electricity box positioning may warrant long leads in some areas (10A). The marina alongside is very attractive, as are the views from the terraces of the rustic restaurant and bar. The shop is similarly uncomplicated but will provide for most of your needs. There is a paved area around the tip of the site for sunbathing and ladders give access to deeper water. This is part of the Plava Laguna Group of sites and the facilities at one of the group's other sites close by are available to guests here. There is no formal entertainment and the children's play area is basic but safe. So if you want to get away from it all in a delightful location with cheerful people try this site. The night views are fabulous and the village of Funtana is typically Croatian and relatively unspoilt. There is a lot of choice by way of eateries. Sightseeing trips of Istria can be organised.

### Facilities
One main sanitary block is kept clean and has reasonable facilities but is a little short on hot water for washing. British and Turkish style toilets with one locked unit for disabled campers. Washing machines and dryers operated by the 'laundry lady'. Small shop. Restaurant and bar. DIY motorcaravan services (lift the flap etc). Fishing. Basic playground for children. Gas barbecues permitted. Fridge box hire. Boat launching. Marina facilities. Bicycle hire. Watersports from collocated marina. Scuba diving. Off site: Bicycle hire 500 m. Riding 500 m. Funtana town 500 m.

**Open:** 23 April - 1 October.

### Directions
Site is on the main road between Porec and Vrsar, near the village of Funtana, 7 km. south of Porec. Just watch for the yellow camping signs.
GPS: N45:10.600 E13:36.050

### Charges 2007
| | |
|---|---|
| Per person | € 2,90 - € 5,00 |
| child (4-10 yrs) | free - € 3,10 |
| pitch | € 3,40 - € 8,20 |
| incl. electricity | € 4,60 - € 13,70 |

## CR6728 Camping Orsera

Sv. Martin 2/1, HR-52450 Vrsar (Istria)
Tel: 052 441 330. Email: valamar@riviera.hr

Part of the Camping on the Adriatic group, this site is very close to the fishing port of Vrsar, and there is direct access from the site. The views of the many small islands from the site are stunning and it is very relaxing to sit on the beaches and enjoy the Croatian sunshine with a beer in your hand. The site is very proud of its beach's Blue Flag status and a safe rock pool has been created for children and a splash pool is at the base of a large flume in the beach area. This is a 30 hectare site with 833 pitches of which 593 are available to tourists. Marked and numbered, the pitches vary in size with 90 sq.m. being the average. The sandy and grassy ground slopes towards the sea and there is some terracing. Ample shade is provided by mature pines and oak trees. Over 200 pitches have 16A electricity and water and 60 pitches also have waste water drainage. The site has no pool but a long beach area with attractive coves provide easy access for sea bathing from rock surfaces. A public area is in the centre of the beach areas but fenced off. A new beach has been constructed using pebbles - a great contrast to the usual concrete blocking. The restaurant is excellent, with superb views and there is a snack bar and beach bar. The direct route to the old town of Vrsar is very popular as it gives easy access to its huge range of cafés, bars and restaurants.

### Facilities
Many of the toilet blocks have been renovated and one completely new block provides very good facilities. Mainly British style WCs, washbasins and showers, mostly with hot water. Some have facilities for disabled campers, private cabins, baby and children Off site: Golf 7 km. Riding 3 km. Excursions. Shops in Vrsar, although the nearest serious shopping centre is at Porec.

**Open:** 1 April - 8 October.

### Directions
Site is on the main Porec (7 km) - Vrsar (1 km) road, well signed.

### Charges 2007
| | |
|---|---|
| Per person | € 3,45 - € 6,15 |
| child (4-10 yrs) | free - € 4,50 |
| pitch incl. electricity | € 5,75 - € 13,65 |
| with water | € 8,55 - € 14,65 |
| dog | € 3,35 - € 4,75 |

Prices for pitches by the sea are higher.

## CR6732 Camping Polari
Polari bb, HR-52210 Rovinj (Istria)
Tel: 052 801 501. Email: crs@maistra.hr

This 60 hectare site has excellent facilities for both textile and naturist campers, the latter having a reserved area of 12 hectares called Punta Eva. Prime places are taken by permanent customers but there are some numbered pitches which are very good. An impressive swimming pool complex is children friendly with large paddling areas. The site, which is part of the Maistia Group has undergone a massive improvement programme and the results make it a very attractive option. There is something for everyone here to enjoy or you may prefer just to relax. Enjoy a meal on the huge restaurant terrace with panoramic views of the sea. Many of the pitches have also been thoughtfully upgraded and now a new pitch (100 sq.m) is offered with full facilities. Pitches are clean, neat and level and there will be shade when the young trees grow.

### Facilities
All the sanitary facilities have been renovated to a high standard with plenty of hot water and good showers. Washing up and laundry sinks. Washing machines and dryers. Laundry service including ironing. Motorcaravan service point. Two shops, one large and one small, one restaurant and snack bar. Tennis. Minigolf. Children's animation with all major European languages spoken. Bicycle hire. Watersports. Sailing school. Off site: Riding 1 km. Five buses daily to and from Rovinj (3 km).

**Open:** 25 March - 30 September.

### Directions
From any access road to Rovinj look for red signs to AC Polari (amongst other destinations). The site is 3 km. south of Rovinj.

### Charges 2007
| | |
|---|---|
| Per person | € 3,80 - € 7,10 |
| child (5-11 yrs) | free - € 4,20 |
| pitch incl. electricity | € 6,40 - € 14,90 |

For stays less than 3 nights in high season add 20%.
Camping Cheques accepted.

---

## CR6731 Naturist Camping Valalta
Cesta Valalta-Lim bb, HR-52210 Rovinj (Istria)
Tel: 052 804 800. Email: valalta@valalta.hr

This is a most impressive site for up to 6,000 naturist campers but there is a pleasant open feel about it. The passage through reception is efficient and pleasant and this feeling is maintained around the well organised site. A friendly, family atmosphere is to be found here. Single males are not admitted and continuous cautious monitoring within the site ensures the well being of all the naturist guests. An outer and inner reception adds to the security. All pitches are the same price with 16A electricity, although they vary in size and surroundings. The impressive pool is in lagoon style with water features and cascades. Unusually for Croatia, the beach has soft sand (with some help from imported sand). All manner of sports are available and a marina forms part of the site. We were impressed by this well ordered and smart naturist site.

### Facilities
Twenty high quality sanitary blocks of which four are smaller units of plastic 'pod' construction. Hot showers (coin operated). Facilities for disabled campers. Washing machines. Dryers. Supermarket. Four restaurants. Pizzeria. Two bars. Large pool complex. Beauty saloon. Fitness club. Massage. Minigolf. Tennis. Bocce. Sailing. Play area. Bicycle hire. Beach. Marina. Diving. Windsurfing. Internet. Animation all season. Kindergarten. Dogs not accepted.

**Open:** 24 April - 2 October.

### Directions
Site is located on the coast 8 km. north of Rovinj. If approaching from the north turn inland (follow signs to Rovinj) to drive around the Limski Kanal. Then follow signs towards Valalta about 2 km. east of Rovinj. Site is at the end of the road.

### Charges 2007
| | |
|---|---|
| Per person | Kn 37,00 - 60,00 |
| child (4-14 yrs) | Kn 19,00 - 30,00 |
| pitch incl. electricity | Kn 55,00 - 100,00 |

## Croatia

### CR6730 Camping Amarin

Monsena bb, HR-52210 Rovinj (Istria)
Tel: 052 802 000. Email: ac-amarin@maistra.hr

Situated 4 km. from the centre of the lovely old port town of Rovinj this site has much to offer. The complex is part of the Maistra Group. It has 12.6 hectares of land and is adjacent to the Amarin bungalow complex. Campers can take advantage of the facilities afforded by both areas. There are 670 pitches for touring units on various types of ground and between 80-120 sq.m. Most are separated by foliage, 10A electricity is available. A rocky beach backed by a grassy sunbathing area is very popular, but the site has its own superb, supervised round pool with corkscrew slide plus a splash pool for children. Boat owners have a mooring area and launching ramp. The port of Rovinj contains many delights, particularly if you are able to contend with the hundreds of steps which lead to the church above the town from where the views are well worth the climb.

#### Facilities

Thirteen respectable toilet blocks have a mixture of British style and Turkish toilets. Half the washbasins have hot water. Some showers have hot water, the rest have cold and are outside. Some blocks have one private cabin on the female side and a unit for disabled visitors (shower, toilet and washbasin). Fridge box hire. Washing machines. Security boxes. Motorcaravan service point. Supermarket. Small market. Two restaurants, taverna, pizzeria and terrace grill. Swimming pool. Flume and splash pool. Watersports. Bicycle hire. Fishing (subject to permit). Daily animation. Barbecues are not accepted. Hairdresser. Massage. ATM. Off site: Hourly minibus service to Rovinj. Excursions including day trips to Venice. Riding nearby.

**Open:** 20 May - 23 September.

#### Directions

Follow signs towards Rovinj and if approaching from the north turn off about 2 km. before the town towards Amarin and Valalta. Then follow signs to Amarin and the campsite. Watch for a left turn after approx. 3 km. where signs are difficult to see.

#### Charges 2007

| | |
|---|---|
| Per person | € 4,20 - € 7,20 |
| child (5-12 yrs) | free - € 3,60 |
| pitch incl. electricity | € 6,00 - € 11,60 |
| dog | € 3,10 - € 6,20 |

For stays less than 3 nights in high season add 10%.

---

### CR6735 Naturist-Textile Camping Kazela

Kazela, HR-52203 Medulin (Istria)
Tel: 052 576 050. Email: info@campkazela.com

Camping Kazela, the larger sister site of Camping Bi Village and part naturist, is close to Medulin, a fishing port with only 1,700 inhabitants, and just 10 km. from Pula, a bustling seaside resort in southern Istria. This is a rough coastline with numerous little, uninhabited islands along the Medulin Bay. The site can accommodate over 2,000 units on large, unmarked pitches, taking 1,754 touring units with 1,000 electricity connections (16A) and 500 pitches with electricity, water and drainage. The site is open, with young trees, and from the lower pitches there are pleasant views over the sea. Some clusters of mature trees provide a little shade, but generally this site is something of a sun-trap.

#### Facilities

Six adequate toilet blocks have British and Turkish style toilets, open washbasins with cold water only and controllable hot showers. Motorcaravan service point. Shop. Bar, beach bar, restaurant and pizzeria. Sailing and diving schools. Water skiing. Parasailing. Sightseeing train for children. Animation team. Disco. Live music. Off site: Pula 10 km. Medulin 2 km.

**Open:** 7 April - 13 October.

#### Directions

Follow the road south from Pula to Medulin. At Medulin, follow signs for hotels and site is 1km. after the hotels. GPS: N44:48.324 E13:57.330

#### Charges 2007

| | |
|---|---|
| Per person | € 2,70 - € 7,00 |
| child (6-11 yrs) | free - € 4,00 |
| pitch incl. electricity | € 5,20 - € 14,70 |

Camping Cheques accepted.

## CR6736 Camping Valdaliso

Monsena bb, HR-52210 Rovinj (Istria)

Tel: **052 815 025**. Email: **info@rovinjturist.hr**

Unusually Camping Valdaliso has its affiliated hotel in the centre of the site. The advantage for campers is that they can use the hotel and, as breakfast is served there but not in the restaurant, it may appeal to some. The fine Barabiga restaurant within the hotel offers superb Istrian and fish cuisine and the pool is also within the hotel. You are close to the beautiful old town of Rovinj and parts of this site enjoy views of the town. A water taxi makes exploring Rovinj very easy, compared with the impossible parking for private cars. A bus service is also provided but this involves considerable walking. The pitches are mostly flat with shade from pine trees and the site is divided into three sections all with 16A electricity. The choice of formal numbered pitches, informal camping or proximity to the sea impacts on the prices. The kilometre plus of beach has crystal clear water and a pebble beach. The animation programme is extremely professional and there is a lot to do at Valdaliso, which is aimed primarily at families. The variety of activities here and the bonus of the use of the hotel make this a great choice for campers

### Facilities

Two large clean sanitary blocks have hot showers (coin operated). The northeastern block has facilities for disabled campers. Hotel facilities. Shop. Pizzeria. Restaurant. Table tennis. Volleyball. Basketball. Tennis. Fitness centre. Games room. Billiards. Children's games. Bicycle hire. Summer painting courses. Exchange. Water taxi. Bus service. Boat rental. Watersports. Boat launching. Fishing. Gym. Diving school. Internet in both receptions. Animals are not accepted. Off site: Town 1 km.

**Open:** 23 March - 15 October.

### Directions

Site is 7 km. north of Rovinj on the main coast road between Vsrar and Rovinj. Watch for the signs to Monsena and the site.

### Charges 2007

| | |
|---|---|
| Per person | € 3,90 - € 6,50 |
| child (12-18 yrs) | € 1,95 - € 3,25 |
| child (under 12 yrs) | free |
| pitch | € 5,50 - € 13,50 |

---

**Camping VALDALISO ***  Rovinj  Istria** Green Mediterranean.

Just in front of the old town of Rovinj, in the shadow of olive and pine trees lies the camping Valdaliso. With 1 mile of its own pebbles beach, with new modern toilet facilities, 2 restaurants, beach bar, grocery store, pizzeria, tennis, beach volley, surfing, table tennis and diving centre, a hotel with fitness, game room and rich day and evening animation entertainment programme and mobilhomes with air conditioning and SAT TV!

tel.: 00385 52 805 505 / fax: 00385 52 811 541 / e-mail: info@rovinjturist.hr   www.valdaliso.info

---

## CR6739 Camping Indije

Banjole, HR-52100 Pula (Istria)

Tel: **052 573 066**. Email: **marketing@arenaturist.hr**

Camping Indije, with 422 pitches, is one of the smaller sites in Croatia. It is on the beautiful Adriatic coast in Banjole (Medulin), only a few kilometres away from Pula. Medulin fronts a beautiful bay, dominated by a bell tower, with a wealth of little peninsulas and islands, all melting together with the blue sea and the green of the Mediterranean vegetation and Banjole is on one edge of it. The 250 grass and gravel pitches for tourers are mostly under mature trees, off tarmac access roads. All with electricity, the pitches vary in size (50-120 sq.m) and from some there are views of the sea. Indije has its own diving centre. The site also organizes sightseeing tours to Rovinj by boat, the Mali Brijun island in the National Park Brijuni and even to Venice in Italy, a cruise of about two hours.

### Facilities

Three comfortable toilet blocks with British and Turkish style toilets, open plan washbasins and showers. Washing machine. Motorcaravan service point. Supermarket. Bar and restaurant. Miniclub. Live music. Rock plateau beach. Diving centre. Boat mooring. Fishing. Boat launching. Off site: Historic towns of Pula and Rovinj are close.

**Open:** 1 May - 30 September.

### Directions

From Pula follow signs for Prematura and Banjole southwards. From Banjole follow site signs.
GPS: N44:49.429 E13:51.047

### Charges 2007

| | |
|---|---|
| Per person | € 2,20 - € 5,70 |
| child (2-12 yrs) | € 1,40 - € 3,00 |
| pitch incl. electricity | € 4,40 - € 13,50 |

*Check real time availability and at-the-gate prices...*
www.alanrogers.com

## CR6734 Medulin Camping Village

HR-52203 Medulin (Istria)

Tel: 052 572 801. Email: marketing@arenaturist.hr

Medulin is part of the Arenaturist group and it has a fabulous setting near Pula on the tip of the Istrian peninsula, enjoying great views of the offshore island and the twin church towers in the town above. Consisting of a peninsula about 1.5 km. long and a small island accessed by a road bridge, the site is thickly wooded with mature pine trees producing a carpet of needles. Pitches are marked and separated into three sizes. The land is undulating but there is no shortage of level areas. There are 1,106 touring pitches, all with 10/16A electricity and some mobile homes which are not intrusive. The site has no swimming pool but has a huge water chute into a plunge pool. It is able to offer swimming at one of its hotels close by (small charge) and as the sea virtually surrounds it via a gently sloping rocky beach, swimming and sunbathing are convenient and safe as lifeguards are provided. There are areas of coarse sand which are brilliant for children and other paddlers. This is a very pleasant family site with lots of fun things to do; we visited in peak season and everyone seemed happy. With the competitive prices a very pleasant stay can be had by families and others.

### Facilities

The sanitary blocks are kept clean but are really in need of renovation. Toilets are mostly dated Turkish style and the search for British styles is tedious. Washbasins and showers are a mixture of outdoors and under cover. Most have hot water (relying on solar power). Shop, market and produce stalls. Eight restaurants or snack bars provide a large range of fare. Cocktail bar. Ice for sale. Fridge rental. Watersports. Barbecues are not permitted on pitches but the site provides fixed barbecues. Dogs allowed in some areas. Off site: Golf, fishing (with permit) and riding near. Restaurants and bars in Medulin village or in Pula. Regular bus service into Pula or a 20 minute drive to town centre.

**Open:** 30 March - 21 October.

### Directions

Approaching from the north (Koper, Rovinj), on outskirts of Pula turn to follow signs for Medulin and site. Site is at far end of village and is well signed.

### Charges 2007

| | |
|---|---|
| Per person | € 4,10 - € 7,20 |
| child (4-10 yrs) | € 2,80 - € 4,50 |
| pitch incl. electricity | € 7,10 - € 14,90 |
| small tent pitch | € 5,00 - € 10,00 |
| electricity | € 3,00 |

## CR6737 Camping Stupice

Premantura, HR-52100 Pula (Istria)

Tel: 052 575 101. Email: marketing@arenaturist.hr

Camping Village Stupice, part of the Arenaturist group, is situated in a delightful strip of coast on the Istrian peninsula near the small village of Premantura. Most of the site is covered with undulating, dense pinewood providing ample shade with a carpet of pine needles. There are 1000 pitches in total with 588 touring pitches in three sizes (ranging from 60-120 sq.m). They are sloping or level and about a fifth have sea views. Access roads are bitumen or gravel. A narrow pebble beach separates the sea from the site and it is not crowded due to the length of the sea access. Water areas are netted off from motor sports for safe swimming. There is boat launching with a marina as well as many sporting activities. For those who enjoy a sunny position, a small circular rocky spit of land approximately 500 m. in diameter extends from the site. Surrounded by water and enjoying excellent views, there is room for about 60 pitches, although with no shade or facilities on the spit (it is generally occupied with motorcaravans). The very attractive restaurant serves an affordable simple menu of mainly pasta, meat and seafood dishes on a hillside location overlooking the sea. The 130 permanent pitches are kept to one side of the site away from the water, and the 110 centrally located bungalows are unobtrusive. This rustic site provides a lovely secluded setting with easy access to the Istrian region and historic port of Pula where ferries are available to many Croatian islands.

### Facilities

The six toilet blocks, whilst clean when we visited, are all in need of updating. Toilets are a mixture of Turkish and British style. The low numbers of hot showers (common in Croatia) are unisex. Washing machines. Good supermarket. Kiosk and several good small bars and grills. Minigolf. Modern playground. Animation for children, disco and some live entertainment at the restaurant in high season. Ample sea access with rocky and pebble beach. Beach volleyball. Marina, boat launching, jetty and scuba diving. Bicycle and beach buggy hire. Aquapark. Off site: Premantura 1 km. Bicycle hire 500 m.

**Open:** May - 1 September.

### Directions

Site is 11 km. southeast of Pula. Follow signs to Premantura from Pula where there are site signs.

### Charges 2007

| | |
|---|---|
| Per person | Kn 27,01 - 47,45 |
| child (4-12 yrs) | Kn 18,25 - 29,20 |
| pitch | Kn 46,72 - 97,82 |
| electricity | Kn 21,90 |

Check real time availability and at-the-gate prices...
www.alanrogers.com

## Croatia

### CR6742 Camping Stoja
Stoja 37, HR-52100 Pula (Istria)
Tel: 052 387 144. Email: marketing@arenaturist.hr

Camping Stoja in Pula, one of the famous little Istrian harbour towns, is on a little peninsula and therefore almost completely surrounded by the waters of the clear Adriatic. In the centre of the site is the old Fort Stoja, built in 1884 for coastal defence. Some of its buildings are now used as a toilet block or laundry and its courtyard is used by the animation team. The pitches here vary greatly in size (50-120 sq.m) and are marked by round, concrete, numbered blocks and separated by young trees. About half have shade from mature trees and all are slightly sloping on grass and gravel. Pitches close to the pebble and rock beach have beautiful views of the sea and Pula. This site is an ideal base for visiting Pula, considered to be the capital of Istrian tourism and full of history, tradition and natural beauty, including a spectacular Roman Coliseum.

#### Facilities
Five toilet blocks with British and Turkish style toilets, open plan washbasins with cold water only and controllable hot showers. Child-size basins. Facilities for disabled visitors. Laundry and ironing service. Fridge box hire. Dishwashing under cover. Dog shower. Motorcaravan service point. Chemical disposal. Supermarket. Bar/restaurant. Miniclub and teen club. Bicycle hire. Water skiing. Boat hire. Boat launching. Surfboard and pedalo hire. Island excursions. Off site: Pula (walking distance).

**Open:** 24 March - 1 November.

#### Directions
From Pula follow site signs.
GPS: N44:51.583 E13:48.870

#### Charges 2007
| | |
|---|---|
| Per person | € 4,10 - € 7,20 |
| child (4-12 yrs) | € 2,80 - € 4,50 |
| pitch | € 5,00 - € 10,00 |
| with electricity | € 7,10 - € 14,90 |
| dog | € 2,50 - € 4,50 |

---

### CR6745 Camping Bi-Village
Dragonja 115, HR-52212 Fazana (Istria)
Tel: 052 380 700

Camping Bi-Village is large new holiday village, close to the historic town of Pula and opposite the Brioni National Park. The location is excellent and there are some superb sunsets. The site is landscaped with many flowers, shrubs and rock walls and offers 1,522 pitches, of which 922 pitches are for tourers, the remainder being taken by bungalows and chalets. The campsite is separated from the holiday bungalows by the main site road, that runs from the entrance to the beach. Pitches are set in long rows accessed by gravel lanes, slightly sloping towards the sea, with only the pitches at the bottom having shade from mature trees and good views over the Adriatic. Pitches are separated by young trees and shrubs. Bi-Village has 800 m. of pebble beach, but also offers three attractive swimming pools with a fun pool, a whirlpool, slides and flumes. In front of the touring pitches is a commercial centre with a supermarket and several restaurants and bars. Tour operators take about 200 pitches. The site open all year.

#### Facilities
Four modern toilet blocks with toilets, open plan washbasins and controllable hot showers. Child-size washbasins. Baby room. Facilities for disabled visitors. Washing machine. Dishwashing under cover. Shopping centre. Several bars and restaurants. Bazaar. Gelateria. Pastry shop. Three swimming pools. Playground on gravel. Playing field. Tennis. Basketball. Trampolines. Minigolf. Fishing. Jet skis, motorboats and pedaloes for hire. Boat launching. Games hall. Sports tournaments and professional entertainment organised. Massage. Salsa lessons. Model making. Internet point. Off site: Historic towns of Pula and Rovinj are close.

**Open:** All year.

#### Directions
Follow no. 2 road south from Rijeka to Pula.
In Pula follow site signs. Site is close to Fazana.

#### Charges 2007
| | |
|---|---|
| Per person | € 3,50 - € 9,00 |
| child | free - € 4,50 |
| pitch incl. electricity and water | € 5,50 - € 18,00 |
| dog | € 2,00 - € 3,00 |

Camping Cheques accepted.

## Croatia

### CR6600 Motel Plitvice – Autokamp

Lucko Bb, HR-10250 Zagreb (Central)

Tel: 016 530 444. Email: motel@motel-plitvice.hr

This is a typical transit site or possibly a site for a visit to the Croatian capital. As they put it themselves, this is the only campsite around Zagreb. Nothing special, the logistically efficient location (on the motorway) fortunately does not stand in the way of a normal night's rest, as the site is far enough from the road to reduce noise to acceptable levels. The pitches are of average size and have electricity hook-ups; the toilet building is fairly old but acceptable. Despite the name, this site has nothing to do with the Plitvice Lakes National Park that is roughly 150 kilometres south from here.

#### Facilities

Shop, restaurants and bars in the Motel facilities connected to the site. Off site: Zagreb.

**Open:** 1 May - 30 September.

#### Directions

Motel Plitvice is located above and on both sides of motorway 1 circling Zagreb, just southwest of the capital between the junctions with motorway 12 to Karlovac (E65) and with National Road 4 (E70) to Ljubljana, Slovenia. Site is signed.

#### Charges guide

| | |
|---|---|
| Per person | € 5,00 |
| pitch incl. electricity | € 22,50 |

### CR6750 Autocamp Selce

Jasenova 19, HR-51266 Selce (Kvarner)

Tel: 051 764 038. Email: kamp-selce@ri.t-com.hr

Selce is a small site in the village of Selce on the Dalmatian Coast. It has 500 pitches, all with 10A electricity, with 300 used for touring units and the others taken by seasonal guests. The pitches are mostly on level terraces on the steeply sloping terrain on a grass and gravel surface. (Firm tent pegs may be needed). They are under low trees that provide useful shade in the hot Mediterranean summer. Pitches are 50-80 sq.m. and there are several gravel hardstandings for larger units. From the top of the site it is an easy ten minute stroll downhill to the seaside promenade where there are numerous bars and restaurants, a diving school, parasailing possibilities and a small marina.

#### Facilities

Seven good toilet blocks with British and Turkish style toilets, open style washbasins and controllable, hot showers (free). Laundry service. Dishwashing. Fridge box hire. Dog shower. Shop. Bar/restaurant with covered and open-air terrace. Barbecues permitted only in communal area. Fishing. Off site: Boat rental and water skiing 150 m. Boat launching and jetty 500 m.

**Open:** 1 April - 1 November.

#### Directions

From Rijeka, follow the no. 8 coastal road south towards Senj. In Selce, follow the camp signs.
GPS: N45:09.246 E14:43.508

#### Charges 2007

| | |
|---|---|
| Per person | € 3,30 - € 5,75 |
| child (5-13 yrs) | € 2,05 - € 3,30 |
| pitch | € 6,25 - € 10,90 |
| car | € 2,33 - € 3,56 |

### CR6755 Camping Pila

Setaliste Ivana Bruscia 2, Punat, HR-51521 Krk Island (Kvarner)

Tel: 051 854 020. Email: pila@hoteli-punat.hr

Autocamping Pila is right beside the bustling seaside resort of Punat on the biggest Croatian island Krk, which is connected to the mainland by a bridge. Krk is the first island you reach as you travel south into Croatia and the Romans called it the 'Golden Island'. Autocamp Pila is just 100 m. from the Adriatic and has 600 pitches for tourers, all with 10A electricity on grass and gravel. Some are slightly sloping. Some 250 of the pitches are marked and numbered, most with shade from mature trees. The remainder are unmarked on a separate field. It can get very busy in high season and pitching can become cramped.

#### Facilities

Four modern, comfortable toilet blocks with toilets, basins and showers. Child-size showers and basins. Facilities for babies and disabled visitors. Campers kitchen with cooking rings. Dishwashing area. Motorcaravan service point. Supermarket, bar with terrace and restaurant. Snack bar. Small playground. Minigolf. Aerobics and aquarobics. Video games. Daily evening programme for children. Internet. Pebble beach. Off site: Punat with shops, bars, restaurants. Pedalo and boat hire 200 m.

**Open:** 1 April - 15 October.

#### Directions

On Krk follow no. 29 road and take exit for Punat. In Punat follow good site signs.
GPS: N45:00.998 E14:37.724

#### Charges 2007

| | |
|---|---|
| Per person | € 3,70 - € 5,80 |
| child | free - € 3,80 |
| pitch | € 6,00 - € 10,10 |
| with electricity | € 8,90 - € 13,90 |

Camping Cheques accepted.

Check real time availability and at-the-gate prices...
www.alanrogers.com

## CR6756 Naturist Camping Konobe

Obala 94, Punat, HR-51521 Krk Island (Kvarner)

Tel: **051 854 036**. Email: **konobe@hoteli-punat.hr**

Naturist Camping Konobe is situated south of the historic fishing port of Punat on the island Krk in a remote and quiet location. Access is down a long, tarmac road which leads to a landscaped terrain, with terraces built from natural stone. The 800 slightly sloping pitches are part open, part wooded, with some shade from mature trees and some with beautiful views over the Adriatic. Unmarked pitches for tents are on small terraces, with numbered pitches for caravans and motorcaravans of 80-100 sq.m. on gravel hardstanding off tarmac access roads. The remote location makes this site ideal for quiet camping among the wild charm of a rocky and still green environment, while the bustling seaside resort of Punat is only 4 km. away. Pitching is adapted to the natural setting of the site which can become a real sun-trap due to the high, white rocks surrounding it. Small ferries take guests to Punat from the pebble beach and one can moor small boats.

### Facilities

Three modern, comfortable toilet blocks with toilets, open basins and pre-set showers. Child-size washbasins. Facilities for disabled visitors. Dishwashing under cover. Campers' kitchen with connections (no rings). Gas. Supermarket. Bar/restaurant with open air terrace. Tennis. Minigolf. Fishing. Pebble beach. Boat launching. Evening entertainment programme for children. Croatian language lessons. Off site: Punat 4 km.

**Open:** 1 May - 1 October.

### Directions

On Krk follow 29 road and take exit for Punat and follow main road through town. Site is 4 km. south of Punat and well signed.
GPS: N44:59.464 E14:37.839

### Charges 2007

| | |
|---|---|
| Per person | € 3,70 - € 5,80 |
| child | free - € 3,80 |
| pitch | € 6,00 - € 10,10 |
| with electricity | € 8,90 - € 13,90 |
| dog | € 1,60 - € 2,80 |

Camping Cheques accepted.

---

## CR6760 Naturist Camping Bunculuka

Baska, HR-51523 Krk Island (Kvarner)

Tel: **051 856 806**. Email: **fkk-bunculuka@ri.hinet.hr / lolic@hotelibasta.hr**

Bunculuka is on the opposite side of the port of Baska from Camping Zablace. In an enclosed environment, bordered by trees on one side and the sea on the other, it has 400 pitches (270 for tourers) in two areas. One is open and sloping downwards to the sea, the other is wooded and more hilly to the rear of the site (and mainly used for tents). From the front row of pitches, there are beautiful views over the sea and the private pebble beach. Varying in size from small to average, most pitches are fairly level, although the ground is a little rocky. A bar/restaurant is beside the beach, but from the site entrance it is only 500 m. to the promenade in the centre of Baska where there are several bars, restaurants and pizzerias. From the port one can take a ferry to the islands of Rab or Cres or visit the island of Kosaljun with its Franciscan monastery, that now houses an art museum.

### Facilities

One new (2005) and two refurbished toilet blocks with toilets, open style wash basins and controllable hot showers. Dishwashing under cover. Supermarket. Bar/restaurant with covered and open air terrace. Snack bar. Bread kiosk at beach. Newspaper, fruit and tobacco kiosks. Tennis. Minigolf. Fishing. Volleyball. Table tennis. Off site: Baska with bars, restaurants and shops 500 m.

**Open:** 1 May - 30 October.

### Directions

On Krk follow 29 road south to Baska and then site signs. Turn right before Baska, then left (east) and follow signs for ferry and site.
GPS: N44:58.154 E14:46.021

### Charges guide

| | |
|---|---|
| Per person | € 4,00 - € 5,00 |
| child | € 2,00 - € 2,50 |
| pitch | € 8,00 - € 9,00 |
| incl. electricity | € 9,40 - € 10,50 |
| dog | € 3,20 |

Camping Cheques accepted.

---

Check real time availability and at-the-gate prices...
www.alanrogers.com

## Croatia

### CR6765 Camping Kovacine

HR-51557 Cres Island (Kvarner)
Tel: 051 573 150. Email: campkovacine@kovacine.com

Camping Kovacine is located on a peninsula on the beautiful Dalmatian island of Cres, just 2 km. from the town of the same name. The site has 750 numbered, mostly level pitches, of which 750 are for tourers (300 with 12A electricity). On sloping ground, partially shaded by mature olive and pine trees, pitching is on the large, open spaces between the trees. Some places have views of the Valun lagoon. Kovacine is partly an FKK (naturist) site, which is quite common in Croatia, and has a pleasant atmosphere. Here one can enjoy Croatian camping with local live music on a stage close to the pebble beach (Blue Flag), where there is also a restaurant and bar. The site has its own private beach, part concrete, part pebbles, and a jetty for mooring boats and fishing. It is close to the historic town of Cres, the main town on the island, which offers a rich history of fishing, shipyards and authentic Dalmatian-style houses. There are also several bars, restaurants and shops.

#### Facilities

Five modern, comfortable toilet blocks (two refurbished) offer British style toilets, open plan washbasins (some cabins for ladies) and hot showers. Bathroom for hire. Facilities for disabled people (although access is difficult). Laundry sinks and washing machine. Fridge box hire. Dishwashing under cover. Motorcaravan service point. Dog shower. Car wash. Supermarket. Bar, restaurant and pizzeria. Playground. Daily children's club. Evening shows with live music. Boat launching. Fishing. Diving centre. Motorboat hire. Airport transfers. Off site: Historic town of Cres with bars, restaurants and shops 2 km.

**Open:** 16 April - 15 October.

#### Directions

From Rijeka take no. 2 road south towards Labin and take ferry to Cres at Brestova. Continue to Cres and follow site signs. GPS: N44:57.713 E14:23.790

#### Charges 2008

| | |
|---|---|
| Per person | € 4,80 - € 9,60 |
| child (3-11 yrs) | € 2,30 - € 3,50 |
| pitch | € 4,60 - € 8,40 |
| dog | € 1,00 - € 3,00 |

---

### CR6761 Camping Zablace

E Geistlicha 38, HR-51523 Baska (Kvarner)
Tel: 051 856 909. Email: campzablace@campzablace.into

Camping Zablace is at the southern end of the beautiful island of Krk, in the ancient ferry port of Baska. Like most sites in Croatia it has direct access to a large, pebble beach and from the bottom row of pitches one has views over the Adriatic and the little island of Kosljun with its Franciscan Monastery. The site has 500 pitches with 400 used for touring units. Zone 1 (nearest the beach) provides 200 individual pitches with electricity and water. The quietest zone, if further away (and across a public road that splits the site in two) has electricity and water taps. There is not much shade anywhere. There are not many amenities on the site, but it is an easy five minute walk along the promenade to the centre of Baska where there are bars, restaurants and pizzerias. Ferries leave from Baska to the other islands and well worth visiting is the little church on the top of the hill, where there are beautiful views over the bay and the Seniska Vrata channel.

#### Facilities

Four toilet blocks (three new, one old) with toilets, open plan basins and controllable hot showers (key access for the toilets nearest the beach; with deposit). Facilities for disabled visitors. Dishwashing under cover. Motorcaravan service point. Shop. Kiosks with fruit, cold drinks, tobacco, newspapers and beach wear. Fishing. Beach volleyball. Off site: Giant slide and games hall. Tennis and minigolf 200 m.

**Open:** Easter - 15 October.

#### Directions

On Krk follow the no. 29 road south to Baska, then good signs to site. GPS: N44:58.001 E14:44.707

#### Charges 2008

| | |
|---|---|
| Per person | Kn 30,00 - Kn 45,00 |
| child (7-11 yrs) | Kn 15,00 - Kn 22,00 |
| pitch with electricity | Kn 75,00 - Kn 130,00 |
| dog | free - Kn 25,00 |

Camping Cheques accepted.

**Shuttle service/Airport-transfer: Airport Rijeka – Cres and back: only € 19,99/person**

# CAMP KOVAČINE
### CRES-CHERSO

A crystal clear sea, beautiful beaches and pine and olive trees which provide plenty of shade, make Kovacine a unique holiday destination. The campsite is situated on the Cres peninsula and is close to the village with the same name. There are 1500 pitches which offer all the comfort you might wish.
**Room (with breakfast), direct on the beach with sea view.**

*Mobile homes – the freedom of camping with all the comforts of home. To book a pitch in advance possible!*

## We offer you a range of facilities:

- Bar, buffet, restaurant, Self service shop
- Modern, new sanitary facilities
- Boat mooring for your boat and boat crane
- Children's animation programme
- Various sport facilities
- First aid service on site

Camping »Kovačine« Cres • HR-51557 Cres • Tel. 00-385/51/573-150
Fax 00-385/51/571-086 • campkovacine@kovacine.com • www.camp-kovacine.com

## Croatia

### CR6768 Camping Slatina
Martinscica, HR-51556 Cres Island (Kvarner)
Tel: 051 574 127. Email: info@camp-slatina.com

Camping Slatina lies about halfway along the island of Cres, beside the fishing port of Martinscica on a bay of the Adriatic Sea. It has 370 pitches for tourers, some with 10A electricity, off very steep, tarmac access roads, sloping down to the sea. The pitches are large and level on a gravel base and enjoy plenty of shade from mature laurel trees, although hardly any have views. Whilst there is plenty of privacy, the site does have an enclosed feeling. Some pitches in the lower areas have water, electricity and drainage. Like so many sites in Croatia, Slatina has a private diving centre, which will take you to the remote island of Lastovo. Lastovo is surrounded by reefs and little islands and the crystal clear waters of the Adriatic make it perfect for diving. Martinscica owes its name to the medieval church of the Holy Martin and has a Glagolite monastery, standing next to the 17th century castle, built by the Patrician Sforza. Both are well worth a visit.

#### Facilities
Two new and three refurbished toilet blocks provide toilets, open style washbasins and controllable hot showers. Facilities for disabled visitors. Laundry with sinks and washing machine. Fridge box hire. Dog shower. Car wash. Shop. Bar, restaurant, grill restaurant, pizzeria and fish restaurant. Playground. Minigolf. Fishing. Bicycle hire. Diving centre. Boat launching. Beach volleyball. Pedalo, canoe and boat hire. Excursions to the 'Blue Cave'. 'Pet projects'. Off site: Martinscica with bars, restaurants and shops 2 km.

**Open:** Easter - 30 September.

#### Directions
From Rijeka take no. 2 road south towards Labin and take ferry to Cres at Brestova. From Cres go south towards Martinscica and follow site signs.
GPS: N44:49.400 E14:20.450

#### Charges 2007
| | |
|---|---|
| Per person | € 4,49 - € 7,31 |
| child (3-12 years old) | € 1,35 - € 3,40 |
| pitch | € 3,74 - € 7,70 |

---

### CR6772 Camping Poljana
Poljana bb, Mali Losinj, HR-51550 Losinj Island (Kvarner)
Tel: 051 231 726. Email: info@poljana.hr

Autocamp Poljana lies on the narrow strip of land in the southern part of Losinj island, just north of the pleasant town of Mali Losinj. With 600 pitches, this side is bigger than it looks. Only some of the pitches are numbered and many guests find their own place between the mature trees and close to one of the 600 electricity connections. Campers may be able to experience both sunset and sunrise from the same pitch! The toilet facilities are new and well maintained, while a shop and a series of bars and restaurants are available close by. On the far and quiet side of the island, a private (rock and concrete) shore strip with a cocktail bar is available.

#### Facilities
New toilet blocks are entirely up-to-date and adequate. Facilities for disabled people. Baby changing rooms. Motorcaravan service point. Washing machine (expensive). Daily animation programmes. Bicycle hire. Off site: The bustling town of Mali Losinj is the summer capital of the island with plenty of activities and life around the port and in the streets. Getting there is possible by bus, taxi or water taxi.

**Open:** 30 March - 21 October.

#### Directions
About 2 km. north of the town, the site occupies both sides of the road along the waterline and opposite the little marina.

#### Charges 2008
| | |
|---|---|
| Per pitch incl 2 persons and electricity | € 12,80 - € 38,40 |
| extra person | € 0,80 - € 6,40 |
| child (3-9 yrs) or senior (over 60) | free - € 4,80 |
| dog | € 3,50 - € 7,00 |

---

**UnityPlus CARD — Unique Discounts FOR CAMPERS AND CARAVANNERS**
Full details at www.unity-plus.com Request your UnityPlus Card today!

Check real time availability and at-the-gate prices...
www.alanrogers.com

## CR6773 Camping Rapoca

Rapoca, Nerezine, HR-51554 Losinj Island (Kvarner)
Tel: 051 237 145. Email: rapoca@lostur.hinet.hr

Camping Rapoca is located beside the historic town of Nerezine, an ancient seafaring and shipbuilding settlement, close to Mount Osorscica on the east coast of the Losinj island. This private site offers an oasis of tranquillity when compared to its bigger, commercial brothers. It has just 250 pitches, including 100 for tourers with 10A electricity. The touring pitches are in a separate area from the seasonal units, on one large, open field with little shade. Pitches are marked, level and vary in size, but are not separated. The site has its own restaurant with good value meals and a small bar. It is an easy ten minute walk alongside the Adriatic to Nerezine and here one can enjoy ancient Dalmatian style houses and several bars, restaurants and shops or climb the Osorscica, reputedly the most beautiful island mountain in the Adriatic region, in the footsteps of Rudolph of Habsburg who climbed it in 1887. At the top is a church and from the highest point, Televrin at 589 m, there are beautiful views of the Adriatic and Nerezine.

### Facilities
Two modern, comfortable toilet blocks have toilets, open style basins with cold water only and pre-set hot showers. Shop, newspaper stand and fruit kiosk. Restaurant and bar. Fishing. Small playground. Boat launching. Beach and promenade. Off site: Historic town of Nerezine with shops, bars and restaurants.

**Open:** 1 April - 31 October.

### Directions
On Cres take no. 58 road south towards Mali Losinj. Site is on the left in Nerezine and has a sharp, narrow left turn to it which may be difficult for large units. GPS: N44:39.873 E14:23.886

### Charges 2007
| | |
|---|---|
| Per person | € 5,50 - € 7,00 |
| child | € 2,75 - € 3,50 |

---

## CR6776 Camp Strasko

Novalja, HR-51291 Otok Pag (Dalmatia)
Tel: 053 661 226. Email: turno@turno.hr

Auto Camp Strasko is a very large, part FKK, part textile camp site, close to Novalja on the Dalmatian island Pag. The naturist part is separated from the textile area by a high, rock wall. All 2,000 pitches (1,800 for touring units of which 1,000 have electricity) are in the shade of mature oak, pine and olive trees. Just 200 pitches are marked and numbered, on grass and gravel off hard access roads. The site can get very busy in July and August and the lack of marked pitches may make it difficult to find space in high season. The beauty of this site is clearly its 1,650 m. long sand and pebble beach and the sports centre next to it. From the beach about every possible watersport is available and the sports centre provides 11 tennis courts, table tennis, a basketball court and a football field. The site has a full animation programme for children and evening entertainment for all ages, which is best enjoyed with the delicious Pag lamb with cheese, smoked ham and fish.

### Facilities
Ten traditional toilet blocks, three new and seven refurbished, provide British and Turkish style toilets, open style washbasins and controllable hot showers. Three washing machines. Dishwashing (inside). Large supermarket and several kiosks. Bars, restaurant, self-service restaurant and pizzeria. Sports centre. Trampolines. Table tennis. Aerobics. Minigolf. Bicycle hire. Gymnastics. Games machines. Billiards. Daily children's club. Art workshops. Dance nights. Bungalows to rent. Off site: Novalja with bars, restaurants and shops is close.

**Open:** 1 May - 30 September.

### Directions
Take no. 2 coast road south from Rijeka and at Prizna take the ferry. From the ferry follow signs for Novalja and site. GPS: N44:32.330 E14:53.176

### Charges 2007
| | |
|---|---|
| Per person | € 3,20 - € 6,30 |
| child | free - € 3,90 |
| pitch | € 5,00 - € 18,00 |
| dog | € 3,00 - € 4,00 |

## CR6778 Camping Simuni
Otok Pag, HR-23251 Simuni (Dalmatia)
Tel: 023 697 441. Email: info@camping-simuni.hr

The Simuni site is landscaped with low rock walls alongside the access roads and many varieties of shrubs and flowers, giving it a pleasant, welcoming atmosphere. It is close to the fishing port of Simuni and just 8 km. from Pag on the island of Pag. There are 800 pitches, most for tourers, about half with electricity and with a water tap between four pitches. Tent pitches are small, pitches for caravans are larger and fairly level, most with hardstanding and off tarmac or paved access roads. Shade is provided by mature laurel trees and all pitches are separated by low rock walls on grass and gravel. The site has a private pebble beach and offers many sporting facilities, as well as a pizzeria, a restaurant and several bars. Almost the whole eating area enjoys pleasant views of the sea through the trees and is very popular serving good local fish as a speciality. The open fronted reception building and other site buildings have been constructed in a remarkable style using recycled materials. The site is very dark at night and torches are essential. Being so close to Pag, one should not miss out on the speciality of the island, the Pag cheese, ham and lamb.

### Facilities
Three new sanitary blocks will be ready for 2007 we are told (construction on the site is ongoing). Laundry service from reception. Dishwashing under cover. Supermarket and fruit kiosks. Bar, pizzeria and restaurant. Tennis, minigolf and table tennis (charged). Aerobics. Beach volleyball. Boat launching. Games hall with video games. Table football. Trampolines. Football tournaments for children. Latin and ballroom dancing lessons.
Off site: Simuni (walking distance) and Pag 8 km.

**Open:** 1 May - 1 October.

### Directions
Take no. 2 road south from Rijeka to Prizna and take the ferry to Pag. From ferry follow signs for Pag and site. GPS: N44:27.912 E14:58.027

### Charges 2007
| | |
|---|---|
| Per person | € 2,90 - € 7,80 |
| child | free - € 5,50 |
| pitch with electricity | € 6,30 - € 19,60 |

Camping Cheques accepted.

---

## CR6782 Camping Zaton
P.O. Box 363, Siroka ulica bb, HR-23232 Zadar (Dalmatia)
Tel: 023 280 280. Email: camping@zaton.hr

Zaton Holiday Village is a newly built, family holiday park, close to the historic town of Nin and just a few kilometres from the bustling seaside resort of Zadar. This park itself is more like a town and has every amenity one can think of for a holiday on the Dalmatian south coast. The village is divided into two areas separated by the shopping centre and a large parking area, one for campers close to the sea, the other for a complex with holiday bungalows. Zaton has 1,400 mostly level pitches for tourers, of which about 1,060 have electricity, water and waste water, the rest having electricity only. All numbered pitches have shade from mature trees and some have views over the extensive, pebble beach and the sea. Access is off hard access roads and some of the pitches at the far end are on terraces. Zaton caters for everybody's needs on site with numerous bars, restaurants, shops and two swimming pools. Excursions are organised to the Krka waterfalls, the Zrmanja Canyon and the Kornati, Paklenica and Plitvice National Parks.

### Facilities
Five modern and one refurbished toilet blocks have British and Turkish style toilets, washbasins (some in cabins) and controllable hot showers. Child-size washbasins. Facilities for disabled visitors. Campers' kitchen with gas hobs. Motorcaravan service point. Dog shower. Car wash. Shopping centre. Restaurants, bars and kiosks. Water play area for older children. Heated swimming pool. Mini-car track. Riding. Trim track. Scuba diving. Professional animation team (high season). Teen club. Games hall. Internet point. Live shows on stage by the beach.
Off site: Historic towns of Zadar and Nin.

**Open:** 1 May - 25 September.

### Directions
From Rijeka take no. 2 road south and leave at exit for Zadar. Drive north towards Nin and Zaton Holiday Village is signed a few kilometres before Nin. GPS: N44:14.086 E15:09.862

### Charges 2007
| | |
|---|---|
| Per person | € 4,70 - € 8,70 |
| child | € 2,30 - € 6,80 |
| pitch incl. electricity | € 8,90 - € 28,00 |
| dog | € 4,00 - € 7,60 |

Camping Cheques accepted.

# Croatia

### CR6830 Kamp Paklenica

Dr. Franje Tudmania 14, HR-23244 Paklenica (Dalmatia)
Tel: 023 209 050. Email: alan@bluesunhotels.com

This is a relatively small site next to the Alan Hotel in Plaklenica. It has 250 pitches, all for tourers and 150 with 16A electricity, on level, grass and gravel ground (firm tent pegs needed) under mature trees that provide useful shade. The front pitches have beautiful views of the blue waters of the Adriatic. Paklenica is only 100 m. from the entrance of the Paklenica National Park and excursions to the Park and to the Zrmanja Canyon can be booked on the site. Paklenica has its own beach, paved with rock plates, that gives access to a sheltered lagoon for swimming and boating. On site are a pizzeria and good value restaurant with a large, open-air terrace and a supermarket is only a 200 m. walk. The Alan Hotel provides a children's club, an outdoor swimming pool, games room with billiards and a fully equipped fitness centre (all free of charge for camp guests). Some entertainment is organised with live musical nights (quality variable) and games (you could win a five day free stay).

#### Facilities

Two good toilet blocks provide British and Turkish style toilets, open washbasins and controllable, hot showers (free). Child-size toilet, shower and basin. Excellent facilities for disabled visitors. Dishwashing. Fridge box hire. Motorcaravan service point. Bar/restaurant and pizzeria. Oval shaped pool (150 sq.m) with paddling pool. New playground (on gravel). Tennis. Minigolf. Fishing. Bicycle hire. Beach volleyball. Jet ski, boat and scooter hire. Children's club. Live music night with entertainment. Games room with billiards and arcade machines. Communal barbecue area. Off site: Supermarket 200 m.

**Open:** Easter - 15 October.

#### Directions

From Rijeka, take no. 8 coast road south along the Dalmatian coast towards Starigrad-Paklenica. In town turn right at sign for 'Hotel Alan'. Turn right to site. GPS: N44:17.236 E15:26.857

#### Charges guide

| | |
|---|---|
| Per person | Kn 20,50 - 49,00 |
| child (3-12 yrs) | Kn 11,50 - 30,00 |
| pitch incl. car | Kn 37,50 - 71,50 |

---

### CR6833 Autocamp Rio

Put Primorja 66, HR-23207 Sv. Filip I Jakov (Dalmatia)
Tel: 023 388 671. Email: levyzd@yahoo.co.uk

In a village close to Biograd, the small, Autocamp Rio provides 54 pitches of which 29 are available for tourers. All have old-type (two-pin) electricity connections. The fairly unofficial reception, the toilet block and the house of the Croatian owner are situated on the street front while behind, the site ends on a cliff directly above the sea. Below, a little sandy beach and a pier for boats are accessible from the site and used by campsite guests only. The partly shaded, marked pitches are laid out in two wings around a central grassy area so nobody is entirely surrounded by campers. There is no bar or restaurant on the site, but the village centre is within walking distance. The atmosphere here is pleasant, most of the guests being Dutch, and the site is popular, especially in high season. Opportunities for day trips include visits by boat to the wonderful National Park of the Kornati Archipelago with 146 little islands and islets, or a trip to the freshwater bird reserve at Vransko Jezero 10 km. away.

#### Facilities

Decent but simple toilet block has showers with curtains and no facilities for babies or disabled persons. Washing machine. No bar or restaurant. Off site: Village within walking distance. City of Zadar 25 km. Komati Archipelago National Park. Vransko Jezero bird reserve 10 km.

**Open:** Easter - 15 October.

#### Directions

From centre of Sv Filip I Jakov village, leave main coast road and follow signs for 'centar' and little site sign for Rio. Continue around a little park and keeping right (in southeastern direction, parallel to the sea) for almost 1 km. Rio is on the right, not far from the end of the village.

#### Charges guide

| | |
|---|---|
| Per person | € 3,00 |
| child (under 12 yrs) | € 1,00 |
| pitch | € 5,00 |
| electricity | € 3,00 |

---

Check real time availability and at-the-gate prices...
www.alanrogers.com

## CR6840 Autocamp Jezera Lovisca

HR-22242 Jezera Lovisca (Dalmatia)
Tel: 022 439 600. Email: info@jezera-kornati.hr

Jezera Lovisca is a family site of 75 acres with 400 informal pitches and would be a good choice for a relaxing beach holiday as it is on the island of Murter. In high season the site provides a full animation program for children with games, music, drawing and swimming. For adults there are live musical nights at the bar/restaurant which has a large, welcoming terrace from where there are beautiful views of the lagoon. There are 360 grass and gravel pitches for touring units, all with 10A electricity (long leads may be necessary). They are mostly on level terraces, attractively built with low rock walls in the shade of mature trees and from the front row there are sea views. In front of the site is a pebble beach with a concrete sunbathing area. The more active can take diving lessons at the site's own diving centre, enjoy day trips around the Murter peninsula, the Plitvice and Kornati National Parks, or visit the bustling seaside resort of Zadar and the historic towns of Nin and Jezera.

### Facilities

Six modern and comfortable toilet blocks have British style toilets, open washbasins and controllable, hot showers (free) - all of a very high standard. Campers' kitchen. Dishwashing. Fridge box hire. Shop. Bar/restaurant and takeaway. Tennis. Minigolf. Fishing. Diving centre. Animation program for children. Internet access. Fishing. Watersports. Boat launching. Bicycle hire. Excursions organised. Live musical nights. Barbecues permitted only in communal area. Off site: Harbour town of Jerz 500 m. Buses from gate to local attractions.

**Open:** 15 April - 15 October.

### Directions

From Rijeka take no. 8 coast road south towards Zadar and Split. 58 km. south of Zadar is the town of Pirovic. Turn right 4 km. south of Pirovec towards O Murter and continue through town of Trisco keeping to the coast road. This will take you to Jereza Lovisca. Site is well signed in Jezera and is just through the village.

### Charges 2007

| | |
|---|---|
| Per person | Kn 33,80 - 55,50 |
| child (3-12 yrs) | Kn 21,00 - 41,30 |
| pitch incl. car | Kn 52,50 - 97,50 |
| electricity | Kn 28,90 |
| dog | Kn 30,00 - 45,80 |

Site does not accept euros.
Camping Cheques accepted.

---

## CR6845 Kamp Adriatic

Huljerat bb, HR-22202 Primosten (Dalmatia)
Tel: 022 571 223. Email: info@camp-adriatic.hr

As we drove south down the Dalmatian coast road, we looked across a clear turquoise bay and saw a few tents, caravans and motorcaravans camped under some trees. A short distance later we were at the entrance of Camping Adriatic. With 530 pitches that slope down to the sea, the site is deceptive and enjoys a one kilometre beach frontage which is ideal for snorkelling and diving. Close to the delightful town of Primosten (with a taxi boat service in high season) the site boasts good modern amenities and a fantastic location. Tour operators use some pitches on the sea front and there are seven caravans to rent. Most pitches are level and have shade from pine trees. There are 212 numbered pitches and 288 unnumbered, all with 10/16A electricity available.

### Facilities

Four modern sanitary blocks provide clean toilets, hot showers and washbasins. Facilities for disabled visitors. Bathroom for children. Washing machine and dryer. Kitchen facilities. Small supermarket (15/5-30/9). Restaurant and bar (all season). Sports centre. Miniclub for children. Beach. Diving school. Sailing school and boat hire. Entertainment programme in July/Aug. Internet point.

**Open:** 1 May - 15 October.

### Directions

Take the new A1 motorway south and leave at the Sibenik exit. Follow the 33 road into Sibenik and then go south along the coast road (no. 8), signed Primosten. Site is 2.5 km. north of Primosten.
GPS: N43:36.391 E15:55.257

### Charges 2007

| | |
|---|---|
| Per person | Kn 31,00 - 43,00 |
| child (5-12 yrs) | Kn 22,00 - 28,00 |
| pitch | Kn 30,00 - 60,00 |

Camping Cheques accepted.

## CR6850 Camp Seget

Hrvatskih zrtava 121, HR-21218 Seget Donji (Dalmatia)

Tel: 021 880 394. Email: kamp@kamp-seget.hr

Seget is a simple site which is pleasant and quiet with only 120 pitches, just 2 km. from the interesting old harbour town of Trogir. It is an ideal base for exploring this part of the Dalmatian Coast, or for visiting Trogir and Split. The site is set up on both sides of a tarmac access lane that runs down to the Adriatic Sea. Pitches to the left are off three separate, gravel lanes. They are fairly level and from most there are views of the sea. Pitches to the right are slightly sloping and mostly used for tents. Of varying sizes (80-100 sq.m) the pitches are on grass and gravel (firm tent pegs may be needed), mostly in the shade of mature fig and palm trees and some are numbered. All have access to 16A electricity (long leads may be necessary). To the front of the site a paved promenade gives access to the pebble beach. Via the promenade it is an easy five minute stroll to the first restaurants (we can recommend Frankie's), where you can enjoy good quality, good value meals.

### Facilities

Two sanitary blocks (one half remaining a 'portacabin' style). British style toilets, washbasins and controllable, hot showers (free). Facilities for disabled visitors. Campers' kitchen. Fridge box hire. Dishwashing. Shop. Beach. Fishing. Boat rental. Barbecues permitted only on communal area. Off site: Bus at gate for touring. Golf, riding and bicycle hire 1 km. Boat launching 500 m.

**Open:** 15 April - 15 October.

### Directions

Follow no. 8 coastal road south from Zadar towards Split and in Trogir look for prominent site signs, finishing in a sharp right turn.

### Charges 2007

| | |
|---|---|
| Per person | Kn 21,00 - 28,00 |
| child (5-12 yrs) | Kn 14,00 - 17,00 |
| pitch incl. car | Kn 43,00 - 81,00 |
| electricity | Kn 16,50 |

## CR6860 Autocamp Galeb

Vukovarska bb, HR-21310 Omis (Dalmatia)

Tel: 021 864 430. Email: camping@galeb.hr

Galeb is 25 km. south of Split and sits below the Cetine Canyon which can deliver strong winds from the east. The river Cetine in just to the north of the site and the pretty port where river meets sea is another powerful attraction, complemented by the ancient forts and pirate buildings above. A dramatic 1,000 metre rock backdrop to the whole site reflects the light differently as the day progresses and the superb sunsets here paint it with amazing orange and red hues. The 500 tourist pitches are informal and security was a little laissez faire when we stayed. Flat and mostly shady, some pitches are right at the water's edge and very long leads are required if you want to get away from it all. Many bungalows are on site but they are set back from the beach in their own areas as are the few tour operator pitches. The site sits between the road and the sea with a long beach frontage of gravel and sand. It is not too noisy, although the campsite broadcast is used periodically to announce the entertainment. There is a smart, newly renovated restaurant and bar by reception with a patio and a pizzeria is on the beach with a terrace from where you can enjoy those wonderful sunsets. A large range of activities is available on site and the village of Omis is 100 metres from the gate with many bars and restaurants, plus banks. The shop on site sells basics only as the nearest supermarket is at the gate with much choice of produce. This is a sound site in a very interesting location and can be enjoyed by all the family.

### Facilities

Three sanitary blocks have been renovated to a good standard and two have facilities for disabled campers. Hot water for showers is plentiful and there is a regular cleaning routine. Motorcaravan service point. Shop. Restaurant. Pizzeria. Tennis. Volleyball. Play areas. Bicycle hire. Animation all season. TV. Security boxes. Cold boxes. Exchange. Doctor. Beach. Boat launching and boat hire. Beach volleyball. Windsurfing. Sailing. Off site: Busy village 100 m. Port 1 km. Island of Brac for tours and exploration. Rafting and canyoning. Climbing.

**Open:** 1 June - 30 September.

### Directions

Site is off the main coast road between Split and Dubronvik, about 25 km. southeast of Split and is well signed from the road.

### Charges 2007

| | |
|---|---|
| Per person | Kn 31,50 - 42,50 |
| child (5-12 yrs) | Kn 20,50 - 25,50 |
| pitch | Kn 30,50 - 58,50 |
| electricity | Kn 10,00 |
| car | Kn 20,50 - 31,00 |

## Croatia

### CR6865 Camp Vira
HR-21450 Hvar (Dalmatia)
Tel: 021 741 803. Email: viracamp@suncanihvar.com

Camp Vira has been recommended to us by our Croatia agent and we plan to undertake a full inspection next year. Located only 4 km. from the town of Hvar, it is said to be a nature lover's paradise that combines Hvar's natural beauty and clean sea with an environmentally friendly array of modern amenities. Solar power units supply the bulk of the camp's energy needs, while pine trees provide natural shade for the 90 pitches and 72 camping places. Vira's private cove has a pebble beach making it ideal for sunbathing, swimming and variety of water activities.

#### Facilities
Amenities include newly renovated shower and bathroom facilities. Laundry and ironing services. Grocery shop and souvenir shop. Aloe Vera bar and grill. Playground. Recreation rentals and beach shop. Fridge hire. Tent hire. Off site: Bus service to Hvar.

**Open:** 15 May - 31 October.

#### Directions
Site is 4 km. northwest from the town of Hvar. From Hvar go forward leaving the central car park on the left and follow roadside directions to site.

#### Charges 2007
| | |
|---|---|
| Per person | € 6,00 - € 7,00 |
| child (3-11 yrs) | € 3,00 - € 4,00 |
| pitch | € 11,00 - € 22,00 |
| dog | € 4,00 - € 5,00 |

### CR6870 Kamp Dole
Zivogosce bb, HR-21331 Zivogosce (Dalmatia)
Tel: 021 628 749

Dole is a basic site in southern Croatia, close to the beautiful island of Hvar. It has 500 pitches, of which 400 are for tourers, the other pitches taken by Czech tour operators. The beachside pitches are numbered and marked, the remainder are used informally and are mostly in the shade of mature trees. There are great views of the sea as the site is raised 7 metres above the pebble beach which stretches for over a kilometre in front of the site. The pitches at the back have beautiful views of the impressive mountains. Facilities on site include several fruit and vegetable kiosks and there is a market. Close to reception is a welcoming bar with terrace for drinks. There is no restaurant on site but two restaurants are nearby. In high season a full entertainment programme for children is organised with carnival, gymnastics and aquarobics.

#### Facilities
Four toilet blocks, three of which have been renovated to a reasonable level and offer high quality British WCs, washbasins and controllable, hot showers (free). The fourth block is due to be completed in 2008. Fridge box hire. Dishwashing. Several kiosks and supermarket. Bar. Beach volleyball. Jet ski hire. Paragliding. Pedalo and canoe hire. Full entertainment programme in high season. Excursions to Korcula. Barbecues only in communal area. Off site: Boat launching 200 m. Paintball adjacent to site.

**Open:** 1 May - 30 September.

#### Directions
From Split take no. 8 coast road south towards Dubrovnik. Site is on the right in Zivogosce, 12 km south east of Makarska, and signed 4 km. before village and also in village.

#### Charges 2007
| | |
|---|---|
| Per person | Kn 21,00 - 32,00 |
| child (5-12 yrs) | Kn 12,50 - 20,00 |
| pitch | Kn 60,00 - 140,00 |
| electricity | Kn 22,00 |

## www.alanrogers.com

Around 500 of Europe's finest campsites, all bookable at the click of a mouse.

All campsites are inspected & selected by Alan Rogers.

**Just Click and Go!**

INSPECTED CAMPSITES SELECTED

## CR6874 Autocamp Kalac

Dubrovacka cesta 19, HR-20260 Korcula (Dalmatia)
Tel: 020 726 693. Email: kalac@htp-korcula.hr

Close to the historical town of Korcula, Camping Kalac is a good choice for a relaxing holiday on the Dalmatian coast. Not one of the typically large sites of the area, this is a modestly sized one with only 230 pitches. Most of these are suitable only for tents or reserved for the season, but 70 pitches are available for tourers. Located under trees, there is sufficient shade and all have electricity connections. Many visitors leave their cars outside the camping areas as the pitches are fairly small and not always easy to access. A restaurant and several bars are close to the sea.

### Facilities
The two sanitary blocks are modern and convenient, but lack facilities for disabled persons or special areas for children. Washing machine. Fridge hire. Large shop. Restaurant and bars. On-site entertainment is limited. Scooter, bicycle and boat hire. Table tennis. Minigolf. Torches are advised at night. Off site: Town 2 km.

**Open:** 15 May - 1 October.

### Directions
The island of Korcula can be reached by ferry from Orebic. Leaving the ferry, the road winds up and leads to Korcula town via a loop through the forest. Access to site is on the right (signed, near Hotel Bon Repos) in a built-up area 500 m. from ferry landing.

### Charges 2008
| | |
|---|---|
| Per person | Kn 19,50 - 45,00 |
| child (2-12 yrs) | Kn 9,75 - 22,50 |
| caravan or motorcaravan | Kn 30,00 - 72,00 |
| electricity | Kn 19,50 |

## CR6875 Autocamp Nevio

Dubravica bb, HR-20250 Orebic (Dalmatia)
Tel: 020 713 100. Email: info@nevio-camping.com

This little campsite is a first class option in the southern part of Dalmatia. Everything on the site is brand new including a comfortable main building with a bar, restaurant and terrace (summer only). The 70 level pitches are slightly terraced and of 80-120 sq.m. All have electricity and water, 10 also have sewage connections. There is little shade as yet, but this will develop. Located on the peninsula of Peljesac, there is the atmosphere of Dalmatia and its islands without the need for a ferry from the mainland to reach the site. From the almost vertical, 50 m. cliffs there are great views of Korcula town on the opposite island. A road winds down to a private beach and boat pier.

### Facilities
New sanitary facilities include rooms for children and babies rooms and a fully equipped unit for disabled persons. Small kitchen. Laundry facilities. Small bar and restaurant (summer). Fridge hire. Bicycle hire. Boat launching. Mobile homes for hire. Off site: Shop 100 m. Orebic within 2 km. Korcula (by ferry). Dubrovnik 125 km.

**Open:** All year.

### Directions
Approaching from the mainland, site is just over 1 km. before the town of Orebic, on the left (signed). GPS: N42:58.440 E17:11.580

### Charges 2008
| | |
|---|---|
| Per person (over 5 yrs) | € 4,40 |
| pitch | € 8,00 - € 14,00 |
| dog | € 1,00 |

## CR6890 Camping Solitudo

Vatroslava Lisinskog 17, HR-20000 Dubrovnik (Dalmatia)
Tel: 020 448 686. Email: camping-dubrovnik@valamar.com

Solitudo belongs to the Camping on the Adriatic Group. The location is excellent, just a few kilometres from the historic old town of Dubrovnik. It also has a beach which makes it an ideal base for both sightseeing and relaxing. There are 238 pitches, all for tourers, all with 12A electricity and 30 with water, arranged on four large fields that are opened according to demand. Field D is mainly used for tents and pitches here are small. The A field has pitches of up to 120 sq.m. and takes many motorcaravans (long leads required). All pitches are numbered, some are level, other are on terraces and most are shaded by mature trees. The ground is hard and stony (firm tent pegs needed). There is a mini-market for essentials plus the affiliated hotel complex 1 km. down the road.

### Facilities
Clean and modern toilet blocks have British style toilets, open washbasins and controllable, hot showers. Good facilities for disabled visitors. Laundry and dishwashing facilities. Motorcaravan service point. Mini-market. Attached restaurant/bar. Snack bar. Fishing. Bicycle hire. Beach with pedalo, beach chair, kayak and jet ski hire. Excursions to the Elafiti Islands. WiFi. Off site: Outdoor pool 500 m. Bar, disco and restaurant 500 m.

**Open:** 1 April - 1 November.

### Directions
From Split follow no. 8 road south towards Dubrovnik. Site is very well signed, starting 110 km. before reaching Dubrovnik, and throughout the city.

### Charges 2007
| | |
|---|---|
| Per person | € 3,74 - € 7,00 |
| child (4-10 yrs) | free - € 4,90 |
| pitch with services | € 9,63 - € 15,30 |
| dog | € 2,92 - € 4,73 |

Camping Cheques accepted.

# Slovenia

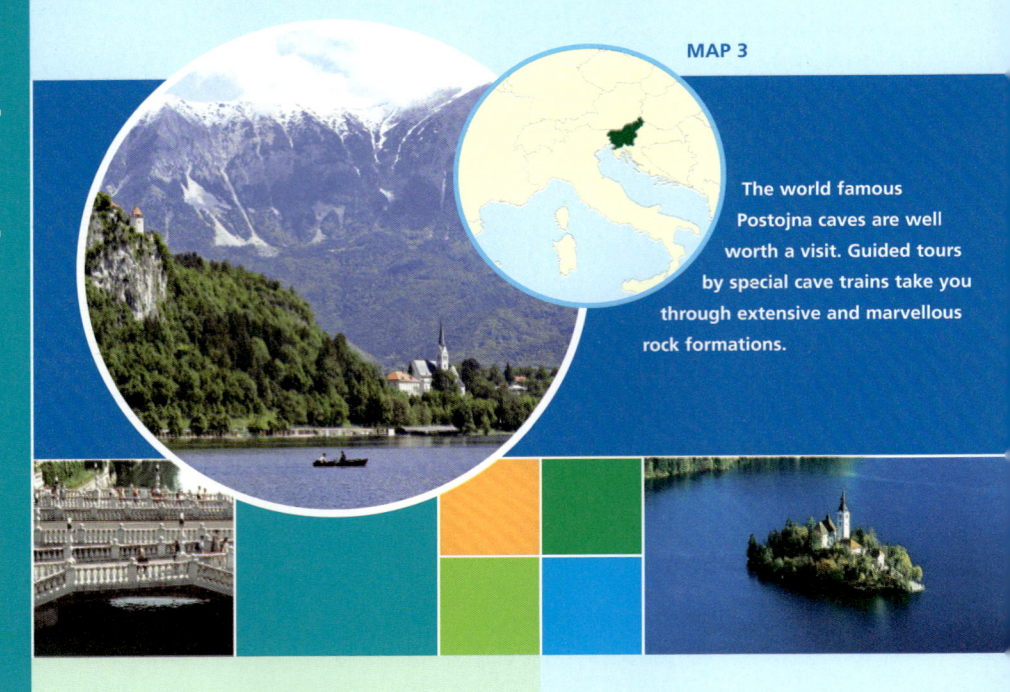

**MAP 3**

The world famous Postojna caves are well worth a visit. Guided tours by special cave trains take you through extensive and marvellous rock formations.

With its snow capped Julian Alps and the picturesque Triglav National park that include the beautiful lakes of Bled and Bohinj, and the peaceful Soca River, it is no wonder that the northwest region of Slovenia is so popular. Stretching from the Alps down to the Adriatic coast is the picturesque Karst region, with pretty olive groves and thousands of spectacular underground caves, including the Postojna and Skocjan caves. Although small, the Adriatic coast has several bustling beach towns such as the Italianised Koper resort and the historic port of Piran, with many opportunities for watersports and sunbathing. The capital Ljubljana is centrally located; with Renaissance, Baroque and Art Nouveau architecture, you will find most points of interest are along the Ljubljana river. Heading eastwards the landscape becomes gently rolling hills, and is largely given over to vines (home of Lutomer Riesling). Savinja with its spectacular Alps is the main area for producing wine.

**Population**
2 million

**Capital**
Ljubljana

**Climate**
Warm summers, cold winters with snow in the Alps.

**Language**
Slovene, with German often spoken in the north and Italian in the west.

**Currency**
Euro

**Telephone**
The country code is 386

**Banks**
Mon-Fri 8.30-16.30 with a lunch break 12.30-14.00, plus Saturday mornings 8.30-11.30.

**Shops**
Shops usually open by 08.00, sometimes 07.00. Closing times vary widely.

# Slovenia

**WHAT SLOVENIA LACKS IN SIZE IT MAKES UP FOR IN EXCEPTIONAL BEAUTY. SITUATED BETWEEN ITALY, AUSTRIA, HUNGARY AND CROATIA, IT HAS A DIVERSE LANDSCAPE WITH STUNNING ALPS, RIVERS, FORESTS AND THE WARM ADRIATIC COAST.**

### Public Holidays
New Year 1, 2 Jan; Preseren Day 8 Feb; Easter Monday; Resistance Day 27 Apr; Labour Day 1-2 May; National Day 25 Jun; Assumption; Reformation Day 31 Oct; All Saint's Day; Christmas Day; Independence Day 26 Dec.

### Motoring
Small but expanding network of motorways radiating from Ljubljana (there may be tolls). Secondary roads often poorly maintained. Tertiary roads are often gravel (known locally as 'white roads' and shown thus on road maps). Road markings and signs are generally good. Do not drink and drive. Police regularly carry out random breath checks and you will be prosecuted if any trace of alcohol is found in your system.

### Tourist Office
The Embassy of the Slovenian Republic
10 Little College Street
London SW1P 3SH
Tel: 020 7222 5400  Fax: 020 7222 5277
E-mail: vlo@gov.si
Internet: www.slovenia.info

### British Embassy
4th Floor Trg Republike 3
1000 Ljubljana
Tel: (386) (1) 200 3910

### Places of interest
*Adriatic Coast:* Venetian Gothic architecture can be found at Piran, the best beach along the coast is at Fiesa.

*Julian Alps:* Mt Triglav is the country's highest peak, Bled's Castle, Bled Island has a 15th century belfry with a 'bell of wishes', Lake Bohinij.

*Ljubljana:* Municipal Museum, National Museum, Museum of Modern Art all along the banks of the Ljubljana River, Tivoli Park with bowling alleys, tennis courts, swimming pools and a roller-skating rink.

*Skocjan Caves:* filled with stalactites and stalagmites and housing 250 plant varieties and five types of bats.

### Cuisine of the region
Traditionally the cuisine mainly consists of venison and fish, but there are Austrian, Italian and Hungarian influences.

*Dunajski zrezek:* wiener schnitzel

*Golaz:* goulash

*Klobasa:* sausage

*Njoki:* potato dumplings

*Paprikas:* chicken or beef stew

*Struklji:* cheese dumplings

*Zavitek:* strudel

# Slovenia

## SV4210 Camping Sobec

Sobceva cesta 25, SLO-4248 Lesce
Tel: 045 353 700. Email: sobec@siol.net

Sobec is situated in a valley between the Julian Alps and the Karavanke Mountains, in a pine grove between the Sava Dolinka river and a small lake. It is only 3 km. from Bled and 20 km. from the Karavanke Tunnel. There are 500 unmarked pitches on level, grassy fields off tarmac access roads (450 for touring units), all with 16A electricity. Shade is provided by mature pine trees and younger trees separate some pitches. Camping Sobec is surrounded by water – the Sava river borders it on three sides and on the fourth is a small, artificial lake with grassy fields for sunbathing. Some pitches have views over the lake, which has an enclosed area providing safe swimming for children. This site is a good base for an active holiday, since both the Sava Dolinka and the Sava Bohinjka rivers are suitable for canoeing, kayaking, rafting and fishing, whilst the nearby mountains offer challenges for mountain climbing, paragliding and canyoning.

### Facilities

Three traditional style toilet blocks (two refurbished, one old) with mainly British style toilets, washbasins in cabins and controllable hot showers. Child size toilets and basins. Well equipped, attractive baby room. Facilities for disabled visitors. Laundry with sinks, washing machines and dryer. Dishwashing under cover. Motorcaravan service point. Supermarket, bar/restaurant (all open all season) with stage for live performances. Playgrounds on grass and stone. Rafting, canyoning and kayaking organised. Miniclub. Tours to Bled and the Narodni National Park organised. Off site: Golf and riding 2 km.

**Open:** 21 April - 30 September.

### Directions

Site is off the main road from Lesce to Bled and well signed just outside Lesce.
GPS: N46:21.364 E14:08.995

### Charges 2007

| | |
|---|---|
| Per person | € 9,70 - € 11,50 |
| child (7-14 yrs) | € 7,30 - € 8,60 |
| electricity (16A) | € 3,00 |
| dog | € 3,00 |

Check real time availability and at-the-gate prices...
www.alanrogers.com

## SV4200 Camping Bled

Kidriceva 10c, SI, SLO-4260 Bled
Tel: 045 752 000. Email: info@camping.bled.si

On the western tip of Lake Bled is Camping Bled. The waterfront here is a small public beach immediately behind which gently runs a sloping narrow wooded valley. Pitches at the front, used mainly for over-nighters, are now marked, separated by young trees and enlarged, bringing the total number down to 280. In areas at the back, visitors are free to pitch where they like. Unlike at many other Slovenian sites the number of statics (and semi-statics) here appears to be carefully controlled with touring caravans, motorcaravans and tents predominating. Some visitors might be disturbed by the noise coming from trains as they hurtle out of a high tunnel overlooking the campsite on the line from Bled to Bohinj. But this is a small price to pay for the pleasure of being in a pleasant site from which the lake, its famous little island, its castle and its town can be explored on foot or by boat.

### Facilities

Toilet facilities in five blocks are of a high standard (with free hot showers). Two blocks are heated. Solar energy used. Backpackers' kitchen. Washing machines and dryers. Chemical disposal point. Motorcaravan services. Gas supplies. Fridge hire. Supermarket. Restaurant. Play area and children's zoo. Table tennis. Games hall. Beach volleyball. Trampolines. Organised activities in July/Aug. including children's club, excursions and sporting activities. Mountain bike tours. Live entertainment. Fishing. Bicycle hire. Internet access. Off site: Riding 3 km. Golf 5 km. Within walking distance of waterfront and town.

**Open:** 1 April - 15 October.

### Directions

From the town of Bled drive along south shore of lake to its western extremity (some 2 km) to the site. GPS: N46:21.693 E14:04.845

### Charges 2007

| | |
|---|---|
| Per person | € 8,50 - € 11,50 |
| child (7-13 yrs) | € 5,95 - € 8,05 |
| electricity | € 3,00 |
| dog | € 1,50 - € 2,50 |

Less 10% for stays over 6 days.
Camping Cheques accepted.

**CAMPING BLED**

*Come and find yourself...*

Camping Bled, Kidričeva 10c, 4260 Bled, Slovenija
Tel: +386 (0) 4 575 20 00
Fax: +386 (0) 4 575 20 02
www.camping-bled.com
E-mail: info@camping.bled.si

## SV4100 Autocamp Spik

Jezerci 21, SLO-4282 Gozd Martuljek
Tel: 045 877 100. Email: recepcija.spik@hitholidays-kg.si

Most British motorists enter Slovenia on the E55 from Villach through the easy Karawanka tunnel. On the Slovenian side they will join national route 202 and could proceed to Kransjska Gora, this pleasant resort town being the main northern gateway for the Julian Alps. Close to Kransjska Gora is the small village of Gozd Martuljek and here, directly on route 202, is Kamp Spik, named after the peak which dominates the spectacular view from the site of the jagged Julian Alps skyline. This is the highest site in Slovenia (altitude 750 m, nearly 2,500 ft). It is large and flat, covering eight hectares of spruce woodland, with 200 touring pitches, all with electricity (6A). The site is shared with the modern Spik Hotel and the facilities are extensive. As a result of its spectacular location and its extensive facilities many of the pitches are occupied by caravans which may not be statics but which are clearly not tourers.

### Facilities

Two toilet blocks include open plan washbasins (cold water only) and controllable hot showers. Motorhome service point. Supermarket. Tennis. Beach volleyball. Fishing. Bicycle hire. Climbing school. Mountaineering. Off site: Riding 6 km.

**Open:** All year.

### Directions

Site is well signed on the 202 just outside Gozd Martuljek. GPS: N46:28.887 E13:50.235

### Charges guide

| | |
|---|---|
| Per person | € 5,84 - € 9,60 |

Less 5% for stays over 7 days
and 10% for 10 days or longer.

Check real time availability and at-the-gate prices...
www.alanrogers.com

# Slovenia

## SV4150 Kamp Kamne

Franc Voga, Dovje 9, SLO-4281 Mojstrana
Tel: 045 891 105. Email: info@campingkamne.com

For visitors proceeding down the 202 road, from Italy or the Wurzen Pass, towards the prime attractions of the twin lakes of Bled and Bohinj, a delightfully informal little site is to be found just outside the village of Mojstrana. For those arriving via the Karavanke Tunnel the diversion along the 202 is very well worth it. Owner Franc Voga opened the site as recently as 1988, on a small terraced orchard. He has steadily developed the facilities, adding a small pool, two tennis courts and improved all other facilities. The little reception doubles as a bar where locals wander up for a beer and a chat while enjoying the view across the valley of the Julian Alps. The site is popular with walkers as three valleys lead west into the mountains from Mojstrana, including the trail to the ascent of Triglav, at nearly 3,000 m. the highest point of the Julian Alps.

### Facilities

The small excellent sanitary block is of a high quality and well maintained. Reception/bar. Small swimming pool. Two tennis courts. Table tennis. TV room. Mountain bike hire. Franc's English is good and his daughter Anna is fluent. Twice weekly excursions to the mountains (free) in July and August. Two new apartments and bungalows now available to rent. Off site: Walking trails.

**Open:** All year.

### Directions

Site is well marked on north side of the 202 4 km. from Jesenice, just to west of exit for Mojstrana. Site is 4 km. from the Karawanken tunnel.
GPS: N46:27.872 E13:57.472

### Charges 2008

| | |
|---|---|
| Per person | € 7,00 - € 6,00 |
| child (7-17 yrs) | € 4,50 - € 5,00 |
| electricity | € 2,00 - € 2,50 |

## SV4250 Camping Danica Bohinj

Triglavska 60, SLO-4265 Bohinjska Bistrica
Tel: 045 747 820. Email: info@camp-danica.si

For those wanting to visit the famous Bohinj valley, which stretches like a fjord right into the heart of the Julian Alps, an ideal site is Danica Bohinj which lies in the valley 3 km. downstream of the lake. Danica was set up in 1989 to supplement the camping accommodation then only available at Zlatorog. The fact that the manager on the site, Marjan Malej, is the director of the local tourist association is an indication of the local community's well deserved pride in their own campsite. Danica occupies a rural site that stretches from the main road leading into Bohinj from Bled (25 km. away), to the bank of the newly formed Sava river. It is basically flat meadow, broken up by lines of natural woodland. This excellent site has 165 pitches, 145 for touring units, all with 10A electricity and forms an ideal base for the many sporting activities the area has to offer.

### Facilities

Two good toilet blocks with toilets, open plan washbasins and hot showers. Facilities for disabled visitors. Laundry with washing machines and dryers. Ironing board. Chemical disposal point. Motorcaravan service point. Volleyball. Football. Tennis. Small shop. Café. Fishing. Bicycle hire. Organised excursions in the Triglavski National Park. Off site: Riding 6 km. Canoeing, kayaking, rafting and numerous walking and mountain bike trails.

**Open:** May - September.

### Directions

Driving from Bled to Bohinj, the well signed site lies just behind the village of Bohinjska Bistrica on the right-hand (north) side of the road.
GPS: N46:16.401 E13:56.921

### Charges 2007

| | |
|---|---|
| Per person | € 7,00 - € 10,00 |
| child (7-14 yrs) | € 5,60 - € 7,50 |
| electricity | € 2,50 |
| dog | € 2,00 |

Less 10% for stays over 7 days.

have you visited www.alanrogers.com yet?

INSPECTED CAMPSITES & SELECTED

Alan Rogers

Check real time availability and at-the-gate prices...
www.alanrogers.com

## SV4235 Kamp Klin

Lepena 1, SLO-5232 Soca
Tel: 053 889 513. Email: kampklin@volja.net

Kamp Klin is next to the confluence of the Soca and Lepenca rivers and is surrounded by mountains. The park is close to the Triglavski National Park and from here it is only a short drive to the highest point of Slovenia, the Triglavski mountain and its beautiful viewpoint with marked walking routes. Being next to two rivers, the site is also a suitable base for fishing, kayaking and rafting. Kamp Klin is privately owned and there is a 'pension' next door, all run by the Zorc family, who serve the local dishes with compe (potatoes), cottage cheese, grilled trout and local salami in the restaurant. The campsite has only 50 pitches, all for tourers and with electricity, on one large, grassy field, connected by a circular, gravel access road. The site is attractively landscaped with flowers and young trees, but this also means there is not much shade. Some pitches are right on the bank of the river (unfenced) and there are beautiful views of the river and the mountains. Like so many Slovenian sites in this area, this is a good holiday base for the active camper.

### Facilities
One modern toilet block and a 'portacabin' style unit with toilets and controllable showers. Laundry with sinks. Dishwashing (inside). Bar/restaurant. Play field. Beach volleyball. Fishing (permit required). Torch useful. Off site: Riding 500 m. Bicycle hire 10 km.

**Open:** All year.

### Directions
Site is on the main Kranjska Gora - Bovec road and is well signed in Soca. Access is via a sharp turn from the main road and over a small bridge that may be difficult for larger units.
GPS: N46:19.804 E13:38.640

### Charges guide
| | |
|---|---|
| Per person | € 5,50 - € 7,20 |
| child (7-12 yrs) | € 2,80 - € 3,60 |
| electricity | € 2,40 |

## SV4265 Lazar Kamp

Gregorciceva, SLO-5222 Kobarid
Tel: 053 885 333. Email: edi.lazar@siol.net

This new campsite high above the Soca river has a good location and is ideally situated for the many sporting activities this region of Slovenia has to offer. However, the road to the site from the Napoleon Bridge is narrow, twisting and unmade and is not really suitable for most modern motorcaravans or larger caravans. The owner of the site does insist that larger rigs do get down there, but I certainly was not going to try. With a large overhanging cliff face on the left and a low stone wall, or rusting railings on the right (before the 100 foot drop into the river) it is not for the fainthearted. The site is very suitable for tents and those with small outfits and offers 50 pitches (all with electricity) and good facilities. Kobarid is a delightful town and has much to offer the interested visitor.

### Facilities
The sanitary block is of a good standard and includes facilities for disabled visitors. Dishwashing sinks. Fridge. Washing machine. Bar. Crêperie and grill with terrace area. Internet access. Ranch style clubroom. Excursions and lots of local sporting activities.

**Open:** 1 April - 31 October.

### Directions
Site is on a side road leading east out of Kobarid towards Bosec, just beyond the so-called Napoleon's Bridge. It is not well signed but follow Kamp Koren signs to the bridge then the site is straight on down the narrow unmade road.

### Charges 2007
| | |
|---|---|
| Per person | € 8,00 - € 10,00 |
| child (7-14 yrs) | € 4,00 - € 5,00 |
| electricity | € 2,00 |

Check real time availability and at-the-gate prices...
www.alanrogers.com

## SV4270 Kamp Koren Kobarid

Drenzniske Ravne 33, SLO-5222 Kobarid
Tel: 00386 53 891 311. Email: info@kamp-koren.si

The campsite, run to perfection by Lidija Koren, occupies a flat, tree-lined meadow on a wide ledge which drops down sharply to the Soca river and a new, terraced area behind reception. A small, site with just 60 pitches, it is deservedly very popular with those interested in outdoor sports, including paragliding, canoeing, canyoning, rafting and fishing. Equally, a pleasant atmosphere is generated for those seeking a quiet and relaxing break. The Julian Alps and in particular the Triglav National Park is a wonderful and under-explored part of Slovenia that has much to offer. Kobarid, probably best approached via Udine in Italy, is a pleasant country town, with easy access to nearby rivers, valleys and mountains which alone justify a visit to Kamp Koren. But most British visitors will remember it for the opportunity it provides to fill that curious gap in their knowledge of European history. The local museum in Kobarid was voted European Museum of the year recently and is excellent.

### Facilities
Two attractive log-built toilet blocks are of a standard worthy of a high class private sports club. Facilities for disabled visitors. Laundry facilities. Chemical disposal point. Motorcaravan services. Shop (March - Nov). Café dispenses light meals, snacks and drinks apparently without much regard to closing hours. Sauna. Play area. Bowling. Fishing. Bicycle hire. Canoe hire. Climbing walls for adults. Off site: Riding 5 km. Golf 20 km. Town within walking distance.

**Open:** 15 March - 1 November.

### Directions
Site is on side road leading east out of Kobarid towards Bosec, just beyond the so-called Napoleon's Bridge, well signed on the left.
GPS: N46:15.045 E13:35.195

### Charges 2007
| | |
|---|---|
| Per person | € 7,50 - € 9,00 |
| child (7-13 yrs) | € 3,75 - € 4,50 |
| electricity | € 3,00. |

## SV4280 Camping Polovnik

Ledina 8, SLO-5230 Bovec
Tel: 053 896 007. Email: kamp.polovnik@siol.net

The Polovnik site is little more than a large, circular field, with trees in the centre that provide useful shade, and an open part to one side. There are 50 unmarked pitches (45 for tourers) all with 16A electricity, off a circular, gravel access road. To the back of the site is a separate field for groups. All pitches have good views of the surrounding mountains. This site is useful as a stop over on your way to the Postojna Caves, the Slovenian Riviera or Italy and for touring the local area with kayaking, rafting and canoeing possible. At the front of the site are a little bar and restaurant (not connected). Bovec and the Bovec district have much to offer culturally – you can visit the art works of Tone Kralj in the church of Soca or visit the Church of the Virgin Mary to listen to violin music and admire the ancient frescoes by Jerney of Loka. This area also provides possibilities for canyoning, paragliding and climbing.

### Facilities
One traditional style toilet block with British style toilets, open style washbasins with cold water only and pre-set hot showers (€ 0,50 token). Washing machine.
Off site: Fishing 1 km. Bovec town. Restaurant at the entrance.

**Open:** 1 April - 16 October.

### Directions
Bovec is on main road (54) from the Italian/Slovenian border to Postojna. Site is just outside Bovec next to a church. GPS: N46:20.173 E13:33.502

### Charges 2007
| | |
|---|---|
| Per person | € 5,00 - € 7,00 |
| child (7-14 yrs) | € 3,75 - € 5,25 |
| electricity | € 2,00 |

## SV4300 Hotel Camping Belvedere

Dobrava 1A, SLO-6310 Izola
Tel: 056 605 100. Email: belve@siol.net

Under the management of Hotel Belvedere, this site has developed into a massive leisure complex of which camping is a small part. It may be suitable for a short stay but is not recommended for a beach holiday. There are 280 pitches, with 200 for touring units. All have 6A electricity, but pitching is haphazard and that may make it difficult to find a place in high season. The site is divided into five different areas, divided by a narrow public road which has to be crossed to reach the toilet facilities (watch out for local drivers). Two fields are dedicated to static and seasonal units, the other three are for tourers. From the furthest area there are some sea views. A restaurant is close to the holiday bungalow complex, but we can also recommend the Italian trattoria, just 150 m. down the road, for a good value meal and beautiful, countryside views from its terrace. Access to the beach is a 500 m. walk down the road.

### Facilities

Two identical toilet blocks provide modern fittings but cleaning is under pressure in high season. Very comprehensive leisure facilities, including a huge swimming pool, restaurant, night club (can be very noisy late into the night) and hotel. Kiosk for basics (25/6-1/9). Beach shop. Torch useful. Off site: Historic town of Izola is close. Beach 500 m. Riding and bicycle hire 5 km.

**Open:** April - September.

### Directions

Follow the main A2 coast road west just beyond the Izola by-pass; the site is clearly signed but the exit is on a rather confusing summit road junction (the original entrance and exit have been closed so access is not easy). GPS: N45:31.857 E13:37.997

### Charges 2007

| | |
|---|---|
| Per person | € 6,50 - € 9,00 |
| child (4-14 yrs) | € 4,00 - € 6,00 |
| electricity | € 2,50 |
| dog | € 1,30 |

## SV4310 Camping Adria

Jadranska Cesta 25, SLO-6280 Ankaran
Tel: 056 637 350. Email: adria.tp@siol.net

Camping Adria is on the south side of the Milje/Muggia peninsula, right on the shore of the Adriatic Sea and just beyond the large shipyard and oil storage depot. It has a concrete promenade with access to the sea, complemented by an Olympic size pool with children's pool, both filled with sea water. The site has 500 pitches (250 for tourers), all with 10A electricity, set up on one side of the site close to sea. Pitches are off tarmac access roads, running down to sea and most are between 80 and 90 sq.m. There are six fully serviced pitches for motorcaravans with electricity, water and waste water. Pitches at the beach (used by static caravans) have beautiful views of the Adriatic and the historic ports of Koper and Izola. This part of the Slovenian Riviera is suitable for a beach holiday (although the sea could be a lot cleaner) and also has much to offer architecturally and culturally. You can visit the Adria hotel (once the Benedictine monastery of St Nicholas) and the site organises boat trips to the historic fishing ports of Piran and Portoroz. The site recently opened its new wellness centre with indoor spa pool, jacuzzi, sauna and gym (extra charge).

### Facilities

Five modern toilet blocks with British and Turkish style toilets, open style washbasins (cold water only) and pre-set showers (on payment). Facilities for disabled visitors. Laundry room with sinks. Fridge box hire. Dishwashing (inside). Supermarket. Beach shop. Newspaper kiosk. Bar/restaurant with terrace. Swimming pool (40 x 15 m.) with large slide. Playground on gravel. Playing field. Tennis. Minigolf. Fishing. Basketball. Table tennis. Jetty for mooring boats. Boat launching. Canoe hire. Disco and bowling club. Off site: Historic towns of Koper, Izola, Piran and Portoroz are close.

**Open:** 1 May - 30 September.

### Directions

From Koper drive north to Ankaran. The campsite is immediately on the left after entering Ankaran. GPS: N45:34.678 E13:44.180

### Charges 2007

| | |
|---|---|
| Per person | € 4,10 - € 8,40 |
| child (2-8 yrs) | € 3,40 - € 6,60 |
| pitch | € 8,95 - € 14,40 |
| electricity | € 2,85 |
| dog | € 2,60 |

Camping Cheques accepted.

## Slovenia

### SV4330 Camping Pivka Jama
Veliki Otok 50, SLO-6230 Postojna
Tel: 057 203 993. Email: autokamp.pivka.jama@siol.net

Postojna is renowned for its extraordinary limestone caves which form one of Slovenia's prime tourist attractions. Among campers it is also renowned for the campsite situated in the forest only four kilometres from the caves. Pivka Jama is a most convenient site for the visitor, being midway between Ljubljana and Piran and only about an hour's pleasant drive from either. This good site is deep in what appears to be primeval forest, cleverly cleared to take advantage of the broken limestone forest bedrock. The 300 pitches are not clustered together but nicely segregated under trees and in small clearings, all connected by a neat network of paths and slip roads. Some level, gravel hardstandings are provided. The facilities are both excellent and extensive and run with obvious pride by enthusiastic staff. It even has its own local caves (the Pivka Jama) which can spare its visitors the commercialisation of Postojna.

#### Facilities
Two toilet blocks with very good facilities. Washing machines. Motorcaravan service point. Chemical disposal point. Campers' kitchen with hobs. Supermarket. Bar/restaurant. Swimming pool and paddling pool. Volleyball. Basketball. Tennis. Table tennis. Bicycle hire. Daytrips to Postojna Caves and other excursions organised. Off site: Fishing 5 km. Riding or skiing 10 km. Golf 30 km.

**Open:** March - October.

#### Directions
Site is 5 km. from Postojna. Take the road leading east from Postojna and then north west towards the Postojna Cave. Site is well signed 4 km. further along this road. GPS: N45:48.320 E14:12.274

#### Charges 2007
| | |
|---|---|
| Per person | € 9,50 - € 10,30 |
| child (7-14 yrs) | € 7,50 - € 8,10 |
| electricity | € 3,70 |

---

### SV4340 Camping Ljubljana Resort
Dunajska Cesta 270, SLO-1000 Ljubljana
Tel: 015 683 913. Email: ljubljana.resort@gpl.si

Located only five kilometres north of central Ljubljana on the relatively quiet bank of the river Sava, Ljubljana Resort is an ideal city campsite. This relaxed site is attached to – but effectively separated from – the sparklingly modern Laguna pool complex (opens 1/6-15/9). The site has 220 pitches, largely situated between mature trees and all with 16A electricity connections. A modern toilet block is operational in summer while a smaller heated block is opened in winter. The main building and the pool complex provide several bars, restaurants and takeaways to cater for the campsite guests and day visitors. In the far corner of the site an 'adrenaline park' (only under supervision) offers a quick introduction to the Slovenian lifestyle, while a range of more conventional sports (tennis, beach volleyball, indoor badminton and a gym) are here as well.

#### Facilities
The modern toilet block includes facilities for disabled people, a baby room and children's toilet and shower. Chemical disposal. Motorcaravan service point. Laundry service. Internet access. Airport transfer service. Bicycle hire. Off site: Ljubljana centre 5 km.

**Open:** All year.

#### Directions
From either direction on the northern city ring road, take exit for Ljubljana-Jezica north towards Crnuce for a little over 1 km. (through Dunajska cesta). Site is signed (blue sign) on the right just before railway crossing and bridge over the river.

#### Charges 2007
| | |
|---|---|
| Per person | € 7,00 - € 13,00 |
| child (7-12 yrs) | € 5,25 - € 9,75 |
| electricity | € 3,00 |
| dog | € 3,00 |

---

Check real time availability and at-the-gate prices...
www.alanrogers.com

## SV4360 Camp Smlednik

Dragocajna 14a, SLO-1216 Smlednik
Tel: 013 627 002. Email: camp@dm-campsmlednik.si

Camp Smlednik is relatively close to the capital, Ljubljana, yet within striking distance of Lake Bled, the Karawanke mountains and the Julian Alps. It provides a good touring base, set above the river Sava, and also provides a small, separate enclosure for those who enjoy naturism. Situated beside the peaceful tiny village of Dragocajni, in attractive countryside, the site provides 190 places for tourers each with electricity (6/10A). Although terraced, it is probably better described as a large plateau with tall pines and deciduous trees providing some shade. Among the many species of birds, you have every chance of seeing the Golden Oriole. Near reception and the security barrier is a bar that provides limited food at weekends. Complete with dartboard, it radiates an atmosphere typical of a British pub and is used by local villagers in the evenings, accentuating that feeling. From a grass sunbathing area there is stepped access to the river for swimming. Good size fish can be caught by anglers (licence required). The Sava is excellent for canoeing or kayaking. The naturist area measuring only some 30 x 100 m. accommodates 15 units in a delightful setting adjacent to the river (INF card not required).

### Facilities

Three fully equipped sanitary blocks are of varying standards, but it is an adequate and clean provision. In the main camping area a fairly new, solar powered two storey block has free hot showers, the lower half for use within the naturist area. Normally heated showers in the old block are on payment. Dishwashing and laundry sinks. Washing machine. Toilet for disabled visitors (level access). Supermarket at entrance. Bar (all year), limited food at weekends. Two good quality clay tennis courts (charged). Table tennis, basketball and area to kick a ball. Swings for children. River swimming and fishing. Internet access.

**Open:** 1 May - 15 October.

### Directions

Travelling on road no.1, both Smlednik and the site are well signed. From E61 motorway, Smlednik and site are again well signed at the Vodiice exit.
GPS: N46:10.455 E14:24.977

### Charges 2007

| | |
|---|---|
| Per person | € 7,00 |
| child (7-14 yrs) | € 3,50 |
| electricity (6-10A) | € 3,00 |

## SV4400 Camp Dolina Prebold

Vozlic Tomaz Dolenja vas 147, SLO-3312 Prebold
Tel: 041 790 590. Email: camp@dolina.si

Prebold is a quiet village about 15 kilometres west of the large historic town of Celje. It is only a few kilometres from the remarkable Roman necropolis at Sempeter. Dolina is an exceptional little site and more than the garden of the house, taking 50 touring units, 15 with 6A electricity. It belongs to Tomaz and Manja Vozlic who look after the site and its guests with loving care. It has been in existence for 40 years and is one of the first private enterprises in the former Yugoslavia. To the south of Prebold lies some of Slovenia's best walking country and to the north lies the upper Savinja valley. It is an easy drive up the Savinja to its spectacular source in the Logar Valley; beyond its semi-circle of 2,000 m. peaks lies Austria. Excursions are organised to the Pekel Caves and Roman remains.

### Facilities

The small, heated toilet block would certainly qualify for Slovenia's 'best loo' award. Washing machine and dryer. Reception with bar in the old stable. Small swimming pool (heated, 1/5-30/9). Sauna. Bicycle hire. WiFi.
Off site: Good supermarket and restaurant 200 m. Tennis and indoor pool within 1 km. Fishing 1.5 km.

**Open:** All year.

### Directions

Site is well signed in a small side street by turning right in the centre of Prebold. Best reached via a signed exit on the Ljubljana - Celje motorway.
GPS: N46:14.420 E15:05.273

### Charges 2007

| | |
|---|---|
| Per person | € 6,25 |
| electricity | € 3,33 |
| dog | € 2,00 |

No credit cards.

## Slovenia

### SV4402 Camping Park Plevcak-Povse

Latkova vas 227, SLO-3312 Prebold
Tel: 037 001 986. Email: info@campingpark.si

Park Plevcak is only a few years old on a grassy field directly beside the Savinja river and close to the Sempeter/Prebold motorway junction. It provides 50 pitches (all for tourers) and is attractively landscaped with young trees. Pitching is haphazard on one large field, with some shade provided by mature trees and the high hedge surrounding the site. Pitches are not separated, but when it is quiet you can take as much space as you need. There are 18 electricity connections. The site has a restaurant and a bar and tennis courts and a riding centre are just 1 km. It is possible to fish and swim in the Savinja river (an outdoor swimming pool is only 2 km). The site organises excursions to the nearby Pekel Cave in Sempeter, the Roman Nekropolis, the Lasko, Dobrna and Topolsica health resorts, and to the castles in Celje and Velenje. Somewhat further, but close enough for a day trip, are the Logarska Dolina valley, the Savinjske Alps and the Poborje mountains.

#### Facilities

One traditional style toilet block with modern fittings with toilets, open plan washbasins and controllable hot showers. Laundry with sinks and washing machine. Fridge boxes (free). Dishwashing (inside). Bar/restaurant. Basketball. Fishing. Large barbecue area. Torch useful. Off site: Riding 1 km. Golf 20 km.

**Open:** 20 April - 30 October.

#### Directions

Follow E57 northeast from Ljubljana towards Celje and leave at the Sempeter/Prebold exit. Site is 250 m. from the motorway exit first turn right and then left. GPS: N46:15.353 E15:05.950

#### Charges 2007

| | |
|---|---|
| Per person | € 6,30 |
| electricity | € 3,50 |
| dog | € 1,50 |

### SV4405 Camping Menina

Varpolje 105, SLO-3332 Recica ob Savinji
Tel: 035 835 027. Email: info@campingmenina.com

The Menina site is in the heart of the 35 km. long Upper Savinja Valley, surrounded by 2,500 m. high mountains and unspoilt nature. It is being improved every year by the young, enthusiastic owner, Jurij Kolenc and has 200 pitches, all for touring units, on grassy fields under mature trees and with access from gravel roads. All have 6-10A electricity. The Savinja river runs along one side of the site, but if its water is too cold for swimming, the site also has a lake which can be used for swimming as well. This site is a perfect base for walking or mountain biking in the mountains (a wealth of maps and routes is available from reception). Rafting, canyoning and kayaking, or visits to a fitness studio, sauna or massage salon are organised.

#### Facilities

The traditional style toilet block has modern fittings with toilets, open plan basins and controllable hot showers (incl. 8 new) and the site reports that a new second block is ready. Chemical disposal point. Motorcaravan service point. Bar/restaurant with open air terrace (evenings only) and open air kitchen. Sauna. Playing field. Fishing. Mountain bike hire. Giant chess. Russian bowling. Excursions (52). Live music and gatherings around the camp fire. Indian village. Hostel. Off site: Fishing 2 km. Recica and other villages with much culture and folklore are close. Indian sauna at Coze.

**Open:** 1 April - 15 November.

#### Directions

From Ljubljana take A1 towards Celje. Exit at Trnava and turn north towards Mozirje. Follow signs Recica ob Savinj from there. Continue through Recica to Nizka and follow site signs.
GPS: N46:18.701 E14:54.548

#### Charges 2008

| | |
|---|---|
| Per person | € 8,00 |
| child (5-15 yrs) | € 5,00 |
| electricity | € 2,50 |
| dog | € 2,50 |

74

Check real time availability and at-the-gate prices...
www.alanrogers.com

## SV4410 Camping Moravske Toplice

Kranjceva ulica 12, SLO-9226 Moravske Toplice
Tel: 025 121 200. Email: info@terme3000.si

Moravske Toplice is a large site with 450 pitches. There are 250 places for touring units (all with 10A electricity), the remaining pitches being taken by seasonal campers. On a grass and gravel surface (hard tent pegs may be needed), the level, numbered pitches are of 50-80 sq.m. There are hardstandings available in the newer area of the site. While there are a few activities on the site, it is only 200 metres from the enormous thermal spa and fun pool complex under the same name. Here there are over 5,000 sq.m. of water activities – swimming, jet streams, water falls, water massages, four water slides (the longest is 170 m.) and thermal baths. The complex also provides bars and restaurants and a large golf course. Access to the pool complex is free for campsite guests. Once you have had enough of the 22 indoor and outdoor pools, you could go walking or cycling through the surrounding woods and fields or try the delicious wines of the Goricko region.

### Facilities
Modern and clean toilet facilities include British style toilets, open washbasins and controllable, free hot showers. Laundry, dryers, iron and ironing board. Dishwashing. Football field. Tennis. Archery. Handball. Volleyball. Gymnastics. Daily activity programme for children (3 times a day). Off site: Large water complex with shop, bars, restaurants and takeaway. Golf.

**Open:** All year.

### Directions
From Maribor, go east to Murska Sobota. From there go north towards Martjanci and then east towards Moravske Toplice. Access to the site is on the right before the bridge. GPS: N46:46.706 E16:13.294

### Charges 2007
| | |
|---|---|
| Per person | € 13,50 - € 14,50 |
| electricity | € 3,50 |
| dog | € 3,00 |

## SV4415 Camping Terme Catez

Topliska cesta 35, SLO-8250 Catez ob Savi
Tel: 074 936 000. Email: camp@terme-catez.si

Terme Catez is part of the modern Catez thermal spa, renowned for its medical programmes to treat rheumatism and for a wide range of programmes to improve or maintain your health. The campsite has 590 pitches, with 190 places for tourers, the remainder being taken by privately owned mobile homes and cottages. The site is in the centre of a large complex, which includes indoor and outdoor pools with giant slides, holiday bungalows and a shopping centre. One large, open field, with some young trees – a real sun trap – provides level, grass pitches which are numbered by markings on the tarmac access roads. All have 10A electricity connections. This complex caters for most needs with its pools, large shopping centre, gym and the numerous events that are organised, such as the Magic School and Junior Olympic Games for children. It would be a very useful stop over on a journey to Croatia in the low season or for an active family holiday.

### Facilities
Two modern toilet blocks with British and Turkish style toilets, open style washbasins and controllable hot showers. Child size washbasins. Facilities for disabled visitors. Laundry with sinks and washing machines. Motorcaravan service point. Supermarket. Kiosks for fruit, newspapers, souvenirs and tobacco. Restaurants. Bar with terrace. Several large indoor and outdoor pools (free, max. two entries per day per person). Go karts. Pedaloes. Rowing boats. Jogging track. Fishing. Golf. Bicycle hire. Sauna. Solarium. Riding. Magic shows, dance nights and fashion shows organised. Casino. Video games.

**Open:** 25 March - 1 November.

### Directions
From Ljubljana take no. 1 road south east towards Zagreb and follow signs for Terme Catez (close to Brezice). GPS: N45:53.482 E15:37.559

### Charges 2007
| | |
|---|---|
| Per person | € 13,70 - € 14,90 |
| child (4-12 yrs) | € 6,85 - € 7,45 |
| electricity | € 3,40 |
| dog | € 3,00 |

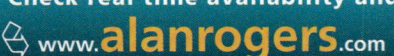

Check real time availability and at-the-gate prices...
www.alanrogers.com

## Slovenia

### SV4440 Camping Terme Ptuj
Pot v toplice 9, SLO-2251 Ptuj
Tel: 027 494 100. Email: info@terme-ptuj.si

Camping Terme Ptuj is close to the river, just outside the interesting town of Ptuj. It is a small site with only 100 level pitches, all for tourers and all with 10A electricity. In two areas, the pitches to the left are on part grass and part gravel hardstanding and are mainly used for motorcaravans. The pitches on the right hand side are on grass under mature trees, off a circular, gravel access road. In this area a promising new toilet block was being built when we visited. The main attraction of this site is clearly the adjacent thermal spa and fun pool complex that also attracts many local visitors. It has several slides and fun pools, as well as a sauna, solarium and spa bath. The swimming pools are free for campsite guests. This site would also be a useful stopover en-route to Croatia and the beautiful historic towns of Ptuj and Maribor are well worth a visit.

#### Facilities
Modern toilet block with British and Turkish style toilets, open washbasins and controllable, hot showers (free). En-suite facilities for disabled with toilet and basin. Two washing machines. Dishwashing. Football field. Torch useful. Off site: Large thermal spa 100 m. Bar/restaurant and snack bar 100 m.

**Open:** All year.

#### Directions
From Maribor go southeast towards Ptuj and follow the site signs. Site is on the left before you cross the river and not very well signed.
GPS: N46:25.361 E15:51.297

#### Charges 2007
| | |
|---|---|
| Per person | € 12,50 - € 15,50 |
| child (7-14 yrs) | € 8,75 - € 10,85 |
| child (4-7 yrs) | € 6,25 - € 7,75 |
| electricity | € 3,50 |
| dog | € 3,00 |

No credit cards.
Camping Cheques accepted.

---

**TERME PTUJ**
SAVA HOTELS & RESORTS

Pot v toplice 9, 2251 PTUJ
Tel.: +386 (0)2 74 94 100
Fax: +386 (0)2 74 94 520
Email: info@terme-ptuj.si
www.terme-ptuj.si

---

## Need a low cost ferry?

**It couldn't be simpler** - just click, choose a ferry and book...

- Special deals for caravans and motorhomes
- View routes and compare prices
- Fully searchable by route and operator

**ferries 4 campers.co.uk**

norfolkline DOVER - DUNKERQUE FERRIES | P&O Ferries | EURO TUNNEL | SEAFRANCE DOVER-CALAIS FERRIES | Brittany Ferries | Condor ferries

Check real time availability and at-the-gate prices...
www.alanrogers.com

# mycamping.info

## myexperience, myvoice

The Alan Rogers Guides have long been the authoritative voice when it comes to an independent assessment of a campsite's quality. But now is the chance to hear your voice – your opinions, your assessments, your tips...

A beta version of the website is now up and running – and it needs YOUR input before it goes fully live!

- Personal **reviews**
- Real **holiday makers**
- Inside **knowledge**
- Honest **advice**

It's all about **YOU** and **YOUR** experiences...

So get involved today!
Visit www.mycamping.info

# Romania

MAP 4

Forests cover over one quarter of the country and the fauna is one of the richest in Europe including bears, deer, lynx, chamois and wolves. Whilst driving through Transylvania it is easy to get caught up in the Dracula tale.

Romania's territory features splendid mountains, beautiful rolling hills, fertile plains and numerous rivers and lakes. The Carpathian Mountains traverse the centre of the country bordered on both sides by foothills and finally the great plains of the outer rim. The legendary Danube River ends its journey through eight European countries at the Black Sea by forming one of the most interesting wetlands in the world, the Danube Delta.

Romania's history has not been as peaceful as its geography. Over the centuries, various migrating people invaded Romania. The provinces of Wallachia and Moldova offered furious resistance to the invading Ottoman Turks, while Transylvania was successively under Hapsburg, Ottoman or Wallachian rule. Romania's post WWII history as a communist-block nation is more widely known, primarily due to the excesses of the dictator Nicolae Ceausescu. In 1989 a national uprising led to his overthrow. The 1991 Constitution established Romania as a republic with a multiparty system, market economy and rights of free speech and private ownership.

**Population**
22.5 million (2005 est.)

**Capital**
Bucharest (Bucuresti)

**Climate**
Temperate, four distinct seasons: pleasant temperatures during spring and autumn, hot summers, cold winters

**Language**
Romanian; German and Hungarian are spoken in some provinces

**Currency**
The Leu (pl. Lei), with its fractional coin, the ban. ATMs are available at large banks, airports and shopping centres in cities. American Express, MasterCard and Visa are accepted in the main cities. It is advised to travel with some Euros in cash in case of difficulty using credit cards or Travellers' cheques.

**Telephone**
The country code for Romania is 00 40. The country is well covered with two GSM 900 mobile phone networks. Email and Internet are freely available in the cities and larger towns.

# Romania

ROMANIA IS IN THE SOUTHEASTERN PART OF CENTRAL EUROPE AND SHARES BORDERS WITH HUNGARY, SERBIA AND MONTENEGRO, BULGARIA, THE BLACK SEA, MOLDAVIA AND UKRAINE. ABOUT A THIRD OF THE COUNTRY CONSISTS OF THE CARPATHIAN MOUNTAINS. ANOTHER THIRD IS HILLS AND PLATEAUX, RICH WITH ORCHARDS AND VINEYARDS. THE FINAL THIRD IS A FERTILE PLAIN, LARGELY DEVOTED TO AGRICULTURE.

### Passport & Visa Requirements

UK passport holders require a valid passport. No visa is needed for stays of up to 90 days.

### Public Holidays

New Year 1, 2 Jan; Monday following Orthodox Easter; Labour Day 1 May; National Day 1 Dec; Christmas 25-26 Dec.

### Motoring

Driving in the mountains can be a challenge in poor weather conditions. Make sure to have plenty of fuel as filling stations can be few and far between outside the major cities. Traffic travels on the right and trams are the only vehicles that can be passed on the right. Vehicles entering on the right of a roundabout are given priority. Police can levy fines on the spot. Parking is allowed only on the right side of the street and cars must be parked in the direction of traffic.

### Tourist Office

Romanian Tourist Office
22 New Cavendish Street
London W1M 7LH.
Tel: (020) 7224 3692
Fax: (020) 7935 6435
E-mail: infouk@romaniatourism.com
Internet: www.romaniatourism.com

### British Embassy

24 Jules Michelet, 010463 Bucharest
Tel: (40) (21) 201 7200

### Places of interest

*Baile Herculane (Herculane Spa):* this is one of the country's oldest spas - first used for its curative effects 1,850 years ago. The resort is located in the forested Cerna river valley.

*Danube delta:* the delta of the Danube is a region of lakes, desolate marshes and swamps, broken by tree-covered elevations. It is a refuge for many rare species of bird, fish, animal and plant.

*Bucharest*: in 2005 the entire historic centre of the city was declared a car-free zone. There are markets selling shabby clothing, textiles, antiques, bric-a-brac, and an increasing amount of cafes, restaurants and bars.

### Cuisine of the region

*Sarmale:* meat rolls in sauerkraut leaves, a famous dish served in Romanian restaurants around the world.

*Zacusca*: pickles made from aubergines, bell peppers, onions and tomato juice.

*Saramura:* carp broiled on the stove or in a spit, is served with polenta and garlic sauce.

*Baclava and sarailie*: cakes with walnuts and syrup.

*Ciorba de potroace:* chicken soup with carrot, onion, parsley, and a spoonful or two of rice.

*Oltenian sausages:* made from beef and pork chopped finely and mixed with garlic, pepper and salt.

## Romania

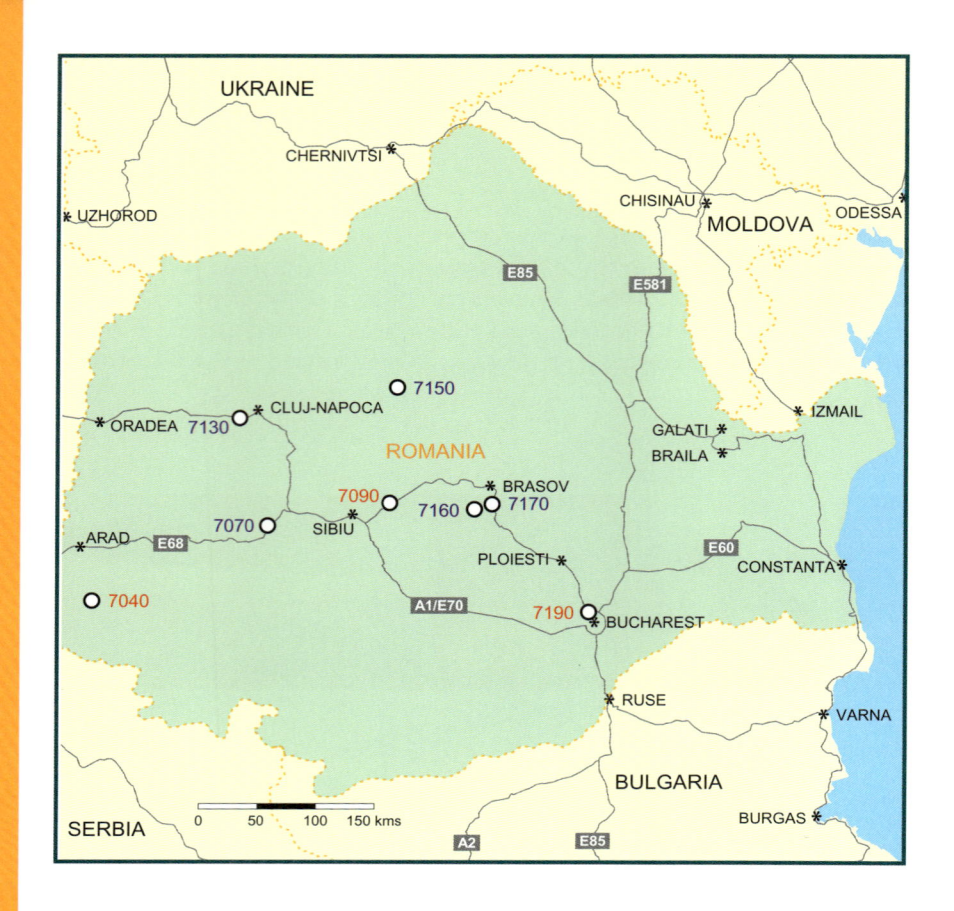

### RO7070 Camping Aurel Vlaicu

Strada Principale 155, RO-335401 Aurel Vlaicu (Jud. Hunedoara)

Tel: 025 424 5541. Email: aurelvlaicu@email.ro

The town of Aurel Vlaicu is named after the famous Romanian aviator of the same name who was born here in 1882. A small museum near the campsite details his life and most towns in Romania have a street and a school named after him. He is also depicted on the new 50 Lei note. The village is typically Romanian – one made up street, a stork's nest, geese and ducks walking around in family groups and the locals sitting outside watching the world pass by. This Dutch owned campsite is small but has good views across open farmland to the mountains beyond. The front entrance has restricted access but an alternative is available to deal with larger units. There are 30 level and marked pitches, all with 10A electricity.

#### Facilities

The modern sanitary block has clean toilets, hot showers and washbasins. Washing machine. Chemical toilet disposal point. Dishwashing facilities. Restaurant. Off site: Aurel Vlaicu Museum (300 m). Corvinestilor Castle and much more within an easy drive.

**Open:** 15 April - 30 September.

#### Directions

Aurel Vlaicu is north of the 1/E68 between Sebes and Deva and east of Orastie. Drive slowly through the village to the site, which is signed.
GPS: N45:54.896 E23:16.765

#### Charges 2008

| | |
|---|---|
| Per person | € 4,00 |
| child (3-12 yrs) | € 2,00 |
| pitch | € 2,00 - € 3,50 |

Prices in Euros. No credit cards.

## RO7040 Complex Turistic International

Aleea Padurea Verde 6, RO-300310 Timisoara

Tel: 025 620 8925. Email: campinginternational@yahoo.com

This large tourist complex provides 124 touring pitches (67 with 6A electricity) in a heavily wooded site next to a busy and noisy main road (24 hours). There are 17 places for motorcaravans or caravans with hardstanding, water and drainage, but the access road is narrow and there are low stone walls which impede access. The very tall trees mean you have no views whatsoever. However, Timisoara is close at hand and as Romania's fourth largest city, known by the locals as Primul Oras Liber (First Free Town), it is somewhere you may wish to visit. It was here that the first anti-Ceausecu protests took place that prompted his downfall from power. There is much to see in the old town and every October the town hosts the national beer festival.

### Facilities

The reasonable sanitary block provides sufficient clean toilets, hot showers and washbasins. Chemical toilet disposal point. Restaurant with terrace. Café. Play area. Wooden cabins to rent. Barbecues are not permitted. Dogs are not accepted. Off site: Forest walks. The city of Timisoara.

**Open:** All year.

### Directions

Site is on the north side of the 6/E70 just east of Timisoara. GPS: N45:46.144 E21:15.975

### Charges 2007

| | |
|---|---|
| Per person | RON 10,00 |
| pitch | RON 10,00 |
| tent (per person) | RON 10,00 |
| car | RON 20,00 |

Camping Cheques accepted.

## RO7090 Camping de Oude Wilg

Strada Prundului 311, RO-557070 Carta

Tel: 072 318 6343. Email: de-oude-wilg@yahoo.com

The pretty and typically Romanian village of Carta (or Cirta as it is spelt on some old Russian-era road signs) is almost in the centre of Romania, north of the Fagaras mountains (highest peak Moldoveanu 2544 m.) in a broad valley. Manette Twilt, who gives you a warm welcome at any time, runs this small, campsite owned by a Romanian-Dutch couple. To reach the site you have to cross a small, flat, concrete bridge so those with very large units and those over 3.5 tonnes will find it difficult. However, for a chance to see Romanian rural life at its best you should plan to visit this delightful village and campsite. The site has 30 level pitches, 12 with 6A electricity connections. The town of Sibiu is about 30 minutes away and is worthy of a visit.

### Facilities

Modern sanitary block with clean toilets, hot showers and washbasins. Washing machine and dryer. Chemical toilet disposal point. Small restaurant.

**Open:** All year.

### Directions

Carta (Cirta) is 3 km. north of the 1/E68 road between Sibiu and Fagaras and 1 km. east of the junction with the 7C. As you go through the village turn left on an unmade road towards this small site. GPS: N45:47.032 E24:33.990

### Charges 2007

| | |
|---|---|
| Per person | € 3,15 |
| child (over 4 yrs) | € 2,00 |
| pitch incl. car | € 3,40 - € 4,50 |
| electricity | € 2,50 |

**Check real time availability and at-the-gate prices...**
www.alanrogers.com

## Romania

### RO7130 Camping Eldorado
RO-407310 Gilau
Tel: 026 437 1688. Email: info@campingeldorado.com

If you cross the border into Romania near Oradea this could well be the first campsite you will encounter. You will not be disappointed! Dutch owned but locally managed, it offers excellent facilities and good pitches, although its proximity to the route 1 road does mean there is some background traffic noise. There are 144 level pitches, unmarked but with some shade and all with 8A electricity connection possible. At the edge of the Transylvanian basin, you will have passed the small mountainous area and can now enjoy the rolling countryside with its extensive views. The site offers an excellent base from which to explore the area. The nearby city of Cluj-Napoca has little to offer but it will always be remembered as the home of one of Eastern Europe's most successful pyramid schemes in the early 1990s and its consequences are still felt today. Doomed to collapse, it ended in 1994 and has ingrained the have/have not system in the area and throughout Romania.

#### Facilities
The modern sanitary block provides ample and clean facilities including toilets, hot showers and washbasins. Dishwashing facilities. Laundry. Chemical toilet disposal point. Small shop with essentials. Restaurant. Play area. Small wooden cabins to rent. Free WiFi internet. Off site: Guided walks in July and August. Fishing, hunting and riding.

**Open:** 15 April - 15 October.

#### Directions
The site is easily found on route 1/E60, the road from Oradea to Cluj-Napoca, just after the village of Capusu Mare and about 1 km. before the village of Gilau. GPS: N46:46.022 E23:21.170

#### Charges 2008
| | |
|---|---|
| Per person | € 3,50 |
| child (4-16 yrs) | € 2,00 |
| pitch incl. car | € 4,00 |
| electricity | € 2,50 |

Prices in Euros.

---

### RO7150 Camping Vasskert
Strada Principala 129, RO-3295 Sovata
Tel: 026 557 0902. Email: vasskert@szovata.hu

Sovata has been a popular resort from the early 19th century. Five lovely lakes surround the town all with reputed curative powers. The most popular is the salt water Lacu Usru for its supposed ability to cure infertility. It is impossible to sink in this lake with 150 grams of salt per litre. A 40 cm. thick layer of fresh water covers the lake and maintains warm temperatures year round. This quiet small family run campsite is just 2 km. from Lacu Ursu and is within walking distance of the small town centre where there are shops, cash exchange facilities and restaurants. There are 20 level un-numbered pitches with some shade and all with 6A electricity. In northern Transylvania you are surrounded by beautiful countryside and lots of places to visit, from the salt mine at Praid to the renowned potteries selling their green, brown and cobalt blue wares, on the road south towards Odorheiu Secuiesc.

#### Facilities
Ample and clean, the modern sanitary block provides toilets, hot showers and washbasins. Dishwashing facilities. Small wooden cabins to rent.

**Open:** 1 May - 30 September.

#### Directions
From Targu Mures take the 13/E60 road south. After 24 km. turn left on the 13a towards Sovata. At the village take the left fork, signed Sovata Bai and go towards the village centre. The site is 2 km. from the fork on the right. GPS: N46:35.442 E25:04.388

#### Charges 2007
| | |
|---|---|
| Per person | € 3,50 |
| child (4-24 yrs) | € 1,50 |
| pitch | € 1,50 - € 2,50 |
| dog | € 1,00 |

Prices in Euros.

## RO7160 Vampire Camping

Sohodol Street 77c, RO-2229 Bran

Tel: **062 508 3909**. Email: **info@vampirecamping.com**

Bran Castle, most commonly known as Dracula's Castle, was not built by Vlad Tepes (father of Vlad the Impaler) upon whom the novelist Bram Stoker is (incorrectly) supposed to have based his vampire, Count Dracula. The castle, perched atop a 60 metre peak in the village centre, was built by Saxons from Brasov in 1382 to defend the Bran Pass from Turks. Whatever its history, the castle makes an interesting visit since it was occupied for many years by the Romanian Royal Family as a summer residence. Inevitably the entrance is surrounded by souvenir stalls but there are some good restaurants locally as well. Ideally located, Vampire Camping is a very good, Dutch owned, but locally managed, site opened in 2004. There are 40 pitches, all with 6A electricity, plus a separate area for tents. Tony speaks very good English and is very conscientious and helpful.

### Facilities

The modern toilet block is very well maintained and provides hot showers, WCs and washbasins. Washing machine. Sinks for dishwashing and food preparation. Ice cream, wine, beer and soft drinks available at reception. Off site: Bran Castle and village only 800 m.

**Open:** 1 April - 31 October.

### Directions

Bran is 30 km. south of Brasov on the 73/E574. Entering the village from Brasov site is signed and is just after supermarket and a petrol station, on the right. GPS: N45:31.715 E25:22.221

### Charges 2007

| | |
|---|---|
| Per person | RON 15,00 |
| pitch | RON 11.00 - 22,00 |
| electricity (6A) | RON 12,00 |

Camping Cheques accepted.

## RO7170 Camping Dârste

Strada Calea bucuresti 285, RO-2200 Brasov

Tel: **026 833 9967**. Email: **camp.dirste@dettanet.ro**

Brasov, Romania's second most visited city, lies north of the Prahova valley and was first colonised by the Saxons in the 12th century. Nowadays, the pedestrianised Str Republicii provides respite from the traffic that detracts from the rest of the old town. There is plenty to see and do in the surrounding countryside. Saxon fortresses can be found at Prejmer, Harman and Rasnov and of course Bran, and you can easily visit the mountain resort of Poiana Brasov. Camping Dârste is probably the best equipped site you will find in Romania (at the present time) and is good for short or long stays. There are 84 level, numbered and marked pitches and all have 6A electricity, drainage and a water supply.

### Facilities

Two modern, clean toilet blocks provide ample toilets, hot showers and washbasins. A third block has Turkish style toilets and more hot showers. Washing machine. Chemical toilet disposal point. Kitchen and dishwashing facilities. Bar and restaurant. Off site: Brasov 8 km.

**Open:** 20 April - 30 October.

### Directions

From Brasov take the N1/E60 towards Ploiesti. About 8 km. out of Brasov, just past the junction with the 1A road and on a right hand bend, the site is on the left adjacent to a BMW agent. Look for Motel signs.

### Charges 2007

| | |
|---|---|
| Per unit incl. 2 persons and electricity | RON 48,00 |
| tent (per person) | RON 10,00 |

## RO7190 Camping Casa Alba

Aleea Privighetorilor 1-3, Baneasa-Bucuresti

Tel: **012 305 203**. Email: **info@casaalba.ro**

If you want to visit the Romanian capital then this site near Bucharest airport is the only one available and that is a shame. Attached to the Casa Alba restaurant, it is primarily an enclosure in a wood for 50 cabins to rent. If you want to camp with a caravan or motorcaravan then you have to park on a gravel area in the centre around three large willow trees. Electricity is available. When we were there after continuous rain deep puddles covered the whole area. The cabins seem to be occupied by groups of young people and the noise from music and shouting went on till after 1am. Bucharest is not far away by bus, but we didn't think we would leave our motorcaravan here unattended.

### Facilities

A refurbished toilet block includes showers, WCs and washbasins. Sinks for dishwashing (not very clean). Electric hobs for cooking. Manhole available for emptying chemical toilet. Restaurant. Off site: Bucharest 8 km.

**Open:** All year.

### Directions

From N1 Ploiesti - Bucuresti road turn east at traffic lights just north of airport. Go past police academy and turn left where tree canopy gets very dense. The site is 50 m. GPS: N44:31.040 E26:05.564

### Charges 2007

| | |
|---|---|
| Per unit incl. 2 persons | RON 17,00 - 40,00 |

# Hungary

MAP 5

Try sampling the local wine - Hungary has plenty to offer including the celebrated Bull's Blood.

An increasingly popular destination, Budapest is divided into two parts by the Danube, the hilly side of Buda on the western bank and the flat plain of Pest on the eastern bank. A cruise along the river will enable you to appreciate this picturesque city with its grand buildings, romantic bridges, museums and art galleries. It also has plenty of spas to tempt you. North of the city, the Danube Bend is one of the grandest stretches of the river, along the banks of which you'll find historic towns and ruins. Further afield in the north-eastern hills, the caves at Aggtelek are another firm favourite.

One of the largest in Europe, Lake Balaton covers an area of nearly 600 square miles and is great for swimming, sailing, windsurfing and waterskiing. It has two distinct shores; the bustling south with its string of hotels, restaurants and beaches, and the north offering a quieter pace with beautiful scenery and sights.

**Population**
10.2 million

**Capital**
Budapest

**Climate**
There are four fairly distinct seasons – hot in summer, mild spring and autumn, very cold winter with snow.

**Language**
The official language is Magyar, but German and English are widely spoken.

**Currency**
Hungarian forints

**Telephone**
The country code is 00 36

**Banks**
Mon-Fri 09.00-14.00, Sat 09.00-12.00

**Shops**
Mon-Fri 10.00-18.00, Sat 10.00-14.00. Food shops open Mon-Fri 07.00-19.00, Sat 07.00-14.00.

# Hungary

CENTRALLY LOCATED IN EUROPE, HUNGARY COMPRISES MOUTAIN RANGES, HILLY REGIONS AND FLAT PLAINS, WITH THE RIVER DANUBE RUNNING THROUGH ITS LENGTH. THE COUNTRY ALSO HAS OVER ONE THOUSAND LAKES, AN ABUNDANCE OF THERMAL BATHS, EUROPE'S LARGEST CAVE SYSTEM AND SEVERAL NOTABLE WINE REGIONS.

### Public Holidays
New Year; Revolution Day 15 March; Easter Mon; Labour Day; Whitsun; Constitution Day 20 Aug; Republic Day 23 Oct; All Saints Day 1 Nov; Christmas 25, 26 Dec.

### Motoring
Main roads are very good, as is signposting. Dipped headlights are compulsory at all times but main beams should not be used in towns. Most of the roads are single carriage. Motorway vignettes must be purchased (from petrol stations and post offices for the M1, M3 and M7 motoways. A separate toll is charged on the full length of the M5 (Budapest - Kiskunfelegyhaza). Give way to trams and buses at junctions and if pulling away from the kerb. Cross railways at walking pace. Carrying spare fuel in a can is not permitted. It is illegal to drive having consumed any alcohol.

### Tourist Office
Hungarian National Tourist Office
46 Eaton Place, London SW1X 8AL
Tel: 020 7823 1032
Fax: 020 7823 1459
Internet: www.hungarytourism.hu
www.gotohungary.co.uk

### British Embassy
Harmincad Utca 6
Budapest 1051
Tel: (36) (1) 266 2888

### Places of interest
*Budapest:* Hungary's capital with a reputation as the 'Paris of Eastern Europe', cruise along the Danube, antiques and jewellery shops.

*Eger:* the town centre has 175 protected buildings and monuments and is closed to traffic, castle, cathedral, a minaret with 100 narrow spiral stairs.

*Lake Balaton:* an oblong lake which is one of the largest in Europe.

*Pécs:* renowned for its music, opera and ballet and includes some of Hungary's best leatherwork.

### Cuisine of the region
*Gulyás:* thick beef stew

*Halászlé:* spicy fish soup cooked with paprika

*Hideg gyumolcsleves:* cold fruit soup made from sour cherries

*Jokai bableves:* bean soup

*Palacsinta:* stuffed crepes

*Pörkölt:* stew or 'goulash'

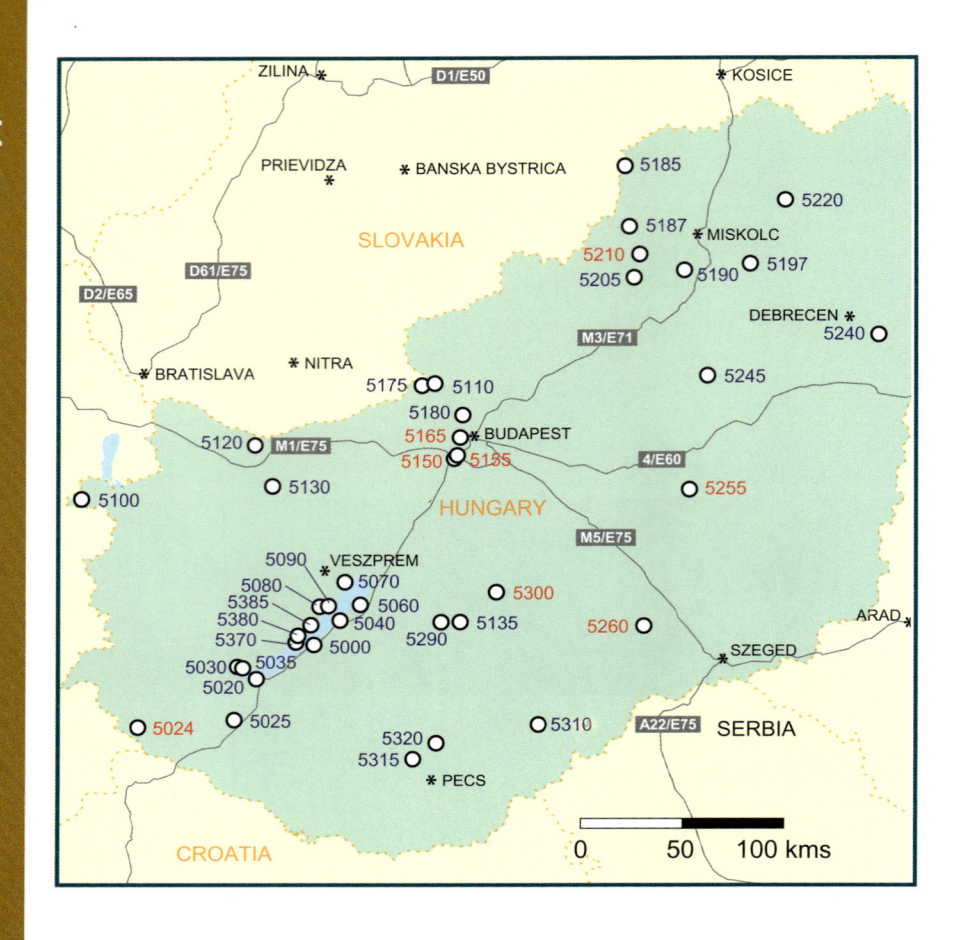

## HU5035 Castrum Camping Keszthely

Mora Ferenc utca 48, H-8360 Keszthely (Zala County)
Tel: 833 121 20. Email: info@castrum-group.hu

Castrum Keszthely is a large site on the southwest corner of Lake Balaton. Although it is next to the main road and a railway and there is a disco nearby, we found it surprisingly quiet at night. It is a real family site with 352 pitches, all for tourers and with electricity (6/12A). It is on the wrong side of the railway that runs along the north side of Lake Balaton and therefore has no direct access to the lake or the beach. However, this is compensated for by a large, well kept outdoor pool with paddling pool and sunbathing area in the centre of the site. The site is also within walking distance of the centre of the bustling lakeside resort of Keszthely. The level pitches of up to 90 sq.m, are numbered on a grass and gravel surface (firm tent pegs necessary) and are separated by hedges with shade from a variety of mature trees. To the front of the site is a small kiosk for bread, some basics and fruit and there is a welcoming restaurant in wine cellar style.

### Facilities
Traditional toilet blocks with British style toilets, open washbasins and pre-set, hot showers (free, hot water variable). Washing machine and spin dryer. Dishwashing. Small shop for basics. Bar/restaurant. Swimming pool (25 x 10 m) with oval paddling pool; daily charge. Tennis. Minigolf. Beach volleyball. Daily activity programme for children in high season. Bus service to Thermal Spa. Bicycle hire. Off site: Fishing and Lake Balaton 1 km.

**Open:** 1 April - 31 October.

### Directions
Follow no. 71 road along Lake Balaton into Keszthely and then follow signs 'Castrum 2900 metres'. Continue straight on for exactly 2,900 metres and turn right towards site. GPS: N46:46.087 E17:15.573

### Charges guide

| | |
|---|---|
| Per person | € 3,00 - € 4,00 |
| child (2-10 yrs) | € 2,43 |
| pitch | € 2,80 - € 10,00 |
| electricity | € 3,00 |

No credit cards. Prices in Euros.

## HU5000 Vadvirág Camping & Bungalows

Arany j.u., H-8636 Balatonszemes (Somogy County)
Tel: 843 601 15. Email: vadvirag@balatontourist.hu

This large Balatontourist site (7 hectares) on the southern shore of Lake Balaton has a beach almost 600 metres long, which is also used by day visitors. On flat grass, just over half the 600 touring pitches are individual ones with electricity connections (16A) for 600. There are 110 pitches for tents. Some shade is provided by a variety of trees. Windsurfing and excellent swimming are possible in the lake and there are pedaloes for hire. A train line runs along the back of the site.

### Facilities

Two standard sanitary blocks include some washbasins in cabins, a few private bathrooms for hire and facilities for disabled visitors. Launderette. Motorcaravan services. Shop. Snack bars. Lake swimming with water slide. Three tennis courts. Table tennis. Minigolf. Bicycle hire. Massage and pedicures. Children's entertainment organised.
Off site: Restaurants and gift shop nearby. Riding 2 km.

**Open:** 3 June - 4 September.

### Directions

Balatonszemes is about halfway round the southern side of Lake Balaton and the site is accessed from road 7/E71 turning towards the lake at 132 km. over the railway.
GPS: N46:47.850 E17:43.715

### Charges 2007

| | |
|---|---|
| Per person | HUF 670,00 - 970,00 |
| child (2-14 yrs) | HUF 510,00 - 770,00 |
| pitch incl. electricity | HUF 2960,00 - 5820,00 |
| dog | free - HUF 770,00 |

No credit cards.

## HU5020 Naturista Camping Balatonbereny

Hétvezér ut 2, H-8649 Balatoberény (Somogy County)
Tel: 853 777 15. Email: naturista@matavnet.hu

A holiday anywhere on the shore of Lake Balaton almost equates to being beside the sea. With a length of 77 km. and a surface area of 600 sq.km. it is the largest fresh water lake in western and central Europe. The quieter, less commercial southern end of Balaton provides the location for this very acceptable 6 ha. naturist site with direct access to the lake. The 117 numbered flat grass pitches each with electricity (16A), are of a good size, many divided by neatly boxed privet hedges. Well spaced mature trees provide a degree of shade. An INF naturist card is not a requirement but gives a 10% reduction. A unique circular pier, that doubles as a sunbathing area, permits access to the shallow waters. One has to walk almost 200 m. into the lake for a suitable swimming depth. Canoes, dinghies and windsurfing are all very popular. This is a quiet site with no entertainment programme but possibly two or three social evenings during the season. Within an acceptable driving distance one can visit Festetics mansion at Keszthely and the internationally famous hot water lake at Heviz. Kanyavar island at Kis-Balaton provides an excellent location for bird watching. Only limited English is spoken.

### Facilities

Two central sanitary blocks are not modern but are adequate and clean, with British style toilets and open washbasins. Water temperature to the showers can be variable. Cold showers by the lake. Dishwashing and laundry sinks with hot water. Washing machine and spin dryers. Four gas hobs. Small shop for basics. Restaurants. Takeaway. Massage. Pre-arranged tours may be booked. Play area. Kayak and pedalo hire. Off site: Two small supermarkets at Balatonbereny (400 m). Restaurant near entrance.

**Open:** 15 May - 15 September.

### Directions

Travelling southeast from Zalaegerszeg on road 76 take left turn signed Balatonbereny. Site is signed in 3.5 km. marked FKK. Turn left to site on right in 150 m. GPS: N46:42.798 E17:18.633

### Charges guide

| | |
|---|---|
| Per person | HUF 820,00 - 950,00 |
| child (2-14 yrs) | HUF 600,00 - 700,00 |
| pitch | HUF 1900,00 - 2400,00 |
| electricity | HUF 550,00 |

Less 10% with INF naturist card.

## Hungary

### HU5040 Balatontourist Camping Autós

Szent István út, H-8621 Zamardi (Somogy County)
Tel: **843 488 63**. Email: **bookings@balatontourists.hu**

If you have young children or non-swimmers in your party, then the southern shores of the lake where this Balatontourist site is situated are ideal as you can walk out for nearly a kilometre before the water rises to more than a metre in depth. It is a large site with its own direct access to the lake offering 480 pitches, 450 with 16A electricity, but there might be the possibility of noise in high season, although it was peaceful during our visit in early June. There are many tall trees and the more attractive pitches are near the lakeside, including some unshaded ones alongside the water. The rest, in a large central area which comprises the majority of the site, are flat, individual ones on grass and these are hedged and vary from small to quite large. A separate tent area is at the back of the site.

#### Facilities

Three modern, tiled sanitary buildings. Three en-suite private bathrooms to rent. Warm water to washbasins with single tap. Showers with changing area. Facilities for disabled visitors. Laundry facilities. Restaurant. Snack bar with terrace (from June). Lake swimming. Fishing. Wooden play equipment by the lake. Off site: Adjacent large water slide area and boats for hire. Shop 50 m.

**Open:** 13 May - 4 September.

#### Directions

Exit road no. 7/E71 between Balatonföldvár and Siófok towards Tihany, and the site is well signed.

#### Charges 2007

| | |
|---|---|
| Per person | HUF 670,00 - 920,00 |
| child (2-14 yrs) | HUF 510,00 - 720,00 |
| caravan | HUF 1000,00 - 1600,00 |
| tent | HUF 600,00 - 900,00 |

Electricity and car incl.

### HU5060 Camping & Bungalows Aranypart

Szent László u.183-185, H-8600 Siófok (Somogy County)
Tel: **843 525 19**. Email: **aranypart@siotour.hu**

Situated right by the famous lake, and near the main tourist town, this very well run site has 682 flat, grassy numbered pitches – 242 for caravans and 437 for tents, just over half being fairly small individual ones. There are 440 electrical connections (10/16A). At the far end of the site is a fenced area where there are 70 excellent bungalows for rent. Groups of younger guests are placed separately from other campers (mainly on the left wing of the site from the entrance. A superb restaurant offers a good menu and there are many sports and entertainment facilities making it very popular with the younger generation. The site is fenced from the lake with good security.

#### Facilities

Five toilet blocks of marginal quality and one good block are spread throughout this long site. Dishwashing and laundry facilities at either end with free hot water. Five washing machines. Fourteen two-burner cookers in the middle of the site. Supermarket and shops. Snack bars and bars. Pizzeria and restaurant. Two play areas and one animator. Moped, bicycle, quad-bikes for children, canoe and pedalo hire. Lake swimming. Off site: Riding 500 m.

**Open:** Easter - 15 September.

#### Directions

Site is 3 km. north of Siófok. From road no. 70, exit at km. 108, cross railway and site is 200 m. well signed. GPS: N46:55.664 E18:06.201

#### Charges 2007

| | |
|---|---|
| Per person | HUF 770,00 - 1130,00 |
| child (2-14 yrs) | HUF 620,00 - 920,00 |
| caravan incl. electricity | HUF 1640,00 - 2350,00 |
| tent | HUF 800,00 - 1130,00 |

Camping Cheques accepted.

### HU5024 Castrum Thermal Camping Lenti

Tancsics M. str. 18-20, H-8960 Lenti (Zala County)
Tel: **923 513 68**. Email: **panzkemp@enternet.hu**

Camping Lenti is one of a series of thermal spa campsites in the Hungarian-Slovenian-Austrian border region. Due to the high temperatures below ground, the water used for the baths is very rich in minerals said to help in rheumatic and vascular diseases. After cooling down to a comfortable 38° Celsius, the water is used to fill four outdoor and three indoor bath, with additional services such as saunas and special therapies also available. While the wider area is not really inspiring, the site itself is well cared for. There are 146 numbered and fenced pitches with 6A electricity connections.

#### Facilities

The modern, heated toilet block is well equipped (including soap containers and toilet fresheners). Washing machine. Restaurant and rooms housed in a modern main building. Off site: Thermal baths. Bars, takeaways and restaurants available inside the thermal bath complex. Shop 500 m.

**Open:** All year.

#### Directions

From roundabout in centre of Lenti, go west towards Rédics for a little under 1 km. Site is on the left (big blue sign) just before the railway station.

#### Charges guide

| | |
|---|---|
| Per person | € 3,00 - € 4,00 |
| pitch incl. electricity | € 6,80 - € 12,00 |

Prices in Euros.

Check real time availability and at-the-gate prices...
**www.alanrogers.com**

## HU5070 Balatontourist Camping & Motel Kristof

H-8220 Balatonalmádi (Veszprem County)
Tel: 885 842 01. Email: ckristof@balatontourist.hu

This is a delightfully small site with just 33 marked pitches and many tall trees. Square in shape, the generously sized pitches are on either side of hard roads, on level grass. There is some shade and all pitches have electricity (6A). It is between the main road and railway line and the lake. Although there is no direct access to the lake, a public lakeside area adjoins the site, and site fees include the entry price. This is a neat little site with a kiosk with terrace for breakfast and dinner (steaks, etc) drinks, bread, milk and ice cream. Balatonalmádi is at the northern end of the lake and well placed for excursions around the lake or to Budapest. Kristof is suitable for anyone seeking a small, friendly site without the bustle of the larger camps. There are also 15 rooms for rent. Good English is spoken.

### Facilities
The excellent, fully equipped toilet facility is part of the reception building. Laundry room with washing machine (small charge), kitchen and sitting room with TV. Motorcaravan service point. Café (12/5-19/9). Playground and entertainment daily except Sunday. Tennis. Paddling pool. Off site: Fishing and beach 50 m. Bicycle hire and boat launching 500 m. Supermarket 500 m. Riding 5 km.

**Open:** 12 May - 24 September.

### Directions
Site is on road no. 71 at Balatonalmádi, between the railway line and the lake and is signed.
GPS: N47:01.507 E18:00.613

### Charges 2007
| | |
|---|---|
| Per person | HUF 620,00 - 1020,00 |
| child (2-14 yrs) | HUF 460,00 - 870,00 |
| pitch | HUF 1790,00 - 3620,00 |

## HU5025 Zalatour Thermal Camping

Gyogyfurdo 6, H-8749 Zalakaros (Zala County)
Tel: 933 401 05. Email: thermal@zalatour.hu

Zalatour at Zalakaros has 280 attractively laid out, level pitches, all with 10A electricity and varying in size from 30-100 sq.m. (the larger pitches need to be reserved). There are 250 for touring units on grass and gravel (firm tent pegs may be needed) and around 10 hardstandings for larger units and motorcaravans. Mature trees provide useful shade and access roads are gravel. Zalatour attracts many elderly people who spend their day at the thermal spa 200 metres down the road – the waters are good for rheumatism and other joint problems. This site is good for rest and relaxation in the shade with the added benefit of the healing waters of the spa. Lake Balaton is close.

### Facilities
Modern and comfortable toilet facilities with British style toilets, open washbasins and controllable, hot showers (free). Facilities for disabled visitors. Full-service laundry including ironing. Campers' kitchen. Motorcaravan service point. Shop. Bar/restaurant. Massage, acupuncture and pedicure. Sauna. Hairdresser. Bicycle hire. Off site: Fishing and beach 3 km. Golf 500 m. Riding 2 km.

**Open:** 1 April - 30 September.

### Directions
On E71 travelling northeast from Nagykanizsa, take exit for Zalakaros. Follow good site signs.
GPS: N46:33.136 E17:07.556

### Charges 2007
| | |
|---|---|
| Per person | HUF 1000,00 - 1200,00 |
| child (2-14 yrs) | HUF 500,00 - 600,00 |
| pitch incl. electricity | HUF 1200,00 - 1650,00 |
| tent | HUF 750,00 - 900,00 |

## HU5030 Panoráma Camping

Panoráma Köz 1, H-8372 Cserszegtomaj (Zala County)
Tel: 833 302 15. Email: matuska78@freemail.hu

Campsites around Lake Balaton generally have the disadvantage of being close to the main road and/or the railway, as well as being extremely busy in high season. Panorama is popular too, but is essentially a quiet site inland from the western end of the lake. It also has the benefit of extensive views from the flat, grass terraces. Only the young or very fit are advised to take the higher levels with the best views of all. The original 50 pitches vary in size from fairly small to quite large, all with 10A electricity, with the lower terraces having fairly easy access. The site is a sun-trap and there is not much shade from the trees. It also has a delightful restaurant offering good value meals.

### Facilities
A new sanitary block, with the original block, are heated and satisfactory, with large, curtained showers (communal changing). Washing machine. Ladies' hairdresser. Massage. Small shop. Restaurant with bar. Small swimming pool. Off site: Riding and bicycle hire 3 km. Fishing and boat launching 6 km. Lake Balaton 7 km.

**Open:** 1 April - 31 October.

### Directions
Site is 2 km. north of Héviz. From the 71 road initially follow the signs for Helvi, then take road to Sümeg. Entering Cserzegtomal, site is signed.

### Charges 2007
| | |
|---|---|
| Per person | € 4,00 |
| pitch | € 10,00 - € 12,00 |

No credit cards. Prices in Euros.

**Check real time availability and at-the-gate prices...**
www.alanrogers.com

## HU5080 Balatontourist Diana Camping

H-8241 Aszófô (Veszprem County)
Tel: 874 450 13. Email: dianacamping@freemail.hu

Once a very large site of about 12 hectares, Diana was developed many years ago as a retreat for the 'party faithful'. Now just 8 hectares are used by Mr and Mrs Keller-Toth, who have leased it from the Balatontourist organisation and run it as a quiet, friendly site. There is a great feeling of space and much woodland around in which you may wander. There are 27 hedged pitches of 120 sq.m. (where two 60 sq.m. ones have been joined) on grass. Many have shade from trees including about 65 smaller individual ones. The remainder are amongst the trees which mark them out. There is no exact number of pitches, but about 150 units are taken, all with electrical connections (2 pin, 6 or 10A) on sloping ground. The fair-sized restaurant, open all season, has tables, benches and flowers in troughs outside. Animation is organised in high season with Hungarian musicians and animators, including occasional 'Diana days' with Hungarian folklore and goulash soup.

### Facilities

Toilet facilities have been largely refurbished and are open 06.00-12.00 and 15.00-23.00 hrs. Very smart, new sections now provide large showers with private dressing for men and women and washbasins with hot water. Splendid, new children's washroom (key from reception), with 3 shower/baths, 2 designed for handicapped children. Washing machines, dryers and ironing (key from reception). Motorcaravan service point. Large kitchen with 3 cookers. Well stocked shop (open 08.00-17.00 low season or 22.00 high season). Restaurant (all season). Children's play area, with animation in high season. Volleyball. Tennis. Club room with video nights for adults at weekends. Off site: Many walking opportunities. Lake fishing 3 km. Riding or bicycle 5 km.

**Open:** 7 May - 17 September.

### Directions

From road 71 on the north side of the lake, turn towards Azsófö just west of Balatonfüred, through the village and follow the signs for about 1 km. along access road (bumpy in places).
GPS: N46:56.368 E17:49.542

### Charges 2007

| | |
|---|---|
| Per pitch incl. electricity | HUF 1250,00 - 2000,00 |
| person | HUF 800,00 - 1100,00 |
| child (6-14 yrs) | HUF 600,00 - 800,00 |

Special rates for disabled persons and low season long stays.

## HU5090 Balatontourist Camping Füred

H-8230 Balatonfüred (Veszprem County)
Tel: 873 438 23. Email: cfured@balatontourist.hu

This is a large international holiday village rather than just a campsite, pleasantly decorated with flowers and shrubs, with a very wide range of facilities and sporting activities. All that one could want for a family holiday can be found on this site. Directly on the lake with 800 m. of access for boats and bathing, it has a large, grassy lying out area, a small beach area for children with various watersports organised. There is also a swimming pool on site with lifeguards. Mature trees cover about two-thirds of the site giving shade, with the remaining area being in the open. The 944 individual pitches (60-120 sq.m), all with electricity (4-10A), are on either side of hard access roads on which pitch numbers are painted. Many bungalows are also on the site. Along the main road that runs through the site, are shops and kiosks, with the main bar/restaurant and terrace overlooking the lake. Other bars and restaurants are around the site. A water ski drag lift is most spectacular with its four towers erected in the lake to pull skiers around the circuit. Coach trips and pleasure cruises are organised. The site is part of the Balatontourist organisation and, while public access is allowed for the amenities, security is good. Some tour operators – Danish and German.

### Facilities

Six fully equipped toilet blocks around the site include hot water for dishwashing and laundry. Private cabins for rent. Laundry service. Gas supplies. Numerous bars, restaurants, cafés, food bars and supermarket (all 15/4-15/10). Stalls and kiosks with wide range of goods, souvenirs, photo processing. Hairdresser. Excellent swimming pool with separate children's pool (20/6-25/9). Sauna. Fishing. Water ski lift. Windsurf school. Sailing. Pedaloes. Play area on sand. Bicycle hire. Tennis. Minigolf. Video games. Internet point. Dogs are not accepted. Off site: Riding 5 km. Close by a street of fast food bars, about 10 in all, offering a variety of Hungarian and international dishes with attractive outdoor terraces under trees.

**Open:** 15 April - 15 October.

### Directions

Site is just south of Balatonfüred, on Balatonfüred - Tihany road and is well signed. Gates closed 1-3 pm. except Sat/Sun. GPS: N46:56.735 E17:52.626

### Charges 2007

| | |
|---|---|
| Per person | HUF 720,00 - 1530,00 |
| child (2-14 yrs) | HUF 500,00 - 1130,00 |
| pitch incl. electricity: | |
| 120 sq.m. | HUF 3960,00 - 6500,00 |
| 100 sq.m. | HUF 2860,00 - 5100,00 |
| 70 sq m | HUF 2400,00 - 3880,00 |

Camping Cheques accepted.

## HU5370 Balatontourist Camping Napfeny

H-8253 Révfülöp (Veszprem County)

Tel: 875 630 31. Email: napfeny@balatontourist.hu

Camping Napfény, an exceptionally good site, is designed for families with children of all ages looking for an active holiday, and has a 200 m. frontage on Lake Balaton. There are steps to get into the lake and canoes, boats and pedaloes for hire. An extensive entertainment programme is designed for all ages and there are several bars and restaurants of various styles. There are souvenir shops and a supermarket. In fact, you need not leave the site at all during your holiday, although there are several excursions on offer, including to Budapest or to one of the many Hungarian spas, a trip over Lake Balaton or a traditional wine tour. The site's 450 pitches vary in size (60-110 sq.m) and almost all have shade – very welcome during the hot Hungarian summers – and 4-10A electricity. As with most of the sites on Lake Balaton, a train line runs just outside the site boundary.

### Facilities

The three sanitary blocks have toilets, washbasins (open style and in cabins) with hot and cold water, spacious showers (both pre-set and controllable), child size toilets and basins, and two bathrooms (hourly charge). Heated, unisex baby room with baby bath. Facilities for disabled people. Launderette. Dog shower. Motorcaravan services. Supermarket. Several bars and restaurants and souvenir shops. Sports field, Tennis. Minigolf. Fishing. Bicycle hire. Canoe, rowing boats and pedalo hire. Entertainment programme for all ages. Off site: Riding 3 km.

**Open:** 1 May - 30 September.

### Directions

Follow road 71 from Veszprém southeast to Keszthely. Site is in Révfülöp.

### Charges 2007

| | |
|---|---|
| Per person | HUF 770,00 - 1230,00 |
| child (2-14 yrs) | HUF 560,00 - 920,00 |
| pitch incl. electricity | HUF 1690,00 - 4700,00 |
| dog | HUF 560,00 - 920,00 |

Camping Cheques accepted.

## HU5380 Balatontourist Camping Venus

H-8252 Balatonszepezd (Veszprem County)

Tel: 875 680 61. Email: venus@balatontourist.hu

For those who want to be directly beside Lake Balaton and would like a reasonably quiet location, Camping Venus would be a good choice and it is also possibly the best site in Hungary. Apart from the rather noisy train that regularly passes the site, this is a quiet setting with views of the lake from almost all the pitches. From the front row of pitches you could almost dangle your feet from your caravan in the warm water of the lake. There are 150 flat pitches all with at least 4/10A electricity. Varying in size (70-100 sq.m), almost all have shade. Given the small size of the site, Mária Ékes, the manager, gets to know every guest in person and she will make you very welcome. This is a well managed site with modern, well kept sanitary blocks and 24 hour security at the gate. Lake Balaton with its water temperature of about 25° Celsius in summer, is obviously the main attraction here, but you can also make several excursions, for example a trip to Budapest or a gipsy night in Riza.

### Facilities

Two good sanitary blocks provide toilets, washbasins (open style and in cabins) with hot and cold water, pre-set showers, facilities for disabled people and child size toilets and basins. Launderette. Motorcaravan services. Shop for basics. Bar. Restaurant. Snack bar. Playground. Daily activity programme with pottery, fairy tale reading, horse shows, tournaments in Sümeg, trips over the lake and to Budapest. Canoe, pedalo, rowing boats and bicycle hire. Dogs are not accepted. Off site: Riding 3 km.

**Open:** 18 May - 9 September, with all services

### Directions

On the 71 road between Balatonfüred and Keszthely, site is in Balatonszepezd on the lake side of the road.

### Charges 2007

| | |
|---|---|
| Per person | HUF 670,00 - 1130,00 |
| child (2-14 yrs) | HUF 510,00 - 820,00 |
| pitch incl. electricity | HUF 1280,00 - 3470,00 |

www.alanrogers.com

All campsites are inspected & selected by Alan Rogers.

Just Click and Go!

INSPECTED CAMPSITES & SELECTED

# Hungary

## HU5100 Ozon Camping

Erdei Malom köz 3, H-9400 Sopron (Gyor-Moson-Sopron County)
Tel: 993 311 44. Email: ozoncamping@sopron.hu

Sopron, close to the Austrian border, was not over-run by the Turks or bombed in WW2, so 350 historic buildings and monuments remain intact, making it the second major tourist centre after Budapest. It also has a music festival from mid-June to mid-July and is close to the Löverek hills. This surprisingly pleasant campsite is just over four kilometres from the centre, with the modern, chalet style reception at the entrance from where the oval site opens out into a little green valley surrounded by trees. It is peaceful and comfortable with many trees within the site offering shade. Concrete access roads lead to 60 numbered grass pitches, all with electricity (6A), and 12 with water and waste water are in the lower level on the left, where siting is more difficult for caravans. They are mostly flat, some with a slight slope, separated by hedges and vary from 40 sq.m. for tents up to 80 sq.m. for larger units. One member of staff spoke English when we visited.

### Facilities
Sanitary facilities in two heated buildings are identical except that one has a laundry (free) whilst the other, near the pool, has a sauna. Curtained showers with communal changing, close to washbasins therefore could be a little cramped. Both blocks have free cookers, fridges and dishwashing. Gas supplies. Restaurant with good value meals (all season). Room with TV. Money exchange at reception. Small swimming pool and paddling pool (1/6-11/10). Off site: Shops 150 m. Bicycle hire 1 km. Tennis and fishing 2 km. Riding 3 km. Bus service to town centre.

**Open:** 15 April - 15 October.

### Directions
From the A3 south of Wien, follow roads numbers 308 (Klingenbach) and 84 to Sopron. Site is on road to Brennerberganya, well signed in Sopron.
GPS: N47:40.664 E16:32.313

### Charges guide

| | |
|---|---|
| Per person | HUF 1200,00 |
| child (3-12 yrs) | HUF 850,00 |
| pitch incl. electricity | HUF 800,00 - 1600,00 |
| dog | HUF 500,00 |

---

## HU5385 Balatontourist Camping Levendula Naturist FKK

H-8243 Balatonakali (Veszprem County)
Tel: 875 440 11. Email: clevendula@balatontourist.hu

Levendula is a naturist site and is the latest addition to the Balatontourist chain of sites on the north side of Lake Balaton. It has 123 level unmarked pitches, varying in size from 60-110 sq.m, and separated by low hedges. Almost all have views of the lake and all have electricity (4/10A). The site is attractively landscaped with shrubs and flowers and there is direct access to the lake. The north side of Lake Balaton has much to offer culturally. Veszprém county has a rich history with baroque towns, castles, old churches and several items of interest such as the watermill and Protestant cemetery from the first decades of the 19th century with its heart shaped tombs. As part of the Balatontourist organisation, Levendula has similar amenities to the other sites, including a full entertainment program for children in high season, but without the noise of its larger brothers. The new toilet buildings are worth mentioning – they are among the best we've seen in Central Europe.

### Facilities
Two toilet blocks with modern fittings, including one washbasin in a cabin for men and women, en-suite facilities for disabled people and a heated baby room with bath and changing mat. Laundry. Campers' kitchen with cooking rings on request. Fish cleaning area. Dog shower. Bar/restaurant with terrace. Shop. Playground with colourful equipment. Watersports. Games room. Animation programme 6 days a week, 3 times a day. Excursions. Off site: Riding 1.5 km.

**Open:** 12 May - 10 September.

### Directions
Follow no. 71 road towards Keszthely and site is signed in Balatonakali. GPS: N46:52.760 E17:44.535

### Charges 2007

| | |
|---|---|
| Per person | HUF 800,00 - 1200,00 |
| child (2-14 yrs) | HUF 600,00 - 900,00 |
| pitch incl. electricity | HUF 2600,00 - 5500,00 |

Camping Cheques accepted.

---

Check real time availability and at-the-gate prices...
www.alanrogers.com

## HU5120 Gasthof Camping Piheno

I-es foút, H-9011 Györszentivan-Kertváros (Gyor-Moson-Sopron County)
Tel: 965 230 08. Email: piheno@piheno_hu

This privately owned site makes an excellent night stop when travelling to and from Hungary as it lies beside the main no. 1 road, near the end of the motorway to the east of Györ. It is set amidst pine trees with pitches which are not numbered, but marked out by small shrubs, in a small clearing or between the trees. With space for about 40 touring units, all with electrical connections (6A), and eight simple, one roomed bungalows and four en-suite rooms. On one side of the site, fronting the road, is the reception, bar and pleasant restaurant with terrace (menu in English). The food is of excellent quality and very well priced (typical main course and coffee £3.50). The management offer a very reasonably priced package (if desired) which includes pitch and meals. A very friendly German speaking owner runs the site and restaurant with his wife and daughters who speak a little English.

### Facilities
A single, small, basic toilet block has just two showers for each sex (10 ft for one minute) and curtained, communal dressing space. Baby room. Room for washing clothes and dishes with small cooking facility. Washing machine. Bar. Restaurant with good menu and reasonable prices. Solar heated swimming and paddling pools (10 x 5 m, open June -Sept). Order bread at reception the previous evening. Off site: Gyor with shops and swimming pool.

**Open:** 1 April - 30 October.

### Directions
Coming from Austria, continue through Györ following signs for Budapest. Continue on road no. 1 past start of motorway for 3 km. and site is on left. From Budapest, turn right onto road no. 10 at end of motorway, then as above.
GPS: N47:43.528 E17:42.883

### Charges 2007
| | |
|---|---|
| Per person | € 4,40 |
| pitch | € 3,40 |
| dog | € 0,87 |
| electricity | € 1,50 |

Less 10% for stays over 4 days, 20% after 8. Prices in Euros.


## HU5110 Dömös Camping

Duna-Part, H-2027 Dömös (Komarom-Esztergom County)
Tel: 334 823 19. Email: info@domoscamping.hu

The area of the Danube Bend is a major tourist attraction and here at Dömös is a lovely modern, well maintained and presented, friendly, peaceful site with large pitches and easy access. The Danube is just over 50 m. away and quite fast flowing. There are views of the river and the hills on the other bank from some pitches. With Budapest just 45 kilometres, Esztergom (the ancient capital of Hungary) 15 kilometres and the small town of Visegrad, with its impressive cliff fortress close by, this could make an ideal base from which to explore the whole area. There are 107 quite large pitches, of which 80 have 6A electricity, in sections on flat grass, numbered and divided by small plants and some with little shade. At the top of the site is an inviting open air swimming pool with a grass lying out area and tiny children's pool with a large bar with pool tables alongside. Sightseeing tours to Budapest, Esztergom and Szentendre are arranged.

### Facilities
The modern, long, brick built sanitary building is tiled with sliding doors and includes large, pre-set hot showers with individual changing, and good facilities for children and disabled visitors. Dishwashing and cooking area. Laundry with washing machines and dryer. Motorcaravan services. New restaurant (all season). Small café with terrace. Bar. Swimming pool (20 x 10 m, all season). Small play area on grass. English is spoken. Off site: Fishing 50 m. Village facilities 300 m. Tennis, minigolf and football field adjacent. Riding 2 km. Bicycle hire 8 km. Mountain walking tours.

**Open:** 1 May - 15 September.

### Directions
Site is between the village and the Danube, off road 11 Esztergom - Visegrad - Szentendre.
GPS: N47:45.927 E18:54.864

### Charges 2007
| | |
|---|---|
| Per unit incl. 2 persons and electricity | HUF 3440,00 - 3770,00 |
| extra person | HUF 880,00 - 990,00 |
| child (2-14 yrs) | HUF 700,00 - 800,00 |
| dog | HUF 400,00 |

No credit cards (cash only).

Check real time availability and at-the-gate prices...
www.alanrogers.com

# Hungary

## HU5130 Panorama Camping

Fenyvesalja 4/A, H-9090 Pannonhalma (Gyor-Moson-Sopron County)

Tel: 964 712 40

In 1982 this became the first private enterprise campsite in Hungary. It offers a very pleasant outlook and peaceful stay at the start or end of your visit to this country, situated just 20 kilometres southeast of Györ, on a hillside with views across the valley to the Sokoro hills. On the edge of the village, it is just below the 1,000 year old Benedictine monastery, which has guided tours and a library of over 300,000 books. The site has its own stairway up to the monastery. The 70 numbered and hedged touring pitches (50 with 16A electricity, long leads necessary) are on terraces, generally fairly level but reached by fairly steep concrete access roads, with many trees and plants around. Some small hardstandings are provided. There are benches provided and a small, grass terrace below reception from where you can purchase beer, local wine and soft drinks, etc. Occasional big stews are cooked in high season and the wine cellar in the village is recommended.

### Facilities

Good sanitary facilities are in a small building near reception and a larger unit halfway up the site. Curtained, hot showers with curtained communal changing. Hot water for dishwashing and laundry. Cooking facilities. Bar and meals (1/6-30/9). Shop. Recreation room with TV and games. Internet access. Small play area and small pool (cleaned once per week). Table tennis. No English is spoken. Off site: Hourly bus service to Györ. Shop for essentials 150 m. Good value restaurant 400 m. away in the village. Riding 3 km. Fishing 4 km.

**Open:** Easter, then 1 May - 15 September.

### Directions

From no. 82 Györ - Veszprém road turn to Pannonhalma at Ecs. Site is well signed – the final approach road is fairly steep
GPS: N47:32.921 E17:45.515

### Charges guide

| | |
|---|---|
| Per person | € 5,00 |
| child (2-14 yrs) | € 3,00 |
| pitch | € 4,00 |
| electricity | € 3,00 |

No credit cards. Prices in Euros.

## HU5135 Aucost Holiday Parc

Termalsor 1, H-7041 Vajta (Fejer)

Tel: 252 297 00. Email: holidayparc@aucost.nl

On arrival at Camping Aucost you will be welcomed at the entrance by an iron stork, made by a local man. This is a good, well kept site under Dutch ownership and only 400 m. from a thermal spa bath. It has 80 pitches for touring units and with 6A electricity on level, grassy fields and 20 mobile homes for rent. Shade is available from mature trees. The main building houses reception and a comfortable lounge with TV and library. To the left is an additional, portacabin toilet block. All the facilities were clean and well maintained during our visit and the site is attractively landscaped with colourful flowers. Aucost is a former tobacco farm and was set up by the Soeterboek family in 1998. They organise several excursions to the historic cities of Pécs, Székesfehérvar, Pannonhalma and Budapest. You could also go walking in the nearby National Park, or enjoy Hungarian meals, a 'Puszta' show and wine tastings on the site.

### Facilities

Good, modern facilities with British style toilets, open washbasins and pre-set, hot showers (free). Laundry with sinks and 2 washing machines. Motorcaravan service point. Bar with takeaway service. Library (English and Dutch) with satellite TV. Hungarian meals. Football field. Boules. Tennis. Games room. Trampoline. Daily activities organised for children in high season. Excursions to several cities organised. Horse shows. Cellar for youngsters. Off site: Thermal spa 400 m. (free for camp guests). Fishing 8 km.

**Open:** 22 April - 16 September.

### Directions

Site is off the main road running to Szekszárd just before entering the village of Vajta. Access road is bumpy. GPS: N46:43.727 E18:39.317

### Charges 2008

| | |
|---|---|
| Per unit incl. 2 persons | € 20,25 |
| incl. electricity | € 22,50 |
| extra person | € 4,25 |
| child (0-12 yrs) | € 3,65 |
| animal | € 2,75 |

No credit cards. Prices in Euros.

Check real time availability and at-the-gate prices...
www.alanrogers.com

## HU5155 Római Camping

Szentendrei ut 189, H-1031 Budapest (Budapest City)

Tel: **138 871 67**. Email: **romaicamping@message.hu**

Római Camping is a large site with 2,000 pitches within the boundaries of Budapest, next to the Római Fürdo Aqualand centre. There are about 500 touring pitches on level, grassy fields, 180 with 4A electricity. Pitches are under mature trees that provide useful shade with access off tarmac roads. A small buffet on site provides drinks, ice cream, fruit and basics, and there is a restaurant with a further restaurant at the Róma' pool complex. The site is an easy half hour by public transport (first stop ten minutes walk) to the bustling and interesting city centre of Budapest. Here you will find numerous museums, the parliament building (open to the public on certain days), the Royal Palace and the Mátyás Church.

### Facilities

Basic toilet facilities (partly refurbished and cleaned twice daily) provide British and Turkish style toilets, open washbasins and controllable, hot showers (free). Laundry with sinks, washing machine and dryer. Dishwashing. Motorcaravan service point. Playground. Volleyball. Buffet and bar. Restaurant. Torch useful. Internet access. Off site: Római open-air pool 100 m. Budapest centre 30 minutes by public transport.

**Open:** All year.

### Directions

Coming into town from the north via main road no. 11, turn left at OMV petrol station. Keep right at the end and continue to keep right until Csalina utca. Turn left at crossing and take first right. Go past swimming pool and turn right again. Coming out of town, take sharp right bend 100 m. after camping sign. GPS: N47:34.480 E19:03.103

### Charges guide

| | |
|---|---|
| Per person | € 4,10 |
| child | € 2,50 |
| pitch incl. car | € 11,00 - € 17,00 |
| dog | € 2,50 |

No credit cards. Prices in Euros.

## HU5150 Fortuna Camping

Dózsa György út 164, H-2045 Törökbálint (Pest County)

Tel: **233 353 64**. Email: **fortunacamping@axelero.hu**

This good site lies at the foot of a hill with views of the vineyards, but Budapest is only 25 minutes away by bus. The owner, Csaba Szücs, will provide visitors with a map and instructions on how to see the town in the best way. The site is surrounded by mature trees and Mr Szücs will proudly name all 150 varieties of bushes and shrubs which edge some of the pitches. The site has a small restaurant with very reasonable prices but it is only open from 18.00-21.00. An open air swimming pool with flume will help you to cool off in summer with an indoor pool for cooler weather. Concrete and gravel access roads lead to terraces where there are 170 individual pitches most bordered with hedges, all with electricity (up to 16A, long leads needed), and 14 with water, on slightly sloping ground. A special field area provides for group bookings, and has separate facilities. Mr Szücs and his family will endeavour to make your stay a comfortable one. His daughter organises tours to Budapest or the surrounding countryside, and will also explain the mysteries of public transport in Budapest.

### Facilities

One fully equipped sanitary blocks and two smaller blocks. Good facilities for disabled people. Dishwashing facilities, plus six cookers in sheltered area. Washing machine and dryer. Gas supplies. Motorcaravan services. Restaurant and bar (all year). Snack bar. Essentials from reception, (order bread previous day). Outdoor swimming pool with slide (15/5-15/9). Indoor pool. Small play area. Excursions organised. English spoken. Off site: Close to bus terminal for city centre 1 km. Riding 3 km. Fishing 4 km.

**Open:** All year.

### Directions

From M1 Gyor - Budapest, exit for Törökbálint following signs for town and then site. Also accessible from M7 Budapest - Balaton road. GPS: N47:25.922 E18:54.066

### Charges 2007

| | |
|---|---|
| Per person | € 6,00 |
| child (4-14 yrs) | € 4,00 |
| pitch | € 5,00 |
| electricity | € 2,00 |
| dog | € 2,00 |

No credit cards. Prices in Euros.

# Hungary

## HU5165 Zugligeti Niche Camping

Zugligeti ut 101, H-1121 Budapest (Budapest City)

Tel: 00 36 1 299 83 46. Email: camping.niche@t-online.hu

Zugligeti Niche is in the Buda Hills on steeply sloping ground. There are 200 pitches, all for tourers, on both sides of a steep and winding access road. Pitches on the first half of the site are mostly hardstandings for motorcaravans, off a tarmac and gravel access road. After a sharp right turn, a sandy road takes you further uphill where there are pitches mostly for tents, varying in size from 20- 40 sq.m. To the front of the site are two old trams; one functions as reception and there are plans for the other to become a small shop. In front of the site a cable track takes you high up in the hills and the bus stop for the city centre is a few minutes walk.

### Facilities

Scattered around the site are several toilet blocks, renewed in 2007. They include British style toilets, open washbasins and controllable showers (free). Basic shower for disabled visitors. Laundry with sinks and washing machine. Campers' kitchen. Bar/restaurant with good value meals. Torch useful. Free breakfast and free WiFi. Off site: Budapest city centre 30 minutes by public transport.

**Open:** All year.

### Directions

Site is in the Budapest district three. Coming from the north follow signs for M1 and M7 motorway. Site is well signed from Moszkva Tér.
GPS: N47:30.550 E18:58.200

### Charges 2007

| | |
|---|---|
| Per person | HUF 1400,00 |
| child | HUF 700,00 |
| pitch | HUF 990,00 - 2550,00 |
| electricity | HUF 1200,00 |
| dog | HUF 600,00 |

No credit cards.

## HU5175 Kek Duna Autoscamping

Főut 70, H-2025 Visegrad (Pest County)

Tel: 263 981 20. Email: hotelhon@t-online.hu

Just opposite a road that runs alongside the beautiful Danube river, this small site has only 40 pitches (all for tourers and with 4A electricity) and two static units. It is owned by the Honti Hotel 50 m. down the road and this is where reception is located. It is attractively landscaped with low trees, shrubs and flowers. The good size pitches are arranged on well kept, grassy lawns, separated by hedges in the middle field. From some there are good views of Visegrád Castle, once the home of King Mátyás Corvinus. Some road noise can be heard from the main road that runs to Budapest. Kék Duna is a good base for exploring the historic towns of Visegrád with its Castle and thermal spa, Esztergom with its Cathedral and Szentendre, a beautiful old town. Kék Duna is also just 40 km. from Budapest, the Hungarian capital. Just opposite the site, a ferry will take you across the Danube and the site rents canoes for trips on the river.

### Facilities

Adequate 'portacabin' style toilet block and a good shower block with British style toilets, open washbasins and controllable showers (free). Basic kitchen with electric cookers and fridge. Bar with small buffet. Fishing. Canoe hire. Off site: Riding 6 km. Golf 7 km. Restaurants close.

**Open:** 1 May - 30 September.

### Directions

Site is on the right of the no. 11 road running to Budapest at km. 43. GPS: N47:46.985 E18:50.034

### Charges guide

| | |
|---|---|
| Per person | HUF 900,00 |
| pitch incl. car | HUF 600,00 - 1200,00 |
| electricity | HUF 650,00 |
| dog | HUF 500,00 |

No credit cards.

Check real time availability and at-the-gate prices...
www.alanrogers.com

## HU5180 Jumbo Camping

Budakalászi út 23-25, H-2096 Üröm (Pest County)

Tel: 263 512 51

Jumbo Camping is a modern, thoughtfully developed site in the northern outskirts of Budapest. The concrete and gravel access roads lead shortly to 55 terraced pitches of varying size, a little on the small size for large units, and some slightly sloping. Hardstanding for cars and caravan wheels, as well as large hardstandings for motorhomes. There is a steep incline to some pitches and use of the site's 4x4 may be required. All pitches have 6A electricity (may require long leads) and there are 8 caravan pitches with water and drain. They are mostly divided by small hedges and the whole area is fenced. Situated on a hillside 15 km. from Budapest centre, with attractive views of the Buda hills and with public transport to the city near, this is a pleasant and comfortable small site (despite the name) where you will receive a warm welcome. It is possible to park outside the short, fairly steep entrance which has a chain across. Reception, where you are given a comprehensive English language information sheet, doubles as a café/bar area.

### Facilities

Sanitary facilities are excellent, with large showers (communal changing). Dishwashing under cover. Terrace with chairs and tables. Washing machine, iron and cooking facilities on payment. Motorcaravan services. Café where bread (orders taken), milk and butter available. Small, attractive swimming pool (10/6-10/9). Playground with covered area for wet weather. Barbecue area. English spoken and information sheet provided in English. Off site: Shop and restaurant 500 m. The 'Old Swabian Wine-Cellar' said to serve extremely good food. Bus to city 500 m. every 30 minutes. Fishing 8 km.

**Open:** 1 April - 31 October.

### Directions

Site signed on roads to Budapest - nos. 11 from Szentendre and 10 from Komarom. If approaching from Budapest use 11 (note: site sign appears very quickly after sharp right bend; signs and entry are clearer if using road 10). Can also approach via Györ on M1/E60 and Lake Balaton on M7/E71. Turn into site is quite acute and uphill.
GPS: N47:36.093 E19:01.200

### Charges 2007

| | |
|---|---|
| Per person | € 5,00 |
| child (3-14 yrs) | € 3,10 |
| pitch acc to size and season | € 2,60 - € 6,40 |
| electricity | € 2,50 |

No credit cards (cash only). Prices in Euros.

## HU5185 Baradla Camping

Baradla Oldal 1, H-3759 Aggtelek (Borsod-Abauj-Zemplen)

Tel: 485 030 05. Email: aggtelek@tourinform.hu

Baradla is located in one of the most beautiful Hungarian National Parks, the Aggteleki Nemzeti Park, within an hour's drive of Hungary's third largest town, Miskolc. Baradla has 180 pitches, all for tourers but only 16 with electricity (4A). The level pitches are on one large, unmarked grassy field with shade from a few low trees on one side, on open ground on the other. At the front of the site there is a welcoming and good value bar/restaurant (separate management) and numerous souvenir shops are opposite. No English is spoken. There are plenty of opportunities for walking and cycling and for visiting several caves. In fact, the Baradla site is at the entrance of the famous Barlang Caves which form a natural border between Hungary and Slovakia and are the largest caves in the Park. Baradla is fenced, but not gated and in high season, tourists coming out of the Caves pass over land belonging to the site.

### Facilities

Toilet facilities are basic and could be pressed in high season, but were clean and well maintained when we visited. They provide British style toilets, open washbasins and controllable showers (free). Basic campers' kitchen. Fridge. Dishwashing. Bar/restaurant. Playground.
Off site: Barlang Caves.

**Open:** 15 April - 15 October.

### Directions

From Miskolc, take no. 26 road north towards Putnok. At Sájoszentpéter, continue on 27 road north towards Perkupa and follow signs for Aggtelek and the campsite. GPS: N48:28.319 E20:29.538

### Charges 2007

| | |
|---|---|
| Per person | HUF 900,00 |
| child | HUF 600,00 |
| pitch | HUF 1000,00 |

*Hungary*

Check real time availability and at-the-gate prices...
www.alanrogers.com

# Hungary

## HU5187 Camping Amedi

Rákóczi út 181, H-3658 Borsodbóta (Borsod-Abauj-Zemplen)

Tel: 48 438 468. Email: info@campingamedi.hu

Amedi is a new site (2005), under Dutch ownership in the quiet village of Borsodbóta in the Bükk National Park in the northeast of Hungary. The site has 40 pitches, on level, grassy fields with gravel access roads. It is landscaped with flowers and fir trees. Neither marked nor numbered, the pitches are up to 120 sq.m. in size, all with 4-10A electricity. There is little shade as yet and the Hungarian summers can be hot. There are beautiful views over the mountains and the village. A good toilet block and a circular pool for a refreshing swim are centrally located. The Wesselink family will welcome you with campfire sing-alongs and weekly 'gulyás' and barbecues. Active campers can join riding trips, biking tours and walks through the Bükk mountains. This is an area of outstanding beauty with special species of birds, butterflies and plants. Amedi is a peaceful and relaxing base.

### Facilities

The central, modern toilet block (plans for a second block afoot) has toilets, open style washbasins and free, controllable, hot showers. Washing machine and dryer. Campers' kitchen. Small bar (15/6-15/9). Small library. Satellite TV. Open air pool (20 sq.m). Weekly campfires with singing, 'gulyás' and barbecues. Mountain bike hire. Rafting, riding, walking and fishing organised. Off site: Shop 100 m. Bar 400 m. Riding 400 m. Fishing 3 km.

**Open:** 15 April - 15 October.

### Directions

From Budapest, follow the M3 motorway east and take exit for Eger. Follow to Eger and from there the 25 road north. After Szarvask, turn right towards Monósbél and then Bélapátfalva and Szilvásvárad. In Szilvásvárad turn left at T-junction. Continue through Bükkmogyoród, Cserneley and Lénárdaróc. After a tunnel, turn left towards Sáta. Follow site signs in Borsodbóta. GPS: N48:12.461 E20:24.247

### Charges 2007

| | |
|---|---|
| Per person | € 2,75 |
| child (4-12 yrs) | € 1,80 |
| pitch | € 2,75 - € 6,75 |
| electricity (10A) | € 2,95 |

Camping Cheques accepted.

## HU5190 Farm Lator

Rózsavári út 95, H-3425 Sály-Lator Puszta (Borsod-Abauj-Zemplen)

Tel: 493 361 33. Email: farmlator@hotmail.com

Farm Lator is a small, privately run site on the edge of one of the Hungarian National Parks, near the Bükk mountains, more or less in the middle of nowhere! This keeps the site really quiet and the surroundings are very suitable for many different types of bird and butterfly that you won't find anywhere else in Europe. The Dutch/Hungarian owners of Farm Lator, Rob de Jong and Barbara Borostyankoi, try to keep the site and its surroundings as natural as possible. This means the site has few amenities, other than a clean and well kept sanitary block, and electricity (16A) is only provided for three pitches. The charm of this site is the peace and quiet of the natural environment that one enjoys here but they also organise excursions. You can also visit the charcoal-burners who show you how to burn chalk and charcoal the old fashioned way – something else that would be hard to find anywhere else in Europe.

### Facilities

One small unisex sanitary block provides a toilet, two washbasins and three controllable showers, all very clean and well maintained. Sinks under cover. Three pitches with 16A electricity. Sitting room with library and table tennis. Weekly meal organised. No shop but bread to order. Fishing. Bicycle hire. Riding. Torches useful. Off site: Eger 1 hour drive. Thermal bath 30 km.

**Open:** 1 May - 1 September.

### Directions

From Budapest take M3 motorway to Miskolc. Take exit for Mezokerestes and follow road through Mezokerestes and Mezonyárad, then turn right on no. 3 road towards Miskolc. In Bükkabrany, at Total petrol station, turn left to Sály and follow road (10 km.) to site (just after small graveyard). GPS: N47:56.735 E20:39.754

### Charges 2007

| | |
|---|---|
| Per person | € 5,00 |
| child (4-16 yrs) | € 3,00 |
| tent | € 5,00 - € 7,00 |
| caravan or motorcaravan | € 9,00 |
| electricity | € 2,00 |

No credit cards. Prices in Euros.

Check real time availability and at-the-gate prices...
www.alanrogers.com

## HU5197 Termál Camping

Szederkényi út 53, H-3580 Tiszaújváros (Borsod-Abauj-Zemplen)
Tel: **49 542 210**. Email: **camping@tujvaros.hu**

Termál Camping was opened in 2004 and is on the outskirts of Tiszaújváros (the former 'Lenin City') and not far from the River Tisza in eastern Hungary. The site has some 166 grass pitches (all for touring units), of which 16 have 25A electricity. To one end of the site are 8 holiday homes and centrally located is a well equipped toilet block. Since this is a new site, the trees and bushes have not yet fully developed and the site can become hot in the Hungarian summer. The site is next to a tributary of the River Tisza, and the area offers good opportunities for walking, cycling, boating and fishing. Opposite the site is the renovated thermal spa of Tiszaújváros with indoor and outdoor pools (some with water of up to 42 degrees), slides, flumes, jacuzzis and numerous outlets for eating and drinking. Behind the pool complex is a sports arena with an athletics track and professional football field. This site would be ideal for a short stay to enjoy the medicinal waters of the pool complex.

### Facilities
One central, modern toilet block with toilets, pre-set hot showers, and facilities for disabled people. Laundry with washing machines. Kitchen with cooking rings, oven and fridge. Communal barbecue areas. Small buffet/bar. Fishing. Bicycle hire. Torch useful. Some English is spoken. Off site: Thermal spa. Supermarket and swimming pool 300 m.

**Open:** 15 April - 15 October.

### Directions
From M3 motorway from Budapest to the east, take exit for Debrecen and then to Tiszaújváros. On entering town follow the signs to the Thermal Spa bath and the site. GPS: N47:53.900 E21:03.900

### Charges 2007
| | |
|---|---|
| Per unit incl. 2 persons | HUF 5000,00 |
| tent | HUF 4600,00 |
| dog | HUF 500,00 |

## HU5205 Øko-Park-Camping

Borsod utca 9, H-3323 Eger-Szarvaskö (Heves County)
Tel: **363 522 01**. Email: **info@oko-park.hu**

Øko-Park Camping is close to the Baroque style town of Eger, on the edge of the protected Bükk National Park. Buildings on the site are all made of natural materials and there is a well used for watering the plants. Øko-Park has 45 pitches off a single gravel access lane that runs to the back of the site. The grass pitches are level, marked and numbered. All have 16A electricity and are in the shade of mature trees. A pond is at the rear of the site and a covered picnic area with a kitchen for campers and a barbecue area are in the centre. To the front of the site is the 'Panzió' where breakfast is served and which also serves as a bar and restaurant. Being in the hills means the site has a sub-alpine climate, which can be welcoming in the hot Hungarian summers. The area around Eger is of outstanding natural beauty and Eger itself is famous for 'Bull's Blood' red wine and its castle. The only disadvantages at Øko-Park is the road running alongside, the railway to the back and pitches which may be small for larger units.

### Facilities
One toilet block to the front provides toilets, open style washbasins and pre-set hot showers. Baby bath and changing mat. Basic facilities for disabled people. Washing machine and spin dryer. Campers' kitchen. Restaurant with bar for breakfast and dinner (April - Oct). Climbing wall. Playground on gravel. Eco tours, walks and wine cave visits organised. Off site: Eger 9 km. Fishing 7 km. Riding 9 km. Shop nearby.

**Open:** 1 April - 31 October.

### Directions
From Budapest, follow M3 motorway east and take exit for Eger. Follow to Eger and, from there, the 25 road north towards Szarvaske. It is the second site on the right. GPS: N47:59.297 E20:19.861

### Charges guide
| | |
|---|---|
| Per person | € 3,90 |
| child | € 2,70 |
| pitch | € 4,90 - € 8,80 |

Prices in Euros.

Check real time availability and at-the-gate prices...
www.alanrogers.com

## HU5210 Diófaház Accommodations

Ady Endre út 12, H-3348 Szilvásvárad (Heves County)
Tel: 363 555 95. Email: info@diofahaz.hu

Diófaház is an ideal base in northeast Hungary for exploring this wooded part of the country, to visit the stud farm of the famous Lipizzaner horses (one of only five in the world) or to visit the town of Eger, world famous for its culture and red wine. The site is in private grounds on the edge of the village and provides a maximum of six pitches, all with electricity, which makes it quiet and peaceful. Gyöngyi Pap, the owner provides a warm welcome and if you're lucky you may arrive for the weekly barbecue or the home made Hungarian goulash soup. There are plenty of opportunities for cycling or walking tours, or there is a lakeside beach within 6 km. Also close are the famous Szalajka waterfalls. In winter this is a skiing resort and there is a local spa. English is spoken.

### Facilities
The single, freshly painted toilet block includes washbasins in cabins with hot and cold water, controllable hot showers and sinks with free hot water. Fresh rolls to order every day with home made jam but no shop. Internet access. Discounts at four restaurants in the village if you show your campers card. Off site: Riding 200 m. Bicycle hire 500 m. Fishing 6 km.

**Open:** All year.

### Directions
Take the no. 25 road from Eger north to Szilvásvárad. Site is signed when entering the village.
GPS: N48:05.890 E20:23.040

### Charges 2007
| | |
|---|---|
| Per unit incl. 2 persons | € 8,75 - € 10,50 |
| extra person | € 3,15 |
| electricity pkWh | € 0,18 |

Prices in Euros.

## HU5220 Tiszavirág Camping

P.f. 27, H-3910 Tokaj (Szabolcs-Szatmar-Bereg Co)
Tel: 473 526 26

From mid-June to mid-September, this site gets quite busy, but either side of these dates it is quiet and very relaxing. Set on the banks of the wide River Tisza, the level grass pitches, 120 in number, are close together and narrow but quite long, off a hard circular access road so siting should be quite easy. All the pitches have electricity (mostly 6A) and there is much shade from a variety of trees. There is a high season reception, but at other times, you site yourself and a gentleman calls during the evening to collect the fee. There may well be some day-time noise from watersports on the river but it is very quiet by night. This is a useful base for visiting northeast Hungary, not far from the Ukraine and Romania.

### Facilities
The toilet block is basic, but clean, and has recently been largely refurbished. It has WCs (external entry) British style WCs and curtained showers with communal undressing. Kitchen with gas hob. Kiosk and bar with terrace (partly covered). Simple restaurant. Wine shop. Barbecue places and large outdoor grill area for baking bread and barbecues. Newly built area for Hungarian goulash parties. River sports. No English spoken (German is). Off site: Shops for basics outside the main season are in the town over the bridge, 600 m. walk. Bicycle and boat hire 200 m. Riding 3 km.

**Open:** 1 May - 30 September.

### Directions
Tokaj is east of Miskolc and north of Debrecen. Site is just south of the river bridge on road no. 38. (Note: beware the noisy campsite signed on the other side of the road). GPS: N48:07.400 E21:25.086

### Charges guide
| | |
|---|---|
| Per unit incl. 2 persons | HUF 2200,00 |
| tent | HUF 1800,00 |

## HU5240 Dorcas Christian Camping Centre

Vekeri Tó, H-4002 Debrecen (Hajdu-Bihar County)

Tel: 525 410 28. Email: dorcascenter@debrecen.com

Debrecen is an interesting old town, close to the Hortobagy National Park and convenient if you are looking for a break travelling to Romania or the Ukraine. Dorcas is a Dutch Christian organisation and the campsite provides holidays for special causes – indeed, while we were there, 40 children arrived from Chernobyl for a trip abroad. The site is about 10 km. from Debrecen in a forest location, fenced and covered with trees. The 40 flat and grassy touring pitches are off tarmac access roads, arranged in four groups. Some pitches are divided by hedges, others marked out by trees and all have electricity available (6A). There is room in the large tenting area for more units, also with electricity, if necessary. A very pleasant restaurant and terrace offers good value meals. Through the site is an area for walks and a lake for fishing.

### Facilities

The new, central toilet building is large, tiled and of excellent quality with large, curtained showers (external changing), British style toilets and some washbasins. Facilities for laundry (key at reception). Shop for basics. Good value restaurant (menu in English) with terrace. Small swimming pool (June - Aug). Children's playgrounds. Church services (in English) fortnightly or more often if requested. Conference hall and meeting rooms. Bicycle hire. TV rental. Good walks. English spoken. Off site: Riding 2 km. Lake nearby with fishing.

**Open:** 1 May - 30 September.

### Directions

From Debrecen take road no. 47 south for 4 km. then left towards Hosszupalyi for 8 km. Site is signed on the right. GPS: N47:26.919 E21:41.360

### Charges 2007

Per unit incl. 2 persons and electricity  € 18,00
Prices in Euros.

---

## HU5245 Camping Füzes

Strand utca 2, H-5241 Abádszalók (Jász-Nagkyun-Szolnok County)

Tel: 059 535 345. Email: info@fuzescamping.hu

Füzes Camping is beside the beaches of one of the most popular holiday resorts in Eastern Hungary. The site is arranged with grass pitches in the shade of mature 'Füz' trees which provide a cooler environment in the heat of the Hungarian summer. There are around 200 pitches (all for touring units) on both sides of a long tarmac access lane, including 40 with 16A electricity. The popular beaches of Abádszalók are only 200 m. away and here there are many possibilities for water sport, plus restaurants and bars to enjoy the Hungarian lifestyle. Füzes Camping has its own restaurant and bar at the front of the site, where you can experience traditional Hungarian meals and drinks. Toilet facilities were basic during our visit in 2007, but plans are afoot to renovate them for 2008. Many events are organised around the Tisza lake during the summer months. Bird watchers will enjoy the 1500 m. long pathway at the lake where many species of birds are to be found.

### Facilities

One basic toilet block with toilets, controllable hot showers and open style washbasins. Bar and restaurant (all season). Tisza lake with sandy beaches. Fishing. Watersports. Torch useful. German is spoken.
Off site: Fishing and beach 200 m. Boat launching 20 km.

**Open:** May - September.

### Directions

From the M3 motorway from Budapest to the east, take the exit for Tiszafüred and continue south after passing Tiszafüred towards Abádszalók. On entering town, turn right towards the beaches and the site. GPS: N47:28.770 E20:35.409

### Charges 2007

| | |
|---|---|
| Per person | HUF 1400,00 |
| child (under 14 yrs) | HUF 1100,00 |
| caravan or motorcaravan with electricity | HUF 1400,00 |
| dog | HUF 200,00 |

## HU5260 Jonathermál Motel-Camping

Kökút 26, H-6120 Kiskunmajsa (Bacs-Kiskun County)
Tel: 774 818 55. Email: jonathermal@mail.datanet.hu

Situated three kilometres to the north of the town of Kiskunmajsa, a few kilometres west of road no. 5 (E75) from Budapest (140 km.) to Szeged (35 km.) this is one of the best Hungarian campsites. The camping area is large, reached by tarmac access roads, with 250 unmarked pitches in several areas around the motel and sanitary buildings. Some shade is available and more trees are growing. All the 120 large pitches have electricity (6A) and are set on flat grass where you place the pitch number allocated to you. Entrance to the pool complex is charged (daily or weekly tickets available) which gives you a huge 100 x 70 m. open air pool with a beach along one side, the indoor pool, children's pool, thermal, sauna and cold dip and an open air thermal pool, plus various places to eat and drink. This professionally run site offers the chance of relaxation but is also well placed for visiting Szeged, Csongrad or Szolnok, as well as being close to the borders with Romania and the former Yugoslavia.

### Facilities

A heated sanitary block provides first class facilities including washbasins in cabins and a unit for disabled visitors. Launderette. Gas supplies. Kiosk on site for bread and basics. etc. Smart bar and rest room. Restaurant by pool complex. Large swimming and thermal complex with other facilities (1/5-1/10). Massage (on payment). Children's playground including carved wooden animals. Volleyball, tennis and minigolf. Fishing lake (day permits). Bicycle hire. Riding. German spoken. Accommodation to rent. Off site: Shop opposite entrance, 120 m. Restaurants near. Riding 100 m.

**Open:** All year.

### Directions

From no. 5 (E75) Budapest - Szeged road take Kiskunmajsa exit and site is well signed 3 km. north of the town on road 5402.
GPS: N46:31.280 E19:44.812

### Charges 2007

| | |
|---|---|
| Per person | HUF 660,00 - 840,00 |
| child (6-14 yrs) | HUF 300,00 - 360,00 |
| pitch incl. car | HUF 600,00 - 840,00 |
| electricity | HUF 780,00 |
| dog | HUF 480,00 - 600,00 |

Less 5-10% for longer stays. No credit cards.

---

## HU5255 Martfü Health & Recreation Centre

Tüzép utca, H-5435 Martfü (Jász-Nagkyun-Szolnok County)
Tel: 565 805 19. Email: martfu@camping.hu

The Martfu campsite is new and modern with 61 tourist pitches on newly developed, grassy terrain with rubber hardstandings. Each of around 90 sq.m. and separated by young bushes and trees, all have electricity (16/25A), waste water drainage, cable and satellite TV. There is a water tap per two pitches. There is no shade as yet, which may cause the site to become a real suntrap in summer, when temperatures may rise up to 34 degrees Celsius. A small lake and its beach on the site will cool you off. The main attraction at this site is the thermal spa, which was still under construction when we visited, but is said to aid people with dermal and rheumatic problems. Martfu is right on the banks of the River Tisza, which also makes it an excellent spot for those who enjoy watersports and fishing. The village of Martfu is close with numerous shops, restaurants and bars.

### Facilities

Two modern, heated toilet blocks with British style toilets, open style washbasins, and free, controllable hot showers. Children's toilet and shower. Heated baby room. En-suite facilities for disabled visitors. Laundry with washing machines and dryer. Dishwashing. Kitchen with cooking rings. Motorcaravan services. Shop for basics (daily in season). Takeaway for bread and drinks. Welcoming bar with satellite TV with English, Dutch and Danish programmes (daily in season) and internet. Bowling. Library with English and Dutch books. Sauna. Jacuzzi. Playing field. Tennis. Minigolf. Fishing. Bicycle hire. Watersports. English and Dutch spoken. Off site: Fishing 50 m. Riding 5 km. Boat launching 1,5 km.

**Open:** All year.

### Directions

Driving into Martfu from the north on the 442 road, take the first exit at the roundabout (site is signed). Continue for about 800 m. and site is signed on the right. GPS: N47:01.196 E20:16.111

### Charges guide

| | |
|---|---|
| Per person | HUF 1200,00 |
| child (5-14 yrs) | HUF 600,00 |
| pitch | HUF 900,00 - 1200,00 |
| electricity | HUF 250,00 |

No credit cards.

## HU5310 Sugovica Camping

Petöfi-sziget, H-6500 Baja (Bacs-Kiskun County)

Tel: 793 217 55

If you are exploring Southern Transdanubia or en-route south, then Baja is an acceptable stop, on the east banks of the Danube. The site is on a small island, quiet and relaxed, next to the hotel which owns it, where there is a small swimming pool on payment and a terraced restaurant. The 180 fair sized pitches (80 sq.m), all with 10A electricity and 7 with hardstandings for motorcaravans (even if they are a little uneven), are on flat, grassy (but uncut), firm ground, easily accessed from tarred roads and with some shade from the many trees.

### Facilities

Sanitary facilities are just about adequate. Showers have communal changing, but all was clean when seen. Laundry and kitchen with fridge and freezer. Small shop. TV room. Tennis. Table tennis. Riverside walks. Fishing. Boat Launching. No English spoken. Off site: Town facilities close.

**Open:** 1 May - 30 September.

### Directions

Site is on Petoti island (sziget), well signed from just southwest of the junction of roads 51 from Budapest and 55 from Szeged. The bridge is close to a cobbled town square. GPS: N46:10.491 E18:56.804

### Charges guide

| | |
|---|---|
| Per person | HUF 440,00 - 800,00 |
| child (6-14 yrs) | HUF 220,00 - 400,00 |
| caravan or motorcaravan | HUF 850,00 - 1200,00 |
| tent | HUF 590,00 - 850,00 |
| car | HUF 300,00 |

## HU5315 Camping Forras

Bokréta u. 105, H-7394 Magyarhertelend (Baranya)

Tel: 725 211 10. Email: egyesulettelehaz@magyarhertelend.hu

This well established site is close to the historic city of Pécs, in a part of Hungary with a Mediterranean style climate. Camping Forras, or 'Bij Balázc' as it is called by some Dutch guests, is also close to the Mescék National Park, where there are many marked walking routes. The site has 120 pitches, all for tourers, off gravel and grass access roads. Of these, 80 are marked and have 6A electricity connections. The remaining pitches are used mainly for tents. The whole site looks well cared for with many different varieties of trees giving a pleasant atmosphere and providing useful shade in summer. Forras is opposite a pool – not a thermal spa according to the owner, although it is advertised as such! There is a restaurant here, with a small bar on the site for drinks. This is a good site for those seeking relaxation in beautiful, natural surroundings.

### Facilities

The traditional toilet block provides acceptable facilities with British style toilets, open washbasins and controllable showers (free). Washing machine and spin dryer. Dishwashing. Bar with library. Basic playground. Minigolf. Torch useful. Off site: Fishing 3 km. City of Pécs is close.

**Open:** 7 May - 30 September.

### Directions

From Pécs, take no. 66 road north towards Sásd. Turn left in Magyarszék towards Magyarhertelend and follow signs. Site is just outside the village on the left. GPS: N46:11.453 E18:08.506

### Charges guide

| | |
|---|---|
| Per person | HUF 750,00 |
| child (2-13 yrs) | HUF 450,00 |
| pitch incl. car | HUF 900,00 |
| electricity | HUF 500,00 |
| dog | HUF 450,00 |
| No credit cards. | |

## Hungary

### HU5320 Máré Vára Camping

Várvölgyi utca 2, H-7332 Magyaregregy (Baranya)
Tel: 724 204 03. Email: annevelink@axelero.hu

Máré Vára takes its name from an ancient castle situated a few hundred metres down the road where the German noble family of Mariën once lived. The site is on archaeological ground: where now the main house stands, there used to be a monastery and centuries before that there was an ancient Roman settlement. The Dutch Annevelink family opened this campsite in 2002. When we visited there were just 50 pitches (35 with 10A electricity) but there are plans to extend the site further. The pitches are on slightly sloping, well-kept, grassy fields and are separated by young trees and attractive lamp posts (a gift from the local brewery). Toilet facilities are in the old cow shed and here in the walls one can see remains of the former monastery. All the facilities were clean and tidy when we were there. Máré Vára is a good base from which to explore this relatively unknown part of Hungary and is only 20 minutes by bus from the interesting historic town of Pécs.

#### Facilities
Modern and clean toilet facilities with British style toilets, open washbasins and controllable showers (free, hot water variable). Washing machine. Dishwashing. No shop, but bread to order. Buffet with terrace for drinks and ice cream. Swimming pool (7 x 3 m). Playground. Social events organised. TV room with satellite, DVD and video. Off site: Máré Vára Castle 500 m. Fishing 10 km. Riding 3 km.

**Open:** 1 April - 30 September.

#### Directions
Magyaregregy is northeast of Pécs. Site is just outside Magyaregregy on the left and well signed.
GPS: N46:14.032 E18:18.490

#### Charges guide
| | |
|---|---|
| Per unit incl. 2 persons | € 15,00 |
| extra person | € 2,40 |
| child (4-12 yrs) | € 2,00 |
| electricity | € 2,00 |
| dog | € 1,00 |

No credit cards. Prices in euros.

---

### HU5290 Kemping Nap a Szivemben

Petőfi Sándor u. 38-D, H-7081 Simontornya (Tolna County)
Tel: 745 860 60

This small, immaculate looking site is under Dutch ownership and was newly opened in 2004. It only has 15 pitches on well kept, grassy lawns, all with 18/22A electricity. The toilet block is amongst the best we have seen in Central Europe. The site is on the main road but it did not appear to be too disturbing. The owner, Mrs Van Rijn, organises Hungarian breakfasts with visits to the Castle (where a Dutch noble family once lived) and wine tastings in their own vineyard. A cycle route has been set out in the local area. Nap a Szivemben is about 35 km. from Lake Balaton and close to the historic city of Pécs. There is a swimming pool in the town but according to Mrs Van Rijn, this is not clean – she suggests that you use the site's own small pool (10 x 5 m). There is a small bar in one of two former garages with an interesting painting of a tow truck on the wall – the site owners also operate a towing service for stranded Dutch and German drivers.

#### Facilities
One immaculate, modern toilet block has British style toilets, open washbasins and controllable, free showers. Facilities for disabled visitors. Laundry service at the owner's house. Outdoor pool (10 x 5 m). Excursions and activities organised. Bar with Dutch satellite TV.
Off site: Fishing and riding 2 km.

**Open:** Easter - 15 October.

#### Directions
Site is on the main 61 road running through town. Take exit just before the petrol station on the right on leaving Simontornya.
GPS: N46:45.454 E18:32.698

#### Charges guide
| | |
|---|---|
| Per unit incl. 2 persons and electricity | € 20,00 |
| child | € 3,00 - € 3,50 |

No credit cards. Prices in euros.

## HU5300 Kek-Duna Camping

Hösök Tere 23, H-7020 Dunafoldvar (Tolna County)

Tel: 755 411 07. Email: postmaster@camping_gyogyfurdo.axelero.net

Dunaföldvár is a most attractive town of 10,000 people and you are in the heart of it in just two or three minutes by foot from this site, easily reached via the wide towpath on the west bank of the Danube. For a town site, Kék-Duna is remarkably peaceful. Apart from the obvious attractions of the river, with a large island opposite and pleasant walks possible, the ancient town has a most interesting museum, the 'Burg', with a genuine dungeon and cells, Roman relics and with a panoramic view of the town and river from its top floor. There are in fact too many places of interest within easy reach to list here. This is a pleasant small site on the banks of the Danube, fenced all round and locked at night, with flat concrete access roads to 50 pitches. All have 16A electricity, the first half of the site being open, the remainder well shaded.

### Facilities

Modern, tiled sanitary building with nicely decorated ladies' section offers curtained showers with communal changing. The rest of the facilities are of above average standard. Dishwashing outside with cold water. Washing machine. Shop and café (from mid June), town shops close. Bicycle hire. Excursion information. German speaking receptionist. Off site: Tennis 50 m. Thermal swimming pool 200 m. (under the same ownership). Riding 5 km.

**Open:** All year.

### Directions

From the roundabout south of Dunafoldvar turn towards the town centre. At the traffic lights turn right and go down as far as the Danube then turn left, under the green bridge and follow the towpath about 300 m. to the site.

### Charges guide

| | |
|---|---|
| Per person | HUF 500,00 |
| pensioner, student or child | HUF 250,00 |
| caravan, car and electricity | HUF 1200,00 |
| motorcaravan and electricity | HUF 1100,00 |
| tent and car | HUF 550,00 |

---

# www.alanrogers.com

## Around 500 of Europe's finest campsites, all bookable at the click of a mouse.

- View 'at-the-gate' prices and availability
- Book as many or as few nights as you like
- Book direct - no middleman fees or 'extras'
- 24-hour convenience
- Pitches and mobile homes
- Secure on-line payment

All campsites are inspected & selected by Alan Rogers.

## Just Click and Go!

INSPECTED CAMPSITES & SELECTED

Check real time availability and at-the-gate prices...
www.alanrogers.com

# Slovakia

MAP 6

Slovakia is described as a small scale country at the heart of Europe, situated as a crossroads for European travellers and traders for centuries.

Slovakia has a lot to offer the visitor with an abundance of year round natural beauty. Its terrain varies impressively; the Carpathian Arc Mountains take up nearly half the country and include the Tatra Mountains, with their rugged peaks, deciduous forests and lakes. Southern and eastern Slovakia is mainly a lowland region and home to many thermal springs, with several open to the public for bathing. Over the years many Hungarians have moved to this area and there is a strong Hungarian influence.

Slovakia has over four thousand registered caves, twelve are open to the public and vary from drop stone to glacial; each one claims to have healing benefits for respiratory disorders. The capital, Bratislava is situated on the river Danube and directly below the Carpathian Mountains. Although it may not be as glamorous as Prague, it contains many fascinating buildings from nearly every age and is a lively cheerful city.

**Population**
5.4 million

**Capital**
Bratislava

**Climate**
Cold winters and mild summers. Hot summers and some rain in the eastern lowlands.

**Language**
Slovak

**Currency**
The Koruna

**Telephone**
The country code is 00 421

**Banks**
Mon-Fri 08.00-13.00 and 14.00-17.00.

**Shops**
Mon-Fri 09.00-12.00 and 14.00-18.00.
Some remain open at midday.
Sat 09.00-midday.

# Slovakia

SLOVAKIA CONSISTS OF A NARROW STRIP OF LAND BETWEEN THE SPECTACULAR TATRA MOUNTAINS AND THE RIVER DANUBE. IT IS PICTURESQUE AND BEAUTIFUL, WITH MANY HISTORIC CASTLES, EVERGREEN FORESTS, RUGGED MOUNTAINS, CAVE FORMATIONS, AND DEEP LAKES AND VALLEYS.

## Public Holidays

New Year; Easter Mon; May Day; Liberation Day 8 May; Saints Day 5 July; Festival Day 5 July; Constitution 1 Sept; All Saints 1 Nov; Christmas 24-26 Dec.

## Motoring

A full UK driving licence is acceptable. The major route runs from Bratislava via Trencin, Banska, Bystrica, Zilina and Poprad to Presov. A windscreen sticker which is valid for a year must be purchased at the border crossing for use on certain motorways. Vehicles must be parked on the right. Do not drink and drive, there is no permitted level of alcohol and police regularly carry out random breath checks.

## Tourist Office

Czech & Slovak Tourist Centre
16 Frognal Parade
Finchley Road
London NW3 5HG
Tel: 020 7794 3263/4
Fax: 020 7794 3265
E-mail: cztc@cztc.demon.co.uk
Internet: www.slovakiatourism.sk

## British Embassy

Panska 16
811 01 Bratislava
Tel: (421) (2) 5998 2000

## Places of interest

*Bratislava:* Municipal Museum, Museum of Wine Production, Slovak National Museum and National Gallery.

*Malá Fatra National Park:* Vrátna at the heart is a beautiful mountain valley surrounded by forested slopes, a popular ski resort in winter.

*Spissky hrad:* the largest castle in Slovakia.

*Vysoké Tatry:* one of the smallest high mountain ranges in the world, a network of 600 km of hiking trails, Stary Smokovec is the best centre for visitors.

## Cuisine of the region

A basic cuisine consisting of meat, dumplings, potatoes or rice topped with thick sauce, and a well cooked vegetable or sauerkraut. Commonly used ingredients are caraway seed, bacon and lots of salt.

# Slovakia

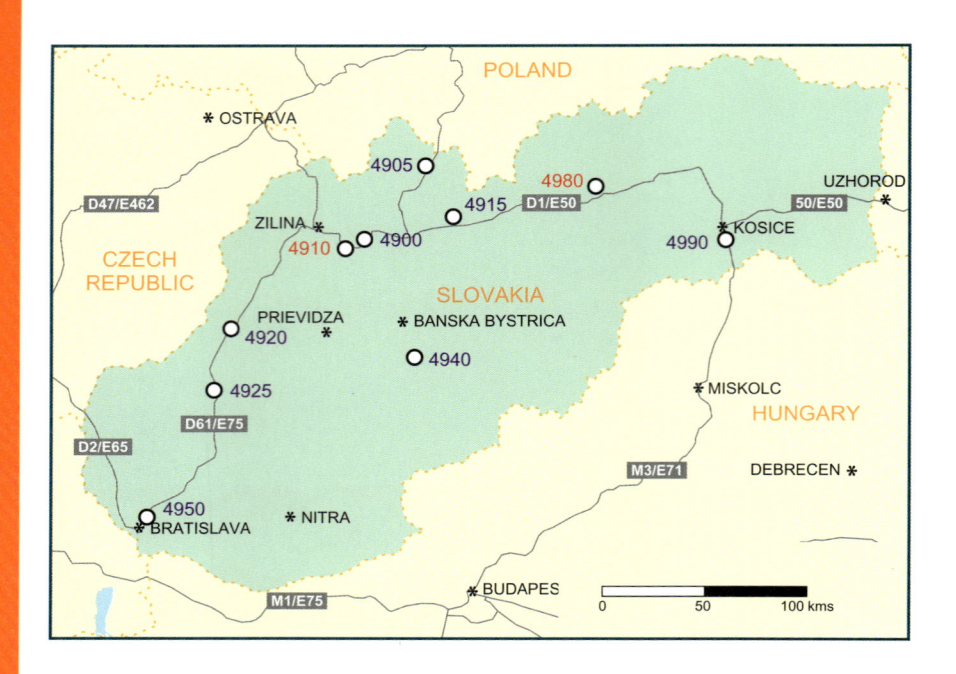

## SK4925 Camping Lodenica

Slnava 1, SK-92101 Piestany (Trnava)
Tel: 033 76 26 093

This site is 1.5 kilometres south of the most important spa in the Slovak Republic and lies in a quiet forest setting on the shores of the Sinava lake, close to the town of Piestany. The site is only four kilometres from the main motorway between Bratislava and Trencin and therefore useful as a night stop when travelling between Poland and Hungary or the Czech Republic. Lodenica is divided into three main camping areas with 250 pitches (150 with electricity), the first right behind the entrance and a large, circular field with pitching close to the electricity boxes. Pitches on the second field to the back are separated by low hedges and the third field is in the 'Arena' and surrounded by a wooden fence, rather like a fortress. Among the pitches are mature trees which provide shade. The lake offers numerous possibilities for watersports and in the town of Piestany are swimming pools, tennis courts, a fitness centre and some historic monuments. Right at the entrance of the site stands a welcoming and good value restaurant. Very disappointing at this site are the toilet blocks, which are old and need refurbishing.

### Facilities

One traditional toilet block with toilets, open style washbasins (cold water only) and hot showers. Laundry with 5 sinks. Campers' kitchen with gas hob and oven. Good value bar/restaurant. Playing field. Rowing boats, canoes and surfboards for hire at the lake. Waterskiing. Bicycle hire. Off site: Fishing and beach 200 m. Piestany town with shops, hot food, bars, indoor and outdoor pools 1.5 km. Riding 5 km.

**Open:** 1 May - 30 September.

### Directions

Take motorway form Bratislava towards Trencin and exit at Piestany. At first main junction turn right at traffic lights and go south. Turn left at the hospital towards site. GPS: N48:39.450 E17:49.442

### Charges 2007

| | |
|---|---|
| Per person | SKK 90,00 |
| child (5-14 yrs) | SKK 40,00 |
| pitch | SKK 120,00 |
| electricity | SKK 80,00 |
| dog | SKK 20,00 |

No credit cards.

## SK4950 Autocamping Zlaté Piesky

Senecka cesta c 2, SK-82104 Bratislava (Bratislava)
Tel: 024 445 0592. Email: kempi@netax.sk

Bratislava undoubtedly has charm, being on the Danube and having a number of interesting buildings and churches in its centre. However, industry around the city, particularly en-route to the camp from the south, presents an ugly picture and gives no hints of the hidden charms. Zlate Piesky (golden sands) is part of a large, lakeside sports complex which is also used during the day in summer by local residents. The site is on the northeast edge of the city with 200 touring pitches, 120 with electrical connections, on level grass under tall trees. Twenty well equipped and many more simple bungalows for hire are spread around the site. An attractive lakeside recreation area also has pedaloes for hire and fitness area in the park, plus water skiing/boarding where you are propelled by something akin to a ski lift. For a night stop or a short stay, this might suit.

### Facilities
Four toilet blocks, two for campers and two for day visitors, are good and clean. Two restaurants, one with waiter service, the other self service. Many small snack bars. Shops. Lake for swimming and watersports with large beach area. Table tennis. Minigolf. Play areas. Room with billiards and electronic games. Disco. Off site: Tesco supermarket nearby.

**Open:** 1 May - 15 October.

### Directions
From E75 Bratislava - Trencin motorway exit towards Zlate Piesky just north of the airport. Head towards Bratislava on the 61/E571 and immediately after the footbridge turn left at the traffic lights. The site is a little way ahead on the left.

### Charges 2007
| | |
|---|---|
| Per person | SKK 100,00 |
| child (4-15 yrs) | SKK 50,00 |
| pitch | SKK 110,00 - 160,00 |
| electricity | SKK 90,00 |
| dog | SKK 40,00 |

No credit cards.

---

## SK4920 Autocamping Trencin

Na Ostrove, P.O. Box 10, SK-91101 Trencin (Trencin)
Tel: 032 743 4013. Email: autocamping.tn@mail.pvt.sk

Trencin is an interesting town with a long history and dominated by the partly restored castle which towers high above. The small site with room for 30 touring units (all with electricity) and rooms to let, stands on an island about one kilometre from the town centre opposite a large sports complex. Pitches occupy a grass area surrounded by bungalows, although when the site is busy, campers park between and almost on top of the bungalows. The castle is high on one side and woods and hills on the other. There is some rail noise. This is a very neat, tidy friendly site with German spoken during our visit.

### Facilities
Toilet block is old but tiled and clean with hot water in the washbasins (in cabins with curtains) and showers (doors and curtains) under cover but not enclosed. Hot water for washing clothes and dishes. Electric cookers, fridge/freezer, tables and chairs. Little shade. Bar in high season. Boating and fishing in river. Off site: Restaurants 200 m. Shops 300 m. Tennis, indoor and outdoor swimming pools within 400 m.

**Open:** 1 May - 15 September.

### Directions
Initially you need to follow signs for 61 Zilina and having crossed the river, bear left. Turn left at first main traffic lights, under the railway and left again. Then turn right after the stadium. Site is over the canal, on the left. GPS: N48:52.996 E18:02.440

### Charges 2007
| | |
|---|---|
| Per person | SKK 170,00 - 200,00 |
| child (6-12 yrs) | SKK 100,00 |
| pitch | SKK 50,00 - 150,00 |
| electricity | SKK 100,00 |
| dog | SKK 30,00 |

No credit cards.

---

**Check real time availability and at-the-gate prices...**
www.alanrogers.com

*Slovakia*

## Slovakia

### SK4940 Autocamping Neresnica

Neresnická cesta, SK-96001 Zvolen (Banská Bystrica)
Tel: 045 533 2651

If you are travelling through Slovakia from Hungary to Poland and looking for a night stop or exploring the central Slovak area, Neresnica is well situated, being on the main 66/E77 highway just to the south of the town. There is inevitably some traffic noise but we did not notice this during our one night stay. The glories of Zvolen lie in the past rather than the present, but this basic but clean site, under private ownership, is surrounded by trees with a rushing steam along one side. The level site has room for 65 units with unmarked pitches of grass from tarmac roads and electrical connections (10A) for about 60%. Apart from Slovak, only German is spoken.

#### Facilities

Two sanitary blocks, one at either end of the camp, are basic rather than luxurious but clean with cold water in cabins for washing and hot water for washing dishes under cover. A few showers have been installed in former WC compartments, but they are at least 16 inches high and, if you are over 5 ft tall, you might have a problem. Still, it is remarkable what you can do with corrugated plastic and sheet metal! Special covered areas have barbecue pits with tables and benches. Restaurant (at entrance) has an extensive menu with good value meals and sometimes provides music from a violin, cello, zither trio. Off site: Shops 200 m. Swimming pool 200 m.

**Open:** 1 April - 20 October.

#### Directions

From Zvolen centre take road 66/E77 towards Sahy. Site is signed as Neresnica and/or Camping Salas at junction with 50/E571 road to Lucenec. The site is on the left just beyond the Slovnaft petrol station.
GPS: N48:33.868 E19:08.049

#### Charges 2007

| | |
|---|---|
| Per person | SKK 100,00 |
| child (10-18 yrs) | SKK 50,00 |
| pitch | SKK 90,00 - 120,00 |
| electricity | SKK 65,00 |

---

### SK4900 Autocamping Trusalová

SK-03853 Turany (Zilina)
Tel: 043 4292 636. Email: autocampingtrusalova@zoznam.sk

Autocamping Trusalová is situated right on the southern edge of the Malá Fatra National Park, northeast of the historic town of Martin which has much to offer to tourists. The town is perhaps best known for the engineering works which produced most of the tanks for the Warsaw Pact countries, but is now the home of Volkswagen Slovakia. Paths from the site lead into the Park making it an ideal base for walkers and serious hikers who wish to enjoy this lovely region. The site is in two halves, one on the left of the entrance and the other behind reception on a slight slope. Surrounded by trees with a stream rushing along one side, pitches are grass from a hard road with room for about 150 units and there are some bungalows. Information on the area is available from reception. We received a most friendly welcome from the German speaking staff. A quiet, orderly and pleasant campsite.

#### Facilities

Each half has its own old, but clean and acceptable, toilet provision including hot water in basins, sinks and showers. Motorcaravan service point. Each section has a covered barbecue area with raised fire box, chimney, tables and chairs. Volleyball. Table tennis. TV lounge. Playground. Outdoor chess board. Bicycle hire. Off site: Bar just outside site. Restaurants 500 m. or 1 km. Shops in the village 3 km.

**Open:** 1 June - 15 September.

#### Directions

Turn north between the Auto Alles car dealer and the Restaurica of the same name on road no. 18/E50 near the village of Turany to campsite.
GPS: N49:08.300 E19:03.000

#### Charges 2008

| | |
|---|---|
| Per person | SKK 100,00 |
| pitch | SKK 100,00 - 170,00 |
| electricity | SKK 100,00 |

No credit cards.

---

Check real time availability and at-the-gate prices...
www.alanrogers.com

## SK4905 Autocamping Stara Hora

Oravska Priehrada, SK-02901 Namestovo (Zilina)
Tel: 043 55 22 223. Email: camp.s.hora@stonline.sk

Stara Hora has a beautiful location on the Orava artificial lake. It is in the northeast of Slovakia in the Tatra Mountains and attracts visitors from all over Europe which creates a happy and sometimes noisy atmosphere. The site has its own pebble beach with a large grass area behind it for sunbathing. The lake provides opportunities for fishing, boating and sailing and the area is good for hiking and cycling and in winter, it is a popular skiing area. Autocamping Stara Hora is on steeply sloping ground with 160 grassy pitches, all for touring units and with 10A electricity. The lower pitches are level and have good views over the lake, pitches at the top are mainly used by tents.

### Facilities
The modern toilet block has British style toilets, open washbasins and controllable hot showers (free). It could be pressed in high season and hot water to the showers is only available from 07.00-10.00 and 19.00-22.00. Shop for basics. Bar and lakeside bar. Small restaurant. Basic playground (new playground planned). Pedalo, canoe and rowing boat hire. Waterskiing. Fishing (with permit). Torch useful. Off site: Slanica Island.

**Open:** May - September.

### Directions
From Ruzomberok take E77 road north towards Trstena. Turn left in Tvrdosin on the 520 road towards Námestovo. Site is on the right.
GPS: N49:23.135 E19:31.657

### Charges 2007
| | |
|---|---|
| Per person | € 2,42 |
| child | € 1,21 |
| pitch incl. electricity | € 5,75 |

Prices in Euros.

## SK4910 Autocamping Turiec

Kolonia hviezda 92, SK-03608 Martin (Zilina)
Tel: 043 428 4215. Email: recepcia@autocampingturiec.sk

Turiec is situated in northeast Slovakia, 1.5 km. from the small village of Vrutky, 4 km. north of Martin, at the foot of the Lucanska Mala Fatra mountains and with castles nearby. This good site has views towards the mountains and is quiet and well maintained. Holiday activities include hiking in summer, skiing in winter, both downhill and cross-country. There is room for about 30 units on grass inside a circular tarmac road with some shade from tall trees. Electrical connections are available for all places. A wooden chalet by the side of the camping area has a TV rest room and a small games room. You will receive a friendly welcome from Viktor Matovcik and his wife Lydia who are constantly improving the site.

### Facilities
One acceptable sanitary block to the side of the camping area, but in winter the facilities in the bungalow at the entrance are used. Cooking facilities. Restaurant/snack bar in summer. Badminton. Volleyball. Swimming pool 1.5 km. Rest room with TV. Small games room. Covered barbecue. Off site: Shop outside entrance.

**Open:** All year.

### Directions
Site is signed from E18 road (Zilina - Martin) in the village of Vrutky, 3 km. northwest of Martin. Turn south on the bend and follow signs to Martinské Hole.

### Charges 2007
| | |
|---|---|
| Per unit incl. 2 persons and electricity | SKK 430,00 |

## SK4980 Autocamping Levocská Dolina

Kovásvá vila 2, SK-05401 Levoca (Presov)
Tel: 053 451 2701. Email: rzlevoca@pobox.sk

According to the owner, Mr Rusnák, this campsite is one of the top ten sites in Slovakia and we agree. The site forms part of a restaurant and pension business and the good value restaurant is welcoming. The entrance is attractively landscaped with varieties of shrubs and colourful flowers and the whole site looks well cared for. There are 60 pitches (all for tourers) and 27 electricity connections. On grassy fields with views of the mountains, there is some terracing. The main road runs steeply uphill and then continues on grass roads. This may cause larger units some difficulty in bad weather. This is a good base from which to explore the Tatra Mountains or visit the Ice Caves.

### Facilities
Well renovated toilet block with British style toilets, open washbasins and controllable, hot showers (free). Campers' kitchen. Sauna. Whirlpool. Bar/restaurant. Basic playground. Torch useful. Off site: Lake with pedalo hire 300 m. Dobsinska Ice Caves and Slovakian Paradise. Town of Levoca.

**Open:** All year.

### Directions
From Liptovsky Mikulás, take E50 road east towards Levoca. In Levoca follow site signs. Site is 3 km. north of the town. GPS: N49:02.939 E20:35.210

### Charges 2007
| | |
|---|---|
| Per person | SKK 85,00 |
| child | SKK 45,00 |
| pitch | SKK 40,00 - 150,00 |

# Slovakia

## SK4915 Autocamping Liptovsky Trnovec

SK-03222 Liptovsky Trnovec (Zilina)
Tel: 044 55 98 458. Email: atc.trnovec@atctrnouec.sk

This is a good Slovakian site beside the Liptovská Mara reservoir, also close to the Tatra Mountains which are popular for climbing, hiking and mountain biking. The lake can be used for sailing, surfing, boating and pedaloes and some of this equipment may be rented on the site. Bicycles are also available for hire. The site is close to the historic cities of Liptovsky Mikulás (6 km), Vlkolinec (on the UNESCO World Heritage list) and Pribylina. There are 250 pitches, all used for touring units and with 14A electricity. With tarmac access roads, the level pitches are on a circular, grassy field and as pitching is rather haphazard, the site can become crowded in high season. Mature trees provide some shade, but in general this is an open site. There are several bars with snack and takeaway services on site with a restaurant nearby (300 m).

### Facilities

Two good modern toilet blocks have British style toilets, washbasins in cabins and showers. Facilities for disabled visitors. Washing machines. Campers' kitchen. Bar with covered terrace and takeaway service. Basic playground. Minigolf. Fishing. Bicycle hire. Basketball. Volleyball. Canoe hire and boat rental. Games room with arcade machines. Beach. Off site: New Tatralandia Aqua Park nearby. Walking in the Lower Tatra Mountains, or rock climbing in the Higher Tatra Mountains.

**Open:** 1 May - 15 October.

### Directions

From E50 road take exit for Liptovsky Mikulás and turn left towards Liptovsky Trnovec on 584 road. Continue alongside the lake to site on the left. GPS: N49:06.668 E19:37.767

### Charges 2007

| | |
|---|---|
| Per person | SKK 70,00 - 110,00 |
| child (4-15 yrs) | SKK 25,00 - 60,00 |
| pitch incl. car | SKK 105,00 - 220,00 |

---

## SK4990 Autocamping Salas Barca

Alejova ul, SK-04001 Kosice (Kosice)
Tel: 055 623 3397. Email: kulik.stk@napri.sk

Salas Barca is close to the motorway that connects the E571 and the E71 south towards Hungary. It is therefore a useful site when travelling this way and would also provide the opportunity to visit the historic town of Kosice. There are 60 pitches on two large, well kept grassy lawns arranged amongst 12 rental cabins. Pitching is rather haphazard as the places are not marked or numbered but there is some shade from mature trees. Good value meals are available at the site's bar/restaurant. From here it is an easy 1 km. drive to a large shopping centre and it is possible to visit the historic inner city by public transport. Some English is spoken.

### Facilities

Basic facilities with British style toilets, open washbasins and controllable hot showers (free). Basic kitchen also used for dishwashing. Basketball. Bar/restaurant. Off site: Centre of Kosice close. Shopping centre 1 km.

**Open:** 15 May - 15 October.

### Directions

Site is well signed south of Kosice on the connecting road between the E571 running southwest from Kosice and the E71 running south. Site is in the Barca area. GPS: N48:41.261 E21:15.370

### Charges 2007

| | |
|---|---|
| Per person | SKK 80,00 |
| child | SKK 40,00 |
| pitch incl. car | SKK 140,00 - 180,00 |
| electricity | SKK 60,00 |

---

Check real time availability and at-the-gate prices...
www.alanrogers.com

# Paying too much for your mobile home holiday?

**NEW** EXTENDED MID-SEASON DATES AVAILABLE

## Pay from Just £24.75 per night with Holiday Cheque

Holiday Cheque gives you exclusive access to quality mobile homes and chalets on over 100 of Europe's finest campsites - in off peak periods and now closer to high season dates too. You'll find superb family facilities, including sensational pools, great value restaurants, friendly bars and real hospitality. And the kids can have the time of their lives!

**All from just £24.75 per night.**

### HUGE SAVINGS - BUT HURRY

HOLIDAY CHEQUES ARE PRICED AT A SPECIAL PROMOTIONAL RATE, SAVING UP TO 50% OFF CAMPSITE'S STANDARD PRICES. BUT IT'S FIRST COME, FIRST SERVED.

# HOLIDAY CHEQUE

- Over 100 top campsites
- From just £24.75 per night
- High quality mobile homes
- Luxury high specification chalets
- Fully equipped - down to the corkscrew!
- Plus unbeatable ferry prices

Call today for your **FREE** brochure
**01580 214114**

IT WILL SAVE YOU £££'S ON YOUR HOLIDAY

www.**holidaycheque**.co.uk

# Czech Republic

MAP 7

Try the locally produced beer and wine. Pilsen, is the home of Pils, and brewery tours are available.

Although small, the Czech Republic is crammed with attractive places to explore. Indeed, since the new country first appeared on the map in 1993, Prague has become one the most popular cities to visit in Europe. Steeped in history with museums, architectural sights, art galleries, and theatres, it is an enchanting place. The beautiful region of Bohemia, known for its Giant Mountains, is popular for skiing, hiking and other sports. The town of Karlovy Vary, world famous for its regenerative waters, is Bohemia's oldest Spa town, with 12 hot springs containing elements that are said to treat digestive and metabolic ailments. It also has many picturesque streets to meander through and peaceful riverside walks. Moravia is quieter, the most favoured area is Brno and from here it is easy to explore historical towns such as Olomouc and Kromeriz. North of Brno is the Moravian Karst, with around 400 caves created by the underground Punkya River. Some caves are open to the public, and boat trips are available along the river and out of the caves.

**Population**
10.3 million

**Capital**
Prague

**Climate**
Temperate, continental climate with four distinct seasons. Warm in summer with cold, snowy winters.

**Language**
The official language is Czech

**Currency**
The Koruna

**Telephone**
The country code is 00 420

**Banks**
Mon-Fri 08.30-16.30

**Shops**
Mon-Fri 08.00-18.00, some close at lunchtime. Sat 09.00 until midday.

# Czech Republic

THE CZECH REPUBLIC IS A LAND FULL OF FASCINATING CASTLES, ROMANTIC LAKES AND VALLEYS, PICTURESQUE MEDIEVAL SQUARES AND FAMOUS SPAS. IT IS DIVIDED INTO TWO MAIN REGIONS, BOHEMIA TO THE WEST AND MORAVIA IN THE EAST.

## Public Holidays

New Year; Easter Mon; May Day; Prague Uprising 5 May; National Day 8 May; Saints Day 5 July; Festival Day 6 July; Independence Day 28 Oct; Democracy Day 17 Nov; Christmas 24-26 Dec.

## Motoring

There is a good and well signposted road network throughout the Republic and, although stretches of cobbles still exist, surfaces are generally good. An annual road tax is levied on all vehicles using Czech motorways and express roads, and a disc can be purchased at border crossings, post offices and filling stations. Do not drink any alcohol before driving. Dipped headlights are compulsory throughout the winter months. Always give way to trams and buses.

## Tourist Office

Czech Tourism
13 Harley Street,
London W1G 9QG
Tel. 0207 631 0427  Fax. 0207 631 0419
Email: info-uk@czechtourism.com
Internet: www.czechtourism.org

## British Embassy

Thunovska 14
118 00 Prague 1
Tel: (420) 257 402 111

## Places of interest

*Karlovy Vary:* the oldest of the Bohemian Spas, famous for its regenerative waters.

*Krivoklat:* late 13th century castle. If you are feeling energetic there is an 18 km trail up the Berounka valley to Skryje.

*Prague:* a compact medieval centre with a maze of cobbled lanes, ancient courtyards, churches and its 1100-year-old castle.

*Moravian Karst:* picture-postcard views, wooded hills, canyons and caves.

*Moravské Slovácko Region:* lively and full of traditional folk culture.

## Cuisine of the region

Basically central European, with German, Hungarian and Polish influences. Lots of meat with dumplings, potatoes or rice topped with thick sauce and a heavily cooked vegetable or sauerkraut. Commonly used ingredients are caraway seed, bacon and lots of salt.

*Knedlo-zelovepro:* the standard quick meal consisting of dumplings, sauerkraut and roast pork.

115

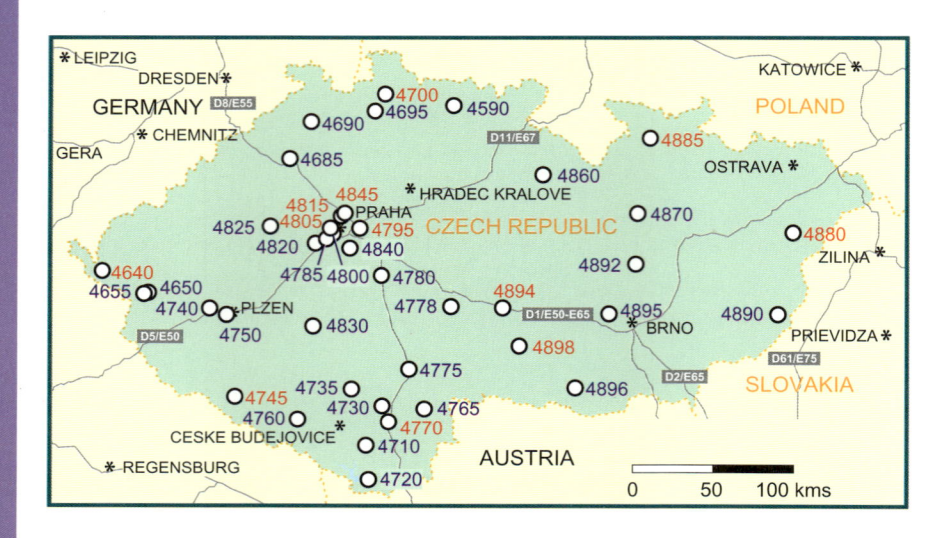

# Czech Republic

### CZ4650 Autocamping Luxor

Plzenska, CZ-35301 Velká Hledsebe (Zapadocesky)

Tel: 354 623 504. Email: autocamping.luxor@seznam.cz

An orderly site, near the German border, Luxor is adequate as a stopover for a couple of days. Now under new management, it is in a quiet location by a small lake on the edge of the village of Velká Hledsebe, 4 km. from Marianbad. The 100 pitches (60 for touring units) are in the open on one side of the entrance road (cars stand on a tarmac park opposite the caravans) or in a clearing under tall trees away from the road. All pitches have access to electricity (10A) but connection in the clearings section may require long leads. Forty bungalows occupy one side of the site. There is little to do here but it is a good location for visiting the spa town of Marianbad.

#### Facilities

Toilet buildings are old and should be refurbished, but the provision is more than adequate. Cleaning could be better. No chemical disposal point. Restaurant with self-service terrace (1/5-30/9). Rest room with TV, kitchen and dining area. Small playground. Fishing. Bicycle hire. Off site: Very good motel restaurant and shops 500 m. in village. Riding 5 km. Golf 8 km.

Open: 1 May - 30 September.

#### Directions

Site is directly by the Stribo - Cheb road (no. 21), 500 m. south of Velká Hledsebe.
GPS: N49:57.145 E12:40.100

#### Charges 2007

| | |
|---|---|
| Per unit incl. 2 persons and electricity | CZK 160,00 - 250,00 |
| extra person | CZK 60,00 |
| child (under 10 yrs) | CZK 40,00 |

No credit cards.

Check real time availability and at-the-gate prices...
www.alanrogers.com

## CZ4640 Autocamping Areal Jadran

Jezerni 84/12, CZ-35101 Frantiskovy Lazne (Zapadocesky)
Tel: **354 542 412**. Email: **atc.jadran@centrum.cz**

Autocamping Jadran is on the outskirts of the spa town Frantiskovy Lázné and is the perfect base to visit the many restored spa baths and tour the beautiful West Bohemian countryside. Marie Novotny with her husband Jiri, owner of the site, welcomed us warmly and are busy making many improvements. During 2005 40 new 'super' pitches were under construction out of a planned total of 90. There are 180 pitches for tourers, all with 16A electricity, and the site has its own lake for cooling down in the hot summer months. The pitches are partly shaded and some are of at least 120 sq.m. Adjacent to the site is Hotel Jadran which serves fine meals for very reasonable prices and has a pleasant bar.

### Facilities
The heated toilet blocks (two older, one refurbished) are simple, but are clean and tidy. They include toilets, washbasins with hot and cold water, controllable showers. Washing machines and sinks with free hot water. Restaurant (1/4-31/10). No shop but fresh bread available every morning in the restaurant. Giant chess, draughts and other games. Russian bowling. Volleyball. Fishing. Riding. Bicycle hire. Inflatables allowed in the lake. Off site: Riding 400 m. Fishing 6 km.

**Open:** All year.

### Directions
Frantiskovy Lazne is north of Cheb. Stay on the no. 21 road to the north of route 6 and leave by the first slip road to the village. Turn sharp left at the Hotel Bohemia and then right. Follow the lakeside road for 2 km. and then turn right to the site.
GPS: N50:07.022 E12:19.801

### Charges 2007
| | |
|---|---|
| Per person | € 4,10 |
| child (3-12 yrs) | € 2,10 |
| pitch incl. electricity | € 4,10 - € 6,20 |

Less 10% for stays over 7 days or repeat visits.
Camping Cheques accepted. Prices in Euros.

---

## CZ4740 Transkemp Hracholusky

Lodnt Doprava, Hracholusky 139, CZ-33023 Nyrany (Zapadocesky)
Tel: **377 914 113**. Email: **info@hracholusky.com**

Set beside the River Mzi where the Hracholusky dam has created a wide basin, this site enjoys a quiet location adjacent to an hotel amidst gentle hills and pleasant trees. The 200 pitches here are spread along three terraces looking over the water with 120 having electrical connections (6/10A). Two kiosks dispense drinks and basic supplies. There is swimming, boating and water skiing on the lake and, during high season, a steamer makes 40 km. round trips along the river. This is a pleasant site but the presence of a large car park at the entrance may mean that it becomes crowded with day visitors in the summer. A new building houses rooms to rent and a sauna, with a new minigolf course.

### Facilities
The large, single sanitary block also contains a rest room with TV, kitchen with electric rings and fridges. All was neat and clean when visited. Washing machines, dryers and irons. Bar and shop (1/1-15/9). Takeaway (1/3-1/10). Watersports. Swimming. Table tennis. Boat trips. Fishing. Off site: Riding 5 km.

**Open:** 1 March - 31 December.

### Directions
Take the E50/605 road west from Plzen (Pilsen). After Kozolupy turn right to Nord Jezna. 2 km. east of Ulice. Follow site signs from here.
GPS: N49:47.456 E13:10.106

### Charges 2007
| | |
|---|---|
| Per person | CZK 35,00 - 50,00 |
| child (6-15 yrs) | CZK 20,00 - 35,00 |
| pitch | CZK 120,00 - 150,00 |
| electricity | CZK 80,00 |

Less 10% for stays over 30 days. No credit cards.

---

Check real time availability and at-the-gate prices...
www.alanrogers.com

## CZ4655 Camping Stanowitz

Stanoviste 9, CZ-35301 Mariánské Lázne (Zapadocesky)
Tel: 354 624 673. Email: info@stanowitz.com

The town of Mariánské Lázne (better known among westerners as Marienbad) is an old-style health resort in the heart of Western Bohemia, a region full of historical and natural beauty. However, this is not the only reason to stay at Camping Stanowitz. This comfortable, family-sized campsite has only 35 pitches on a slightly sloping, unmarked field. There are electricity connections and water taps. Drainage is good. Toilet facilities are in a wing of the main building and are clean and modern. The owner makes a real effort to show off his beautiful country to interested visitors and probably has more brochures than the average tourist office. Attached to the site is a pension and restaurant.

### Facilities
Completely refurbished, fully equipped and modern toilet block. Washing machine. Internet. Off site: Basic groceries can be found in the village or in town (3.5 km). Activities nearby include walking, biking, golf.

**Open:** 1 April - 1 November.

### Directions
Site is in the hills of Stanoviste village just to the southeast of Mariánské Lázne (Marienbad), accessible from road 230 running between Becov nad Teplou/Karlovy Vary and Planá/Plzen. Site is signed.

### Charges 2007
| | |
|---|---|
| Per unit with 2 persons and electricity | € 12,70 |
| extra person | € 3,00 |
| child (3-14 yrs) | € 1,50 |

No credit cards. Prices in Euros.

## CZ4745 Camping U Dvou Orechu

SPLZ 13 Strazov, CZ-34021 Janovice (Zapadocesky)
Tel: 376 382 421. Email: info@camping-tsjechie.nl

At an altitude of 1,700 feet, this small quiet site sits in the centre of a beautiful, green valley. The only sound is from the birds and the campsite terraces enjoy excellent views in all directions. The Dutch owners, Hans and Freda Neuteboom, are painstakingly developing the site to the highest possible standards and it is clearly one of the best in the Czech Republic. There are 35 large grass pitches, all with 6 or 10A electricity. Some are terraced next to the owners' house. There are ample opportunities for walking and cycling or just watching the rural scene change as the day progresses.

### Facilities
The sanitary facilities provide excellent showers and toilets. Chemical toilet emptying facilities. Washing machine and spin dryer plus 2 sinks and hot water for dishwashing. Bar. Off site: Winter skiing 30 km. Swimming 3 km.

**Open:** All year.

### Directions
From Klatovy go south on the 27 to Besiny and turn right towards Strazov. Continue on the road towards Desenice/Depoltice for 3 km. then turn left in the direction of Splz/Hajek. The site is alongside the first house on the left. GPS: N49:16.906 E13:14.402

### Charges 2007
| | |
|---|---|
| Per person | CZK 90,00 |
| pitch | CZK 65,00 - 105,00 |
| electricity | CZK 90,00 - 150,00 |

## CZ4750 Camping Bilá Hora

Ul. 28.rijna 49, CZ-30162 Plzen (Zapadocesky)
Tel: 377 562 225

Even non-drinkers probably know that Pilsen is famous for its beer (Pils) and as the home of the Skoda car factory. Traffic in the town centre is heavy so, if you wish to visit the city where beer has been brewed since 1295, find the campsite and use the bus. Visits to the brewery may be arranged. Camping Bilá Hora is a suitable site and is situated amidst trees in the suburb of Bilá Hora, about three kilometres north of the city centre on the edge of town. The 50 pitches are on a slope in a clearing, but level concrete tracks have been made for caravans and motorcaravans, with electricity available at 30 pitches. It is a pleasant, quiet site with its own restaurant.

### Facilities
The toilet block in the camping area has British style WCs, bath and a laundry, and there is another with the bungalows - they are good by Czech standards. Washing machine and iron. Motorcaravan services. Kitchen. Restaurant. Kiosk with small terrace. Bicycle hire. Table tennis. Playground. Volleyball. Off site: Shops 200 m. Fishing 500 m. Swimming nearby. Bus stop at entrance.

**Open:** 15 May - 30 September.

### Directions
Site is to the north of the town on the Plzen(Pilsen) - Zruc no. 231 road where it is signed. GPS: N49:46.719 E13:24.548

### Charges guide
| | |
|---|---|
| Per person | CZK 50,00 |
| child (10-15 yrs) | CZK 70,00 |
| pitch | CZK 2150,00 |
| electricity | CZK 70,00 |

### CZ4785 **Camp Drusus**

K Reporyjim 4, CZ-15500 Praha 5 - Trebonice (Prague)
Tel: 235 514 391. Email: drusus@drusus.com

Camp Drusus is a friendly, family site on the western edge of Prague. It provides a good base from which to explore this beautiful city with the metro station only 15 minutes walk away. The site has 70 level pitches (all for tourers), 66 with 10A electricity and varying in size (60-90 sq.m), with access off a circular, grass and gravel road. There is no shop here but basics can be ordered at reception and one of the biggest shopping areas in Prague is only 2 km. You could enjoy a real Czech breakfast in the restaurant which also opens for dinner and serves as a bar. This is a pleasant, well kept and quiet site with good connections to the Czech capital.

#### Facilities

Portacabin style toilet facilities that look basic but are clean, contain British style toilets, open washbasins and free, controllable hot showers. Laundry with sinks, two washing machines and dryer. Kitchen. Dishwashing. Motorcaravan service point. No shop, but basics to order at reception. Bar/restaurant. Small fitness centre. Volleyball and basketball. Playground. Games room with billiards. Off site: Shops 2 km. Metro station for Prague 15 minutes. Golf 12 km. Riding 10 km.

**Open:** 15 April - 15 October.

#### Directions

On E50/E48 from Pilsen to Brno take exit 19 for Reporyje, from Brno to Pilsen take exit 23a. In the centre turn left on K Trebonicum to site on the right. GPS: N50:02.645 E14:17.053

#### Charges 2007

| | |
|---|---|
| Per person | CZK 100,00 - 120,00 |
| child (6-14 yrs) | CZK 50,00 - 60,00 |
| pitch with electricity | CZK 150,00 - 290,00 |
| electricity | CZK 90,00 |

---

### CZ4800 **Caravancamp Prague**

Plzenská 279, CZ-15000 Praha (Prague)
Tel: 257 213 080

Caravancamp is on sloping ground with some terracing in a quiet location about 8 km. from the centre of Prague. With 200 pitches, electricity is available for most caravan places but the grass pitches are neither numbered nor marked out and the site may become crowded in high season. There are hard access roads but with the high turnover of visitors the pitches may be a bit muddy. It is a pleasant situation with trees and a hill on one side and some shade in parts. Caravancamp is a simple site suitable for a couple of days to visit Prague. However, charges are expensive.

#### Facilities

The toilet blocks are satisfactory. Bar (1/4-31/10). Tennis. Minigolf. Off site: Shops 200 m. Golf 3 km. Riding 10 km. Bicycle hire 1 km.

**Open:** 1 April - 31 October.

#### Directions

Site is well signed on main highway from Pilsen, road no. 5/E50, near Hotel Golf.
GPS: N50:04.025 E14:20.828

#### Charges guide

| | |
|---|---|
| Per person | € 5,00 - € 5,50 |
| child (6-12 yrs) | € 2,50 |
| dog | € 1,50 |
| pitch | € 6,50 - € 10,00 |
| electricity | € 2,00 |

No credit cards. Prices in Euros.

## Czech Republic

### CZ4795 Cisarska Louka Caravan Park

Cisarska Louka 599, CZ-15000 Praha 5 (Prague)
Tel: 257 318 681. Email: convoy@volny.cz

This city site on the Cisarská Louka Island is about the closest campsite you can get to the centre of Prague. Right behind the site, which is on the premises of the local Yacht Club, a ferry takes you across the Moldau River to the nearest metro station for the city centre (hourly until 22.00). This is a useful site for a visit to Prague if you can cope with the basic toilet facilities. The site is arranged on one large, well fenced field providing 50 touring pitches, 25 with electricity (10A). Pitching is rather haphazard off a gravel access road running half way up the site. Some pitches have views over the river and all have views of the attractive church on the opposite side of the water. Scattered around the site, mature trees provide useful shade after a hot day in the city. Close to the site (100 and 300 m.) are two restaurants for breakfast, lunch, dinner and drinks and in front of the site a taxi boat will take you to the centre (CZK 50 per person with a minimum of six persons per trip).

#### Facilities

Basic toilet facilities with British style toilets, open washbasins and controllable hot showers (on payment). Facilities for disabled people. Dishwashing. Motorcaravan service point that also services as chemical disposal. River fishing. Boat launching. Off site: Two bar/restaurants close.

**Open:** All year.

#### Directions

Coming in from the west on the E50 continue alongside the river towards the town centre. Take a sharp right bend just before Shell petrol station. Site is the second site on the Cisacská Louka Island in the Moldau River. GPS: N50:03.745 E14:24.333

#### Charges 2007

| | |
|---|---|
| Per person | CZK 95,00 |
| child (0-15 yrs) | CZK 50,00 |
| pitch incl. electricity | CZK 265,00 - 325,00 |
| dog | CZK 50,00 |

---

### CZ4805 Camp Dzban Praha

Nad Lavkou 5, CZ-16000 Praha (Prague)
Tel: 235 358 554. Email: skaritma@mbox.vol.cz

Dzbán is close to the centre of Prague, the site is only 200 m. from one of the lakes in Prague and when you return tired after a hot day in the city centre, it is good to come back to its refreshing beaches. There are 150 numbered touring pitches here, all of which have electricity, on level, grassy fields plus some concrete hardstandings. Off paved access roads, the pitches are separated by young trees and in summer there is not much shade. This is a large, rather anonymous site but facilities are functional. A sports centre is nearby with tennis courts, football and a fully equipped fitness centre. Behind the site is a golf practice course.

#### Facilities

Rather basic toilet block with British style toilets, open washbasins and open style, pre-set showers. Washing machine. Kitchen. Motorcaravan service point. Basic shop. Bar/restaurant. Off site: Lake with beach. Golf practice course and sports centre 200 m.

**Open:** All year.

#### Directions

Coming from the northeast on R7 'Europska' road, pass the lake and turn left at OMV petrol station. Site is signed with small camp signs. Follow the road past the sports complex to the start of the lake. GPS: N50:05.918 E14:20.182

#### Charges 2007

| | |
|---|---|
| Per person | CZK 135,00 |
| child (3-12 yrs) | CZK 80,00 |
| pitch incl. car | CZK 230,00 - 280,00 |
| electricity | CZK 90,00 |

---

It's all about YOU and YOUR experiences...
So get involved today!
Visit www.mycamping.info

mycamping.info

Check real time availability and at-the-gate prices...
www.alanrogers.com

## CZ4840 Camping Oase Praha

Zlatniky-Liben, CZ-25241 Dolni Brezany (Prague)

Tel: **241 932 044**. Email: **info@campingoase.cz**

Camping Oase Praha is an exceptional site, only five kilometres from Prague and with easy access. You can take the bus (from outside the site) or drive to the underground stop (10 minutes). The site has 110 pitches, all around 100 sq.m, with 6A electricity and 55 with water and drainage, on level, well kept fields. The site is very well kept and has just everything one may expect, including a new Western style toilet block, a well maintained, heated swimming pool and separate paddling pool, a restaurant and a bar. Children can amuse themselves with trampolines, the new playground or volleyball and basketball. The main attraction here is, of course, the Czech capital. However, this site will provide a relaxing environment to return to and another advantage is that Mr Hess, the helpful owner, speaks English.

### Facilities

An outstanding, new toilet block includes washbasins (open style and in cabins) with hot and cold water, spacious, controllable showers and child size toilets. Facilities for disabled visitors. Laundry with washing machines and dryer. Campers kitchen with hob, fridge and freezer. Motorcaravan services. Restaurant and bar. Basic groceries are available in the shop. Swimming pool (9 x 15 m) and separate paddling pool with slide (both 15/5-20/9). New adventure style playgrounds. Minigolf. Internet point and WiFi. TV and video. Board games. Bicycle hire. Closed circuit security cameras. Barbecues are permitted. Off site: Fishing 2 km. Riding 3 km. Golf 10 km. Boat launching 15 km.

**Open:** 20 April - 20 September.

### Directions

Go southeast from Prague on the D1 towards Brno and take exit 11 to Jesenice via road 101. At Jesenice turn right then immediately left, following camping signs to the site in Zlatniky where you turn left at the roundabout. Site is 700 m. after the village. GPS: N49:57.087 E14:28.510

### Charges 2008

| | |
|---|---|
| Per person | CZK 120,00 |
| child (under 12 yrs) | CZK 90,00 |

Less 20% discount 15/4-31/5 and 1/9-30/9.
Less 3% discount for payment in cash.

Camping Cheques accepted.

## CZ4815 Triocamp Praha

Ustecka Ul, CZ-18400 Praha (Prague)

Tel: **283 850 795**. Email: **triocamp.praha@telecom.cz**

This site on the northern edge of Prague is a great place to stay for a few days to visit the city. It has 70 pitches (all for tourers) with 6/15A electricity. Most are in the shade of mature trees, which can be very welcoming after a hard day sightseeing. The ground is slightly sloping but most pitches are level and access is off one circular, tarmac road, with cabins and pitches on both sides. There is one hardstanding for a motorcaravan. Triocamp has a bar/restaurant with a comprehensive menu and covered terrace attractively decorated with a variety of flowers. Toilet facilities are in good order and comfortable. Bus tickets can be purchased at the site including bus tours through the city or for a boat excursion on the Moldau River.

### Facilities

Modern, comfortable toilet facilities provide British style toilets, open washbasins and free, pre-set hot showers. Facilities for disabled people. Laundry with washing machine. Motorcaravan services. Shop. Attractive bar/restaurant. Play area and children's pool. Off site: Prague is a few kilometres by public transport.

**Open:** All year.

### Directions

On E55 in either direction, take exit 1 towards Zdiby and continue straight ahead on 608 road. Site is on right after about 3 km. GPS: N50:09.137 E14:27.019

### Charges 2007

| | |
|---|---|
| Per person | CZK 140,00 - 180,00 |
| electricity | CZK 90,00 |
| dog | free - CZK 80,00 |

Czech Republic

Check real time availability and at-the-gate prices...
www.alanrogers.com

## Czech Republic

### CZ4845 Camping Busek Praha

U parku 6, CZ-18200 Praha 8 - Brezineves (Prague)

Tel: **283 910 254**. Email: **campbusekprag@volny.cz**

No trip to the Czech Republic would be complete without a visit to the capital, Prague. At this site you can do just that without getting tangled up with the city traffic. Just about 8 km. from the centre, there is an excellent bus link from the site to the new metro station at Ladvi that is a part of the new integrated transport system. For CZK 20 (50p) and in 40 minutes you can be in the heart of Prague, without the normal hassle, free to enjoy everything this vibrant city has to offer. The site is part of a small motel complex and provides 20 level and unnumbered pitches, all with 10A electricity. It is on the edge of a small, rural village, which offers peace and quiet at the end of a long day's sightseeing; what more could you want!

#### Facilities

Modern sanitary block with clean toilets, hot showers and washbasins. Washing machine and dryer. Chemical disposal point. Kitchen and dishwashing facilities. Small restaurant (all year). Off site: Prague city centre only a bus and metro ride away. Outdoor swimming pool.

**Open:** All year.

#### Directions

From the Prague - Teplice (Dresden) motorway, the D8/E55, take exit to Brezineves and head towards the village. The site is before the village on the right. Turn towards the small fire station and the site is on the right. GPS: N50:09.844 E14:29.118

#### Charges 2008

| | |
|---|---|
| Per person | CZK 80,00 |
| child | CZK 40,00 |
| pitch | CZK 60,00 - 170,00 |
| electricity | CZK 50,00 |

No credit cards.

---

### CZ4825 Camping Bucek

Tratice 170, CZ-27101 Nové Straseci (Stredocesky)

Tel: **313 564 212**. Email: **campingbucek@seznam.cz**

Camping Bucek is a pleasant Dutch owned site 40 km. west of Prague. Its proprietors also own Camping Frymburk (CZ4720). Bucek is located on the edge of woodland and has direct access to a small lake – canoes and rowing boats are available for hire, as well as sun loungers on the site's private beach. The toilet blocks have been recently renovated and a further block was added in 2004. An indoor pool was added in 2006. There are 100 pitches here, many with pleasant views over the lake, and all with electrical connections (6A). Shade is quite limited. Nearby, Revnicov is a pleasant small town with a range of shops and restaurants. The castles of Karlstejn and Krivoklát are also within easy access, along with Karlovy Vary and Prague itself.

#### Facilities

Renovated toilet blocks with free hot showers. Washing and drying machine. Direct lake access. Pedaloes, canoes, lounger hire. Minigolf. Volleyball. Play area. Off site: Revnicov 2 km. with shops (including supermarket), bars and restaurants. Prague 40 km. Karlovy Vary 10 km. Koniprusy caves.

**Open:** 27 April - 15 September.

#### Directions

From the west, take no. 6/E48 express road towards Prague. Site is close to this road, about 3 km. after the Revnicov exit and is clearly signed from this point. Coming from the east, ignore other camping signs and continue until Bucek is signed (to the north). GPS: N50:10.210 E13:50.350

#### Charges 2007

| | |
|---|---|
| Per person | CZK 85,00 |
| child (under 12 yrs) | CZK 50,00 |
| pitch incl. electricity | CZK 350,00 |
| dog | CZK 60,00 |

Reductions in low season.
No credit cards.

---

**UnityPlus CARD** — **Unique Discounts** FOR CAMPERS AND CARAVANNERS

Full details at www.**unity-plus**.com Request your UnityPlus Card today!

Check real time availability and at-the-gate prices...
www.**alanrogers**.com

## CZ4780 Autocamping Konopiste

CZ-25601 Benesov u Prahy (Stredocesky)

Tel: 317 729 083. Email: reserve@cckonopiste.cz

Benesov's chief claim to fame is the Konopiste Palace, the last home of Archduke Franz Ferdinand whose assassination in Sarajevo sparked off the First World War in 1914. Autocamp Konopiste, now under new ownership, is part of a motel complex with excellent facilities situated in a very quiet, tranquil location south of Prague. On a hillside, rows of terraces separated by hedges provide 65 grassy pitches of average size, 50 with electricity (10A). However, 34 are occupied all year by a tour operator's tents. One of the best Czech campsites, Konopiste has many different varieties of trees and much to offer those who stay there. A fitness centre and heated swimming pool are shared with motel guests. The whole complex has a well tended, cared for air. Near the motel, is the Stodola restaurant, open each evening from 6 pm. until 1 am. and this attractive replica of an old Czech barn is well worth a visit. With local specialities served by girls in local costume in a candle lit atmosphere and accompanied by a small, live music quartet, it is an evening to remember (booking essential).

### Facilities

The good quality sanitary block is central to the caravan pitches. Washing machine and irons. Kitchen. Site's own bar/buffet (high season) with simple meals and basic food items. Motel bar and two restaurants (all year). Swimming pool (1/6-31/8). Tennis. Minigolf. Volleyball. Table tennis. Bicycle hire. Badminton. Fitness centre. Playground. Club room with TV. Chateau and park. Off site: Shop 200 m. Fishing 1.5 km. Riding 5 km. Prague 48 km. (public transport available).

**Open:** 1 May - 30 September.

### Directions

Site is signed near the village of Benesov on the main Prague - Ceske Budejovic road no. 3/E55.

#### Charges 2007

| | |
|---|---|
| Per person | CZK 90,00 - 120,00 |
| child (6-15 yrs) | CZK 60,00 - 90,00 |
| pitch incl. electricity | CZK 100,00 - 390,00 |
| dog | CZK 50,00 |

## CZ4830 Camping Horjany

Horejany 3 Tochovice, CZ-26272 Breznice (Stredocesky)

Tel: 723 178 023. Email: sophiartgouda.BV@12move.nl

The Dutch owners, the de Baans, have developed this site on an old farm. The location of the site alone is worth a stay for a couple of days to enjoy the wide views over the woods and the fields, especially from the pitches at the back of the site under the trees. Camping Horjany is truly a 'back to nature' campsite – not all of the 50 pitches (40 with 3A electricity) are marked out. If you need extra space on your pitch (adding up to 200 sq.m!) Arthur just mows an extra piece for you. The site is friendly and cosy and many campers return every year. The bar is a real piece of art, designed to fit into the old barn. With a warm and comfortable atmosphere, there are a few pleasant sofas for relaxing with a drink after a long day's walking or cycling.

### Facilities

The single toilet block in a converted stable provides toilets, washbasins (open style and in cabins) with hot and cold water, controllable showers, child size washbasins, baby bath, sinks for washing up, a dryer, freezer and sinks (inside) with free hot water. No shop but bread to order. Swimming pool (12 x 6 m). Swings for children. Tennis. Soccer competitions against locals. Library. Board games. Torches are necessary. Off site: Riding 2.5 km.

**Open:** July and August only.

### Directions

Follow road no. 20 Plzen - Pisek road and turn onto no. 19 road towards Rozmital and Breznice. Go left over the bridge in Breznice and turn immediately left towards Tochovice and turn right in Tochovice to Horejany. The site is signed on the right before the village. Follow the A4 from Prague to Pribram and from there towards Strakonice. Turn right towards Kletice, Tusovice and Tusovicky which leads to Horejany and the site.

#### Charges 2008

| | |
|---|---|
| Per unit incl. 2 persons | € 14,00 |
| extra person (max 6 per pitch) | € 3,00 |
| electricity | € 2,00 |
| dog | € 1,50 |

No credit cards. Prices in Euros.

# Czech Republic

## CZ4820 Caravan Camp Valek

Chrustenice 155, CZ-26712 Lodenice (Stredocesky)

Tel: 311 672 147. Email: info@campvalek.cz

Only 2.5 km. from the E50 motorway, this well-maintained, family owned site creates a peaceful, friendly base enjoyed by families. Surrounded by delightful countryside, it is possible to visit Prague even though it is about 28 km. from the city centre. The medium sized, gently sloping grass site is divided in two by a row of well established trees (some shade) and the toilet block. Most pitches are relatively flat, in the open and not specifically marked. However this does not appear to cause overcrowding and generally there is plenty of space. Electricity (10A) is available. Some places have pleasant views of the sunbathing area in front of the pool with a pine-forested hillock as a backdrop. The 20 x 60 metre pool is fed by a river and better classified as a lake with rough concrete sides, access steps and a water chute but the water is now filtered, clean and clear. Very small dinghies, air beds and large rubber rings can be used in the 'lake' allowing children to really enjoy themselves. To visit Prague, it is best to use public transport and at Zlicin, a ten minute drive from the site, there is a 'park and ride' with guarded car parks costing 20p per day (no height restriction, arrive before 09.00). This is also the start of the 'B' metro line transporting one rapidly to Mustek, the heart of the city and the main sights (return fare 50p! – tickets can be bought in advance from reception). On leaving the car park to return, there is a large shopping centre including a Tesco superstore!

### Facilities

The single clean toilet block has limited numbers of toilets and showers, but during our visit in high season coped well. Small shop with fresh rolls daily. Waiter service restaurant with terrace has an extensive menu. Natural swimming pool (20 x 60 m; June - Sept) with constantly changing water checked regularly by the authorities to ensure its purity. Extensive games room with arcade machines and internet. Live musical nights on Saturday. Tennis. Off site: Prague 28 km. Plzen 69 km.

**Open:** 1 May - 30 September.

### Directions

From E50 (D5) motorway take exit 10 for Lodenice. Follow camping signs and or Chrustenice. Site is 300 m. on right on leaving Chrustenice.
GPS: N50:00.687 E14:09.033

### Charges 2007

| | |
|---|---|
| Per unit with 2 persons and electricity | CZK 480,00 |
| person | CZK 115,00 |
| child (6-14 yrs) | CZK 55,00 |
| dog | CZK 45,00 |
| electricity | CZK 95,00 |

Less 10% in May and Sept.

---

## CZ4685 Slavoj Autocamp Litomerice

Strerelecky Ostrov, CZ-41201 Litomerice (Severocesky)

Tel: 416 734 481. Email: kemp.litomerice@post.cz

Slavoj is a pleasant, small site with a friendly atmosphere and welcoming people. The site was totally destroyed during the flood of 2002 and has been rebuilt with help from many camp guests from all over Europe. For example, an American visitor painted the little landscape on the restaurant. Located centrally, the bar/restaurant is the main focus on the site and here you can enjoy a good value breakfast, as well as lunch and dinner. The site is on level ground, with 50 unmarked pitches, all for tourers. Some look out over the river Laba which is well fenced. Around 24 electricity connections (8/16A) are available. In high season the site can become rather crowded. Adjacent to the site is a tennis court complex and a large outdoor pool is about 10 minutes walk. Slavoj is an ideal base for a visit to the authentic inner city of Litomerice and also for a visit to one of the first and most gruesome concentration camps, Theresiënstadt.

### Facilities

The basic but clean toilet block has British style toilets, open washbasins and free, controllable hot showers. Laundry with sinks and washing machine. Kitchen. Dishwashing. Motorcaravan service point. Basics from restaurant. Bar/restaurant with covered and open-air terrace. River fishing. Canoeing. Off site: Tennis adjacent. Boat launching 500 m.

**Open:** 1 May - 30 September.

### Directions

On E55 in either direction, take exit 45 towards Litomerice. Cross the river, the railway bridge and turn left. Take first left and go left again. Cross under railway bridge and continue to site.
GPS: N50:31.920 E14:08.320

### Charges 2007

| | |
|---|---|
| Per person | CZK 75,00 - 80,00 |
| child (6-12 yrs) | CZK 45,00 - 50,00 |
| pitch incl. car | CZK 90,00 - 150,00 |
| electricity | CZK 65,00 |
| dog | CZK 30,00 |

Check real time availability and at-the-gate prices...
www.alanrogers.com

## CZ4690 Camping Slunce

CZ-47107 Zandov (Severocesky)
Tel: 487 861 116

Away from larger towns, near the border with the former East Germany, this is pleasant countryside with a wealth of Gothic and Renaissance castles. Zandov has nothing of particular interest but Camping Slunce is a popular campsite with local Czech people. There is room for about 50 touring units with 35 electrical connections (12A) on the level, circular camping area which has a hard road running round. Outside this circle are wooden bungalows and tall trees. The general building at the entrance houses all the facilities including reception. This is a fairly basic site, but is good value for money.

### Facilities

The satisfactory toilet block is good by Czech standards. Kitchen with electric rings, full gas cooker and fridges. Restaurant (all year) but under separate management has live music during high season. Kiosk for basics (May - Sept). Tennis. Table tennis. Swimming pool. Mountain bike hire. Playground. Large, club room for games and TV. Barbecues are not permitted. Dogs are not accepted. Off site: Fishing 1 km. Riding 2 km.

**Open:** 15 May - 28 August.

### Directions

Zandov is 20 km. from Decin and 12 km. from Ceske Lipa on the 262 road. Signed in the centre of Zandov village. GPS: N50:43.278 E14:24.179

### Charges 2007

| | |
|---|---|
| Per person | CZK 64,00 |
| child | CZK 40,00 |
| piitch incl. car | CZK 82,00 - 125,00 |
| electricity per kWh | CZK 8,00 |

---

## CZ4695 Camping 2000

Janov Dul 15, CZ-46352 Januv Dul (Severocesky)
Tel: 0485 179621. Email: camping2000@wanadoo.nl

Created from pleasant farm buildings and the fields behind them, Camping 2000 is especially popular with Dutch visitors. It is a good base for exploring Northern Bohemia with Prague (90 km.) and the Krkonose mountains (50 km.) from a pleasant, rural location. Most of the pitches are of average size (up to 100 sq.m.) and numbered, all with 6A electricity. There is little shade and cars parked on the pitches make the curved rows feel a bit crowded during high season. Further off, however, there are a few larger pitches catering for larger units. The social heart of the site is a large barn with a bar and a takeaway serving pizzas and typical Dutch snacks. Outdoors, a terrace overlooks a paddling pool and a larger, circular swimming pool featuring a 48 m. slide.

### Facilities

Until an extra new block is built (planned for 2008), in high season, portacabin units are used next to the main toilet block. Facilities for disabled persons. Chemical toilet. Washing machine and dryer. Bar and takeaway. Swimming and paddling pools. Bicycle hire. TV room. Five wooden cottages (fully equipped) for hire. Off site: Liberec 15 km. with the Nordic World Ski Championships in 2009, during which the slopes will be open for 1.5 months.

**Open:** 1 May - 15 September.

### Directions

From E65/E442 (Prague - Liberec) motorway take exit 35 for Hodkovicevia Ceske Dub and on to Osecna, then to Januv Dul hamlet where site is signed.
GPS: N50:42.200 E14:56.320

### Charges 2007

| | |
|---|---|
| Per unit with 2 adults, 2 children (under 14 yrs) and electricity | € 20,05 |
| dog | € 2,50 |

Prices in Euros.

## CZ4700 Autokemp Paulovice Jaroslav Kohoutek

Ul. Letná - Pavlovice, CZ-46001 Liberec (Severocesky)
Tel: 485 123 468. Email: info@autocamp-liberec.cz

Autocamp Kohoutek is a good site, nicely situated on the edge of the town near the sports ground. Just outside the entrance are the inevitable drab multi-storey flats, but trees screen these from view on the site. The Jested mountain at 1,012 m. dominates the distant sky line and is accessible by cable way for winter skiing and summer sightseeing. There are 130 touring pitches, 80 with electricity (10A), between the excellent bungalows and different varieties of trees which give a peaceful air. Some caravan pitches are divided by low hedges on the edge of the site with views across open countryside. Tarmac roads lead to the camping places. There is a good welcome and a nice bar and restaurant. Although Liberec does not have too much to write home about, it does have a zoo, botanical garden and a Renaissance château. It is set in grand countryside near the Jizera mountains and not far from the Polish town of Gorlitz.

### Facilities
The single, good quality sanitary block has toilets, washbasins and good hot showers (on payment) plus a kitchen with electric rings. Restaurant, with café, snack bar and raised terrace. Good size swimming pool (1/7-31/8). Tennis. Table tennis. Playground. Off site: Shops outside entrance. 'Centrum Babylon' leisure park nearby. Fishing, golf, riding and bicycle hire within 5 km.

**Open:** All year.

### Directions
Coming from the south on the E442 to Liberec, ignore exit for Liberec and take exit for Frydlant Pavloice shopping centre instead. Keep right at first roundabout, and at second roundabout follow sign for Pavlovic. Pass shopping centre and immediately after footbridge turn left to site.
GPS: N50:47.050 E15:02.556

### Charges 2007
| | |
|---|---|
| Per person | CZK 60,00 - 80,00 |
| child (6-15 yrs) | CZK 40,00 - 50,00 |
| pitch with electricity | CZK 170,00 - 210,00 |
| dog | CZK 50,00 |
| electricity | CZK 70,00 |

## CZ4590 Holiday Park Lisci Farma

Dolni Branna 350, CZ-54362 Vrchlabi (Vychodocesky)
Tel: 499 421 473. Email: info@liscifarma.cz

This is truly an excellent site that could be in Western Europe considering its amenities, pitches and welcome. However, Lisci Farma retains a pleasant Czech atmosphere. The helpful young manager welcomes many Dutch visitors throughout the year, but in the winter months, when local skiing is available, snow chains are essential. The 260 pitches are fairly flat, although the terrain is slightly sloping and some pitches are terraced. There is shade. The site is well equipped for the whole family to enjoy with its adventure playground offering trampolines for children, archery, beach volleyball, Russian bowling and outdoor bowling court for older youngsters. A beautiful sandy, lakeside beach is 800 m. from the entrance. The more active amongst you can go paragliding or rock climbing, with experienced people to guide you. This site is very suitable for relaxing or exploring the culture of the area. Excursions to Prague are organised and, if all the sporting possibilities are not enough, the children can take part in the activities of the entertainment team, while you are walking or cycling or enjoying live music at the Fox Saloon. The site reports the addition of completely new electrical connections, restaurant, games room and mini-market.

### Facilities
Two good sanitary blocks, near the entrance and another modern block next to the hotel, both include toilets, washbasins and spacious, controllable showers (on payment). Child size toilets and baby room. Toilet for disabled visitors. Launderette with sinks, hot water and a washing machine. Shop (15/6-15/9). Bar/snack bar with pool table. Games room. Swimming pool (6 x 12 m). Adventure style playground on grass. Trampolines. Tennis courts. Minigolf. Archery. Russian bowling. Bowling court. Beach volleyball. Paragliding. Rock climbing. Bicycle hire. Excursions to Prague. Shuttle bus for skiing. Off site: Fishing and beach 800 m. Riding 2 km. Golf 5 km.

**Open:** 1 December - 31 March and 1 May - 31 October.

### Directions
Follow road no. 14 from Liberec to Vrchlabi. At the roundabout turn in the direction of Prague and site is about 1 mile on the right.
GPS: N50:36.516 E15:36.056

### Charges 2008
| | |
|---|---|
| Per person | CZK 115,00 |
| child (4-14 yrs) | CZK 90,00 |
| pitch incl. electricity | CZK 410,00 - 570,00 |
| dog | CZK 90,00 |

Various discounts available in low season.
Camping Cheques accepted.

---

**Check real time availability and at-the-gate prices...**
www.alanrogers.com

## CZ4860 Autocamping Orlice

P.O. Box 26, CZ-51741 Kostelec n Orlici (Vychodocesky)

Tel: **494 323 970**. Email: **orlice@wo.cz**

Kostelec does have an ancient castle and a large Ferodo factory, although not a lot else to commend it, but is a good centre from which to explore the interesting town of Hradec Kralove, East Bohemia, the Orlicke Hory and other high districts near the Polish border. Autocamping Orlice, situated on the edge of town near the swimming pool, has a river running by and is in a quiet location (except when children play in the weir!) and a pleasant appearance. Surrounded by tall trees, the grass pitches are of generous size although not marked or numbered, on each side of a concrete grid road which runs the length of this rectangular site. There is room for 80 units, half having electric points (16A) and with shade in parts. The friendly manageress speaks good English and will be pleased to advise on local attractions. There is a hotel alongside the camp but advice is to seek a better restaurant in town for meals. A good site for those seeking rest and quiet and not needing organised activities, there is a friendly welcome.

### Facilities

The central sanitary block includes hot water in washbasins, sinks and good showers – it is of a good standard for the Czech Republic. Unlike most Czech sites, showers have dividers, space for dressing, a door that locks, and even a chair! Chemical disposal point. Limited food supplies are available in a bar/lounge during July/Aug. Café/bar (15/5-30/9). Off site: Town swimming pool near (15/6-31/8). Tennis 100 m. Fishing 500 m. Riding 5 km.

**Open:** 15 May - 30 September.

### Directions

Site is signed from the centre of town.
GPS: N50:06.949 E16:13.010

### Charges 2007

| | |
|---|---|
| Per person | CZK 46,00 - 50,00 |
| child (6-14 yrs) | CZK 22,00 - 26,00 |
| pitch with electricity | CZK 157,00 - 225,00 |
| dog | CZK 42,00 - 46,00 |
| electricity | CZK 65,00 |

## CZ4710 Camping Chvalsiny

Chvalsiny 321, CZ-38208 Chvalsiny (Jihocesky)

Tel: **380 739 123**. Email: **info@campingchvalsiny.nl**

Camping Chvalsiny is Dutch owned and has been developed from an old farm. It has been developed into real camping fields which are terraced and level. A newly built toilet block houses excellent facilities and everything looks well maintained. The 200 pitches are of average size but look larger because of the open nature of the terrain which also means there is little shade. Chvalsiny is a real family site and children are kept occupied with painting, crafts and stories. Older youngsters take part in soccer, volleyball and rafting competitions. The location in the middle of the Blanky Les nature reserve, part of the vast Sumava forest, provides excellent opportunities for walking, cycling and fishing but it also has a rich culture and heritage. You can visit charming villages of which Cesky Krumlov with its impressive castle and scenic centre is the most important.

### Facilities

Modern, clean and well kept toilet facilities include washbasins in cabins and controllable showers (coin operated). Laundry. Dishwashing under cover. Kiosk (1/6-13/9) with bread and daily necessities. Snack bar (1/6-15/9). Play attic. Lake swimming. Climbing equipment and swings. Crafts, games, table tennis and soccer. Torches useful. New for 2007, family showers and baby room. Off site: Village restaurants close. Riding 10 km.

**Open:** 26 April - 15 September.

### Directions

Take exit 114 at Passau in Germany (near the Austrian border) towards Freyung in the Czech Republic. Continue on this road to Philipsreut and take no. 4 road towards Vimperk. Turn right on no. 39 road to Horni Plana and Cesky Krumlov. Turn left 4 km. before Cesky Krumlov on no. 166 to Chvalsiny and follow camp signs through the village.
GPS: N48:51.350 E14:12.510

### Charges 2007

| | |
|---|---|
| Per person | CZK 100,00 |
| child (under 12 yrs) | CZK 60,00 |
| pitch | CZK 300,00 |
| with electricity | CZK 350,00 |
| dog | CZK 50,00 |

No credit cards.

# Czech Republic

## CZ4720 Camping Frymburk

Frymburk 184, CZ-38279 Frymburk (Jihocesky)

Tel: 380 735 284

Camping Frymburk is beautifully located on the Lipno lake in southern Bohemia and is an ideal site. You could enjoy a real Czech meal in one of the restaurants in Frymburk. The site has 170 level pitches on terraces (all with 6A electricity) and from the lower terraces on the edge of the lake there are lovely views over the water. A ferry crosses the lake from Frymburk where one can walk or cycle in the woods. The Dutch owner, Mr Wilzing, will welcome the whole family, personally siting your caravan. Children will be entertained by 'Kidstown' and the site has a small beach.

### Facilities

Two new toilet blocks are immaculate with toilets, washbasins (open style and in cabins) with cold water only, pre-set showers on payment (with curtain) and an en-suite bathroom with toilet, basin and shower. Launderette with washing machines, dryers and ironing board. Bar (15/5-30/9). Takeaway (1/5-15/9). Playground. Canoe, bicycle, pedaloes, rowing boat and surfboard hire. Kidstown. Volleyball competitions. Rafting. Bus trips to Prague. Torches useful. Off site: Shops and restaurants in the village 900 m. from reception. Golf 7 km. Riding 20 km.

**Open:** 25 April - 1 October.

### Directions

Take exit 114 at Passau in Germany (near Austrian border) towards Freyung (Czech Republic). Continue till Philipsreut and then follow the no. 4 road towards Vimperk. Turn right a few kilometres after border towards Volary on no. 141 road. From Volary follow no. 163 road to Horni Plana, Cerna and Frymburk. Site is on 163 road, right after the village.

### Charges 2007

| | |
|---|---|
| Per unit incl. 2 persons and electricity | CZK 416,00 - 580,00 |
| extra person | CZK 72,00 - 90,00 |
| child (under 12 yrs) | CZK 48,00 - 60,00 |

No credit cards.

## CZ4730 Camping Kostelec

Kostelec 8, CZ-37341 Hluboka Nad Vltavou (Jihocesky)

Tel: 731 272 303. Email: info@campingkostelec.nl

Located in the little hamlet of Kostelec, finding this new site is not straightforward, although there are campsite signs from the town of Tyn nad Vltavou which is roughly 15 km. away. The pretty rural campsite was started in 2005 using old farm buildings and the terraced field below. There are 55 pitches (52 with electricity). Drainage problems on the slope and a troublesome steep access road will make manoeuvring difficult during wet weather. There is little shade. Slowly developing, this site will in time become a pleasant base for a quiet holiday in the Czech countryside.

### Facilities

Toilet facilities are modern and up-to-date. Washing machine. Shop and bar planned. Small paddling pool. Off site: Village shop offers basic necessities only. Nearest town 14 km.

**Open:** 15 May - 15 September.

### Directions

From Tyn nad Vltavou centre near bridge, a small road leads along northern bank of river into the countryside (south). From bridge, small site signs direct you over small roads to site in Kostelec (14 km).

### Charges 2007

| | |
|---|---|
| Per person | CZK 105,00 |
| child (under 12 yrs) | CZK 65,00 |
| pitch with electricity | CZK 300,00 |

No credit cards.

## CZ4735 Camping Blanice

Chelcickeho 889, CZ-39811 Protivin (Jihocesky)

Tel: 721 589 125. Email: info@campingblanice.nl

In the pretty, flat valley of the Blanice river, this Dutch-owned campsite is an adequate place to stay near to the countryside and the historical town of Ceské Budejovice. Located between two arms of the river, the site is accessed over a little bridge. The site is well drained, but floods are imaginable. There are 40 large, marked pitches with electricity connections (Europlug). There is not much shade. A mini-shop operates in high season, together with a small restaurant (limited choice) and a bar.

### Facilities

Sanitary facilities can be heated. Washing machine. Small shop, restaurant and bar (high season). Bicycle and canoe hire. Swimming in the river possible. Off site: Historical town of Ceské Budejovice.

**Open:** 1 May - 30 September (other by arrangement).

### Directions

Site is at the southern end of Protivin (30 km. northwest of Ceské Budejovice). On entering town from the south, turn right to the river. Site is signed.

### Charges 2007

| | |
|---|---|
| Per person | CZK 100,00 |
| child (under 8 yrs) | CZK 60,00 |
| pitch incl. electricity | CZK 290,00 |

No credit cards.

Check real time availability and at-the-gate prices...
www.alanrogers.com

## CZ4760 Naturist Camping Mlécna Dráha

Racov 15, CZ-38472 Zdikov (Jihocesky)

Tel: 388 426 222. Email: md.schaak@iol.cz

Opportunities for campers who enjoy a naturist lifestyle are extremely limited within the Czech Republic. We have explored all the possibilities and feel that this 12 hectare, Dutch owned site with 100 pitches in southern Bohemia provides acceptable facilities near interesting attractions and pleasant scenery. It is very popular with families. Previously a farm, this spacious, open and sloping site has a number of well spaced mini-terraces creating both views and distance between you and your neighbours. The gradual descent through the site is via a track but the owners will help with a tractor should there be problems in siting a caravan. The focal point of the site is the main building and adjacent small river-fed lake. The latter is extremely popular with parents and children alike but used entirely at your own risk. The main building, some distance from most pitches houses all the facilities and accommodation. Electricity hook-ups (16A) may need a long lead. Owners Wils and Bert have integrated well with the local people and this is reflected both in the quality of food at the restaurant and the prices of such services as a massage or a haircut. Within a reasonable distance are many places of interest including the UNESCO World Monument town of Cesky Krumlov, Ceske Budejovice and the powerful impressive castle at Hluboka.

### Facilities

New toilet block with immaculate provisions. Sauna. The chemical disposal system is ecological and does not accept 'blue' chemicals. The product must be either green or none used. Bar, restaurant, terrace. Bread to order daily. Warm and comfortable community room with library. Boules. Off site: Nearest shops 3.5 km. Prague is too far for a day visit but the site owners can arrange overnight accommodation and it is possible to travel by public transport. Fishing 1 km. Golf 40 km. Riding and bicycle hire 10 km.

**Open:** 1 May - 15 September (all year by arrangement).

### Directions

From no. 4 Prague - Passau road at Vimperk, take road 145 to Zdikov. On approach to village, site is well signed to the right. Follow to next village of Racov and site is on the outskirts on leaving the village. GPS: N49:05.649 E13:44.318

### Charges 2007

| | |
|---|---|
| Per person | CZK 170,00 |
| child (under 15 yrs) | CZK 90,00 |
| pitch with electricity | CZK 280,00 |
| dog | CZK 50,00 |
| electricity | CZK 80,00 |

## CZ4765 Autocamp Trebon

Libusina 601, CZ-37901 Trebon (Jihocesky)

Tel: 384 722 586. Email: info@autocamp-trebon.cz

Autocamp Trebon offers a happy Czech atmosphere especially around the bar/restaurant and is located on a lake where swimming, surfing and boating (the site rents out canoes) are possible. It is close to the interesting fortifications of Trebon and not far from the historic cities of Cesky Krumlov and Ceske Budejovice, which are certainly worth a visit. Being next to a large forest, it also makes a great location for walking and cycling. The site has 200 pitches, all for tourers and with 7A electricity, plus 35 cabins. Pitching is off tarmac access roads in two area. The lower field is a single large, grassy area with a circular road around it and pitches on both side of the road. The front pitches look out over the lake which is not fenced. The top field is smaller and more cramped. In the evening everybody seems to gather on the terraces near the bar and self-service restaurant where the enjoyable mix of nationalities creates an easygoing atmosphere. Ordering food at the restaurant may cause some confusion and the order in which it is served may be interesting, if incomprehensible.

### Facilities

An older toilet building has some old and some new facilities, including British style toilets, open washbasins and controllable hot showers (token from reception). Washing machine. Dishwashing. Kiosk for bread and drinks. Bar with terrace. Self-service restaurant with open air and covered terrace. Play area. Basketball. Volleyball. Fishing. Canoe rental. Boat launching. Beach. Off site: Riding 200 m. Bicycle hire 100 m.

**Open:** May - 30 September.

### Directions

Take no. 34 road to Trebon; and in town follow the site signs. GPS: N48:59.561 E14:46.049

### Charges guide

| | |
|---|---|
| Per person | CZK 50,00 |
| child | CZK 30,00 |
| pitch incl. car and electricity | CZK 215,00 |
| dog | CZK 50,00 |

## CZ4770 Camping Dlouhá Louka

Stromovka 8, CZ-37001 Ceské Budejovice (Jihocesky)

Tel: 387 203 601

The medieval city of Céske Budejovice is the home of Budweiser beer and is also an industrial centre. It lies on the River Vltava with mountains and pleasant scenery nearby. Dlouhá Louka is a motel and camping complex two kilometres south of the town on the Céske Budejovice - Cesky Krumlov road. The camping part is a flat, rectangular meadow surrounded by trees which give some shade around the edges. There are some marked, hedged pitches and hardstanding, but many of the grass pitches are not marked or numbered so pitching can be rather haphazard. In total, 100 units are taken and there are 50 electricity connections (10A). This is a useful night stop between Prague and Linz or for longer stays if this region is of interest.

### Facilities

The single sanitary block, with British style WCs, is at one end making a fair walk for some. Washing machine and irons. Kitchen with electric rings. Very pleasant restaurant (1/6-31/8). Tennis. Volleyball. Table tennis. Playground. Off site: Shops 200 m. Bicycle hire 2 km. Fishing and golf 10 km.

**Open:** All year.

### Directions

From town follow signs for Ceske Krumlov. After leaving ring road, turn right at Motel sign. Take this small road and turn right 60 m. before Camp Stromovky. Campsite name cannot be seen from the entrance – only the word Motel.
GPS: N48:57.984 E14:27.630

### Charges guide

| | |
|---|---|
| Per person | CZK 50,00 - 70,00 |
| child | CZK 30,00 |
| pitch | CZK 120,00 - 140,00 |
| electricity | CZK 80,00 |
| dog | CZK 30,00 |

No credit cards.

## CZ4775 Autocamping Karvánky

Jiraskova 407, CZ-39201 Sobeslav (Jihocesky)

Tel: 381 521 003. Email: karvanky@post.cz

This good site is owned by the local auto club and managed by enthusiastic volunteers. It surrounds a lake and is near a small river on the southern outskirts of Sobeslav. The 150 pitches are marked and there are 48 new Europlug electricity connections spread around the lakeside. The friendly couple who manage the site tell us that it gets very busy in July and August and it is clearly well used by local tourists. A new sanitary block was nearing completion in May 2005 and this along with the existing provision should be adequate for the busy season. Being close to the busy E55 road, there is inevitably some background traffic noise. Fishing in the lake is permitted but you will need a licence from reception.

### Facilities

Two modern toilet blocks provide toilets, showers (token required) and washbasins. Washing machine. Chemical disposal point. Restaurant and bar with terrace. Internet point in reception (English spoken). Mountain bike and boat hire. Small wooden cabins for rent (sleeping 4). Off site: Sobeslav and a bit further north, Tabor.

**Open:** 15 May - 30 September.

### Directions

Site is on route 3/E55, just south of Sobeslav.
GPS: N49:13.818 E14:43.140

### Charges 2007

| | |
|---|---|
| Per person | CZK 28,00 |
| child (6-15 yrs) | CZK 18,00 |
| pitch | CZK 42,00 - 65,00 |
| electricity | CZK 77,00 |

## CZ4778 Camping Kovarna

Skolni 594, 39601 Humpolec, CZ-39446 Cervená Recice (Jihocesky)

Tel: 565 398 005. Email: campingkovarna@iol.cz

A low intensity, nature-oriented campsite, Kovarna stands in the grounds of a former pioneers' camp in a beautiful river valley between densely forested hills. With an average size of over 100 sq.m. the 50 pitches are spacious and well laid out over 4 hectares of land. All have electricity hook-ups. The site is owned by a Dutch couple who have operated it since 2005. They run their own water purification system (only biologically decomposable agents allowed in chemical toilets).

### Facilities
The sanitary block is not new but modestly renovated and acceptable. Showers with doors and new sanitary equipment. Small swimming pool (no surveillance). Bread service in the mornings. Ice cream and drinks. Off site: Village shop with basic supplies. Supermarket 7 km. Fishing lake 5 km.

**Open:** 1 May - 30 September.

### Directions
From Prague - Brno motorway exit at km. 90 west towards Pelhrimov and Tábor. After 15 km. at Pelhrimov follow signs for Tábor, then turn north to Vlasim (road nr. 112). Arriving in Cervená Recice after 9 km. Site is on the left down in the valley (follow signs). GPS: N49:31.090 E15:09.270

### Charges 2007
| | |
|---|---|
| Per pitch | CZK 85,00 - 95,00 |

No credit cards.

## CZ4870 Autocamping Morava

Bezrucova, CZ-78985 Mohelnice (Severomoravsky)

Tel: 583 430 129. Email: info@atc-morava.cz

This is an interesting area of contrasts – heavy industry, fertile plains and soaring mountains. Mohelnice is a small industrial town but the campsite is in a peaceful setting surrounded by trees on the northern edge. The amenities on offer, particularly for children, may tempt one to stay longer. The site is roughly in two halves with the camping area on a flat, open meadow with a hard access road. The 100 touring pitches are not numbered or marked so siting could be a little haphazard. There are 80 electricity connections (10A). There is little shade but the perimeter trees should screen out road noise. The other part of the site is given over to a two storey motel and bungalows with a good quality restaurant between the two sections. Good English is spoken at reception and it is a very pleasant, well organised site.

### Facilities
The toilet block is satisfactory. Electric cooking rings. Restaurant (May - Oct). Kiosk/snack bar. Small shop (May - Oct). Live music (high season). Swimming pool (May - Oct). Tennis. Minigolf. Bicycle hire. Road track – driving and cycling learning area with tarmac roads, road signs, traffic lights and road markings well set up to give youngsters a practice area without the hazard of normal traffic. Playground. TV room.

**Open:** 15 May - 15 October (motel all year).

### Directions
Site is signed on the western edge of town on road to Svitavy. GPS: N49:46.997 E16:54.571

### Charges 2007
| | |
|---|---|
| Per person | CZK 50,00 |
| child | CZK 25,00 |
| pitch | CZK 80,00 - 120,00 |
| electricity | CZK 40,00 |

No credit cards.
Less 10% for 5 days or more, paid on arrival.

## CZ4880 Camping Roznov

Horni Paseky 940, CZ-75661 Roznov pod Radhostem (Severomoravsky)

Tel: 571 648 001. Email: info@camproznov.cz

Roznov pod Radhostem is halfway up the Roznovska Becva valley amidst the Beskydy hills which extend from North Moravia into Poland in the extreme east of the Republic. It is a busy tourist centre which attracts visitors to the Wallachian open-air museum and those who enjoy hill walking. There are 300 pitches (200 for touring units), some of which are rather small, although there are some new landscaped pitches of 90-100 sq.m. Arranged on flat grass and set amidst a variety of fruit and other trees, there are 120 electrical connections (16A) and shade in some parts. Although right by a main road with some traffic noise, the site is surrounded by trees and hills and was reasonably quiet during our visit. The friendly manager will be pleased to advise on local attractions. Camping Roznov makes a good base for exploring this interesting part of Moravia.

### Facilities

The good quality central toilet block has hot water in showers, washbasins and sinks. This block also has a large, comfortable TV lounge/meeting room. A further well equipped toilet block has washbasins and WCs en-suite for ladies and a washing machine. Only very basic food items available in shop (not always open). Swimming pool (25 m. open July/Aug). Trampolines. Tennis. Off site: Restaurant or snack bar night club at the modern Europlan Hotel some 300 m. towards the town. Fishing and golf 1 km. Riding 4 km.

**Open:** All year.

### Directions

Site is at eastern end of Roznov on the main 35/E442 Zilina - Olomouc road opposite sports stadium. GPS: N49:27.977 E18:09.840

### Charges 2007

| | |
|---|---|
| Per person | CZK 55,00 - 90,00 |
| child (3-15 yrs) | CZK 45,00 - 70,00 |
| pitch | CZK 95,00 - 175,00 |
| electricity | CZK 60,00 - 80,00 |

## CZ4885 Autocamping Bobrovnik

CZ-79061 Lipova Lazne (Severomoravsky)

Tel: 584 411 145. Email: camp@bobrovnik.cz

Lipova Lazne is on the northern edge of the Hruby Jesenik area, which is a protected landscape and is in the shadow of Praded, Moravia's highest mountain (1491 m). It is said that on a clear day you can see both the Krkonose of eastern Bohemia and the Tatras of central Slovakia from its peak. The area is a great for walking and trails abound, as do transport options. From the Cervenohorske Sedlo pass you can take the cable car down to Ramzova or walk the red trail. This quiet and pleasant campsite has 132 level and numbered pitches, 32 with 6A electricity. Facilities are basic but it may suit people interested in a nature oriented holiday.

### Facilities

The toilet block is old but has clean toilets, hot showers and washbasins. Washing machine and drier. Kitchen and dishwashing. Motorcaravan drain down facility. Small restaurant. Off site: Fishing, Riding 10 km. Bicycle hire 3 km. Skiing in winter 1 km.

**Open:** All year.

### Directions

Site is on road 60 between Lipova Lazne and Jesenik. However, from Lipova Lazne follow signs to Sumperk and turn left at the no through road sign towards the site. GPS: N50:13.493 E17:10.510

### Charges 2007

| | |
|---|---|
| Per person | CZK 49,00 |
| child (5-12 yrs) | CZK 30,00 |
| pitch | CZK 186,00 - 199,00 |
| dog | CZK 42,00 |
| electricity (10A) | CZK 50,00 |

## CZ4890 Eurocamping Bojkovice S.R.O.

Stefanikova ATC, CZ-68771 Bojkovice (Jihormoravsky)
Tel: 604 236 631. Email: **eurocamping@iol.cz**

This family site in Bojkovice, close to the Slovak border, is one of the better Czech sites. It is on hilly ground with tarmac access roads connecting the 40 pitches. These are all for touring units on grassy fields taking six or eight units, but the manager will try to fit you in wherever possible. Mostly on terraces in the shade of mature birch trees, all have 6A electricity. A footpath connects the three toilet blocks which offer a more than adequate provision and are cleaned twice daily. It also leads to the bar/restaurant and the centrally located outdoor pool. There is no entertainment programme but we were told that children and teenagers enjoy a stay here. At reception you may borrow a map with extensive tourist information about the local area. This is a good, well run site.

### Facilities

Three toilet blocks (one refurbished) are a good, clean provisions, including British style toilets, open washbasins and controllable, hot showers (free). Washing machine. Campers' kitchen. Bar/restaurant with open air terrace (breakfast and dinner served). Outdoor swimming pool (15 x 8 m, unfenced). Fishing. Bicycle hire. Off site: Riding 3 km.

**Open:** 1 May - 30 September.

### Directions

From Brno take E50 road southeast towards the Slovakian border. Exit onto the 495 road towards Uhersky Brod and follow signs for Bojkovice. In town, turn left uphill and follow the green signs. GPS: N49:02.250 E17:47.835

### Charges 2007

| | |
|---|---|
| Per unit incl. 2 persons and electricity | € 12,00 - € 16,15 |
| extra person | € 2,50 - € 3,05 |
| child (3-15 yrs) | € 1,30 - € 2,00 |
| dog | € 1,85 |

Prices in Euros.

## CZ4892 Camping de Bongerd

Benesov 104, CZ-67953 Benesov (Jihormoravsky)
Tel: 516 467 233. Email: **campingbenesov@hetnet.nl**

This small, well cared for family site is in the part of the Czech Republic said to enjoy the most sun. Under Dutch ownership, and almost exclusively used by Dutch guests, many activities for children are organised such as film nights, excursions, walks through the site's own forest and campfires. Trips to the historic cities of Brno and Olomouc are organised and there is an extensive library. De Bongerd has 70 rather small pitches (all for tourers), 45 with 4/6A electricity, in two fields with pitching off a gravel access road. One field runs down towards the former farmhouse and pitches here are slightly sloping, although some terraces have been created. Pitches on the other field are arranged on level ground in a circular arrangement. The site is attractively landscaped with young pine trees and colourful flowers. A maximum of one dog per pitch is accepted.

### Facilities

Two well maintained 'portacabin' style units supplement facilities in the farmhouse. British style toilets, open washbasins and controllable, hot showers (running free for 7 minutes). Playground on gravel. Football field. Minigolf. Fishing. Riding. Library. Activities for children and excursions. Off site: Riding 1 km. Golf 2 km.

**Open:** 1 May - 10 September.

### Directions

Follow the E461-43 until the exit for Prostejov, Boskovic and follow campsite signs. Site is in the village of Benesov. The distance between Boskovic and Benesov is 10 km. GPS: N49:30.630 E16:46.462

### Charges 2007

| | |
|---|---|
| Per person | CZK 80,00 |
| child (0-10 yrs) | CZK 60,00 |
| pitch | CZK 100,00 - 160,00 |
| electricity | CZK 90,00 |

## CZ4894 Autocamping Pavov

Pavov 90, CZ-58601 Jihlava (Jihormoravsky)
Tel: 567 210 295. Email: atcpavov@volny.cz

Pávov is a small site, close to the town of Jihlava and just a few hundred metres from the E50 motorway running from Prague to Brno. The site belongs to a hotel and is on a little lake, where boating, windsurfing and swimming are possible. Only really suitable as a transit site, Pávov has 60 pitches on grass (all for tourers), off one circular tarmac and gravel access road. Low hedges separate the pitches on the central field and around 30 pitches have electricity. Day visitors as well as campsite and hotel guests use the lake. Being so close to the motorway, Pávov makes a useful stopover for a night, and if you don't mind the very basic facilities. No English is spoken.

### Facilities
The toilet block is basic and cleaning is variable. British style toilets, open washbasins and controllable hot showers (token from reception). Bar with basic restaurant and terrace. Boat, canoe, pedalo and surfboard rental. Fishing. Beach.

**Open:** April - September.

### Directions
From motorway E50 (Prague - Brno), take exit for Jihlava at km. 112. Go south towards town for 1 km. or so, then exit dual-carriageway at site sign. Then turn left and follow road into the village. Site is near the Pavov lake, signed. GPS: N49:26.863 E15:35.970

### Charges 2007
| | |
|---|---|
| Per person | CZK 50,00 |
| child | CZK 30,00 |
| pitch incl. car | CZK 110,00 - 160,00 |
| electricity | CZK 65,00 |

---

## CZ4895 Camping Hana

CZ-66471 Veverska Bityska (Jihormoravsky)
Tel: 549 420 331. Email: camping.hana@quick.cz

The caves of the Moravian Karst, the site of the battle of Austerlitz and the castles of Veveri, Pertstejn and Spillberk are all within easy reach of this pleasant, small and quiet campsite. Hana Musilova runs the site to very high standards, speaks excellent English and Dutch and is keen to provide lots of local information. There are 55 level, numbered pitches with 10A electricity. Brno, the capital of Moravia and the Czech Republic's second largest city, is a short boat or bus ride away and the village of Veverska Bityska has shops, restaurants, bars and an ATM plus a reasonable small supermarket. In Brno you can enjoy a good meal in one of the many restaurants or the more ghoulish campers may like to visit the Capuchin monastery crypt where the mummified bodies of monks and local dignitaries dating back from the early 1700s are on display. This is an excellent site, on the banks of the river Svratka, at which you can savour Czech life, in a quiet and leisurely way.

### Facilities
The modern sanitary block provides ample and clean toilets, hot showers (token, 1st free per person then CZK 5) and washbasins. Washing machine and dryer. Chemical disposal point. Kitchen and dishwashing facilities. Small shop with essential supplies.
Off site: Fishing 1 km. Golf 10 km. Riding 4 km. Boat cruise to Brno 500 m. Veversak Bityska village 1 km.

**Open:** 1 May - 30 September.

### Directions
From the D1 Prague - Brno autoroute, turn off at Ostrovacice and head towards Tisnov. The site is at Veverska Bityska on the road to Chudcice. From the 43 turn off south of Lipuvka towards Kurim and then follow the signs to Veverska Bityska where the site is on the right before entering the village.
GPS: N49:16.594 E16:27.158

### Charges 2007
| | |
|---|---|
| Per person | CZK 80,00 |
| child (4-12 yrs) | CZK 40,00 |
| pitch with electricity | CZK 180,00 - 220,00 |
| dog | CZK 40,00 |
| Less 5% in low season. | |

## CZ4896 Camping Country

Hluboke Masuvky 257, CZ-67152 Hluboke Masuvky (Jihormoravsky)
Tel: **515 255 249**. Email: **camping-country@cbox.cz**

Camping Country is a well cared for and attractively landscaped site, close to the historical town of Znojmo. It is a rural location close to a National Park and close to the Austrian border which would make it ideal either as a stopover on your way south and for a longer stay to enjoy the new cycling routes which have been set out in the National Park. Camping Country has 60 pitches (all for tourers), 30 with 6A electricity, on two fields – one behind the main house taking 6 or 8 units, the other one larger with a gravel access road. The fields are connected by two wooden bridges (one is only fenced on one side). Varieties of low hedges and firs partly separate the pitches. To the front of the site is a paddock with two horses and facilities for minigolf, volleyball, basketball and tennis. In the garden of the main house is a paddling pool. Colourful flowers and trees give the site a pleasant atmosphere. We feel that Camping Country is certainly one of the better Czech sites.

### Facilities

Modern and comfortable toilet facilities provide British style toilets, open washbasins (cold water only) and free, controllable hot showers. Campers' kitchen. Bar and restaurant with one meal served daily. Play area. Tennis. Minigolf. Riding. Some live music nights in high season. Internet access. Tours to Vienna, Brno and wine cellars organised. Torch useful. Off site: Fishing, boat launching and beach 10 km.

**Open:** 1 May - 31 October.

### Directions

Coming from the northwest on the E59 road exit to the east at Kasarna onto the 408 road and continue north on the 361 road towards Hluboké Masuvky. Site is well signed. GPS: N48:55.240 E16:01.600

### Charges 2007

| | |
|---|---|
| Per person | CZK 120,00 |
| child (3-12 yrs) | CZK 60,00 |
| pitch incl. car | CZK 120,00 - 170,00 |
| electricity | CZK 80,00 |
| dog | CZK 50,00 |

Camping Cheques accepted.

## CZ4898 Camping Vidlak

C.p. 322, CZ-67528 Opatov na Morave (Jihormoravsky)
Tel: **0736 678 687**. Email: **campingvidlak@seznam.cz**

Bordering a quiet lake in a peaceful valley, Camping Vidlak is an island of space with only 50 pitches of over 150 sq.m. each and the site is very well cared for. The owners live in the main building all year round and welcome their guests personally throughout the year – for arrivals between October and April advanced notice will ensure the toilet block will be clean and heated. Most of the pitches have a clear view of and direct access to the lake; families with smaller children may prefer one of the pitches further to the back, as there is no fence around the water. Lake swimming is possible, as well as lighting a campfire on one of the designated fireplaces. A sitting room provides a library (primarily Dutch) and a computer with internet access. There are 48 pitches with electricity (10A).

### Facilities

Modern toilet facilities are in the main building and heated in cool weather. Facilities for dsabled visitors. Washing machine and dryer. Bread to order (June - Aug). sitting room with library and internet access. Play area. Suite for 2-4 persons in the main building for rent. Lake swimming. Off site: Historical towns of South Moravia: Telc, Trebic, Jihlava and Brno.

**Open:** All year.

### Directions

From Prague take E50 to Brno, then exit 112 to Jihlava. From there take E58, road 38 to Znojmo. After 20 km. in Dlouhá Brtnice, turn left towards Opatov. Site is signed to the south of the village. GPS: N49:12.560 E15:39.350

### Charges 2007

| | |
|---|---|
| Per person | CZK 135,00 |
| child (3-11 yrs) | CZK 98,00 |
| pitch incl. electricity | CZK 210,00 |
| dog | CZK 25,00 |

Czech Republic

Check real time availability and at-the-gate prices...
www.alanrogers.com

# Poland

**MAP 8**

Poland has strong theatrical and musical traditions and a rich folklore history. Small local feasts, fairs and contests occur throughout the country, particularly in the summer.

The northern part of Poland is varied, well-forested and gently undulating, with the coastline providing miles of sandy beaches, bays, cliffs and dunes. The flat central plain is the main agricultural area and heading south the terrain rises, with the mountainous regions being dominated by two big ranges, the Sudetens in the west and the Carpathians in the south. Here you'll find plenty of caves to explore. Poland also has over 9,000 lakes; the majority located in the north east in the Pomeranian and Masurian Lake districts. These lakes offer many opportunities for water sports enthusiasts, anglers, nature lovers and bird watchers.

Completely ravaged by the Second World War, Warsaw has been rebuilt and developed into a thriving capital, with plenty of churches, palaces, galleries and museums to visit. Unlike the capital, Kraków still retains its original character and wealth of architecture, having come through the war unscathed to become one of the world's twelve most significant historic sites as listed by UNESCO.

**Population**
38.6 million

**Capital**
Warsaw (Warszawa)

**Climate**
Temperate climate, with warm and sunny summers, cold winters with large snowfalls.

**Language**
Polish

**Currency**
The Zloty

**Telephone**
The country code is 00 48

**Banks**
Mon-Fri 9.00-16.00

**Shops**
Mon-Fri 6.00/7.00 - 18.00/19.00. Sat: 7.00 -13.00. Supermakets usually stay open until 21.00/22.00.

# Poland

SITUATED IN THE HEART OF EUROPE, POLAND IS A COUNTRY RICH IN CULTURE AND HERITAGE. HAVING TRANSFORMED ITSELF AFTER YEARS OF INVASIONS AND INTERFERENCE FROM ITS NEIGHBOURS, IT HAS NOW BECOME AN IDEAL PLACE FOR THOSE LOOKING FOR SOMETHING A LITTLE DIFFERENT.

### Public Holidays
New Year; Easter Mon; Womens' Day 8 Mar; April Fool's Day 1 April; Labour Day; Constitution Day 3 May; Corpus Christi; Assumption 15 Aug; , All Saints 1 Nov; Independence Day 11 Nov; Christmas 25, 26 Dec.

### Motoring
International Driving Permit is required. Between October and March it is compulsory to have headlights switched on at all times while driving. Motorcyclists must keep their lights on all year round. In rural areas horse drawn and slow moving agricultural vehicles are common, even on main roads. There are few dual-cariageways and even main roads between cities and major towns can be narrow and poorly surfaced.

### Tourist Office
Poland National Tourist Office
Level 3, Westec House,
West Gate,
London W5 1YY
Tel: 08700 675 012 Fax: 08700 675 011
E-mail: info@visitpoland.org
Internet: www.poland.gov.pl

### British Embassy
Aleje Roz No 1
00-556 Warsaw
Tel: (48) 22 311 00 00

### Places of interest
*Great Masurian Lakes:* the main lakes are linked by rivers and canals, a prime area for yachting and canoeing.

*Krakow:* a lively city with old architecture from different periods.

*The Tatras:* an alpine range of towering peaks, rocky cliffs and glacial lakes, many walking paths especially the spectacular route to the Zawrat Pass.

*Warsaw:* a grand stretch of road is the Royal Way, lined with churches, palaces, galleries and museums, Royal castle and Lazienki Palace.

### Cuisine of the region
Polish food is rich in meat with plenty of potatoes and dumplings but not so many vegetables. Ingredients often used are dill, marjoram, caraway seeds and wild mushrooms. There are normally four daily meals: early breakfast, a light snack for second breakfast, a substantial lunch and a small supper.

*Barszcz:* beetroot soup

*Bigos:* sauerkraut and meat

## Poland

### PL3002 Auto Camping Park Nr. 130
Ul. Sudecka 42, PL-58-500 Jelenia Góra (Dolnoslaskie)
Tel: 075 752 4525. Email: campingpark@interia.pl

This site is almost in the centre of Jelenia Gora, which is situated at the foot of the Karkonosze Mountains. It is close to the Czech border and the famous 'crystal glass' town of Szklarska Poreba. The 80 level touring pitches are on terraced grass, all with 10A electricity and there are mature trees. A new hotel is adjacent to the site with tennis courts. Some road noise should be expected. Jelenia Gora's historic centre, with a Baroque town hall, is surrounded by arcaded town houses and is just a few minutes walk from this pleasant campsite. Places to visit locally include Cieplice, the Szlarka waterfall, Karpacz and Sobieszow with its Chojnik Castle. Silesia has a varied landscape that distinguishes it from other regions of Poland and it has many hiking trails in the picturesque Sudeten Mountains that make it an area that invites exploration.

#### Facilities
The small, heated sanitary block provides toilets and hot showers which are good and clean. Facilitied for disabled visitors. Kitchen with cookers, sinks and fridges. Sinks for laundry and dishwashing. Motorcaravan service point. Playground. Satelitte TV. Off site: Jelenia Góra and Silesia and in the winter skiing on the nearby slopes.

**Open:** All year.

#### Directions
From the centre of Jelenia Gora follow the signs to Karpacz. As you climb the hill the site is on the right. GPS: N50:50.781 E15:44.576

#### Charges 2007
| | |
|---|---|
| Per person | PLN 10,00 |
| pitch | PLN 8,00 - 17,00 |
| electricity | PLN 6,00 |
| dog | PLN 5,00 |

## PL3000 Camping Sloneczna Polana

Ul. Rataja 9, Cieplice, PL-58-560 Jelenia Góra (Dolnoslaskie)
Tel: 075 755 2566. Email: info@campingpolen.com

This is a small family site located at the foot of 'The Giant Mountains'. It is close to the health resort of Cieplice and the Karkonosze National Park and should provide a useful stop on your way through Poland or for a visit to the many interesting sites around Jelenia Góra. The site provides 70 individual flat, grass touring pitches (up to 100 sq.m.) with electrical connections (10A) and with some shade from mature trees. The Dutch owners, Peter and Liesbeth van Kinderen, organise grill nights in high season and folklore nights with the locals. This site has everything to offer for an active and healthy holiday with several marked walking routes through the mountains and spa and mud baths near. For children there is a play house, trampoline and an open air pool with separate paddling pool. During your stay here you may also enjoy a visit to the 'Huta Julia' crystal factory, the town of Szklarska Poreba with beautiful panoramic views and waterfalls and a day trip by bus to the city of Prague.

### Facilities
Clean and well maintained sanitary facilities with free hot water to vanity style washbasins (one cabin for ladies), showers and dishwashing. Washing machine and dryer. Pool (8 x 4 m.) with paddling pool (3 x 3m). Motorcaravan service point. Bar with covered terrace (all season). Restaurant. Snack bar (June – August, Mondays closed). Small playground. Play house with games. Table tennis. Basketball. Boules. Volleyball. Badminton. Internet access. WiFi. Boules. Off site: Bicycle hire 1 km. Outdoor pool 1.5 km. Fishing 2.5 km. Riding 5 km. Jelenia Góra 7 km.

**Open:** 1 May - 30 September.

### Directions
Jelenia Góra is on road 3 (E65) about 25 km. from the Czech border. Cieplice is about 7 km. southwest of Jelenia Góra and the site is well signed from there. Access to the site is a sharp left turn in a bend right after the bridge. GPS: N50:51.908 E15:39.792

### Charges 2007
| | |
|---|---|
| Per person | PLN 10,40 |
| child (4-12 yrs) | PLN 5,20 |
| pitch | PLN 10,40 - 22,00 |
| electricity | PLN 14,00 |
| car | PLN 8,00 |

## PL3003 Camping Boduwico

Ul. Lesna 1, PL-52-580 Janowice Wielkie (Dolnoslaskie)
Tel: 0757515243. Email: boduwico@dip.pl

The village of Janowice Wielkie lies just south of the Karkonosze mountains of southwest Poland. The area is popular for hiking, biking, climbing and skiing and attracts visitors all year. Nearby is the curius Wang hapel in the town of Karpacz and 15 km. to the west is Jelenia Gora, the gateway to some pf Poland's most popular recreational areas. As a base for any of these activities or for generally exploring the region, Camping Boduwico offers a quiet and pleasant spot. It is a small, partly wooded and sloping grassy site with just 12 touring pitches, all with 6A electric hook-ups. There is occasional noise from a nearby railway.

### Facilities
Tiled and heated sanitary facilities include hot showers and washing facilities. Current facilities are communal, but separate areas are planned. No facilities for disabled visitors. Bar and limited restaurant on request. TV in main house. Multilingual managers. Off site: Nearby mountain walking and skiing areas in Karkonoze National Park.

**Open:** All year.

### Directions
From Jelenia Gora take road E65 direction Wroclaw. After about 2 kms take right turn to Janowice Wilke. Climb hill about 0.5 km and turn left at sign down unpaved steep road to site.

### Charges 2007
| | |
|---|---|
| Per unit with electricity | PLN 27,85 - 34,55 |
| person | PLN 12,05 |
| child (1-11 yrs) | PLN 9,05 |
| dog | PLN 6,50 |

Check real time availability and at-the-gate prices...
www.alanrogers.com

# Poland

### PL3006 Camping Olimpijski Nr. 117

Ul. Paderewskiego. 35, PL-51-612 Wroclaw (Dolnoslaskie)

Tel: **071 348 4651**

Wroclaw sits on the River Oder and boasts over a hundred bridges. The historic town centre has an impressive mixture of architectural influences, from Flemish style, Renaissance mansions to a late Gothic Town Hall, and has a fine collection of open-air restaurants and cafés. The campsite is 5 km. rom the town centre at the Olympic stadium and has convenient tram services to town. It would be a good site for an overnight stop or for a couple of says sightseeing. It is a large site with pitches for 180 touring units on level, grassy ground with some trees.

#### Facilities

Two toilet blocks, both in need of of some updating. Hot and cold showers and washbasins. Small shop at entrance. Bar and snacks (high season). Games room and TV. Basic cottages to rent. Off site: Sports facilities adjacent.

**Open:** All year.

#### Directions

From Wroclaw, follow E67 and signs for 'Stadion Olimpiji' (very large floodlights are a good indicator). Site is about 5 km. from the centre.
GPS: N51:07.002 E17:05.469

#### Charges 2007

| | |
|---|---|
| Per unit with 2 persons and electricity | PLN 13,50 - 20,00 |

---

### PL3010 Camping Lesny Nr. 52

Ul. Sulechowska 39, PL-65-454 Zielona (Lubuskie)

Tel: **032 536 36**

The Silesian town of Zielona Gora largely escaped damage during the war and has a variety of architectural styles, a population of 100,000 and has become the centre of the textile industry. The campsite is 5 km. from the centre of town at the rear of the bright yellow painted Hotel Lesny and one books in at the hotel reception which is open 24 hours. The hotel occupies one side of the site with direct access to the 24 hour bar/restaurant. The 140 flat tourist pitches are on grassy sand between concrete access roads. They are not marked out and where you pitch is determined by 12 electric connection boxes which have points for four units. With tall trees on two sides of the square site and a small area for tents under the pines, it is a quiet site, ideal for a night stop in transit or for a longer stay if wishing to explore the southwest part of Poland. There is no shop but these can be found about 10 minutes walk away or in the town, together with sports facilities in the nearby stadium.

#### Facilities

The single sanitary block in the centre of the site is old, but clean, newly tiled and smelling fresh. Facilities for disabled visitors. Ironing board (iron from reception). Bar/restaurant (24 hrs). Small playground. Games room with table tennis. Parking inside fence and gate with 24 hour security guard (keys to the gate provided). Off site: Zielona Gora 5 km. Riding 5 km. Fishing 20 km.

**Open:** 1 May - 1 October.

#### Directions

From the Polish border coming from Berlin, take no. 29 road to Zielona Góra and continue on no. 32 road to Zielona Góra/Poznan. At first roundabout approaching Zielona Góra, turn left towards Poznan. Proceed on dual carriageway, crossing next roundabout. Turn right at next roundabout, GPS: N51:57.242 E15:31.783

#### Charges 2007

| | |
|---|---|
| Per person | PLN 8,00 |
| caravan or motorcaravan | PLN 12,00 |
| tent | PLN 8,00 |
| electricity | PLN 6,50 |

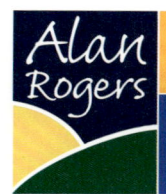

---

**Alan Rogers** www.**alanrogers**.com

All campsites are inspected & selected by Alan Rogers.

**Just Click and Go!**

INSPECTED CAMPSITES & SELECTED

Check real time availability and at-the-gate prices...
www.alanrogers.com

## PL3050 Camping Tramp Nr. 33

Ul. Kujawska 14, PL-87-100 Torun (Kujawsko-Pomorskie)
Tel: **056 654 7187.** Email: **tramp@mosir.torun.pl**

Camping Tramp has a pleasant appearance and lies in a basin below the level of the roads which run on both sides of the site. A variety of trees cover part of the site where pitches (with electric hook-ups) mingle with holiday bungalows. The other, larger field is an open meadow, where half the pitches have electricity. The 100 pitches, reached from hard access roads, are neither marked nor numbered but the position of electric boxes define where to go. Some pitches are separated by low hedging. The main E75 runs along one side of the campsite just before a busy junction and river bridge resulting in continuous traffic noise. Torun, a Gothic jewel built originally by the Teutonic Knights and now listed by UNESCO as a world heritage site, like so many Polish towns has a long, interesting and troubled history. Famous as the birth place of Copernicus, it is today a prosperous university city on the wide River Wisla. The old walled town is worth a visit in its own right, and with a major part of it pedestrianised, walking over the Wisla bridge from the campsite is a perfect way to enjoy your visit. Inevitably the town has a planetarium which has two shows a day in English. Whilst we would not recommend this as a 'holiday' base, it makes a good night stop when travelling between Germany and the Baltic coast or to visit Torun.

### Facilities

One refurbished and fully tiled, traditional style toilet block with toilets, hot showers and washbasins. Clean and smelling fresh when visited but without dressing space. Washing Machine. Dishwashing sinks. Facilities for disabled visitors (ramped access). Welcoming bar/restaurant (good value) with basic food supplies. Basketball. Playing field. Fishing. Off site: Town with restaurants and shops 2 km. Riding 5 km. Golf 10 km.

**Open:** 1 May - 30 September.

### Directions

From the south approaching the town you have a choice – fork left for a restricted height route (max 3.2 m) or straight on. If you fork left go under the bridge and turn right immediately to site 300 m. on left. If straight on, floow blue truck signs for 1 km, then turn back towards main bridge. Site access on right before river crossing. From the north go over the Wisla bridge and turn left before railway to site in 300 m. on left. GPS: N53:00.016 E18:36.451

### Charges 2007

| | |
|---|---|
| Per person | PLN 8,00 |
| child (under 10 rrs) | PLN 4,00 |
| pitch | PLN 5,00 - 26,00 |
| electricity (10A) | PLN 8,00 |

## PL3210 Astur Camping Nr. 123

Ul. Bitwy Warszawskiej 1920 R 15/17, PL-02-366 Warsaw (Mazowieckie)
Tel: **022 823 3748.** Email: **camp123@wp.pl**

Camp 123 is inside the city boundary about 4 km. (20 minutes by bus) from the centre of the Polish capital. The trees on the site provide enough shade in the hot Polish summer and it is nice to come back to a reasonably cool and surprisingly quiet environment after a hard day's visit to this historic and interesting city. With room for about 40 caravans and tents, the site is in an oblong section leading from reception and entrance. At the end of the site are some bungalows for rent. Grass pitches on sand are on either side of concrete paved roads and all have electric connections. Maps of Warsaw can be purchased at reception (English spoken).

### Facilities

One 'portacabin' style, clean refurbished toilet block with toilets, hot showers and basins. En-suite unit for disabled visitors with seat at the washbasin and the shower. Dishwashing with free hot water. Tennis courts and playground next to the site. Off site: Warsaw inner city 20 minutes by bus/tram.

**Open:** 1 May - 15 October.

### Directions

From south via 7/8 roads from Kraków-Katowice-Czestochowa, turn left at junction with Ul. Bitwy Warszawskiej road towards West train/bus station. Site is on left opposite a medical centre. From west via 2 road from Poznan keep right on Wolska road onto Kasprzaka road. Take first right onto Al Prymasa Tysiaclecia road. This continues into Ul. Bitwy Warszawskiej road. Site is on the right. From the north, follow ring road towards Kraków, pass under railway bridge and under road 718 and site is on the right in 300 m. GPS: N52:12.867 E20:57.940

### Charges 2007

| | |
|---|---|
| Per person | PLN 12,00 |
| child (under 4-10 yrs) | PLN 7,00 |
| pitch incl. electricity | PLN 55,00 - 65,00 |
| tent | PLN 14,00 |

**Check real time availability and at-the-gate prices...**
www.**alanrogers**.com

# Poland

## PL3035 Lido Camping Nr. 26

Wroclawska 6, 63-421 Przgodzice, PL-63-422 Antonin (Wielkopolskie)

Tel: **062 734 8194**

In this village, in the heart of a large forest and next to a large recreational lake, Duke Antoni Radziwill built an unusual larchwood hunting lodge in 1822. It has a cruciform plan and an octagonal hall that is surrounded by galleries supported by a large central pillar. It was here that in 1827 that Frederic Chopin taught Wanda, the Duke's daughter, with whom he fell in love. Unfortunately the piano on which the great composer played was chopped up for firewood by the Red Army who were billeted in the lodge. The lodge now houses a Centre for Culture and Art and is the venue for festivals and concerts in honour of Chopin. The campsite here has 45 pitches, all with electricity, but many restricted by tress that cover the site. The site may make a convenient overnight stop.

### Facilities

The old but clean sanitary block has toilets and showers. Chemical toilet disposal. Small campers' kitchen with sinks and electric rings. TV room. Off site: Antonin.

**Open:** 1 May - 30 September.

### Directions

Road 11 runs north from Katowice towards Poznan. This campsite is at Antonin, which is about 28 km. north of Kepno. Just after entering the village the site is on the east side of the main highway. GPS: N51:00.600 E17:50.799

### Charges 2007

| | |
|---|---|
| Per person | PLN 8,00 |
| pitch | PLN 6,00 - 10,00 |

## PL3070 Morski Camping

Ul. Turystyczna 3, PL-84-360 Leba (Pomorskie)

Tel: **059 866 1380**. Email: camp21@op.pl

Situated at the mouth of a small river with a marina, and just north of the village of Leba, Morski Camping is one of three which are about 200 m. from the sea and 300 m. from the centre of the village. This site is in a pleasant, quiet location and attractively landscaped with a number of mature trees and many shrubs and flowers. There are 250 level pitches, all numbered and separated a variety of shrubs and mature trees that provide shade. The whole site is being renewed and both toilet blocks which are surrounded by flowers are a real asset. Unusually for Poland, the whole site is covered by WiFi internet access. Leba is a holiday resort with lots of good value bars and restaurants, close to the Baltic sea and its beaches, but the site is quiet and has night security. This area of Poland is excellent for walking and cycling or spending some time on the beautiful, sandy beaches. Leba is close to the Slowinski National Park, with its 30 m. high sand dunes – there is a good view of them from the viewpoint at Smoldzino. It is advisable to arrive with a plentiful supply of gas, as it is very hard to obtain here.

### Facilities

Two immaculate sanitary blocks with toilets, controllable hot showers, open plan washbasins, child size toilets and en-suite facilities for disabled. Laundry with sinks and two washing machines. Dishwashing sinks. Motorcaravan service point. Bar/restaurant/shop with basic supplies (20 June - Sept). Playground. WiFi. Off site: Beach, bicycle hire and boat launching 200 m. Slowieski National Park. Fishing and golf 1 km. Riding 3 km. Sailing 10 km.

**Open:** 1 May - 30 September.

### Directions

From road no. 6/E28 Koszalin-Wejherowo, turn north on the 214 at Lebork to Leba. Follow signs to campsites on left (keep going left) on main street and continue to site. GPS: N54:45.690 E17:32.296

### Charges 2007

| | |
|---|---|
| Per person | PLN 13,00 |
| child (4-12 yrs) | PLN 6,00 |
| pitch | PLN 8,00 - 18,00 |
| electricity | PLN 9,00 |

Camping Cheques accepted.

## PL3080 Intercamp Nr. 84

Ul. Turystyczna 10, PL-84-360 Leba (Pomorskie)

Tel: 059 866 2230. Email: intercamp@ta.pl

This is a large site with some 800 unmarked pitches. When we visited, in the second week of August, four of the six identical sanitary blocks were out of use. However, the site was very quiet and that was not a problem. Pitching is on large, grassy fields with a tarmac access road. Leba is one of Poland's popular seaside resorts, similar in many ways to a British or Dutch seaside town. With large sandy beaches on the Baltic Sea only 1 km. from the site and the town only a few minutes walk away. Leba is also close to the Slowinski National Park, famous for its large shifting sand dunes which move at a rate of 9 metres a year leaving behind the stumps of dead trees. The sad thing is that in June and July Poland not only enjoys its sunniest hottest days but also has its highest rainfall, so come prepared! The area was once a gulf of which the lakes Lebsko and Gardno are vestiges. The park, a 'World Biosphere' reserve, is a haven for wild birds; more than 250 species, including the rare sea eagle, are found here. The park's highest point, Rowokol, offers a fine view of the dunescape.

### Facilities

Each of the six sanitary block has toilets and showers and is clean, although a little worn. Chemical toilet disposal. Small campers' kitchen with sinks. Small shop. Bar and café. Play area. Bicycle hire. Internet café. Off site: Beach 1 km. Leba, the harbour and the beach plus numerous shops, bars and restaurants.

**Open:** 1 June - 30 September.

### Directions

From Lebork take the 214 to Leba. As you enter the town, just past Orlen petrol station, fork left past the station. At mini-roundabout turn left, go over the bridge and the site is 150 m. on the left.

### Charges 2007

| | |
|---|---|
| Per person | PLN 11,00 |
| child (0-12 yrs) | PLN 6,00 - 10,00 |
| pitch | PLN 8,00 - 25,00 |
| electricity | PLN 9,00 |

## PL3090 Kemping Nr. 19 Kamienny Potok

Ul. Zamkowa Góra 25, PL-81-713 Sopot (Pomorskie)

Tel: 058 550 0445

Kamienny Potok is set back from the beach in Sopot and, by Polish standards, is a large site with 288 touring pitches, some back to back on either side of concrete access roads, others in open meadows. Places are numbered but not marked out, of grass on sand and 150 pitches have electricity (6-10A). With well mown grass, the site was neat and tidy. There are many tall trees around the site, although not much shade in camping areas. It is an easy 25 minute train ride from the site to Gdansk and the station is only 500 m. walk. Dutch clubs rally here and the whole campsite has a pleasant quiet atmosphere, although there is some road and train noise near the entrance. Sopot is a popular seaside resort on the Gulf of Gdansk with a sandy beach, promenade and pier against a background of wooded hills. There are many attractions nearby including 'Opera-in-the-Woods' with 5,000 seats, an annual pop concert and centres of historic interest. From the pier a ferry service departs for Gdansk, Gdynia or to Hel on the Baltic Sea peninsula and it is possible to travel from Gdansk to Finland.

### Facilities

Three toilet blocks (all refurbished to high standards) with toilets, open style washbasins, hot showers and sinks for dishwashing. Facilities for disabled visitors. Motorcaravan service point. Washing machine. Open air bar with food service. Playgrounds. Fishing. Volleyball. Basketball. TV room. Billiard club with electronic dart boards (also sells drinks). Off site: Swimming pool complex with giant slide 200 m. Beaches 500 m. Riding 1 km. Bicycle hire 1.5 km. Boat launching/hiring 2 km. Shell garage with basic food supplies. Ferry service to Gdansk, Gdynia and Hel 1 km.

**Open:** 1 May - 30 September.

### Directions

Site is 2 km. north of Sopot on main road behind Shell garage. Take the exit for the Sopot Aqua Park and immediately turn left.

GPS: N54:27.702 E18:33.311

### Charges 2007

| | |
|---|---|
| Per person | PLN 12,00 |
| child (4-15 yrs) | PLN 6,00 |
| pitch | PLN 5,00 - 9,00 |
| electricity (10A) | PLN 9,00 |

# Poland

## PL3100 Camping Przy Plazy Nr. 67

Ul. Bitwy pod Plowcami 73, PL-81-731 Sopot (Pomorskie)

Tel: 058 551 6523. Email: camping67@sopot.pl

This is a large site for Poland, with 180 unmarked pitches, 160 with electricity (16A). There is shade from mature trees and direct access to the beach. Some road nooise can be heard as the Gdansk - Gdynia coast road runs past the site. Sopot is Poland's most popular seaside resort and one of the large sandy beaches is only 25 m. from this site, with the town only a short walk away. The town was first established as a sea bathing centre in 1824 and its heyday came in the interwar years when it attracted the richest people in Europe. The pier and the main street contain many bars, restaurants and cafes and is a pleasant place to enjoy a beer and the sea air.

### Facilities
Each sanitary block has toilets and showers and is a little worn. Motorcaravan drain down available. Small covered campers' kitchen with sinks. Small shop and buffet. Play area. Off site: Sopot with numerous shops, bars and restaurants. Beach, sailing, bicycle hire and riding within 1 km.

**Open:** 15 June - 31 August.

### Directions
Sopot is between Gdansk and Gydnia on Poland's Baltic coast. To find this site you need to be on the coastal road between Sopot and Gdansk. The site is next to the new Novotel at the southern end of the town and is well signed.

### Charges 2007
| | |
|---|---|
| Per person | PLN 11,00 |
| child (7-16 yrs) | PLN 8,90 |
| pitch incl. electricity | PLN 16,00 - 21,00 |

## PL3155 Camping KamA

Talty 36 k, PL-11-730 Mikolajki (Warminsko-Mazurskie)

Tel: 0487 65 75. Email: akaminski@maxi.pl

A small family campsite on the banks of Lake Talty north of Mikolajki, Camping KamA is run by the Kaminski family. Whilst the site straddles the small rural road, it creates two small unique areas, providing in total 50 pitches with 16A electricity. The first to the left is on the banks of the lake, whilst the second, a little higher on the right, is where reception and all the facilities are to be found. Here the site is also level having climbed the small access road. Both areas provide electricity. Lake Talty is good for canoeing, yachting and swimming and it would be possible to launch small boats.

### Facilities
Small sanitary block with toilets and showers. Facilities for disabled visitors. Motorcaravan services. Chemical disposal point. Bar and restaurant. Pool table. Play area. Fishing. Bicycle hire. Beach. Boat launching. Watersports. Off site: Mikolajki and the Mazurian lakes.

**Open:** 1 May - 30 September.

### Directions
From Mikolajki take no. 16 road towards Elk. Just after railway bridge turn left towards Talty. Go through village and site straddles the road just a few hundred metres to the north. From Elk, just before Mikolajki at 228.5 post, turn right towards Talty.

### Charges 2007
| | |
|---|---|
| Per person | PLN 13,00 |
| child (0-10 yrs) | PLN 6,00 |
| pitch incl. electricity | PLN 30,00 |

## PL3160 Camping Echo

PL-11-511 Rydzewo (Warminsko-Mazurskie)

Tel: 087 421 1186. Email: echo@mazury.info

This is a very good, small family campsite run by the welcoming owner, Barbara Nowakowska. With only space for about 40 pitches, all with 6A electricity, it would be a good choice for a short or medium term stop while you explore and enjoy the Mazurian Lakes. It is on the eastern banks of Lake Neogocin which is popular with watersports enthusiasts and swimmers alike. The Mazurian Lakes area is a very popular holiday spot but despite this the countryside remains unspoiled with many rare plants and birds thriving here. The district is also a paradise for ramblers.

### Facilities
The small sanitary block has toilets and hot showers which are immaculate. Washing machine. Chemical disposal point. Bread to order. Gas. Small restaurant and bar. Fishing. Bicycle hire. Beach. Boat trips on the lake. Boat launching possible. Off site: Mazurian Lakes and not far away the Wolfslair, Hitler's bunker.

**Open:** 1 May - 30 September.

### Directions
Rydzewo is south of Gizycko and the site is easy to find just on the northern outskirts of the village. It is on the eastern banks of Lake Neogocin. Coming from Mikolajki, turn right after Kamin towards Pratski, cross the river and continue north towards Rydzebo.

### Charges 2007
| | |
|---|---|
| Per person | PLN 12,00 |
| child (3-16 yrs) | PLN 8,00 |
| pitch incl. car and electricity | PLN 28,00 |

Check real time availability and at-the-gate prices...
www.alanrogers.com

## PL3110 Camping Stegna Nr. 180

Ul. Morska 15, PL-82-103 Stegna (Pomorskie)
Tel: 055 247 8254

With so much of Poland being flat, it is surprising to find wooded hills so near the sea. The bustling seaside resort of Stegna is about 25 km. east of Gdansk in pleasant countryside and Camping Stegna 180 is right by a sandy beach. The presence of a restaurant and kiosks at the campsite entrance and the beach access suggest that it attracts many day visitors in summer. This pleasant site has 200 pitches (150 for tourers), 140 with 6-16A electricity. Some are on slopes under tall pines, some are flat, but all are within sight and sound of the sea shore. A few pitches at the entrance are reserved for disabled visitors. Some pitches are rather small, depending on the position of the trees and there are several hardstandings for motorcaravans or caravans towards the front of the site. Several picnic tables are provided for tent campers. The site would suit those looking for a beach holiday or a respite from touring and those who would like to visit Gdansk or tour the peninsula, which stretches all the way to the Russian border. In summer the site gets very busy with Polish campers, although all seems very organised and security staff at the gate keep things running smoothly. Just outside the entrance is a small, resort style shopping centre with bars and restaurants.

### Facilities
Two good, heated toilet blocks could be under pressure in high season when hot water and cleaning could be variable. It has toilets, washbasins, hot showers and child-size showers. Facilities for disabled visitors. Covered area with sinks. Wooden chalets with gas hobs. Open air bar. Restaurant at entrance. Volleyball. Basketball. Riding. Fishing. Bicycle hire (children only). Watersports. Outdoor paddling pool. Video games. Off site: Gdansk 25 km. Baltic Sea beaches. Fishing 7 km. Sailing 10 km. Golf 30 km.

**Open:** 1 May - 15 September.

### Directions
From no. 7/E77 Gdansk - Elbag road take road no. 502 at Nowy Dwor signed Stegna to village. Turn right to enter village, then left at church signed 'Stegna Port' with campsite sign.
GPS: N54:45.604 E19:32.288

### Charges 2007
| | |
|---|---|
| Per person | PLN 13,00 |
| child (4-12 yrs) | PLN 10,00 |
| pitch incl. electricity | PLN 24,00 - 33,00 |
| tent | PLN 8,00 - 13,00 |

## PL3170 Camping Pension Galindia Mazurski Eden

Bartlewo 1, PL-12-210 Ukta (Warminsko-Mazurskie)
Tel: 087 423 1416. Email: galindia@galindia.com.pl

Mazurski Eden is in the centre of the beautiful Mazurian Lake District, surrounded by the interesting flora and fauna of the Piska forest. It is a quite amazing place approached by a 1.5 km. sand road, easily negotiable by caravans, with the entrance flanked by tall pine posts of carved figures. Wood carvings abound with statues by the water's edge, on buildings and inside the hotel. The camping area, with room for 100 units, is grass on sand under tall trees which serve to determine the pitches, with electrical connection boxes topped with lamps for night illumination. A wealth of activities includes organised photographic safaris, canoeing and hiking trips, cycle excursions and visits to the Kadzidlowo nature reserve with its wolves, bison, beavers and other wildlife. Sailing and other watersports are arranged and even fishing under the ice in winter. Parties, picnics and barbecues are organised with dancing and folk bands. Various national days are noted, with open air workshops for painters and sculptors and church festivals are celebrated in a family atmosphere. The manager has a great interest in the social history of the ancient people of this area and this is reflected in the entertainment offered to group conferences being held in the hotel, to which campers are invited.

### Facilities
Good tiled sanitary block (caveman style) with toilets, basins and showers. Dishwashing sinks with free hot water. Laundry service in the hotel. Motorcaravan service point. Kayaks, canoes, sailing boats and pedaloes for hire. Beach. Boat mooring. 'Cave men' festivities. Bar in cave under the pension with billiards. Open air bar near the lake. 'Cave men style' restaurant. Lounge with TV with English and German channels. Cave men style events organised with 'Chief Galindia'. Off site: Skiing and sailing.

**Open:** All year.

### Directions
Take 609 road from Mikolajki to Ukta and turn off towards Iznota (signed Iznota 3 km.) on sand road. Pass through Nowy Most to Iznota and follow camp signs. GPS: N53:44.049 E21:33.794

### Charges 2007
| | |
|---|---|
| Per person | PLN 15,00 |
| pitch | PLN 13,00 - 26,00 |
| electricity | PLN 20,00 |

## Poland

### PL3175 Stanica Wodna P.T.T.K. Nowy Most

Osrodek Turystyki Nowy Most, PL-12-210 Ukta (Warminsko-Mazurskie)

Tel: 087 423 6045. Email: biuro@nowymost.pl

This lovely small site, which is on a river bank, offers real peace and quiet, along with Polish hospitality. It has 30 pitches for tents without electricity and there are two pitches with electricity for tourers. The site is used by many nationalities who arrive here with their canoes and usually stay one or two nights before continuing their tour through this marvellous lake area. Others stay for a week or two, as the site has kayaks for rent and organises walking and riding trips in the Mazurskie Lake District – this area of 1,500 square kilometres contains over 3,000 large and small lakes and is one of the biggest tourist attractions in Poland, close to the borders of Lithuania, Belarus and Russia.

**Facilities**

One tiled toilet block (key access) provides toilets, open plan washbasins, hot showers and family showers and facilities for disabled visitors. Separate fish cleaning area. Open air bar. Good value restaurant. Barbecue. Volleyball. Kayaks, canoes and bicycles for rent. Fishing. Organised walking and riding. Off site: Canoeing, walking and biking and riding.

**Open:** 1 May - 30 September.

**Directions**

Take 609 road from Mikolajki to Ukta and turn off at sign for 'Iznota 3 km.' to continue on asphalt road. Site is on the left immediately after the bridge in Nowy Most. GPS: N53:43.923 E21:31.141

**Charges 2007**

| | |
|---|---|
| Per person | PLN 10,00 |
| electricity | PLN 5,00 |

### PL3190 Camping Pension Kruska

Wygryny 52, PL-12-220 Wygryny (Warminsko-Mazurskie)

Tel: 087 423 1597. Email: 2Biqre@orange.pl

If you are looking for a cheaper option with just room for camping and no frills, this small site for about 60 units might suit. Pitches which are neither marked out nor numbered, are on slightly sloping ground between the Pension and the lake. There is some shade available near the lake but the main field is in the open and units group around the electricity boxes (10/16A). It could become crowded in high season with German visitors. The pitches offer beautiful views over the lake and the site has canoes for hire. There is a small jetty which can be used for a variety of watersports and the Mazurskie Lake District also has a lot to offer for walking and cycling.

**Facilities**

Two fully equipped, excellent sanitary blocks. Motorcaravan service point. Bar with light meals. Kiosk for ice and cold drinks. No shop but baker calls daily. Weekend entertainment with meals and live music. Activities organised. Canoe hire. Fishing. Bicycle hire. Boat launching. Torch useful. Off site: Shop, restaurant and bar 10 minutes walk. Sailing 1 km. Riding 3 km.

**Open:** All year.

**Directions**

Wygryny and the site are signed from road no. 610 Ukta - Ruciane-Nida. GPS: N53:41.172 E21:32.835

**Charges 2007**

| | |
|---|---|
| Per person | PLN 10,00 |
| child (under 10 yrs) | PLN 5,00 |
| electricity (16A) | PLN 10,00 |

### PL3300 Camping Polana Sosny Nr. 38

Os. Na Polenie Sosny, PL-34-441 Niedzica (Malopolskie)

Tel: 018 262 9403. Email: dworek@pro.onet.pl

The small village of Niedzica is south of the Pieniny mountain range in the Dunajec valley and about 40 km. northeast of Zakopane. This excellent little campsite is right alongside the Dunajec dam and the river, at the eastern end of the Czorsztynskie lake. With 35 level touring pitches, all with electricity, it is a good short or long stay. Adjacent is the Dwor restaurant which is open from 10.00 to 22.00 all the year. The raft ride on the river that flows through the limestone mountain gorges is one of the best known tourist attractions in Poland.

**Facilities**

The small sanitary block near reception has toilets and showers and two good sets of facilities for disabled visitors. Chemical toilet disposal. Small campers' kitchen with sinks and electric rings. Bar, restaurant and takeaway (all season). Off site: Village park adjacent with children

**Open:** All year.

**Directions**

From Nowy Targ head east on the 969. In village of Debno turn right towards Niedzica (17 km). The Czorsztynskie lake is on the left and Czorsztyn Castle is ahead. After the castle continue through Niedzica-Zamek towards Niedzica. Just before the second Dunajec dam bridge turn right and site is on the left. GPS: N49:24.246 E20:19.963

**Charges 2007**

| | |
|---|---|
| Per person | PLN 5,00 |
| pitch | PLN 15,00 - 30,00 |

Check real time availability and at-the-gate prices...

www.alanrogers.com

## PL3310 Camping Ustup
Ustup K/5, PL-34-500 Zakopane (Malopolskie)
Tel: 018 206 3667. Email: camping.ustup@op.pl

This is a very good, small campsite run enthusiastically by the Jarzabek family in the Polish winter capital, which is on a par with the best alpine resorts as an upmarket ski resort. With only space for about 24 pitches, all with electricity, this a good short or medium term stop while you explore and enjoy the Tatry Mountains and Zakopane. While some go hiking in the mountains, most are content to admire the scenery from the windows of their cable car gliding to the summit of Mt Kasprowy Wierch or from the funicular railway (14PLZ return) ascending Mt Gubalówka. Later in the day many visitors gather in Krupówki, the town's central pedestrian area that is lined with cafés, restaurants and souvenir shops. From the site you can enjoy views over the tree-clad hills to the west or the snow-capped mountain peaks, all over 2,000 m, to the south.

### Facilities
Small sanitary block has toilets and showers which are immaculate. Washbasins are both open and in cabins, with extra ones outside. Chemical toilet disposal. Shop. Bar. Restaurant. Off site: Bicycle hire 2 km. Puls supermarket right next door and McDonalds is 50 m. Zakopane (Winter Olympics 2006). Buses from just outside the site serve the town.

**Open:** 1 April - 15 October.

### Directions
Coming from Krakow on the 47, just after entering Zakopane there is the inevitable McDonalds. Turn right just before Orlen petrol station and McDonalds and then immediately right again. Site is on left in 25 m. GPS: N49:19.326 E19:59.113

### Charges 2007
| | |
|---|---|
| Per person | PLN 15,00 |
| child | PLN 10,00 |
| pitch | PLN 8,00 - 12,00 |
| electricity | PLN 12,00 |

## PL3320 Auschwitz Centre
Ul. M. Kolbego 1, PL-32-602 Oswiecim (Malopolskie)
Tel: 033 843 1000

Oswiecim is a name that many foreigners will not have heard, but any mention of the German equivalent, Auschwitz, evokes fear in almost everyone. Founded in 1992 this centre gives the outward appearance of being a first class hotel. Its aim is to create a venue for meetings, exchanges, education, reflection and prayer for all those who visit Auschwitz and are moved by what happened here. To further this aim campers are welcome to use the landscaped gardens with tents, motorcaravans or caravans and use the centre's facilities. Electricity has been provided (6A) with 20 pitches either on the grass or on the large parking area. The state museum in Oswiecim (Auschwitz/Birkenau), now a UNESCO World Heritage site, is only a few minutes walk away, and is open almost every day of the year. No visitor can leave unmoved. Entrance is free and guided tours are available in English; alternatively you could buy the English guide book and walk around on your own.

### Facilities
Showers and toilets are provided and are clean and well maintained. The restaurant in the centre may be used by campers. Off site: Oswiecim and the museums of Auschwitz and Birkenau.

**Open:** All year.

### Directions
The centre is 600 m. from the Auschwitz museum on the road to the south running parallel to the road that serves the museum. It is on the 950/933 and is situated between a roundabout and a large electricity substation. It appears to be a first class hotel from the outside and has facilities to match. GPS: N50:01.412 E19:11.879

### Charges 2007
| | |
|---|---|
| Per person | PLN 23,00 |

Poland

It's all about YOU and YOUR experiences…
So get involved today!
Visit www.mycamping.info

Check real time availability and at-the-gate prices…
www.alanrogers.com

## PL3340 Camping Smok Nr. 46

Kamedulska 18, PL-30-252 Krakow (Malopolskie)

Tel: 012 429 8300. Email: info@smok.krakow.pl

Just five kilometres or a short bus ride from this site is one of Europe's most beautiful cities, Krakow. It dates back to the tenth century and contains many fine buildings, such as the Cloth Market in the main square. A short (or somewhat longer) stay at Camping Smok is likely to be an essential part of any trip to Poland. It has 50 touring places, all with 6A electricity, in a semi-rural area along the Vistula valley and is only 5 km. from the A4 motorway junction. As you approach the site on the motorway you will see the Camaldolite Monastery at Bielany, high on a cliff. However, monks who are committed to absolute silence and no contact with the outside world inhabit it and visits are severely restricted. For the tourist, it is fortunate that most of the places of interest are located in its fairly compact historic centre. Start your tour in Rynek Glówny and you're spoilt for choice, but don't miss the Wawel, with its fine gothic cathedral and Renaissance castle.

### Facilities
The enlarged toilet block near reception has toilets and showers and is clean and tidy. Chemical toilet disposal. Washing machine. Covered cooking facilities for tents, with tables. Small shop with essentials only. Covered picnic hut. Off site: Kraków. Numerous buses from just outside the site serve the city centre.

**Open:** All year.

### Directions
From the A4 heading north take first exit having crossed the river, signed 'Kraków Centrum'. Turn left towards Kraków and after 2 km. at T-junction turn right onto the 780. After 3 km. (about 300 m. after the 'Hospital' sign) turn left into site. Reception is at the top of the steep climb.
GPS: N50:02.784 E19:52.868

### Charges 2007

| | |
|---|---|
| Per person | PLN 20,00 |
| child (4-14 yrs) | PLN 10,00 |
| car, caravan and electricity | PLN 37,00 |
| motorcaravan with electricity | PLN 30,00 |

No credit cards.

## PL3230 Camping Olenka Nr. 76

Ul. Olenki 22/30, PL-42-200 Czestochowa (Slaskie)

Tel: 034 360 6066. Email: camping@mosir.pl

Czestochowa's main claim to fame is the famous Jasna Góra monastery, one of Europe's most important pilgrimage centres. Camp 76 is located right behind the huge monastery car and coach park, on a slight slope with level pitches of grass and sand and some hardstandings. Pitches on one field are laid out in a circle, in the other along tarmac roads. Pitch size depends on the amount of visitors. Electricity boxes determine pitches which are otherwise not marked or numbered. There is room for about 200 units with the many mature trees, which enhance the site, giving shade in some parts. The icon of the Black Madonna, displayed in the monastery, has attracted thousands of pilgrims for 600 years and still does today because it is said to have healing powers. This site could make a useful night stop when passing through or for a day or two if visiting the monastery but it may be better not be here around 14/15, 25/26 August or 7/8 September – the site will be crowded with over 2,000 pilgrim visitors who come mostly on foot from all over the country.

### Facilities
Two toilet blocks (refurbished to a good standard) plus public toilet facilities in the reception area. Hot showers, toilets and open washbasins. Facilities for disabled visitors. Washing machine. Bar. English spoken. Off site: Jasna Góra Monastery 500 m, fishing 500 m.

**Open:** All year.

### Directions
Follow signs for Jasna Góra (the monastery which, being on a hill, is very obvious from most parts of town) and then camp signs or the signs for the big parking place at the back.
GPS: N50:48.555 E19:05.416

### Charges 2007

| | |
|---|---|
| Per person | PLN 15,00 |
| pitch | PLN 15,00 - 18,00 |
| car | PLN 12,00 |
| electricity | PLN 13,00 |

# Poland

## PL3250 Auto Camping Nr. 215
Ul. Murckowska 6, PL-40 266 Katowice (Slaskie)
Tel: 032 256 5939

Although the Górnóslaski industrial district, of which Katowice is the capital, is not a tourist centre, Camping 215, being near a lake and 5 km. from the town centre in a leafy suburb, makes a good one night stop when travelling from the west to Krakow or for a few days if visiting Auschwitz or Katowice. The site has five rectangular grass lawns, separated by hard access roads. There are just 40 unmarked, slightly sloping pitches for tourers, some being under trees and some in the open, but all having 6A electricity. The disadvantage of this site is that it is next to the main motorway and is therefore noisy. Katowice is an industrial city but has several museums and architectural monuments. Also worth visiting are the market, with the St Wyspianskiego Theatre, and the south part of town where the Kosciólek Park with its 16th century wooden church is situated.

### Facilities
One good, fully equipped toilet block on one side of the site with toilets, pre-set showers and open style washbasins. Dishwashing. Campers Off site: Lake with beach, boat launching and fishing 100 m. Katowice town centre 5 km.

**Open:** 1 May - 30 September.

### Directions
Site is about 5 km. south of Katowice centre, on the west side of Highway 86 (Katowice - Bielsko-Biala) and about 0.5 km. north of motorway A4 (Katowice to Krakow). Site is signed from Highway 86.
GPS: N50:14.646 E19:02.878

### Charges 2007
| | |
|---|---|
| Per person | PLN 10,00 |
| pitch | PLN 8,00 - 20,00 |
| electricity per kWh | PLN 2,50 |
| dog | PLN 5,00 |

---

## PL3280 Korona Camping Nr. 241
Ul. Myslenicka 32, PL-32-031 Gaj (Slaskie)
Tel: 012 270 1318. Email: biuro@camping-korona.com.pl

This attractively landscaped site, with direct access from the main road, is 10 km. from Krakow. It is down a slope, some 100 m. back from the road, so is not noisy and it has lovely views over the village. The site is terraced, but caravans and motorcaravans tend to use a flat area near the toilet block. Tent pitches are slightly sloping. It is a family run site that takes about 100 units, all with 6A electricity, and pitches are separated by young trees. To the back of the site is a large pond for fishing (well fenced) and a large, covered barbecue area. Mrs Trepizynska has fresh bread rolls available each morning and cooks a delicious stroganoff soup. There are buses from the main road into Krakow, but each evening Mr Trepizynska will ask if anyone wishes to make the trip and if he finds ten people, will take them in his own minibus for a small charge. Similarly he will take people to the Wieliczka salt mines (16 km). Ausschwitz is 64 km. and impressive enough to spend a day.

### Facilities
One modern toilet block (could be under pressure in high season) with hot showers (temperature can be variable), washbasins and toilets, all clean and well maintained. Baby bath in both sections. Dishwashing under cover. Shop. Bar with open air terrace and some basics. Fishing pond. Playing field. Volleyball. Playground. WiFi and internet access. Trips to Kraków and the Wieliczka salt mines. Off site: Bus stop outside site. Bar/restaurant 500 m. Tennis 2 km. Riding 3 km. Kraków 10 km. Beach 20 km.

**Open:** May - September.

### Directions
Site is 10 km. south of Kraków off the E77 Kraków - Zakopane road. Take care because access to the site is directly off the motorway and is particularly difficult when coming from Zakopane because one has to cross the motorway.
GPS: N49:57.760 E19:53.412

### Charges 2007
| | |
|---|---|
| Per person | PLN 15,00 |
| child (5-10 yrs) | PLN 10,00 |
| pitch incl. car | PLN 14,00 - 24,00 |
| electricity | PLN 8,00 |

149

Check real time availability and at-the-gate prices...
www.alanrogers.com

## Poland

### PL3330 Camping Ondraszek Nr. 57

Ul. Pocztowa 43, PL-43-309 Bielsko Biala (Slaskie)
Tel: 033 814 6425. Email: kemping57ondraszek@op.pl

If you enter Poland from the Czech Republic, Bielsko Biala could well be the first large town you enter. Formed by the joining of the Silesian town of Bielsko and the Galician town of Biala it was once an important centre for the textile industry. It is a good starting point for excursions into the Beskid Slaski Mountains and the local ski lift will take you to the Szyndzielnia peak 1,026 m. (3,300 feet). The site is located south of the town is in a pleasant park area. With 60 pitches for touring in two areas, some between mature trees, the site is quiet and well kept. Many streets contain miniature versions of old Viennese houses. The castle of the Sulkowski princes is also of interest. If you travel north east from here, about 30 km, you will find Oswiecim which is perhaps better known by its German name: Auschwitz.

#### Facilities

The small sanitary block near reception has toilets and showers and is clean and tidy. Small block near the pitches has WCs and washing troughs and one unisex shower. Motorcaravan service point. Bar and restaurant. Small shop with essentials only. Two small unheated swimming pools. Off site: Bielsko Biala. Park and sports facility adjoining the site.

**Open:** 15 April - 15 October.

#### Directions

Head towards the centre of Bielsko Biala and follow signs for Szczyrk on road 942, heading south. After 4 km, having left the main town, you will see the Parkhotel Vienna on the right. In 300 m. turn right up the hill (signed camping) and at the top turn left to site. GPS: N49:46.819 E19:03.191

#### Charges 2007

| | |
|---|---|
| Per person | PLN 9,00 |
| caravan or motorcaravan | PLN 25,00 |
| tent | PLN 10,00 |
| car | PLN 9,00 |

### PL3335 Camping C'est la Vie

Ul. Krolowej Jadwigi 41, PL-34-300 Zwyiec (Slaskie)
Tel: 033 865 24 27. Email: info@campingcestlavie.com

The town of Zywiec is situated at the southern end of the Jezioro Zywieckie lake, surrounded by the Beskidy mountains. The campsite provides the ideal base from which to visit several places of interest including Krakov, Osweicim (Auschwitz), Zacopane and Walowice (birthplace of Pope John Paul II). In addition the Zywiec area offers holiday activities such as hiking, watersports and an International Folklore festival in early August. The campsite overlooks the lake, is grassed with mature trees and provides 24 pitches for touring. It is a pleasant, peaceful small site. The managers are multi-lingual and very welcoming.

#### Facilities

Two small toilet blocks (one 'portacabin' style) near reception are clean, tiled and well maintained. Separate facilities for disabled visitors. Washing machine. Chemical disposal. Pleasant covered barbecue/fire with seating in centre of the site with views of the lake. Small play area. Three attractive A-frame chalets for rent. Off site: Small attractive town of Zywiec about 5 km. Access to nearby lake with watersports. Close to Auschwitz. Walking and skiing in Tatra mountains.

**Open:** 1 July - 1 September.

#### Directions

Site is on route 946 from Zywiec to Sucha B, about 5 km. from Zywiec on the lake.
GPS: N49:43.130 E19:12.663

#### Charges 2007

| | |
|---|---|
| Per person | € 2,50 |
| child (under 10 yrs) | € 1,50 |
| pitch | € 4,50 - € 6,00 |
| electricity (6A) | € 2,50 |

Prices in Euros.

Check real time availability and at-the-gate prices...
www.alanrogers.com

# Lithuania

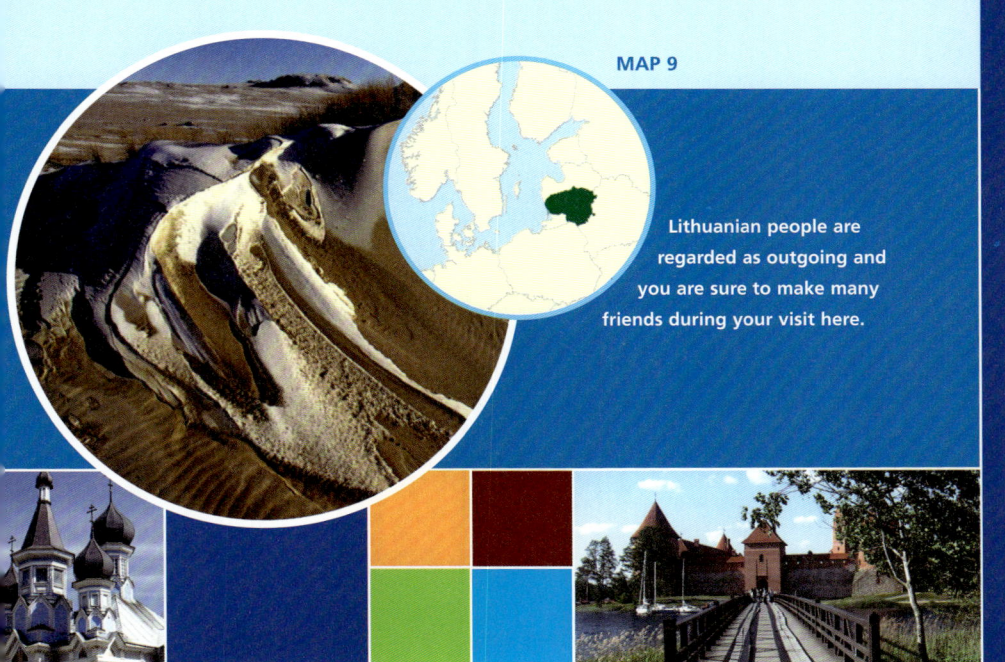

**MAP 9**

Lithuanian people are regarded as outgoing and you are sure to make many friends during your visit here.

For centuries, amber has been washed up onto the golden sands of the coastline and has historically become known as 'Lithuania's gold'. The unique sand spit here, created by wind and water, is an impressive formation stretching from the southwest to Klaipeda and enclosing the vast Curonian Lagoon. Old villages are said to be buried beneath but today there are several fishermen's settlements in their place. The capital Vilnius is often known as 'Baltic Jerusalem' which becomes quite apparent when you see the many churches, towers and medieval courtyards.

Kaunas is the second largest city with numerous buildings that combine together in a mix of arts and architecture of different eras. Klaipeda is well worth a visit as it is the country's main seaport and sits on the strait linking the Curonian Lagoon to the Baltic Sea. It is a modern city of quays and warehouses and a restored fortress, Kopgalis, is now a marine museum, aquarium and dolphinarium.

Throughout the regions, there are five national parks, established for the protection and study of the natural, cultural and historical heritage of the country. This is the place to be for a breath of fresh air and activities such as walking, cycling, horse riding and fishing.

**Population**
3.484 million

**Capital**
Vilnius

**Climate**
Maritime/continental. There is snow on the ground for about three months of the year and summers are warm.

**Language**
Lithuanian. Russian, Polish and German are widely spoken as is English in the major cities.

**Currency**
The Litas (Lt)

**Telephone**
The country code is 00 370

**Banks**
Generally open from 08.00-18.00. (Closed at weekends).

**Shops**
Shopping hours vary. In larger towns and cities, many are open from 09.00-19.00 with reduced hours at weekends.

# Lithuania

THE LARGEST AND MOST SOUTHERLY OF THE BALTIC STATES, THE LANDSCAPE IS MADE UP OF WONDERFUL ROLLING HILLS, GENTLE PLAINS, FLOWING RIVERS AND LAKES. MOST OF THE BALTIC SHORELINE IS SEPARATED FROM THE OPEN SEA BY A LONG NARROW STRIP OF SAND DUNES CALLED THE CURONIAN SPIT. WALKERS SHOULD BE AWARE THAT THE SPIT ALSO FORMS PART OF KALININGRAD, WHICH IS TERRITORY OF THE RUSSIAN FEDERATION.

### Public Holidays

New Year's Day; Freedom Day 13 Jan; Independence Day 16 Feb; Independence Restoration Day 11 March; Easter Sun, Mon; Labour Day 1 May; Mourning and Hope 14 June; State Day 6 July; Assumption 15 Aug; Black Ribbon 23 Aug; Constitution Day 25 Oct; All Saints Day 1 Nov; Christmas 25, 26 Dec.

### Motoring

From the beginning of September through to March, dipped headlights are required at all times. Ensure your car is well equipped during the winter months as weather conditions can be severe.
It is recommended that you use guarded car parks in larger towns, especially if leaving your car somewhere overnight.

### Tourist Office

Lithouanian Tourist Information Centre
86 Gloucester Place
London W1U 6HP
Tel: 020 7034 1222
Fax: 020 7935 4661
E-mail: tourism@lithuanianembassy.co.uk
Internet: www.tourism.lt/en

### British Embassy

Antakalnio 2
Vilnius LT-10308
Tel: (370) 5 246 29 00

### Places of interest

*Curonian Spit:* a 60 mile stretch of sand, dunes and pine forests, freshly smoked fish is a must, jet ski and paddle boat hire in Nida in summer, ice fishing.

*Hill of Crosses:* a forested area with thousands of devotional and memorial crosses.

*Palanga:* premier seaside resort, botanical park, excellent amber museum. A large street carnival, market, song festival and pop concert is held here to mark the opening and closing of the summer season.

*Vilnius:* Cathedral Square at the heart, churches, courtyards, the President's palace.

### Cuisine of the region

Traditional cuisine includes soup (beet, sauerkraut and sorrel), stews, sausages, smoked meat and rye bread.

Main meals consist of pork, chicken and duck or eel, pike and herring for fish.

Dairy products especially used are cottage cheese, curd cheese and eggs for omelets.

*Cepelinai:* potato dough with cheese, meat or mushroom in the centre, topped with a sauce of onions, sour cream and bacon.

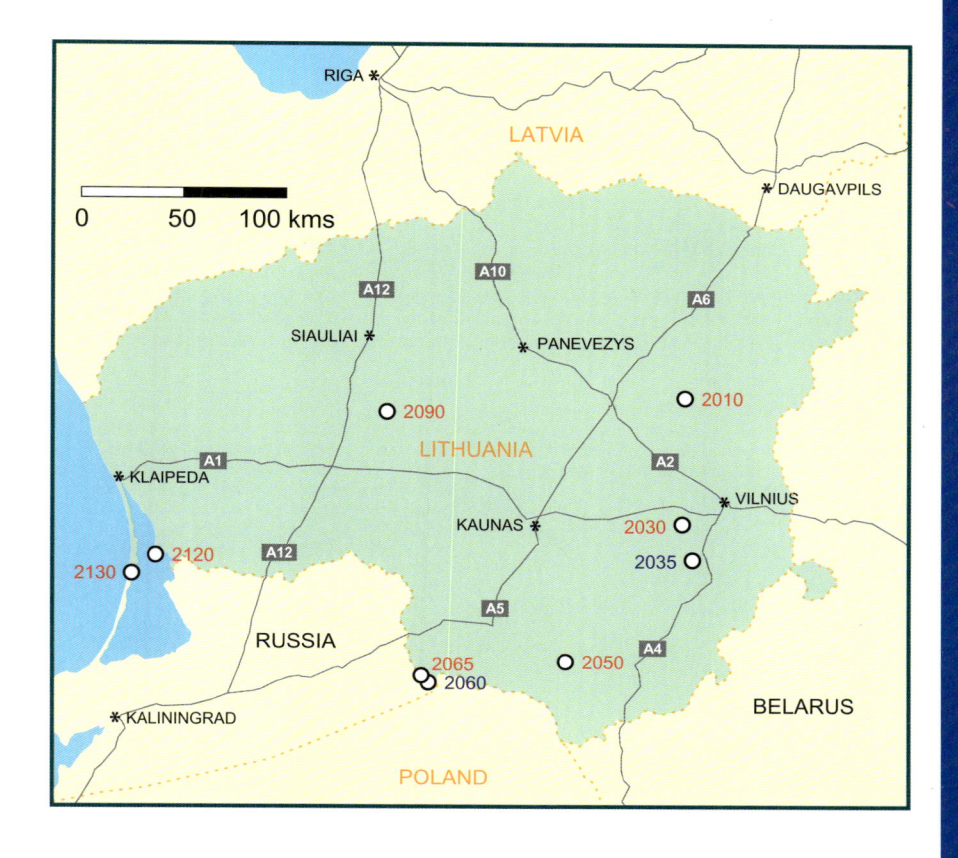

## LI2010 Apple Island
Grabuostas Lake, LT-33001 Zalvariai
Tel: 383 50073. Email: strenko@strenko.lt

Camping Apple Island is a new site, which is attractively located on an island on Lake Grabuostas, around 60 km. north of Vilnius. The site is named after the island where some 2500 apple trees were planted at the beginning of the nineteenth century. This region is predominantly made up of forests, lakes and rolling hills. In all, there are more than 300 lakes, including the largest in Lithuania, Lake Asveja. A little bridge leads to Camping Apple Island and the site offers some attractive tent pitches (no electricity) on sloping terrain in the shade of apple trees. Additionally, there are 24 hardstanding pitches with electricity, water and drainage, all of which are level and of a good size. These pitches also have a grass area with private picnic bench. Leisure facilities here include tennis, boules, volleyball and minigolf, and there is an attractive lakeside beach with barbecue facilities. The central building, formerly a barn, houses a welcoming bar/restaurant with good value meals and an adjacent covered terrace. A games room with table tennis is on the first floor and a billiard table in the cellar. This site, under Dutch ownership, is one of the best that we have seen in Lithuania.

### Facilities
Modern sanitary facilities in the main block provide British style toilets, basins (cold water only) and pre-set hot showers (token operated). Shower tokens are sold at reception (1 lt. each). Washing machine and dryer (free). Bar/restaurant. Minigolf. Fishing. Boules. Tennis. Sauna. Rowing boat hire. Lakeside beach. Internet access. Off site: Riding, walking (many marked footpaths), mountain biking. Moletai (nearest large town with some interesting museums and monuments).

**Open:** All year.

### Directions
From the A14 (Vilnius - Utena) road, follow signs to Luokesa (before reaching Moletai). Follow signs to Ambraziskiai and pass through Zalvariai village. The site is signed on the left, and this road leads across the bridge onto the island.

### Charges 2007
| | |
|---|---:|
| Per person | LTL 10,00 |
| child (1-10 yrs) | LTL 5,00 |
| pitch | LTL 8,00 - 30,00 |
| electricity, water and drainage | LTL 20,00 |

## Lithuania

### LI2030 Kempingas Slenyje

Slenio g. 1, LT-21102 Trakai

Tel: 528 53880. Email: kempingasslenyje@one.lt

This excellent site in a National Park beside Lake Galve is situated north of Trakai and about 35 km. from Vilnius. There are 50 touring pitches, all with 16A electricity and views across the lake to Trakai Castle which was Lithuania's former capital. Vilnius has much to offer the visitor, from the old town – don't miss Pilies Gatve (the gates of dawn) – to the modern, new city centre. Most of the symbols of Soviet occupation have now been destroyed and a modern vibrant city is being constructed. In the old town, for lunch it is worth trying a Cepelinai (literally shaped liked a Zeppelin), which is grated potatoes with meat or mushrooms inside and then boiled for some time – blow the diet! The geographical centre of Europe is only 25 km. north of the capital and is also worth visiting. The adventurous can try a hot air balloon ride direct from the campsite over the lakes surrounding Trakai.

#### Facilities

Small sanitary block has toilets and hot showers which are good and clean. Chemical disposal point. Bar, restaurant and café in adjoining complex. English spoken in reception. Hot air balloon and steamboat rides. Bicycle hire. Off site: Vilnius and Trakai.

**Open:** All year.

#### Directions

From Vilnius, take Vilnius - Kaunas road. After 25 km. near Rykantai, turn right at sign for Trakai. After 7 km. turn right at sign 'Kempingas slenyje 500 m'. Once down the hill, take narrow asphalt road which takes you round the shore of the lake to the site. If you are coming from Kaunas, as soon as you pass Vievis turn right at sign for Trakai. After 13 km. turn left in towards Uztrakis at the sign 'Slenis 2 km.' and then follow the signs.
GPS: N54:40.040 E24:55.430

#### Charges 2007

| | |
|---|---:|
| Per person | LTL 16,00 |
| pitch incl. car | LTL 11,00 - 19,00 |
| electricity | LTL 9,00 |

---

### LI2035 Camping Harmonie

Pusyno 3, LT-70347 Rudiskes

Tel: 614 21560. Email: wim_brauns@hotmail.com

The owner of Camping Harmonie prefers not to call it a campsite, but actually it is one of the better sites in Lithuania. At the entrance, you are greeted by flowering shrubs, colourful flowers and several small ponds with waterfalls. All of this is the work of Mrs Brauns who has taken over 10 years to develop this welcoming environment. Harmonie has 40 pitches (all for tourers) on slightly sloping grass, mostly in the shade of mature trees on two fields. Pitches in the field closest to the entrance are grouped around a pond (fenced), with pitches on the newer field to the right more in the open. In all, there are 30 pitches with 6A electricity. Toilet facilities on this site are excellent and in the evenings, happy discussions take place in the common room (with free coffee). If you want to know more about Lithuania's history, ask Mrs Braun who is an historian and can tell you anything about it. Mr Braun has been the coach of the Lithuanian Olympic cycling team and in earlier years played professional soccer. One big advantage of this site is that loud music is prohibited.

#### Facilities

Clean and comfortable toilet facilities with British style toilets, open washbasins and controllable hot showers. Washing machine. Dishwashing. Fully equipped kitchen. Library. Motorcaravan services and chemical toilet. Bicycle hire (biking trips organised). Lake swimming. Common room with TV and free coffee. Service from site to train station for Vilnius. Torch useful. Dog walks in the forest.

**Open:** May - October.

#### Directions

From Vilnius take the A4 south and exit to the west at Paluknys. Continue for 7 km. on a bumpy access road and the site is signed to the left half way between Paluknys and Rudiskes.
GPS: N54:30.455 E24:53.466

#### Charges 2008

| | |
|---|---:|
| Per unit incl. 2 persons and electricity | LTL 16,00 |

No credit cards.

## LI2050 Camping Vitruna

Meteliai, Seirijai

Tel: 687 70748. Email: vitruna@centras.lt

Camping Vitruna is a small site situated between two lakes in southern Lithuania. It has some 50 pitches on two level, grassy fields. One is a circular area in front of the reception, the other is closer to the lake under mature trees that provide shade. There are 15 pitches with 4A electricity connections. Vitruna is an ideal base for enjoying watersports on the lakes or for simply relaxing by sunbathing on the site's sandy beach. It is also not far to the Grutas Parkas, where a Lithuanian millionaire has collected many Soviet statues and put them in a gulag-style camp as a memorial to harsh times. Although Vitruna has great surroundings, there are strict limitations – there are no showers or toilet facilities (except for two quite unacceptable wooden toilets) – you will need your own facilities.

### Facilities

There are no sanitary facilities. Drinks available from reception. Watersports. Fishing. Beach. Lake swimming. Basketball. Volleyball. Torch useful. No English spoken.

**Open:** All year.

### Directions

From Marijampole, turn south towards Kalvarija and then east on the 131 road towards Simnas. In Simnas, turn south towards Meteliai. Site is signed.

### Charges 2007

| | |
|---|---|
| Per person | LTL 5,00 |
| pitch | LTL 10,00 |

## LI2060 Camping Viktorija

Vilkaviskio Sav, LT-70001 Vistytis

Tel: 342 47521. Email: viktorija@viktorija.lt

Vistytis is just inside Lithuania, near the border at the point where Poland, Russia (Kaliningrad region) and Lithuania meet. In fact most of the adjoining lake is in Russia. At the present time this is probably one of the best campsites in the Baltic States, where standards are generally lower than seen in western Europe and more akin to Russia where there exists what might best be described as pre-war sanitation. Not surprisingly the site gets busy in high season especially at weekends. There are 40 touring pitches, all with electricity, and further open areas for tents beside the lake. The site reports the addition of a swimming pool, sauna and massage bath complex.

### Facilities

A small sanitary block has toilets which are poor. However the new building houses 6 bathrooms, each containing new, clean and modern facilities (WC, washbasin and shower). Chemical disposal point. Bar and restaurant at adjoining hotel. English spoken in reception. Boat and bicycle hire. Old wooden huts for rent. Dogs are not accepted. Off site: Lake Vistytis.

**Open:** 1 May - 1 October.

### Directions

From Kalvarija on A5 (E67) take the road west towards Vistytis. After 35 km. on entering the village, turn left heading south down the side of lake Vistytis. Site is on right after 5 km.

### Charges 2007

| | |
|---|---|
| Per person | LTL 8,00 |
| child | LTL 4,00 |
| pitch incl. electricity | LTL 30,00 |

## Lithuania

### LI2065 Camping Pusele

Zirgenu k, Vistycio sen, LT-70345 Vilkaviskio
Tel: **834 247555**

Pusele is another Lithuanian campsite in a great location. It is on sloping ground on the banks of a lake and is attractively landscaped with flowers and many trees. In a single long, fairly level field with views over the lake, the grass pitches are of normal size and are connected by a circular road. To the rear of the site are 10 wooden cabins, some with toilet and shower, which campers may use if they are not rented out. There was no toilet block at the time of our visit, but we were told that a block with 4 showers and 4 toilets is planned. The bar/restaurant has a lakeside terrace with good views over the lake and towards Russia, which is on the far side of the lake. One disadvantage could be that local youngsters sometimes come here at weekends and holidays to play loud music.

**Facilities**

A toilet block is planned. Welcoming bar/restaurant with good value meals (menu only in Lithuanian). Fishing. Beach. Pedaloes and rowing boats for hire. Torch useful. No English is spoken.

**Open:** All year.

**Directions**

From Marijampole, turn south towards Kalvarija and then west towards Vystytis. In Vystytis, turn south alongside the lake and the site is signed.

**Charges guide**

| | |
|---|---|
| Per person | LTL 2,00 |
| pitch | LTL 18,00 - 25,00 |

### LI2090 Camping Sedula

LT-86482 Tytuvenai
Tel: **842 756795**. Email: **vadybininkas@sedula.lt**

On the shore of Lake Bridvaisis in the Tytuvénai National Park, the attractively landscaped Resort Sedula was only built two years ago on ground that slopes gently down to the lake. It comprises a hotel with a conference centre, some cabins to rent and 30 fairly level camping pitches. Of these, 12 are on hardstanding and 16A electricity connections. Pitches for tents are shaded by a variety of trees and are situated between the rental cabins. From these pitches, there are good views of the lake. All the site buildings are new and at the time of our visit the development did not include a toilet block. However, campers are able to use the facilities of the hotel and the sauna room near the lake. The hotel also houses a comfortable bar/restaurant with good value meals and satellite TV. This is a good site for those who enjoy nature and water sports, or would like to taste the real Lithuanian countryside.

**Facilities**

Showers and toilets at the hotel. Bar/restaurant (all year). Sauna. Beach with slide. Volleyball. Basketball. Pedaloes (free). Playground.

**Open:** All year.

**Directions**

From Kelmé, follow the 157 road east to Tytuvénai. In Tytuvénai, follow the 148 road towards Radsviskis and then sign for Sedula 2 km.
GPS: N55:35.320 E23:12.668

**Charges 2007**

| | |
|---|---|
| Per unit incl. electricity | LTL 35,00 |

### LI2120 Camping Ventaine

Ventes k, Kintai sen, LT-99361 Silutes reaj
Tel: **441 68525**. Email: **ventaine@takas.lt**

Camping Ventaine is a pleasant, quiet site on the Curonian Lagoon, just opposite the Neringa Peninsula and close to the Russian border. It has some 60 pitches on one large field in front of the Ventaine Hotel. The numbered pitches are on level grass, divided by low wooden fences and with no shade. There are 30 with electricity (6/10A), 4 with water and drainage also. The front rows have beautiful views over the water. This area of Lithuania is famous for birdwatching, with many migration routes passing over here. Other attractions could include relaxing in an ancient Roman style steam sauna, fishing or sailing trips, or a visit to the famous small towns of Minia or Silute.

**Facilities**

One toilet block with British style toilets, open washbasins and free, controllable hot showers. Bar/restaurant with good value meals (daily in season). Watersports. Fishing. Boat launching. Bicycle hire. Small beach. Indoor, heated swimming pool (all year).

**Open:** All year.

**Directions**

From Klaipeda, follow the 141 road south towards Silute. In Priekule, turn right towards Vente. In Vente, site is on the right after 300 m.
GPS: N55:22.300 E22:12.180

**Charges 2008**

| | |
|---|---|
| Per person | LTL 10,00 |
| pitch incl. electricity | LTL 40,00 |
| tent | LTL 10,00 |

Check real time availability and at-the-gate prices...
www.alanrogers.com

## LI2130 Camping Nidos

Taikos 45a, Nida, LT-93121 Neringa

Tel: **682 41150**. Email: **info@kempingas.lt**

The Nidos campsite is located on the small stretch of land that connects Lithuania with a part of the Russian Federation. The whole peninsula is designated as a National Park and is on the UNESCO World Heritage List. Close to the site is the beautiful dune landscape of the 52 metre high Parnidzio Dune from where there are wonderful views of the Curonian Lagoon, across the Lagoon to Ventspils and Russia. The site is about 2 km. from the ancient town of Nida. There are 100 pitches, all for touring units and all with 6/10A electricity. Most are on hardstanding, some made of concrete, some in small, rocky bays. This means there is little room to use awnings, although there is space between the trees to put up small tents. The site has a very welcoming ambiance and there is a covered swimming pool and a restaurant (housed in reception) which provides good quality meals for little money. Popular with local people and German, Dutch and Scandinavian campers, in high season the site can become busy.

### Facilities

Refurbished toilet facilities to the back of reception consist of British style toilets, open washbasins and roomy hot showers with a curtain. Laundry with sinks, washing machines and dryer. Sauna. Campers' kitchen. Bar/restaurant with good value meals (all year). Covered swimming pool (8 x 4 m, all year). Hard court tennis. Fishing. Bicycle hire. Watersports. Giant chess. Playground. Fishing trips, riding, folklore and jazz evenings and excursions organised.

**Open:** All year.

### Directions

From Klaipeda take the ferry onto the Neringa peninsula and drive south on the 167 road towards Nida. From Nida follow site signs.
GPS: N55:17.916 E20:58.956

### Charges 2007

| | |
|---|---|
| Per person | LTL 15,00 - 20,00 |
| child (0-14 yrs) | LTL 5,00 - 10,00 |
| caravan or motorcaravan incl. electricity | LTL 40,00 - 65,00 |
| tent | LTL 10,15 - 15,25 |

## Lithuania

# the Baltic States

Whilst there is a good selection of campsites in the three Baltic states, many fall well short of standards which are the norm in western Europe. Sites, whilst in attractive locations, suffer from poor (and sometimes very poor) sanitary facilities. Showers will be poor, often with cold water only, toilets are usually Turkish. Indeed many sites are reminiscent of standards we may have tolerated in the 1950s.

Changes are happening but it is certainly going to take some years for things to change to any substantial extent. Motorcaravan draindown points are very rare, so you may need to resort to other methods. Inevitably, sites of most recent construction offer the best standards. Our recommendations, we feel, are all to a good and reliable standard.

Check real time availability and at-the-gate prices...
www.alanrogers.com

# Latvia

MAP 9

Latvia offers over 12,000 rivers and 3,000 lakes providing a fantastic opportunity for boating, walking and generally enjoying the outdoors.

The capital city of Riga is situated on both banks of the River Daugava, separating it into two parts. It has a very interesting and historic centre with architectural styles ranging from medieval to art nouveau. Here you will find a wealth of theatres, opera houses, concert halls, restaurants and art galleries representing cultural life.

The region of Kurzeme is well known for its many fishing villages, nestled among pine forests and large ice-free ports. The furthest point north is the Kolka Horn, a stretch separating the Baltic Sea from the Riga Gulf. If it's windy you may see waves from the Gulf meeting waves from the open sea. Another water spectacle, near Kuldiga, is the Ventas Rumba, one of the widest waterfalls in Europe.

Vidzeme is the Northern region and houses the Gauja National Park. Along the stretch of the River Gauja you will come across a combination of medieval castles, legendary caves and a wonderful hilly landscape. Sigulda, the 'Switzerland of Latvia' is where you will find Latvia's downhill skiing centre and bobsled track.

The east is the 'land of blue lakes', several hundred in fact, making this region a fisherman's paradise. Particularly beautiful is Lake Ezezers which has more bays and islands than any other in Latvia.

### Population
2.324 million

### Capital
Riga

### Climate
A temperate climate but with considerable temperature variations. Summers are warm and winters can be very cold with snow.

### Language
Latvian. Russian, English and German are also widely spoken.

### Currency
The Lat (LVL)

### Telephone
The country code is 00 371

### Banks
Normal banking hours are 9.00-17.00 Mon-Fri, some are open on Saturdays from 9.00-13.00.

### Shops
Shopping hours vary. In larger towns and cities, many are open from 09.00-19.00 with reduced hours at weekends.

# Latvia

THIS IS THE CENTRAL OF THE THREE BALTIC COUNTRIES, SITTING ON THE EASTERN COAST BETWEEN ESTONIA AND LITHUANIA. IT IS A LAND OF FORESTS, PLAINS, LAKES, RIVER VALLEYS AND WHITE SANDY BEACHES.

### Public Holidays
New Year's Day; Easter Good Friday, Sun, Mon; Labour Day 1 May; Mother's Day - first Sun of May; Midsummer's Eve; Ligo Day 23 June; Jani Day 24 June; Proclamation of the Republic of Latvia 18 Nov; Christmas 25, 26 Dec; New Year's Eve 31 Dec.

### Motoring
Traffic is relatively light in Latvia (except in the capital) and main roads are well maintained. Some rural roads may be unsurfaced. Dipped headlights are required at all times. If involved in an accident do not attempt to remove your vehicle until the police give permission. Motorway speed limits are low (90-100 kph). You will not be allowed to leave Latvia with your car if you do not have the original registration papers.

### Tourist Office
Latvian Tourisms Bureaux
72 Queensborough Terrace
London WH 3SH
Tel: 020 7229 8271
Email: london@latviatourism.lv
Internet: www.latviatourism.lv

### British Embassy
5, J. Alunan Street
Riga LV-1010
Tel: (371) 777 4700

### Places of interest
*Bauska:* principally for its castle (ancient music festivals are often hosted here) and museum.

*Jurmala:* (seashore) beaches, dunes and woodlands perfect for a relaxing break.

*Kuldiga:* a most picturesque and historic town, visitors are able to fish and swim in the Venta River which also has a waterfall.

*Riga:* the capital city, situated on both banks of the River Daugava.

*Sigulda:* gateway to the Gauja National Park and a winter sports centre.

### Cuisine of the region
Wonderfully international, incorporating Swedish, German and Slavic menus. In the capital of Riga you will find other international flavours ranging from French, Italian, Greek, Thai, Chinese and even British and Irish pubs.

Traditional food includes soup, rye breads, and sausages.

Smoked foods are popular, particularly fish which tends to be flounder, eel, herring and pilchards. Berry pies and tarts are popular in summer and autumn.

*Piragi:* meat, bacon and onion pastries.

## Latvia

### LA1020 Camping Meleku Licis

LV-4032 Dzeni
Tel: 371 928 4555. Email: aktivs@apollo.lv

This site is typical of many of the 'Old Russian' standard sites in the Baltic States – an excellent location, great pitches and disgusting sanitary provision. So, unless you are prepared to use your own facilities, give this site a miss. Having said that, it is right next to the Baltic coast with a great sandy beach, it is quiet and there is a pleasant restaurant and bar. There are 75 touring pitches, 20 with electricity. Located about 20 km. south of the Estonian border, it is south of the small town of Salacgriva in the Limbazu Region.

#### Facilities

The small sanitary block has toilets which were filthy and cold showers. If you come here be prepared to use your own facilities. Chemical disposal point. English spoken in reception. Small restaurant and bar. Disco every Friday and Saturday. Off site: Baltic coast.

**Open:** 1 May - 30 September.

#### Directions

This Dzeni did not appear on our map of the Baltic States, however it is 72 km. north of Riga on the Tallinn highway near Salacgriva. It is well signed.

#### Charges guide

Per unit incl. 2 persons and electricity          LVL 7,70

Check real time availability and at-the-gate prices...
www.alanrogers.com

## LA1030 Camping Gauja

Dzirnupes iela 3, LV-2163 Gauja
Tel: **6799 2833**. Email: **kempings.gauja@apollo.lv**

Camping Gauja is close to Riga (the bus to Riga leaves from in front of the site), close to the Baltic Sea and beside the Gauja river which offers excellent opportunities for fishing. A visit to Latvia is not complete without visiting its capital, Riga, and this site is a good starting point. The site also has about 25 holiday homes (some fairly new, others fairly worn down) which take up most of the space. Finding space for a large tent would be difficult. For caravans and motorcaravans there are concrete hardstandings to the back of the site with 6 electricity connections (16A). In all, there is a maximum of 30 touring pitches, mostly in the shade of mature trees. It is an easy 300 m. walk from the site to the Gauja river, the Dzirnupes lake or to sandy Baltic Sea beaches where you can enjoy water sports and fishing. The toilet facilities here are in the guest house.

### Facilities

Partly refurbished toilet facilities are located in a former holiday home with one British style toilet, a washbasin and 4 communal showers (other facilities in the holiday homes). Sauna. Well stocked shop (all year). Bar with satellite TV (open until 05.00 all year). Playground. Fishing. Beach. Off site: Train station 300 m. Riding 300 m. Bicycle hire 2 km. Boat launching 3 km.

**Open:** All year.

### Directions

From Riga, take the A1 road north and exit for Gauja, just after passing the river. Follow the minor road all the way to the end. Site is not signed. GPS: N57:08.537 E24:17.730

### Charges 2007

| | |
|---|---:|
| Per person | LVL 1,00 |
| pitch | LVL 5,00 |
| tent pitch | LVL 1,00 |
| car | LVL 1,00 |

## LA1040 Riga City Camping

Kipsalas iela 8, LV-1048 Riga
Tel: **6706 5000**. Email: **camping@bt1.lv**

The old town of Riga is certainly well worth a visit and this new site provides the opportunity. Based on a small island in the Daugava River in a mixed urban area, this small site provides 100 touring pitches; all with electricity connections. Much of the old town has been rebuilt since the war and the informative and perhaps disturbing Museum of Occupation near the Town Hall is worth visiting as is the Art-Nouveau architecture of Riga's residential area. The market, which occupies the former Zeppelin hangers, should also be seen. Latvia's answer to fast food is also an essential part of your visit – 'pelmeni' (meat dumplings fried, boiled or swimming in soup) and pancakes are cheap, filling and tasty and are served throughout the town.

### Facilities

Two small sanitary blocks in 'portacabin' style units have toilets and hot showers (several new), which are clean and useable and the site reports the addition of a new shower and toilet building. The adjoining building provides a bar and snacks. Chemical disposal point. Bicycle hire. English is spoken in reception. CCTV security and a new power supply have been installed. Off site: Shopping centre within 800 m. Riga 20 minutes walk away.

**Open:** 15 May - 15 September.

### Directions

Kipsalas is a small island in the Daugava River in central Riga. From the old town cross the new suspension bridge and at the end of the bridge go down the slip road, turn right after 300 m. (large campsite sign) and site is 800 m. on the left. GPS: N56:57.379 E24:04.689

### Charges 2007

| | |
|---|---:|
| Per person | LVL 1,50 |
| child (0-16 yrs) | LVL 1,00 |
| pitch | LVL 5,00 - 8,00 |
| electricity | LVL 2,00 |

No credit cards.

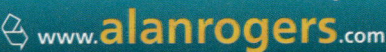

Check real time availability and at-the-gate prices...
www.alanrogers.com

## Latvia

### LA1060 Camping Nemo
Atbalss 1, LV-2008 Jurmala
Tel: 773 2349. Email: nemo@nemo.lv

Jurmala is the favourite seaside resort of the Latvian people, and also many Russians, and the name literally means 'seaside'. Nemo is, in fact, a small water theme park where many of the visitors camp on the flat, grassed areas inside the park. Technically the site has 40 touring pitches, all with electricity, but more than three times that number were camping there when we visited so you should expect little space. There are also many basic wooden huts to rent which sleep four people. During late July and August the park is crowded and the sanitary facilities inadequate and dirty. Riga is about 40 minutes drive to the east and it is possible to use public transport.

#### Facilities
Two small sanitary blocks have toilets and cold communal showers with no screens; with the site so crowded they are over used and dirty. Chemical disposal point. Restaurant and bar. Disco until the early hours every Friday and Saturday. Small water theme park, but no swimming pool. English spoken in reception. Off site: Riga and the Baltic coast.

**Open:** 1 May - 1 October.

#### Directions
Nemo is in the Vaivari area of Jurmala. Approach Jurmala from Riga on the A10, you have a choice – pay 2 Lts (you need change) for a 48 hour toll pass (Nemo 14 km.) or turn right (Nemo 22 km). On the toll road go straight on through Jurmala. Nemo is signed and turn right into site after 14 km.

#### Charges guide
| | |
|---|---|
| Per person | LVL 1,00 |
| caravan or motorcaravan | LVL 8,00 - 9,00 |
| tent | LVL 1,00 |

---

### LA1080 Usma Kempings
Priezkalni, LV-3619 Usma
Tel: 367 3654. Email: usma@usma.lv

Usma Camping is beside Lake Usma, the fourth largest lake in Latvia which is used extensively for watersports. The site is attractively landscaped with a variety of shrubs, colourful flowers and trees. The pitches are on grassy fields with views of the lake, most being level and in the shade of mature trees. There are 16 electricity connections (16A). The site also has 10 cabins for rent. As with so many Baltic sites, the site mainly relies on income from its rental cabins and, as a result, toilet facilities for tourers are not extensive, but they are clean and adequate. A spa hotel has been built with a covered pool, three different saunas and a restaurant and bar and internet. With its lakeside location, Usma Camping opportunities for boating, including yacht and motorboat rental. All in all, this a site for watersport enthusiasts and for people who would appreciate the peace and tranquillity of nature (although at weekends the lake is busy with local visitors).

#### Facilities
One small but good toilet block provides British style toilets, open style washbasins and free, controllable hot showers. Washing machine. Dishwashing. Fully equipped kitchen. Motorcaravan services. Basics and bread from reception. Boat, pedalo and yacht hire. Fishing (permits from site). Bicycle hire. Boat launching. Beach. Musical nights at communal grill in season. Sauna. Torch useful. Off site: Riding 5 km.

**Open:** 1 April - 1 October.

#### Directions
On A10 from Ventspils towards Riga, take exit for Usma and follow site signs.
GPS: N57:14.368 E22:10.117

#### Charges 2007
| | |
|---|---|
| Per person | LVL 1,50 |
| child (0-10 yrs) | LVL 0,50 |
| caravan or motorcaravan | LVL 4,00 |
| tent | LVL 3,00 |

---

Check real time availability and at-the-gate prices...
www.alanrogers.com

## LA1100 Piejuras Camping

56 Vasarnicu St, LV-3601 Ventspils
Tel: **362 7925**. Email: **camping@ventspils.lv**

Piejuras Camping is in the bustling seaside resort of Ventspils where the coastal areas of the town has been attractively modernised, and the same goes for the campsite. There is a new reception, also housing first class toilet facilities and a kitchen with a dining room. Pitching is in two areas, one next to reception opposite some new cabins and used for caravans and motorcaravans, the other for tents under mature trees. In total, there are about 100 touring pitches including 30 for caravans and motorcaravans with 16A electricity and water and 4 with drainage. At the rear of the site there is a large stage with picnic tables and a bar with covered terrace. It is an easy 500 m. walk to the Baltic beaches through a beautifully landscaped park and a 700 m. walk to the centre of Ventspils, where you can enjoy numerous bars and restaurants, stroll along the newly developed promenade or visit the restored 13th century castle. The peace can be disturbed by local youngsters at weekends.

### Facilities
Excellent facilities in reception and a smaller block to the back of the site with British style toilets, open washbasins and free, controllable hot showers. En-suite facilities for disabled visitors. Washing machine. Dishwashing. Fully equipped kitchen with terrace and dining room with TV. Stage with picnic tables. Open-air bar. Football field. Watersports. Playground. Off site: Fishing 500 m. Boat launching 2 km. Blue flag beach 500 m.

**Open:** All year.

### Directions
On entering the town from either direction, follow signs for the recreation area via the Lieslais Prospekts. Turn left at the end onto 'Vasarnicu Iela' and follow signs to the site. GPS: N57:23.053 E21:32.174

### Charges 2007
| | |
|---|---|
| Per caravan or motorcaravan incl. electricity | LVL 6,00 |

## LA1130 Camping Verbelnieki

Bernati, LV-3471 Perkone
Tel: **012 91 38 565**. Email: **verbelnieki@inbox.lv**

In the grounds of the Verbelnieki guesthouse, this site would be an ideal spot to enjoy the quiet beaches of the Baltic Sea. Verbelnieki is only 6 km. south of the impressive harbour town of Liepaja. The site is divided in four large, grassy fields with 200 unmarked touring pitches, although there are only 8 electricity connections. However, since most visitors come to stay in the guesthouse, the campsite is rarely busy. Two fields have some shade from mature trees. It is only a 50 metre walk through the sand dunes to the beach where you can enjoy beautiful sunrises and sunsets. The area around the guesthouse is attractively landscaped with a variety of shrubs, trees, flowers and rocks. Breakfast, lunch and snacks can be ordered in high season from the guesthouse. Since the site doesn't attract many campers, the toilet facilities are not extensive with just two showers and three toilets, although they do have a sauna and an open-air communal bath.

### Facilities
One small block with three British style toilets, three washbasins and two showers. Sauna. Open-air bath. Football field. Beach. Fishing. Bicycle hire. Watersports. Torch useful. Off site: Riding 5 km. Boat launching 5 km.

**Open:** May - October.

### Directions
From the Lithuanian - Latvian border, follow the A13 road north towards Liepaja. Site is signed to the left 7 km. south of Liepaja. Follow the 700 m. long, bumpy access road. GPS: N56:25.602 E20:59.896

### Charges 2008
| | |
|---|---|
| Per person | LVL 2,00 |
| child (0-12 yrs) | LVL 1,00 |
| pitch | LVL 5,00 |
| No credit cards. | |

Check real time availability and at-the-gate prices...
www.**alanrogers**.com

## Latvia

### LA1150 Camping Radi
Lielciecere, LV-3851 Broceni
Tel: 29 53 38 230. Email: radi@radi.lv

Beautifully located on the banks of a small lake, Camping Radi is attractively landscaped with flowers. It offers around 40 grassy touring pitches on sloping ground which include 5 level pitches for caravans and motorcaravans with 16A electricity. Most pitches have good views over the lake. The welcoming Donga family who run this little site also run the adjoining guesthouse and conference centre. Most visitors in fact stay in the guesthouse, and with only a few campers, there are only two toilets and a shower available for touring units. If the site gets busy, campers can also use facilities in the guesthouse. The lake offers possibilities for fishing and boating (canoes and rowing boats are available for rent) and waterskiing is possible with the site's own motorboat. There is no restaurant, but the Donga family prepare breakfasts and small, freshly prepared meals, which you can enjoy on the terrace of the guesthouse (we can recommend the homemade noodle and salmon soup).

#### Facilities
Two toilets and a shower plus facilities in the guesthouse. Daily breakfast and meal of the day. Basketball. Volleyball. Fishing. Boat launching. Small beach. Waterskiing. Canoes and rowing boats for hire. WiFi in the guesthouse.

#### Open: All year.

#### Directions
From Liepaja, go east on the A9, going past Saldus towards Broceni. On entering Broceni, site is signed to the right. Follow the bumpy access road 6 km. to the site.

#### Charges 2007
| | |
|---|---|
| Per person | LVL 1,50 - 4,00 |
| pitch | LVL 1,50 - 5,00 |

No credit cards.

---

## Need a low cost ferry?

Do you have a caravan, motorhome or trailer and want the best deal on your cross-Channel ferry? Then visit www.ferries4campers.co.uk for the lowest prices for campers and caravanners from major ferry operators.

**It couldn't be simpler** - just click, choose a ferry and book...

- Special deals for caravans and motorhomes
- View routes and compare prices
- Fully searchable by route and operator

ferries4campers.co.uk

norfolkline DOVER - DUNKERQUE FERRIES | P&O Ferries | EURO TUNNEL | SEAFRANCE DOVER-CALAIS FERRIES | Brittany Ferries | Condorferries

---

Check real time availability and at-the-gate prices...
www.alanrogers.com

# Estonia

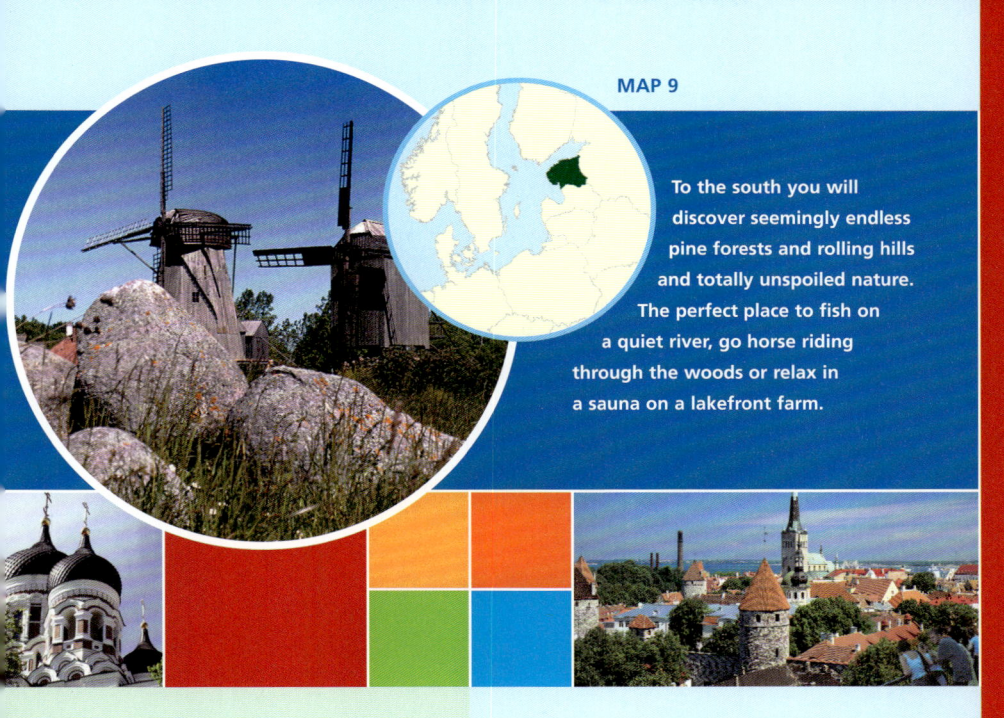

**MAP 9**

To the south you will discover seemingly endless pine forests and rolling hills and totally unspoiled nature. The perfect place to fish on a quiet river, go horse riding through the woods or relax in a sauna on a lakefront farm.

Northern Estonia is the Baltic Sea coast region lined by dramatic cliffs across the Gulf of Finland. Along this 200 km long stretch from Tallinn to Narva, medieval castles, restored manor estates and beautiful waterfalls can be seen. Narva Castle is an impressive hallmark of the region. A nature lover's paradise can be found at Lahemaa National Park, one of Estonia's most popular nature reserves complete with jagged coasts, vast forests, wetlands and numerous hiking trails.

The two largest islands off the coast are Saaremaa and Hiiumaa, both inviting retreats. The smaller islands include Muhu, Kihnu and Ruhnu and, along with their laid-back, and friendly atmosphere are typical examples of the Estonian landscape dotted with windmills, thatched cottages and sleepy fishing villages. Tartu is Estonia's second city and is a good starting point for exploring Southern Estonia. Any visit here should include Polva and Voru, home of the Estonian Setus. Witness a step back in time, villages with wooden huts and small farms where these ancient peoples retain their own unique language and culture and are famous for their colourful folk dress and distinctive style of singing.

**Population**
1.4 million

**Capital**
Tallinn

**Climate**
A temperate climate with warm summers and fairly severe winters.

**Language**
Estonian

**Currency**
Estonian kroon (EEK)

**Telephone**
The country code is 00 372

**Banks**
Mon-Fri 9.00-16.00

**Shops**
Shopping hours vary. In larger towns and cities, many are open from 09.00-19.00 with reduced hours at weekends.

# Estonia

BORDERING THE BALTIC SEA AND SITTING JUST BELOW FINLAND AND NOW RELIEVED FROM ITS COMMUNIST RULE, ESTONIA OFFERS THE CHANCE TO DISCOVER A NEW AND REFRESHINGLY GENUINE EXPERIENCE. A COUNTRY WITH A HISTORY-FILLED PAST, SURROUNDED BY BEAUTIFUL CASTLES, OLD CITIES, MANOR HOUSES, FORESTS, BEACHES AND ISLANDS, TO ONE WITH A PROGRESSIVE FUTURE.

### Public Holidays

New Year's Day; Independence Day 24 Feb; Good Friday; May Day; Whitsun; Victory Day 23 June; Midsummer's Day 24 June; Independence Day 20 Aug; Christmas 25,26 Dec.

### Motoring

Dipped headlights are compulsory at all times and winter tyres must be fitted October-April. You are required to carry wheel chocks in your vehicle. Do not drink any alcohol before driving - the legal limit is zero. When parking in many towns, you must buy and display a ticket (available from local shops).

### Tourist Office

No active tourist office in the UK.

Embassy of the Republic of Estonia
16 Hyde Park Gate, London SW7 5DG
Tel: 020 7589 3428  Fax: 020 7589 3430
Internet: www.visitestonia.com

### British Embassy

Wismari 6
10136 Tallinn
Tel: (372) 667 4700

### Places of interest

*Hiiumaa:* beautiful stretches of coast; the Hill of Crosses at Ristimägi, hand-made crosses where Swedes performed their last act of worship before being deported in 1781.

*Lahemaa National Park:* dense forest, manor houses, lakes, rivers and waterfalls.

*Tartu:* a city with an impressive old quarter, featuring St John's Church - the oldest in Estonia.

*Tallinn:* Estonia's capital, a fantastic mix of old and modern, many major festivals and concerts are held all year round.

### Cuisine of the region

Mainly influenced by the Germans, traditional Estonian food relies heavily on pork, potatoes and garden vegetables. Main meals may also consist of chicken, lamb, veal or beef and fish dishes are mainly eel, cod, herring, plaice or salmon. Porridge, soups, stews, casseroles, rye breads, preserves and pickles also feature as part of the Estonian menu.

In the capital Tallinn you'll find a diverse selection of restaurants comprising Indian, Tex-Mex, Thai, Hungarian, Japanese, Chinese and Greek.

*Suitsukala:* smoked trout

*Verevorst:* blood sausages

*Vere pannkoogid:* blood pancakes

### ET0010 Camping Konse

Suur-Joe 44a, EST-80021 Pärnu
Tel: 534 350 92. Email: info@konse.ee

This newly developed site is some 700 metres from the centre of Pärnu, the summer capital of Estonia. There are 50 pitches, all for touring units and with 16A electricity, arranged in two areas on the banks of the River Pärnu, where it is possible to swim. One area, close to the newly built guesthouse (which also houses excellent sanitary facilities, a bar and the reception) provides small, level, grass pitches, some with views over the river. The other area comprising tarmac hardstandings is mainly used for motorcaravans. There is little shade on the site and it can be hot in summer. Pärnu is Estonia's main seaside resort and its wide, sandy beaches attract many visitors from Finland and Sweden, as well as from Estonia itself. A health spa is close to the beach where you can enjoy mud baths and saunas. The restored centre of Pärnu is within walking distance and well worth a visit to see the wooden fishermen's houses and medieval gates.

#### Facilities

Excellent facilities in the guesthouse include British style toilets, washbasins and free, controllable hot showers. Laundry with washing machine and dryer. Dishwashing. Fully equipped kitchen. Bar with satellite TV and breakfast served. Free internet access. Boat launching. River swimming. Fishing. Off site: Beach 1 km. Outdoor pool 1 km.

Open: All year.

#### Directions

Coming from the south, continue towards the centre of Pärnu. Site is signed to the right after about 2 km.
GPS: N58:23.099 E24:31.574

#### Charges 2007

| | |
|---|---|
| Per unit incl. 2 adults, 2 children (under 12 yrs) | € 12,00 - € 14,00 |
| electricity | € 1,00 |

Prices in Euros.

# Estonia

## ET0015 Camping Pikseke

Männiku tee 34, EST-90506 Haapsalu

Tel: 475 5779. Email: **info@campingpikseke.com**

Pikseke is one of the better campsites in Estonia and it is close to the beautiful seaside resort of Haapsalu. There are 40 good sized, level grass pitches on two fields. All have 10A electricity and most are in the shade of mature trees. The Finnish owner, Mr. Lehtonen, opened the site nine years ago on a former farm and it is now a well established site that attracts mainly Finnish, Dutch and German visitors. The city of Haapsalu has many things to offer. Its beautifully restored old centre has a medieval bishop's castle, which you can visit, and there is a pleasant promenade alongside the shallow waters of the bay. Here there are several statues, including one of the famous composer Pjotr Tchaikovsky who spent his holidays here. Haapsalu is also the ferry port for the island Hiiumaa. After a hard day visiting the town, you can relax in the site's sauna or take a massage. Every week a young couple from a local ostrich farm call at the site to sell ostrich ham and other products (you can also visit their farm).

### Facilities

Three small toilet units contain British style toilets, a washbasin and free, controllable hot showers. Washing machine. Sauna (charge). Dishwashing. Fully equipped kitchen. Motorcaravan services. Baker calls daily (09.00). Massage. Internet access. Bicycle hire. Playground. WiFi. Off site: Haapsalu centre 2 km. Golf 5 km. Riding 10 km. Boat launching 5 km. Beach 2 km.

**Open:** All year.

### Directions

Coming from Talinn on Tallinna Mnt, continue towards Lihula on Lihula Mnt. Cross the railway bridge and then turn right onto Männiku Tee. Site is signed from the centre of Haapsalu.
GPS: N58:55.400 E23:32.150

### Charges 2007

| | |
|---|---|
| Per person | € 1,00 |
| pitch | € 9,00 |

No credit cards. Prices in Euros.

## ET0050 Toila Spa Kamping

Ranna 12, EST-41702 Toila

Tel: 372 332 5328. Email: **info@toilasanetoorium.ee**

Coming to this site after three weeks in Russia and having crossed the border into Estonia at Narva only 30 minutes earlier, we thought it must be a mirage – a clean, level, green field right beside the coast, fenced and secure with clean toilets, hot showers and water! Having quickly settled in, we realised it was not a mirage and set about enjoying all this quiet site has to offer. There are 25 touring pitches all with electricity. Toila, along a former trade route of the Vikings, is famous for its gardens. Here stood the majestic Oru Castle, built by the famous St Petersburg businessman Yelisseyev in the 19th century. Having been used as the Estonian President's summer residence between the wars it was subsequently destroyed. Now the village is home to parts of the parkland that has been reconstructed and the views of the Baltic Glint are quite spectacular. Here the Glint forms part of the Saka-Ontika-Toila landscape reserve. Although the site is next to the coast there are some 120 steps down to the beach. Despite that it is an excellent site in a beautiful location.

### Facilities

Small sanitary block has toilets and hot showers, which are immaculate. Adjoining hotel provides a bar, restaurant and indoor swimming pool, complete with sauna. In addition the spa complex offers a variety of treatments that are all available to campers. Chemical toilet disposal point. English spoken in reception. Internet access in the hotel. Cottage accommodation. Off site: Toila village and park. The Baltic coast.

**Open:** 1 May - 15 October.

### Directions

The village of Toila is 12 km. northeast of Johvi which is on route 1, the Narva - Tallinn highway. Turn north towards Toila and just as you enter the village a sign indicates a left turn towards the Toila Sanatoorium (Spa Hotel). Having turned left, drive about 800 m. and just before the hotel car park turn right, then left and left again. Site is ahead on the right.
GPS: N59:25.330 E27:30.510

### Charges guide

| | |
|---|---|
| Per caravan incl. electricity | EEK 110 |
| tent | EEK 50 |

Check real time availability and at-the-gate prices…
www.alanrogers.com

# Estonia

## ET0020 Camping Peoleo

Pärnu mnt 555, EST-76401 Laagri
Tel: **650 3965**. Email: **hotel@peoleo.ee**

Peoleo is a modern hotel complex where it is possible to park in the gravel car park which has electricity points for campers' use. There are 25 touring places, all with electricity. It was crowded and dusty when we visited in August. It is about 16 km. from Tallinn, which is an essential part of any tour of Estonia. Whilst it is next to the main route 4 there was little noise and it does offer an alternative to Camping Kalev, the other side of Tallinn. In Tallinn it is well worth trying the slightly expensive but excellent Garlic Restaurant next to Molly Malone's in Town Hall Square.

### Facilities
Small sanitary block has toilets and hot showers, which were dirty when we visited but it may be possible to use a bathroom in one of the hotel rooms if you ask. The adjoining hotel provides a bar and two restaurants. Sauna and solarium. Chemical toilet disposal point. English spoken in reception. Off site: Tallinn 15 km.

**Open:** 1 May - 30 September.

### Directions
Laagri is 15 km. southwest of Tallinn on main road no. 4. The site is on the east side of the road so if you are travelling south just go past it and do a U-turn at opening a few hundred metres south.

### Charges 2007
Per pitch incl. electricity         EEK 300

## ET0040 Camping Eesti Karavan

Lepisepa Kula, EST-45501 Vösu
Tel: **324 46 65**. Email: **karavaniklubi@hot.ee**

This site is simply a large, level field screened by trees next to the Baltic Coast. There are 200 touring pitches, most with electricity available. In the village of Vösu there are shops, a bar and a bank (with cash machine). The restored manor house and park at Palmse are well worth a visit if only to see the 'Rolls Royce' used by Khrushchev that broke down during a state visit to Estonia, during the Soviet occupation, and was too expensive to repair so it was left behind. The parks around the manor and the café, in the old bathhouse, are particularly worthy of a visit. There is also a former Soviet Coast Guards barracks at Kasmu, which is now a maritime museum.

### Facilities
Small sanitary block has toilets and showers (including 4 new), which are basic but clean. Chemical toilet disposal point. English spoken in reception. Off site: Lahemaa National Park, Palmse Manor and the Baltic coast.

**Open:** 1 May - 30 September.

### Directions
The village of Vösu is north of Palmse and off route 1 (Narva - Tallinn). Approaching Vösu you can turn left towards Kasmu in which case you turn right at next crossroads and site is 400 m. on the left. If you go on through the village and bear left near the beach car park, site is on the right. It is clearly signed. GPS: N59:34.536 E25:56.182

### Charges 2007
Per unit incl. electricity         € 3,00 - € 12,00
No credit cards. Prices in Euros.

## ET0105 Mändjala Camping

Mändjala küla, Kaarma vald, EST-93822 Saaremaa Island
Tel: **454 4193**. Email: **mandjala@saaremaa.ee**

This campsite is situated within the Mändjala nature reserve, beside the sandy beaches of the Riga Bay area. It shares the site with some 50 holiday homes, but the camping area is towards the rear with direct access to the beach and the shallow waters of the bay. Mändjala offers about 60 touring pitches, most in the shade of mature pine trees, and with 16 electrical connections (10A) available. On grassy, gravel or sandy ground, the pitches are rather small. There are good views of the bay from some pitches. On site, there is a large bar/restaurant with good value meals and film nights with both Estonian and English films in high season. The beach area is open to the public, and whilst during the week this does not cause problems, the site and beach can become crowded at weekends.

### Facilities
Three older, but partly refurbished toilet blocks have British style toilets, washbasins (cold water only) and a few showers (EEK 30) Cleaning and maintenance could be a problem. Sauna. Bar/restaurant with film nights. Fishing. Volleyball. Basketball. Bicycle hire. Watersports. Boat launching. Open-air covered grill.

**Open:** All year.

### Directions
From Kuressaare, follow the 77 road south for about 10 km. Site is signed to the left, just after passing sign for 'Mändjala'. GPS: N58:13.094 E22:19.895

### Charges 2007
| | |
|---|---|
| Per person | EEK 25 - 35 |
| child (0-12 yrs) | EEK 15 - 25 |
| pitch | EEK 125 - 155 |
| electricity | EEK 30 |

## ET0100 Camping Tehumardi

Tehumardi, Salme, EST-93201 Saaremaa Island
Tel: 457 1666. Email: info@tehumardi.ee

Opened in 2004 and offering first class facilities for touring units, Tehumardi Recreation Centre has good toilet facilities, a sauna, a small rowing pond and an Estonian style grill house (both inside and with covered terrace) where you can enjoy organised barbecues. The centre is located at the narrowest part of the largest Estonian Island, Saaremaa, at the start of the Sorve peninsula. It is an easy 300 m. walk from the site to the wide, sandy beaches of Riga Bay, an excellent area for sunbathing or swimming in the shallow waters. The site has two touring fields, one close to reception and the facilities and offering 30 hardstanding pitches with 16A electricity for motorcaravans and caravans under mature pine trees. The other pitches are on a large, grassy field without shade and this is used mainly for tents. At the entrance is a large entertainment hall, which is rented out for folklore festivals. If you are as lucky as we were, you can join the festivities and enjoy local Estonian music and dance.

### Facilities

One excellent toilet block with British style toilets, open washbasins and controllable hot showers (on payment). Toilet and washbasin for disabled visitors. Sauna. Washing machine. Motorcaravan services and chemical disposal. Well equipped kitchen with dining room and covered terrace. Bar in reception with satellite TV. WiFi internet access and internet computer. Bicycle hire. Volleyball. Basketball. New playground. Off site: Fishing 10 km. Beach 300 m.

**Open:** All year.

### Directions

From Kuressaare, follow the 77 road south for about 17 km. Site is signed to the right, just after the sign for Tehumardi.

### Charges 2007

| | |
|---|---|
| Per caravan pitch with electricity | € 11,00 |
| pet | free |

Prices in Euros.

## ET0120 Randmäe Puhketalu

Randmäe Holiday Farm, Mangu, EST-92211 Hiiumaa Island
Tel: 569 13883. Email: puhketalu@hot.ee

Located on the beautiful Tahkuna peninsula on Estonia's second largest island, Hiiumaa, staying at Randmäe Pukhetalu feels like camping at the end of the world. The site has around 60 touring pitches, some with shade from mature trees, and including 10 large pitches with 16A electricity (a further 14 are planned). There are also several tent fields, some with good views to the sea. To the front of the site are 6 wooden cabins and there is a guesthouse. A welcoming young couple, Henry and Kristina Laanemae, are really working hard to develop this relatively new site. They have converted an old shed into a warm and comfortable lounge. There is also a sauna and three cabins with toilet, washbasin and shower. During local holiday periods, the site can become crowded with locals, but normally you should be able to enjoy a relaxing beach holiday in beautiful, natural surroundings.

### Facilities

Good, modern toilet facilities with British style toilets, washbasins and controllable hot showers. Further toilets at the beach. Kiosk with basic supplies, drinks, takeaway meals and a covered terrace. Large communal grill. Football field. Volleyball. Fishing. Watersports. Bicycle hire. Beach. WiFi internet access. Hunting parties organised in winter.

**Open:** All year.

### Directions

From the ferry port in Heltermaa, take the 80 road north towards Kärdla and then on to Korgessaare. Turn onto the peninsula at sign for Tahkuna. At sign 'Posti 4 km.' the campsite is also signed. Continue from there on the bumpy gravel access road.
GPS: N59:01.858 E22:34.800

### Charges 2007

| | |
|---|---|
| Per unit incl. electricity | EEK 200 |
| tent (per person) | EEK 30 |

Check real time availability and at-the-gate prices...
www.alanrogers.com

# Journey to Russia

ONE OF OUR SITE ASSESSOR COUPLES, MIKE AND JUDITH ANNAN, UNDERTOOK A MOTORCARAVAN JOURNEY INTO RUSSIA DURING SUMMER 2004. WITH THE ACCESSION OF THE BALTIC STATES AND POLAND TO THE EUROPEAN UNION, IN MAY 2004, WE FEEL IT IS LIKELY THAT MANY CARAVANNERS AND MOTOR CARAVANNERS WILL BE TEMPTED TO MAKE THE JOURNEY FROM HELSINKI TO ST PETERSBURG AND ONWARD TO TALLINN IN ESTONIA.

WE THEREFORE BELIEVE THAT MIKE AND JUDITH'S ACCOUNT MAY BE OF INTEREST TO MANY AND IT IS THEREFORE REPRODUCED HERE. OUR THANKS TO THEM FOR THIS REPORT.

Although a distance of only 650 km. (430 miles), this is a journey that needs planning and preparation before you leave home and more importantly, it is a journey that offers challenges and excitement. Travelling in the former Soviet Union, now the Russian Federation, is not without difficulty but it is possible and will certainly be enjoyable.

First and foremost anyone contemplating this journey needs to appreciate that campsites in Russia are few and far between and where they exist they do not remotely approach Western European standards. We include details of one site that makes the journey outlined above practical and offers a great opportunity to explore St Petersburg, Peter the Great's city on the Neva River, with all its treasures and world class beauty.

## Before you leave home

### Visa

You will of course need a visa for your journey through Russia and it is essential to get this in the UK. You will need a tourist visa; these are the most straight-forward and inflexible visas available. To obtain this you will need to know your dates of entry and departure. These are effectively fixed dates that cannot be changed without a lot of hassle if at all. So you need to plan your trip carefully. The journey from Helsinki to the campsite north of St Petersburg can be achieved in a day, even allowing for the three to five hour delay at the border. It is probably best to try and make this part of the trip on a Sunday, since then both the roads and the border are likely to be quieter. The campsite listed on page 170 is a basic site and not somewhere with wonderful views where you may wish to spend an extended stay. So the next question is how long do you spend in St Petersburg?

Having spent five days there in August 2004, arriving from Moscow in a motorcaravan, I would say you could easily spend six days, if not more, enjoying all that St Petersburg has to offer. Depending on your tastes you will need to allow whole days for visiting the Hermitage Museum and Peterhof, plus days for wider sightseeing, shopping etc. The journey from the campsite to the city centre, by public transport, is simple, quick and cheap (see details below).

Whatever you do, your dates of entry and departure will be fixed.

## Journey to Russia (continued)

To obtain your visa you will need:
- a valid passport with at least 6 months validity beyond your entry dates.
- three passport size photos.
- completed application form.
- the fee.

In the UK the Russian Embassy is at:
5 Kensington Palace Gardens, London W8 4QS
Tel 0207 229 8027. Fax 0207 229 3215,
or try the Internet www.russianvisas.org

### Documents

Having got your visa you will need to ensure you have other important documents. Ensure that you take your vehicle registration document plus a photocopy (it is wise to copy all your papers, including your passport, credit cards, insurance etc). If the registered owner of the vehicle is not the driver than you need written authority from the owner on a form printed in Russian (available from our travel service). This is required even if the vehicle is registered in your partner's name and they are not driving, so it is a lot easier if the driver is the owner.

### International driving licence

You will also need an International Driving Licence that has information in Cyrillic script (Russian). These can be obtained from either the AA or RAC for about £4 and are valid for one year.

### Insurance

Almost the last and perhaps the most problematic issue is vehicle insurance. Most British insurers do not seem keen to give cover for European Russia and you will need to obtain cover elsewhere. Whilst this may be possible near the border, if you try and obtain it there you will need to speak fairly good Russian. So again, it's well worth arranging before you leave.

One possibility is the Dutch insurer Ingosur B.V. who can be contacted at:
Carnegielaan 10, PO Box 85992, 2508 CR Den Haag, Netherlands
Tel 0031 70 363 3013. Email: ingosur@ingosur.nl

Cover for one month cost 2300 roubles (£ 46) for my motorcaravan (basic cover only). I already had fully comprehensive cover from my French insurer that covered Russia for trips lasting less than three months but nevertheless I still needed Russian third party cover and more importantly the Russian insurance vignette that has to be stuck on the right side of the windscreen. Also, do ensure that you have two copies of the Russian insurance document, normally an A4 sheet – the original and a photocopy will suffice.

### Other issues

The last remaining item, at least as far as your vehicle is concerned, is breakdown cover and recovery. Whilst not absolutely vital, it is certainly recommended, but here you should find it comparatively easy to obtain. Medical cover is of course also highly advisable. Keep all these documents together because you will need them an awful lot as you proceed on your travels.

Having dealt with these issues, you're almost ready to leave. You just need to ensure you have maps that cover Northern Russia and the Baltic States. Sadly most GPS systems don't cover these regions.

### Before you leave Helsinki

I would say the most vital thing before you leave that nice Western European campsite in Helsinki is to ensure you are empty and full. By that I mean that you have a full tank of clean drinking water and an empty waste tank and Thetford cassette. If you don't carry enough water for your stay in Russia then you might consider buying some bottled water. Water is of course available at the campsite in St Petersburg but I would not describe it as drinking water so you should come prepared. We have installed an excellent filter in our

## Journey to Russia (continued)

camper and that coped well but we ensured that water was boiled before drinking and only used the Russian water for washing and dishwashing. It is, of course, also possible to empty Thetford cassettes at the site, but not something you will want to repeat since the hole in the ground is a little unpleasant and you need to take some rinsing water with you.

The journey from Helsinki to the Russian border near Vaalimaa, on route 7/E18, is about 180 km. (112 miles) and, as previously stated, the border formalities can easily take three to five hours. So, an early start is essential as the drive to the campsite on the other side of the border is about 200 km. (125 miles).

### FI2850 Rastila Camping

Karavaanikatu 4, FIN-00980 Helsinki (Uusimaa)
Tel: 09 321 6551. Email: rastilacamping@hel.fi

No trip to Finland would be complete without a few days stay in Helsinki, the capital since 1812. This all year round site has exceptional transport links with the metro; only five minutes walk from the campsite gates. It provides 265 pitches, 165 with electrical hook-ups, plus an additional small field for tent campers. Shrubs have been planted between the tarmac and grass pitches. All visitors will want to spend time in the Capital and a 24 hour bus, tram and metro pass costs a little over € 6 and can be bought at the metro station. Once on the metro you are in the city centre within 20 minutes on this regular fast train service. Essential visits will include Senate Square, in the heart of the city, and Suomenlinna, a marine fortress built on six islands in the 1700s. This garrison town is one of the most popular sights in Finland and is the world's largest maritime fortress. Helsinki, on the other hand, is one of Europe's smallest capitals and walking around the centre and port is popular as well as visiting the market square alongside the ferry port. The city also has a wide variety of art galleries and museums, many of which are free with the Helsinki card.

**Facilities**
Four sanitary blocks (one heated) provide toilets and showers. Kitchens with cooking rings and sinks. Facilities for disabled visitors and babies. Laundry room. Saunas. Motorcaravan service point. Fully licenced restaurant. Playground. Games and TV room. Bicycles, kayaks and rowing boats for hire. Off site: Small beach adjacent. Golf 5 km. Tallinn the capital of Estonia is only 90 minutes away from Helsinki by fast jetliner ferry.

**Open:** All year.

**Directions**
Well signed from 170 or Ring I. From the 170, turn at Itakeskus shopping complex towards Vuosaari. After crossing bridge go up slip road to Rastila. At top of road turn left. Site is directly ahead.
GPS: N60:12.395 E25:07.279

**Charges 2007**
| | |
|---|---|
| Per pitch incl. 2 persons | € 9,00 - € 15,00 |
| electricity | € 4,50 |

Discounts for weekly or monthly bookings.

### Entry into Russia

Firstly, it is important to understand that border formalities in Russia change regularly and it very much seems to depend on the border guards themselves. So, this is based on our experience. Remember – be polite, patient and do not take photos.

When you first arrive at the Russian border you either have to join a queue or go and park in 'park ferme' you will quickly be directed to wherever is appropriate. Your initial concern is that you need Russian roubles and this is the first chance you have to get them, so do that first. Then, armed with registration documents, Russian insurance documents (two copies), passport for the vehicle owner and customs declaration the vehicle driver needs to queue for the payment of 150 RUR (£3). Here you get a form in Russian. Take this to the police office, with the same forms, where they issue the necessary importation clearance.

A fellow traveller told us to limit what cash we took into Russia and disclosed at the border; if you have thousands of euros or dollars it is very tempting for corrupt police or border guards.

Strangely, this seemed to be it. When we were ready, we drove through, just showing the clearance form, and we were in Russia, no one checked the visas or passports for passengers. But these had to be taken to the nearest police when we stopped for the night and another fee of 20 RUR (£0.40) was payable. It is important that you do this because if you don't it might cause problems when you try and leave. The reception staff in the hotel next to the campsite will help.

**Journey to Russia** (continued)

## Russia

Firstly time; Russia is three hours ahead of GMT and from the last Sunday in March to the last Sunday in September 'summer time' is in force, so then it is four hours ahead of GMT.

Russian roads are often in the most appalling condition. Even if a road appears to be a motorway on your map, the surfaces will vary from severely pot-holed to just poor. Even on 'motorways' there will be traffic lights, pedestrian crossings, horses pulling carts and regular police control points. Speed limits are 60 kmh in towns and 90 kmh cross-country but we did well if we could achieve 50 kmh on average.

Diesel and petrol are easy to find and are cheap. In August 2004 diesel cost just 10.2 roubles per litre - that's about 20 pence, and petrol only a few pence more. They are, however, not used to you pulling up and expecting to fill your tank. The accepted procedure is that firstly you have to go to the desk and pay, so you must plan ahead. Don't forget to fill up before you leave Russia at Ivangorod, near the Estonian border, firstly, because it's cheap and secondly because you cannot leave with Russian roubles.

Police Control Points are very common in Russia and sometimes just a few miles apart. You are simply required to drive carefully past them and stop if directed to do so. Usually there won't be a problem.

A few other points about driving in Russia:

- Driving is not allowed after drinking any alcohol.
- Seat belts are compulsory.
- Local drivers do not require third party insurance.
- A vehicle on a roundabout must give way.
- Trams and buses always have right of way.
- Do not overtake near train crossings, crossroads or police control points.
- All accidents must be reported to the Police.

### Nearly there

The Russian border town is Vyborg but it is some distance from the border. To get to the campsite just stay on the M10/E18 towards St Petersburg. Most maps seem to show a ring road north of the city that goes across the island of Kotlin. At the time of our visit, that road had not been built!

Check real time availability and at-the-gate prices...
www.alanrogers.com

## Journey to Russia (continued)

South of Sestroreck the M10 becomes a two lane dual-carriageway with a wide central reservation of grass and trees. You will find the campsite signposted on the right. It is called Hotel Camping Olgino. See our report on the next page. If you enter the urban area with tall high-rise flats, you have missed the site. After the security post, park near the hotel directly ahead and go to reception - take your passports. The campsite is about 200 metres to the left.

Public transport from the site to the city is simple. Directly outside the site is a bus stop. You need either a 110 or 120 bus costing 10 roubles or the 305 minibus costing 30 roubles. All three take you to the metro station. Metro tokens are 10 roubles, and it is worth buying enough for all your journeys.

It is well worth having a good travel guide. We found the Lonely Planet 'Russia & Belarus' very good. Whatever you do, don't miss Peterhof and the Hermitage.

A word of warning. In the city, gangs of gipsy-like females operate. Three or four grab your arms and the others search your pockets or bags taking what they want. This happened to two of our group on different occasions so take sensible precautions and don't carry your passport and other important documents.

### Journey to Tallinn

So, after a hopefully pleasant stay in St Petersburg, it is time to leave. Again, an early start is essential because you have to cope with the border again and it is better to get through the city before the rush hour.

Leaving the city is not difficult. Just turn right as you leave the site and follow the road straight on. Eventually you are alongside the River Neva, which you need to cross to get to the border.

It is best to follow the Tallinn signs – these will take you across the Neva and onto the M11/E20 towards the border town of Ivangorod, about 200 km. (125 miles) in total.

Check real time availability and at-the-gate prices...
www.alanrogers.com

## Journey to Russia (continued)

### Hotel Camping Oglino
Primorskji Chausee 197229 St Petersburg
Tel: 812 336 34 75. Email: info@hotel-olgino.spb.ru

This site is typical of many 'Old Russian' standard sites – excellent location, fair pitches and poor sanitary provision. So - you might choose to use your own facilities, although the site has recently added two new blocks of toilets with hot showers and these were good. Oglino is a hotel/conference centre built in 'Soviet' times, with an adjoining campsite in a small wooded area. There are 35 touring pitches, all with electricity although you may have to share a connection. We are advised that, if anything, it has deteriorated since 'perestroika', but then so has its usage. There is a good restaurant in the hotel and it was also possible to get laundry done overnight at very reasonable cost. A good bus service operates from outside the site, direct to the local metro station. St Petersburg with all its glory is 45 minutes away and there is very much to see and do. Special trips could include Peterhof, Peter the Great's Palace, some way to the east, and accessed by hydrofoil, or a trip to the Russian Ballet.

#### Facilities
Small sanitary block has toilets and hot showers. Chemical toilet disposal point. Small restaurant and bar. The general state of the site is clean but somewhat unkempt. The 'babushka' who looks after the site collects all your rubbish at least twice a day and tries to keep the sanitary facilities clean. Off site: St Petersburg.

**Open:** 1 June - 30 September.

#### Directions
Coming from Finland the site is on the right side of the M10 before you enter the St Petersburg urban area. Coming from the city you want to be on the Neva quay, on the opposite side to the Aurora, with the river to your left and travelling towards Vyborg. Initially this is Neva Quay, but becomes Primorskji Prospekt, then Sawuschkina Street and then Primorskji Chausee where the site is signposted. At this point the road is a dual carriageway with a large central reservation of grass and trees. You turn left through a slip road towards the site.

#### Charges guide
Per motorcaravan incl. two adults and electricity about 300 roubles per night.

### Exit

Just before the town of Kingisepp it is worth stopping and filling up with fuel. At this garage we spent the last of our roubles on vodka, etc. just to ensure we only had what we needed to leave the country, and no more. At the border we had to pay a fee of 50 roubles (£1) but that seems subject to change so we had a 50-rouble note and a handful of coins left.

Before you arrive at Ivangorod and just before the police control point you have to turn right into 'park ferme'. As you enter you get a form and here you have to pay the fee and in return you get a stamp on your form. You are then allowed, a few vehicles at a time, to proceed towards the border. You go through two control points and then join another queue where, one at a time, you have to report to the window with all your documents, not forgetting the customs clearance document you got upon entry. As directed, you then move forward and your vehicle is searched. At the next window all passengers must present their passports - usually to the same guard who has just inspected the vehicle. If you have an unusual vehicle, he may call colleagues from the office to come and have a look. Once this is completed, you can drive out of Russia but not yet into Estonia. The Estonian border guards we encountered spoke English and needed just a quick look at your passport, and you're through! There is a large car park immediately ahead which presents a good opportunity to stop, take a breather, get some Estonian Krone from either the cashpoint or the bureau de change and perhaps have a drink.

In this guide you'll find details of a site at Toila, which is about 50 km. towards Tallinn on much better roads. This is a pleasant site, but again, it's worth remembering that although the water is better - it is still not to UK standards. It is also somewhere to reflect on what you have achieved in the last few days, a trip not undertaken by many and an insight into Russia.

Mike Annan

Check real time availability and at-the-gate prices...
www.alanrogers.com

# Travelling

When taking your car (and caravan, tent or trailer tent) or motorcaravan to the continent you do need to plan in advance and to find out as much as possible about driving in the countries you plan to visit. Whilst European harmonisation has eliminated many of the differences between one country and another, it is well worth reading the short notes we provide in the introduction to each country in this guide in addition to this more general summary.

Of course, the main difference from driving in the UK is that in mainland Europe you will need to drive on the right. Without taking extra time and care, especially at busy junctions and conversely when roads are empty, it is easy to forget to drive on the right. Remember that traffic approaching from the right usually has priority unless otherwise indicated by road markings and signs. Harmonisation also means that most (but not all) common road signs are the same in all countries.

## Your vehicle

Book your vehicle in for a good service well before your intended departure date. This will lessen the chance of an expensive breakdown. Make sure your brakes are working efficiently and that your tyres have plenty of tread (3 mm. is recommended, particularly if you are undertaking a long journey).

Also make sure that your caravan or trailer is roadworthy and that its tyres are in good order and correctly inflated. Plan your packing and be careful not to overload your vehicle, caravan or trailer – this is unsafe and may well invalidate your insurance cover (it must not be more fully loaded than the kerb weight of the insured vehicle).

### Check all the following:

- **GB sticker.** If you do not display a sticker, you may risk an on-the-spot fine as this identifier is compulsory in all countries. Euro-plates are an acceptable alternative within the EU (but not outside). Remember to attach another sticker (or Euro-plate) to caravans or trailers. Only GB stickers (not England, Scotland, Wales or N. Ireland) stickers are valid in the EU.

- **Headlights.** As you will be driving on the right you must adjust your headlights so that the dipped beam does not dazzle oncoming drivers. Converter kits are readily available for most vehicle, although if your car is fitted with high intensity headlights, you should check with your motor dealer. Check that any planned extra loading does not affect the beam height.

- **Seatbelts.** Rules for the fitting and wearing of seatbelts throughout Europe are similar to those in the UK, but it is worth checking before you go. Rules for carrying children in the front of vehicles vary from country to country. It is best to plan not to do this if possible.

- **Door/Wing mirrors.** To help with driving on the right, if your vehicle is not fitted with a mirror on the left hand side, we recommend you have one fitted.

- **Fuel.** Leaded and Lead Replacement petrol is increasingly difficult to find in Northern Europe.

# Travelling continued

## Compulsory additional equipment

The driving laws of the countries of Europe still vary in what you are required to carry in your vehicle, although the consequences of not carrying a required piece of equipment are almost always an on-the-spot fine.

To meet these requirements we suggest that you carry the following:

- Fire extinguisher
- Basic tool kit
- First aid kit
- Spare bulbs
- Two warning triangles – two are required in some countries at all times, and are compulsory in most countries when towing.
- High visibility vest – now compulsory in Spain, Italy and Austria (and likely to become compulsory throughout the EU) in case you need to walk on a motorway.

## Insurance and Motoring Documents

### Vehicle insurance

Contact your insurer well before you depart to check that your car insurance policy covers driving outside the UK. Most do, but many policies only provide minimum cover (so if you have an accident your insurance may only cover the cost of damage to the other person's property, with no cover for fire and theft).

To maintain the same level of cover abroad as you enjoy at home you need to tell your vehicle insurer. Some will automatically cover you abroad with no extra cost and no extra paperwork. Some will say you need a Green Card (which is neither green nor on card) but won't charge for it. Some will charge extra for the Green Card. Ideally you should contact your vehicle insurer 3-4 weeks before you set off, and confirm your conversation with them in writing.

### Breakdown insurance

Arrange breakdown cover for your trip in good time so that if your vehicle breaks down or is involved in an accident it (and your caravan or trailer) can be repaired or returned to this country. This cover can usually be arranged as part of your travel insurance policy (see below).

### Documents you must take with you

You may be asked to show your documents at any time so make sure that they are in order, up-to-date and easily accessible while you travel. These are what you need to take:

- Passports (you may also need a visa in some countries if you hold either a UK passport not issued in the UK or a passport that was issued outside the EU).
- Motor Insurance Certificate, including Green Card (or Continental Cover clause)
- DVLC Vehicle Registration Document plus, if not your own vehicle, the owner's written authority to drive.
- A full valid Driving Licence (not provisional). The new photo style licence is now mandatory in most European countries.

# insure4campers.com

## One call and you're covered

## Travelling on the continent?
## Holidaying on campsites?

Our policies provide exactly the right cover for holidays of this type – at exceptionally low rates. Whatever you need, our policies are tailored to suit self-drive campsite-based holidays.

- Are you covered if you're broken into on site?
- Is your caravan insurance excess reimbursed?
- If your vehicle breaks down will you be able to find someone to fix it?
- Can you get increased car hire limits when towing? (plus policies)
- Do you have access to a 24hr multi-lingual helpline?

### Call us **NOW** for a no-obligation quote
# 01580 214006

Policies despatched within 24 hours

# Travelling continued

### Personal Holiday insurance

Even though you are just travelling within Europe you must take out travel insurance. Few EU countries pay the full cost of medical treatment even under reciprocal health service arrangements. The first part of a holiday insurance policy covers people. It will include the cost of doctor, ambulance and hospital treatment if needed. If needed the better companies will even pay for English language speaking doctors and nurses and will bring a sick or injured holidaymaker home by air ambulance.

The second part of a good policy covers things. If someone breaks into your motorhome and steals your passports and money, one phone call to the insurance company will have everything sorted out. If you manage to drive over your camera, it should be covered. NB – most policies have a maximum payment limit per item, do check that any valuables are adequately covered.

An important part of the insurance, often ignored, is cancellation (and curtailment) cover. Few things are as heartbreaking as having to cancel a holiday because a member of the family falls ill. Cancellation insurance can't take away the disappointment, but it makes sure you don't suffer financially as well. For this reason you should arrange your holiday insurance at least eight weeks before you set off.

Whichever insurance you choose we would advise reading very carefully the policies sold by the High Street travel trade. Whilst they may be good, they may not cover the specific needs of campers, caravanners and motorcaravanners.

Telephone **0870 405 4059** for a quote for our European Camping Holiday Insurance with cover arranged through Green Flag Motoring Assistance and Inter Group Assistance Services, one of the UK's largest assistance companies. Alternatively visit our website at **www.insure4campers.com**.

### European Health Insurance Card (EHIC)

**Important Changes since E111:** Since September 2005 new European Health Insurance Cards have replaced the E111 forms.

Make sure you apply for your EHIC before travelling in Europe. Eligible travellers from the UK are entitled to receive free or reduced-cost medical care in many European countries on production of an EHIC. This free card is available by completing a form in the booklet 'Health Advice for Travellers' from local Post Offices. One should be completed for each family member. Alternatively visit www.dh.gov.uk/travellers and apply on-line. Please allow time to send your application off and have the EHIC returned to you.

The EHIC is valid in all European Community countries plus Iceland, Liechtenstein, Switzerland and Norway. If you or any of your dependants are suddenly taken ill or have an accident during a visit to any of these countries, free or reduced-cost emergency treatment is available – in most cases on production of a valid EHIC. Only state-provided emergency treatment is covered, and you will receive treatment on the same terms as nationals of the country you are visiting. Private treatment is generally not covered, and state-provided treatment may not cover all of the things that you would expect to receive free of charge from the NHS.

Remember an EHIC does not cover you for all the medical costs that you can incur or for repatriation – it is not an alternative to travel insurance. You will still need appropriate insurance to ensure you are fully covered for all eventualities.

## IMPORTANT: TRAVEL HEALTH ALERT

### ! UK HOLIDAYMAKERS COULD BE AT RISK OF DEADLY EUROPEAN VIRUS

**Thousands of British tourists risk contracting a potentially life-threatening disease in Europe this summer.**

The **'Tick Alert'** campaign has been launched warning UK travellers about Tick Borne Encephalitis (TBE), a viral disease contracted via the bite of an infected tick. It can lead to meningitis and, in serious cases, result in paralysis and death.

The warning identifies 16 central and eastern European countries where the TBE infected tick population is officially endemic and therefore poses a high risk to visitors who have not been immunised or taken bite prevention precautions.

According to figures from the Foreign Office, the number of UK tourists visiting central and eastern Europe rose by 38 per cent to 558,000 last summer.

This includes many of the new popular European holiday destinations such as Croatia, the Czech Republic, Estonia, Latvia, Lithuania, Slovenia and Slovakia, where there is a growing adventure travel market.

TBE-infected ticks are found typically in rural and forest areas during the late spring and summer months. At-risk groups include all visitors to rural areas of endemic countries, particularly those participating in outdoor activities such as trekking, hiking, climbing, cycling and camping.

A number of measures can be taken to reduce the risk of infection: these include using an insect repellent, wearing protective clothing to cover all areas of exposed skin, regularly inspecting for tick bites and carefully removing any found. The disease can also be transmitted by the ingestion of unpasteurised milk which should be avoided.

However, the Foreign Office advises that visitors to TBE endemic regions seek inoculation advice from their local surgery or clinic – well before travelling.

Immunisation against TBE is available as a paid-for travel vaccine from specialist travel health clinics and at GP surgeries and healthcare centres.

Further information on the endemic regions of Europe and latest advice for travellers is available at www.masta-travel-health.com/tickalert.

*Travelling in Europe*

## Open All Year

The following sites are understood to accept caravanners and campers all year round. It is always wise to contact the site to check as the facilities available, for example, may be reduced.

### Greece
| | |
|---|---|
| GR8000 | Batis |
| GR8255 | Vrachos Kastraki |
| GR8320 | Olympia |
| GR8330 | Ionion Beach |
| GR8525 | Chrissa |
| GR8560 | Ramnous |
| GR8580 | Bacchus |
| GR8590 | Athens |
| GR8595 | Nea Kifissia |
| GR8685 | Gythion Bay |
| GR8695 | Finikes |

### Croatia
| | |
|---|---|
| CR6745 | Bi-Village |
| CR6875 | Nevio |

### Slovenia
| | |
|---|---|
| SV4100 | Spik |
| SV4150 | Kamne |
| SV4235 | Klin |
| SV4340 | Ljubljana Resort |
| SV4400 | Dolina Prebold |
| SV4410 | Moravke Toplice |
| SV4440 | Terme Ptuj |

### Romania
| | |
|---|---|
| RO7040 | International |
| RO7090 | De Oude Wilg |
| RO7190 | Casa Alba |

### Hungary
| | |
|---|---|
| HU5024 | Lentri |
| HU5150 | Fortuna |
| HU5155 | Római |
| HU5165 | Zugligeti Niche |
| HU5210 | Diófaház |
| HU5255 | Martfü |
| HU5260 | Jonathermál |
| HU5300 | Kek-Duna |

### Slovakia
| | |
|---|---|
| SK4910 | Turiec |
| SK4980 | Levocská Dolina |

### Czech Republic
| | |
|---|---|
| CZ4640 | Areal Jadran |
| CZ4700 | Jaroslav Kohoutek |
| CZ4745 | U Dvou Orechu |
| CZ4770 | Dlouhá Louka |
| CZ4795 | Cisarska Louka |
| CZ4815 | Triocamp |
| CZ4845 | Busek Praha |
| CZ4880 | Roznov |
| CZ4885 | Bobrovnik |
| CZ4898 | Vidlak |

### Poland
| | |
|---|---|
| PL3002 | Camping Park Nr. 130 |
| PL3003 | Boduwico |
| PL3006 | Olimpijski 117 |
| PL3170 | Mazurski Eden |
| PL3190 | Horst Kruska |
| PL3230 | Olenka |
| PL3300 | Polana Sosny |
| PL3320 | Auschwitz Centre |
| PL3340 | Smok |

### Lithuania
| | |
|---|---|
| LI2010 | Apple Island |
| LI2030 | Slenyje |
| LI2050 | Vitruna |
| LI2065 | Pusele |
| LI2090 | Sedula |
| LI2120 | Ventaine |
| LI2130 | Nida |

### Latvia
| | |
|---|---|
| LA1030 | Gauja |
| LA1100 | Piejuras |
| LA1150 | Radi |

### Estonia
| | |
|---|---|
| ET0010 | Konse |
| ET0015 | Pikseke |
| ET0100 | Tehumardi |
| ET0120 | Randmäe |

## Dogs

For the benefit of those who want to take their dogs with them or for people who do not like dogs at the sites they visit, we list here the sites that have indicated to us that they do not accept dogs. If you are, however, planning to take your dog we do advise you to contact them first to check – there may be limits on numbers, breeds, etc. or times of the year when they are excluded.

**Never** – these sites do not accept dogs at any time:

### Greece
| | |
|---|---|
| GR8125 | Comitsa |
| GR8150 | Isa |

### Croatia
| | |
|---|---|
| CR6731 | Valalta (Naturist) |
| CR6736 | Valdaliso |

### Romania
| | |
|---|---|
| RO7040 | International |

### Hungary
| | |
|---|---|
| HU5090 | Füred |
| HU5380 | Venus |

### Czech Republic
| | |
|---|---|
| CZ4750 | Bilá Hora |

### Lithuania
| | |
|---|---|
| LI2060 | Viktorija |

**Maybe** – accepted at any time but with certain restrictions:

### Greece
| | | |
|---|---|---|
| GR8520 | Delphi | - max 1 |

### Czech Republic
| | | |
|---|---|---|
| CZ4892 | Bongerd - max 1 | |

# Save up to 60% on your holiday

## Camping Cheque

- Over 575 sites – all just £10.30 per night
- Maximum flexibility - go as you please
- Fantastic Ferry Deals

Last year 250,000 people used nearly 1.6 million Camping Cheques and enjoyed half-price holidays around Europe. Make sure you don't miss out this year.

### Huge off peak savings

Over 575 quality campsites, in 22 European countries, including the UK, all at just £10.30 per night for pitch + 2 adults, including electricity. That's a saving of up to 60% off normal site tariffs.

## Fantastic Ferry Offers

3 **FREE** Camping Cheques with each return ferry crossing

**CALL NOW** for your **FREE** Holiday Savings guide

FOR FULL INFORMATION VISIT
**www.campingcheque.co.uk**

Buy Cheques, check ferry availability, book everything on-line AND SAVE!

**01580 214002**

# UnityPlus CARD

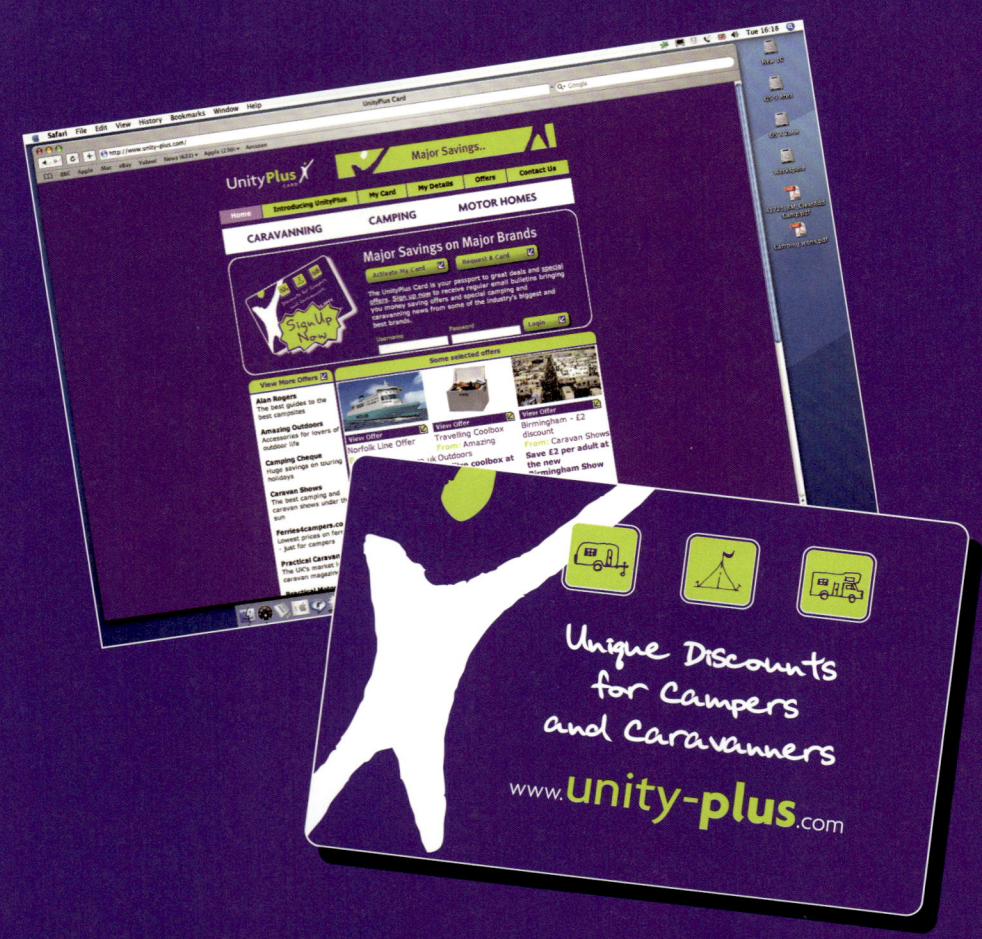

## NEW

Whether you have a caravan, a motorhome or a tent, the UnityPlus Card is for you. It's not a club but it offers great benefits and it's free! Quite simply, it offers unique discounts for campers and caravanners on a range of products including cheap ferry deals, discounted holidays, camping accessories, specialist insurance and more.

Full details at www.**unity-plus**.com

Request your UnityPlus Card today!

# 3 ISSUES FOR £1

Our practical titles are packed full of holiday tips, technical advice, reader reviews, superb photography…and much more! So subscribe to Practical Caravan or Practical Motorhome **for just £1.**

- **YOU** get your first 3 issues for £1
- **YOU** save 20% on the shop price after your trial ends
- **RISK-FREE** offer - you can cancel at any time
- **FREE** delivery, straight to your door!
- **EXCLUSIVE** subscriber offers and discounts

## CALL 08456 777 812 NOW!

or visit **www.themagazineshop.com** quote code ALR08

☐ Please start my subscription to Practical Caravan. I will pay £1 for the first 3 issues and £8.40 every 3 issues thereafter, saving 20% on the shop price.

☐ Please start my subscription to Practical Motorhome. I will pay £1 for the first 3 issues and £7.90 every 3 issues thereafter, saving 20% on the shop price.

**YOUR DETAILS BLOCK CAPITALS PLEASE (MUST BE COMPLETED)**

Mr/Mrs/Ms _____ Name _____ Surname _____

Address _____

_____ Postcode _____

Telephone _____

If you are happy to receive offers, news, product and service information from Haymarket Consumer Media and other carefully selected partners via email and SMS, please tick here ☐

E-mail _____

Mobile _____

This is an introductory offer open to UK residents only and is a Direct Debit only offer. Details of the Direct Debit guarantee are available on request. For international rates please call +44 (0) 1750 724703. Offer ends 31 December 2008. Direct Debit rates will remain the same for one year, after this time they are subject to change. Haymarket Consumer Media may contact you by post or phone from time to time, with special offers and product information. Please tick this box if you prefer not receive this information ☐. Occasionally we may pass your details to carefully selected partners whose products we think would be of interest to you. Please tick this box if you prefer not to receive this information ☐.

**DIRECT DEBIT DETAILS**
Instructions to your Bank or Building Society to pay by Direct Debit

To The Manager: Bank/Building Society _____

Address _____

Postcode _____

Name(s) of Account Holder(s) _____

Branch Sort Code ☐☐ ☐☐ ☐☐

Bank/Building Society account number ☐☐☐☐☐☐☐☐

Reference Number (for office use only) _____

Signature(s) _____

**DIRECT DEBIT** Originators ID No. 850699

**Instruction to your Bank or Building Society**
Please pay Haymarket Consumer Media Direct Debits from the account detailed in this instruction subject to the safeguards assured by the Direct Debit Guarantee. I understand that this instruction may stay with Haymarket Consumer Media and, if so, details will be passed electronically to my Bank/Building Society.

**ALR08**

### Please return this form to:
### Haymarket Consumer Media
### FREEPOST SEA 14716 Haywards Heath RH16 3BR

# Need a **low cost ferry?**

Do you have a caravan, motorhome or trailer and want the best deal on your cross-Channel ferry? Then visit www.ferries4campers.co.uk for the lowest prices for campers and caravanners from major ferry operators. Now there's no need to 'go round the houses' for numerous quotes – all the best deals are in one place.

**It couldn't be simpler** - just click, choose a ferry and book...

## www.ferries4campers.co.uk

- Special deals for caravans and motorhomes
- View routes and compare prices
- Book online at any time of day
- Secure payment guaranteed
- Fully searchable by route and operator
- Instant real-time availability provided

**ferries4campers.co.uk**

norfolkline DOVER - DUNKERQUE FERRIES | P&O Ferries | EURO TUNNEL | SEAFRANCE DOVER - CALAIS FERRIES | Brittany Ferries | Condorferries

# Great magazines for touring, holidays and inspirational ideas!

### Caravan · Motor Caravan · Park Home & Holiday Caravan

For buying information, top tips and technical help, **Caravan, Motor Caravan Magazine** and **Park Home & Holiday Caravan** are all you need — every month!

## Subscribe today and save 30%

☎ **0845 676 7778**

Lines are open seven days a week, 9am – 9pm. Closing date 31 December 2007.
Quote code Caravan XCV 38E or Motor Caravan XMV 39A or
Park Home & Holiday Caravan XPH 35H when calling

30% discount is by quarterly direct debit only.

# mycamping.info

## myexperience, myvoice

The Alan Rogers Guides have long been the authoritative voice when it comes to an independent assessment of a campsite's quality. But now is the chance to hear your voice – your opinions, your assessments, your tips...

A beta version of the website is now up and running – and it needs YOUR input before it goes fully live!

- Personal **reviews**
- Real **holiday makers**
- Inside **knowledge**
- Honest **advice**

It's all about **YOU** and **YOUR** experiences...

So get involved today!
Visit www.mycamping.info

## Reports by Readers

We always welcome reports from readers concerning sites which they have visited. Generally reports provide us with invaluable feedback on sites already included in the Guide or, in the case of those not featured in our Guide, they provide information which we can follow up with a view to adding them in future editions. However, if you have a complaint about a site, this should be addressed to the campsite owner, preferably in person before you leave.

Please make your comments either on this form or on plain paper. It would be appreciated if you would indicate the approximate dates when you visited the site and, in the case of potential new sites, provide the correct name and address and, if possible, include a campsite brochure. Send your reports to:

Alan Rogers Guides, Spelmonden Old Oast, Goudhurst, Kent TN17 1HE

Name of Site and Ref. No. (or address for new recommendations)

_____

_____

Dates of visit: _____

Comments:












Reader's Name and Address: _____

_____

_____

_____

## Reports by Readers

Name and reference number of the campsite (or address for new recommendations):
_____
_____

Dates of visit: _____

Comments:

Reader's Name and Address: _____
_____
_____
_____

# Countries of Central Europe

- Estonia
- Russia
- Sweden
- Latvia
- Lithuania
- Belarus
- Russia
- Poland
- Germany
- Ukraine
- Moldova
- Czech Republic
- Slovakia
- Austria
- Hungary
- Romania
- Slovenia
- Croatia
- Bosnia-Herzegovina
- Serbia
- Bulgaria
- Italy
- Albania
- Macedonia
- Greece

# Greece - Map 1

Sites on this map are featured on pages 14-33 of the guide.
Please refer to the numerical index (page 205) for exact campsite page references.

Red text denotes all year opening

# Croatia - Map 2

Sites on this map are featured on pages 34-63 of the guide.
Please refer to the numerical index (page 205) for exact campsite page references.

# Slovenia - Map 3

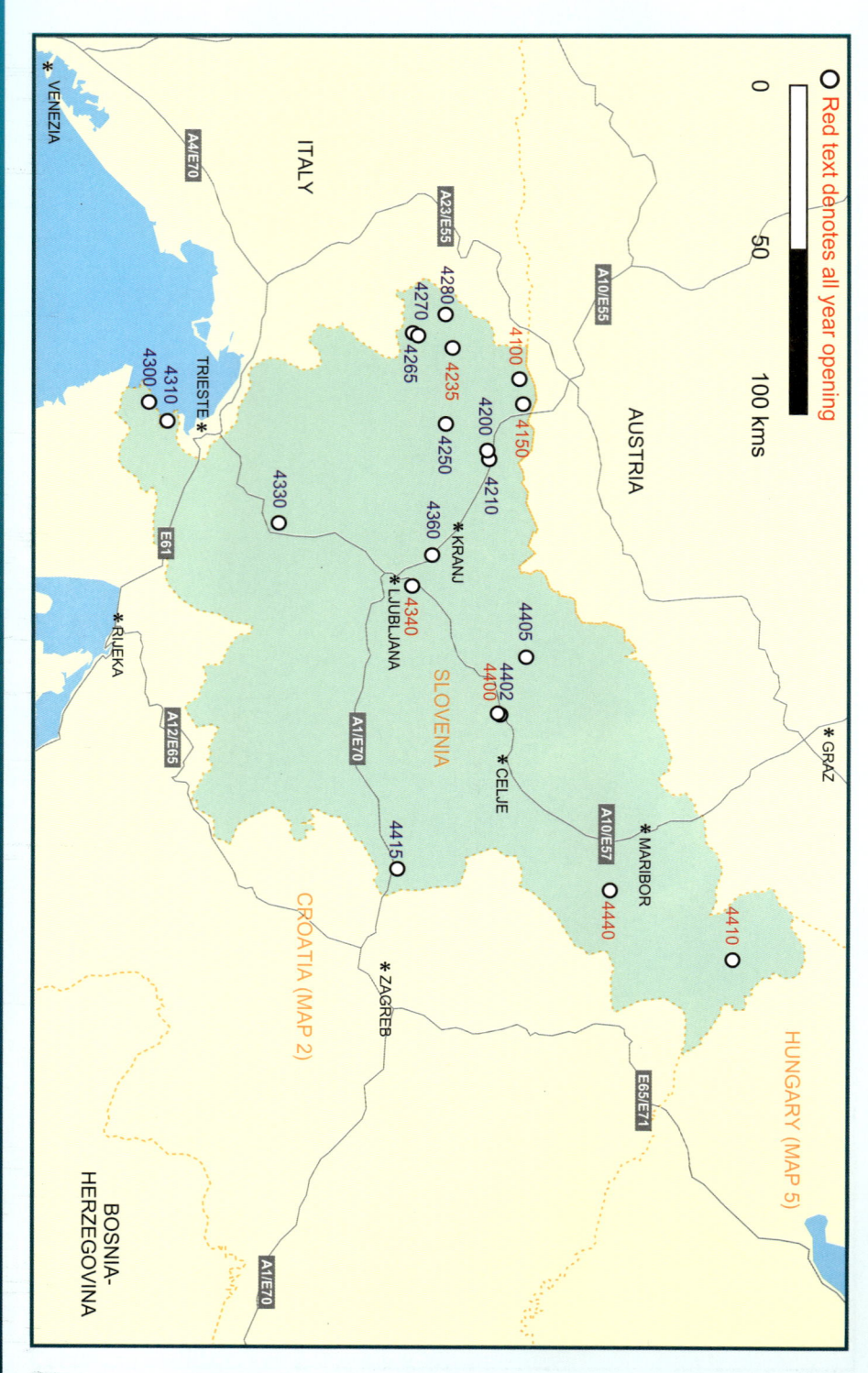

Sites on this map are featured on pages 64-76 of the guide.
Please refer to the numerical index (page 205) for exact campsite page references.

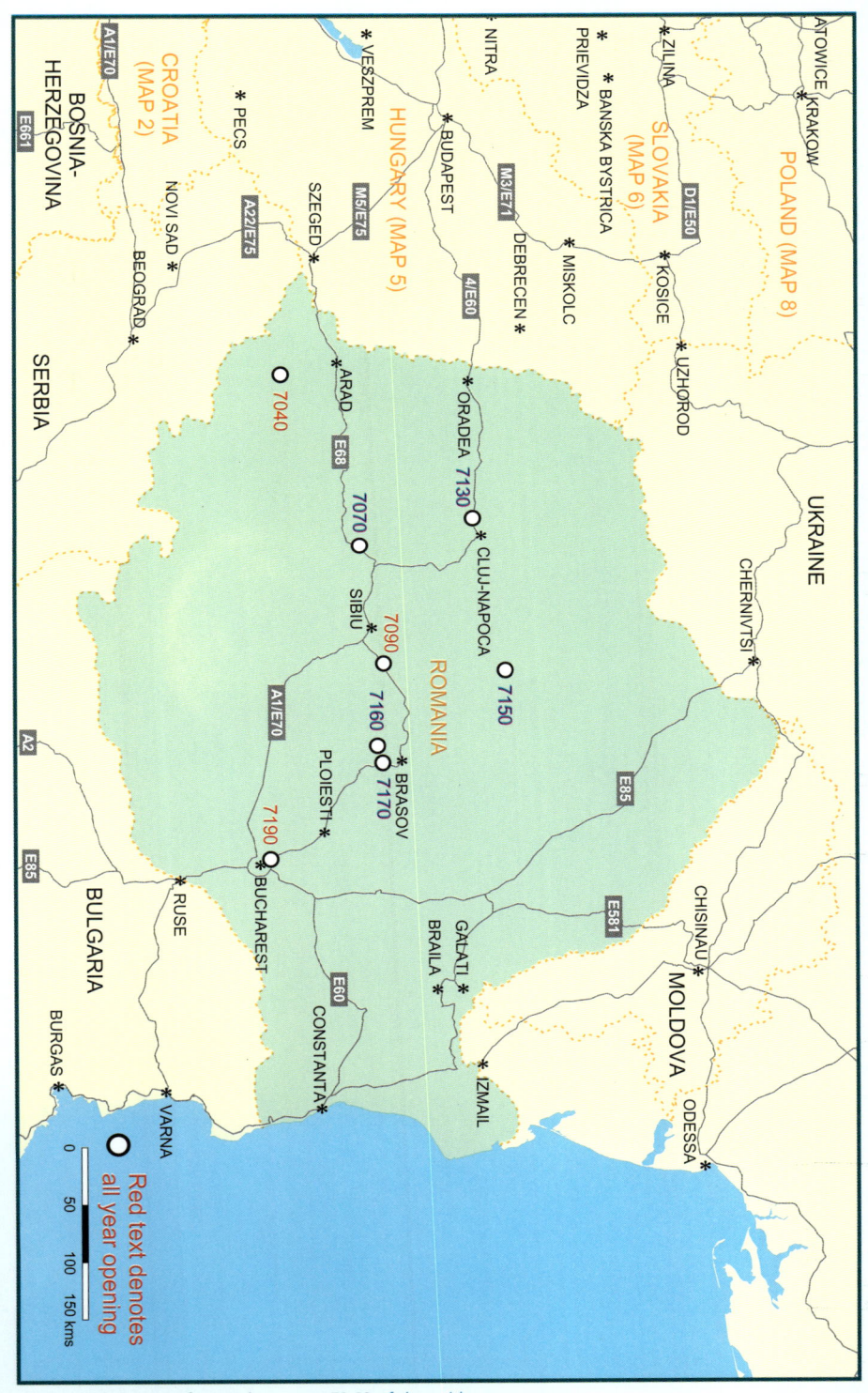

# Romania - Map 4

Sites on this map are featured on pages 78-83 of the guide.
Please refer to the numerical index (page 205) for exact campsite page references.

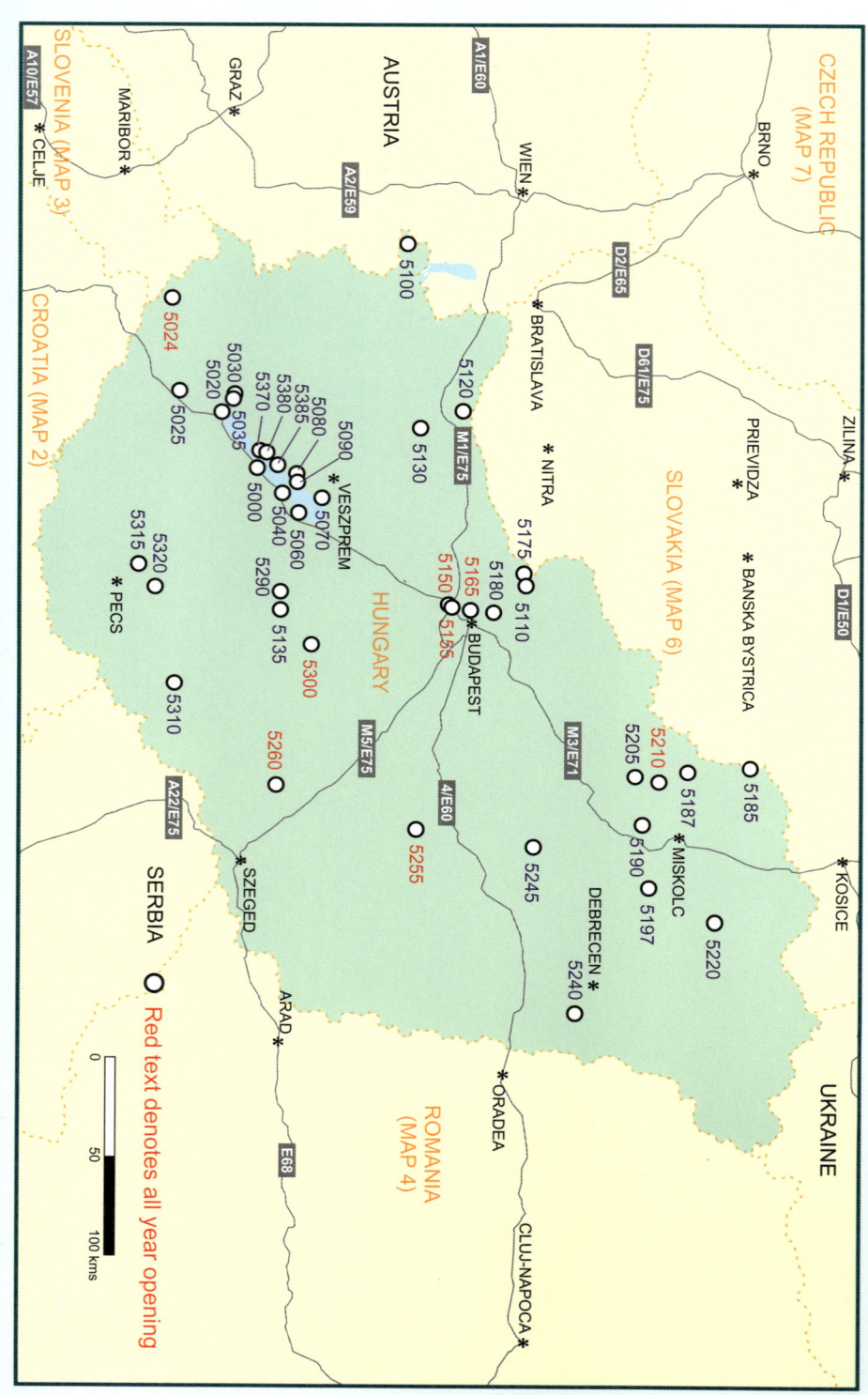

Sites on this map are featured on pages 84-105 of the guide.
Please refer to the numerical index (page 205) for exact campsite page references.

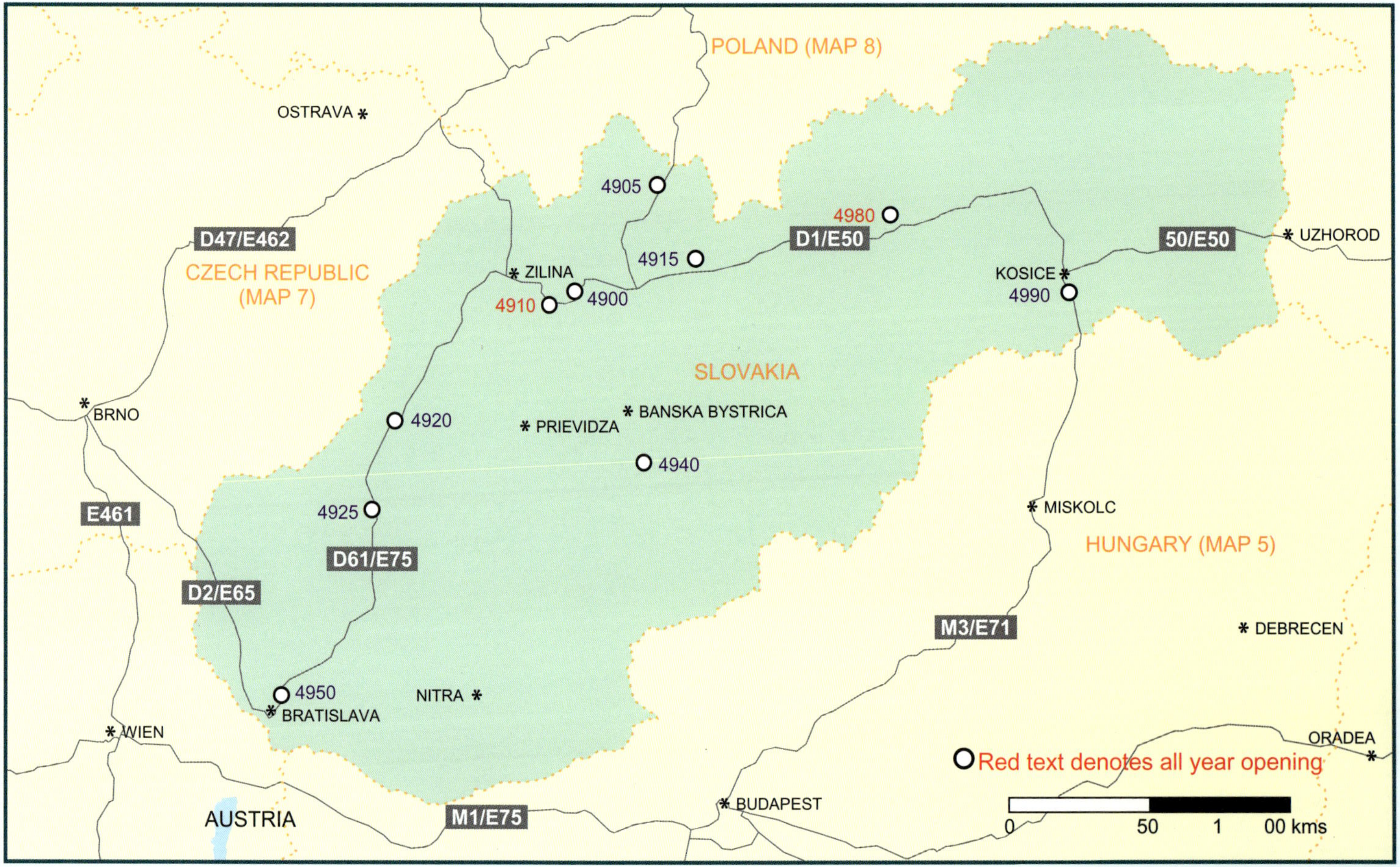

# Slovakia - Map 6

Sites on this map are featured on pages 106-112 of the guide.
Please refer to the numerical index (page 205) for exact campsite page references.

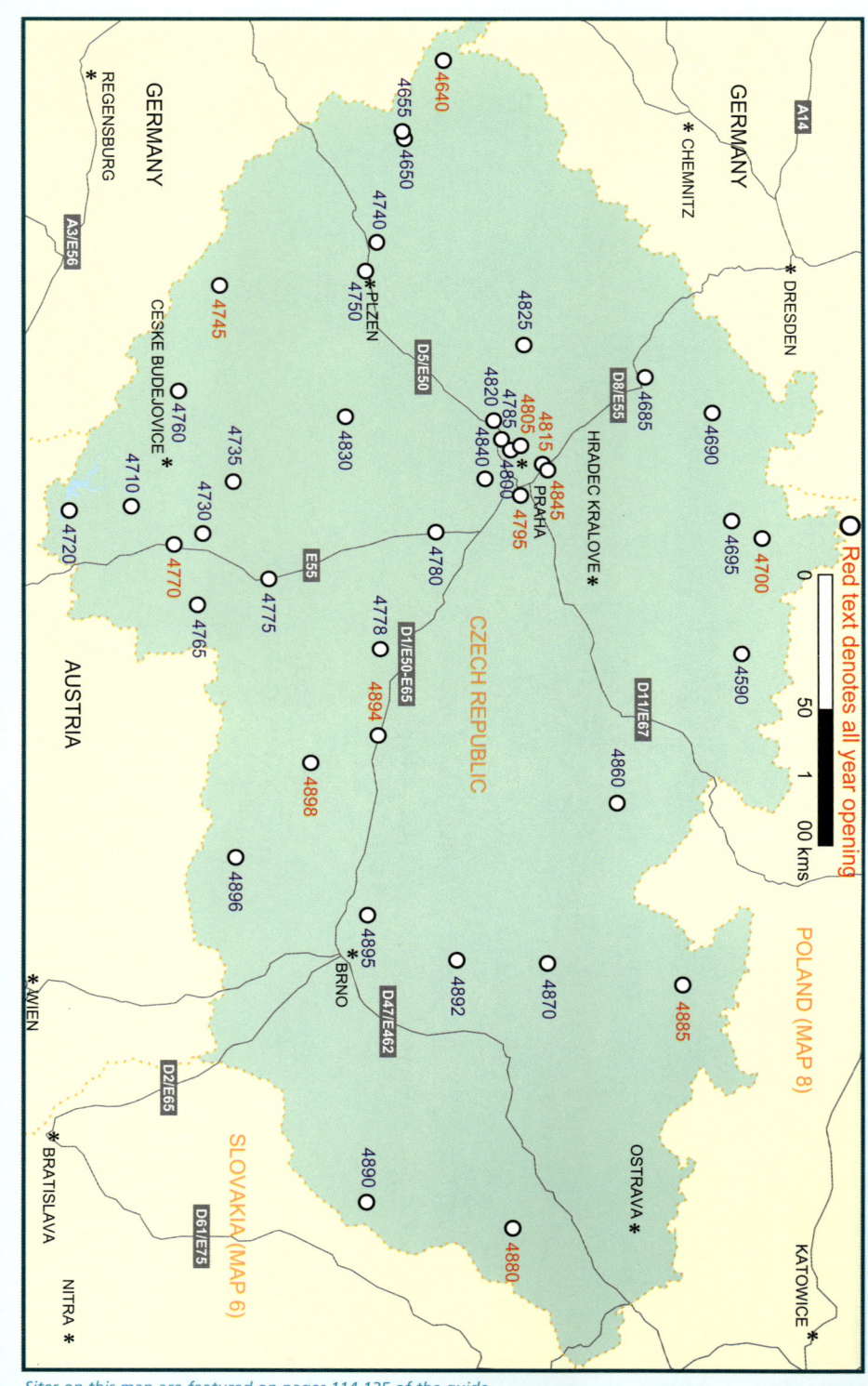

# Czech Republic - Map 7

Sites on this map are featured on pages 114-135 of the guide.
Please refer to the numerical index (page 205) for exact campsite page references.

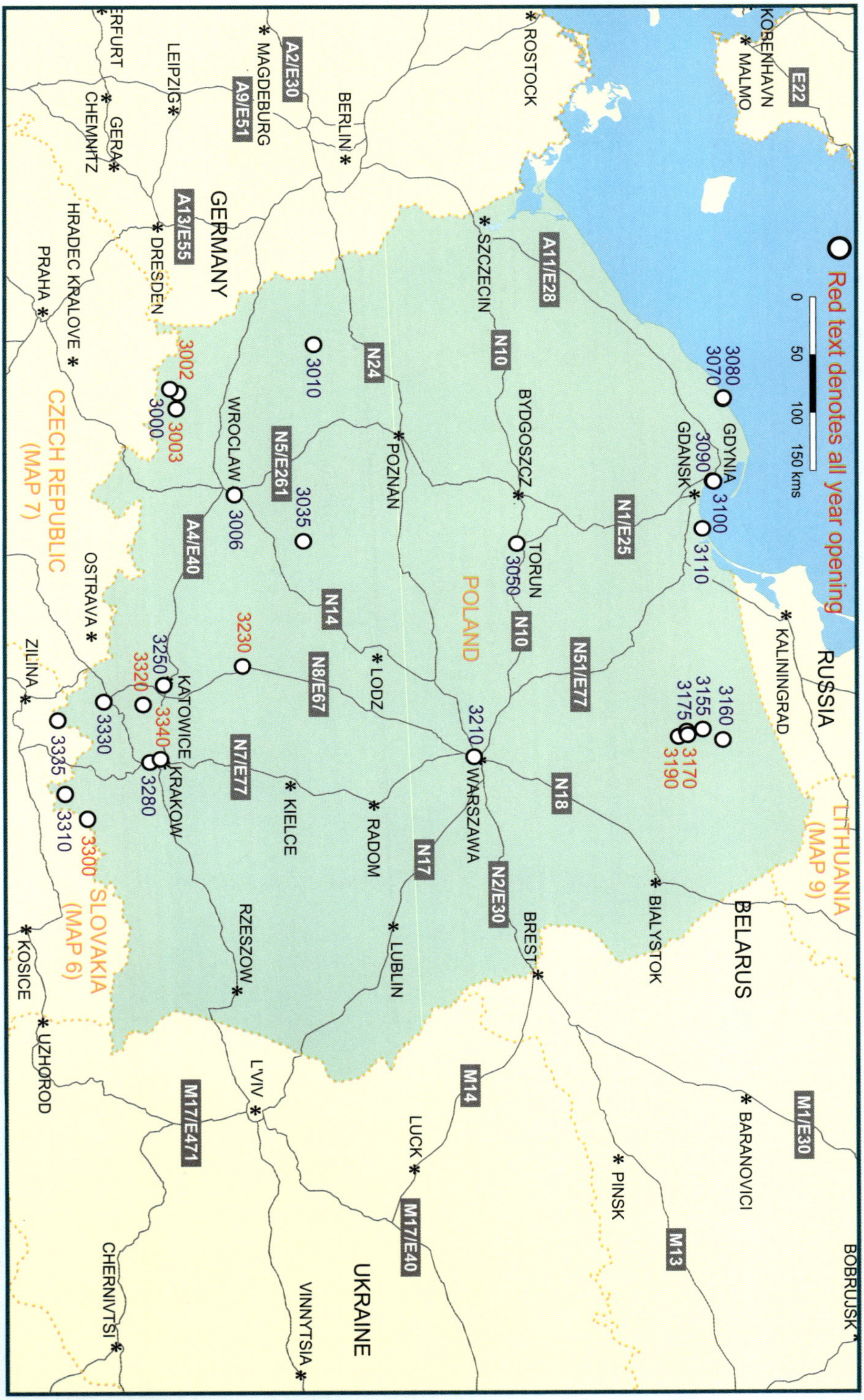


Sites on this map are featured on pages 136-150 of the guide.
Please refer to the numerical index (page 205) for exact campsite page references.

# The Baltic States - Map 9

# Town and Village Index

## Greece

| | |
|---|---|
| Akti Koutloumoussi | 18 |
| Ancient Epidavros | 28 |
| Antirrio | 22 |
| Assini | 29 |
| Athens | 27 |
| Chrisso | 25 |
| Corfu | 31 |
| Corinth | 28 |
| Dassia | 31 |
| Delphi | 25 |
| Eretria | 25 |
| Finikounda | 30 |
| Gerakini | 18 |
| Gialasi | 28 |
| Glifa | 23 |
| Gythion | 29 |
| Igoumenitsa | 20 |
| Kalambaka | 20 |
| Kariotes | 32 |
| Kastraki | 20 |
| Kastro | 22 |
| Kato Gatzea | 21 |
| Kavala | 16 |
| Killinis | 22 |
| Koroni | 30 |
| Lecheon | 28 |
| Lefkada | 32 |
| Lerissos | 17 |
| Lichnos | 19 |
| Marathonas | 26 |
| Nafplio | 29 |
| Nea Kifissia | 27 |
| Nea Roda | 17 |
| Neos Marmaras | 18 |
| Neos Panteleimonas | 17 |
| Nikiti | 18 |
| Olympia | 22-24 |
| Paleokastritsa | 31 |
| Parga | 19 |
| Pefki | 24 |
| Plaka Drepano | 29 |
| Platamon-Pieria | 17 |
| Plataria | 20 |
| Poros | 32 |
| Pylos | 30 |
| Pyrgos | 22 |
| Rafina | 26 |
| Rovies | 24 |
| Schinos | 28 |
| Sounio | 26 |
| Tristinika | 19 |
| Valtos Beach | 19 |
| Vartholomino Ilias | 23 |

## Croatia

| | |
|---|---|
| Banjole | 49 |
| Baska | 53-54 |
| Bijela Uvala | 41 |
| Cervar | 40 |
| Cres Island | 54, 56 |
| Dubrovnik | 63 |
| Fazana | 51 |
| Funtana | 42, 46 |
| Hvar | 62 |
| Jezera Lovisca | 60 |
| Kazela | 48 |
| Korcula | 63 |
| Koversada | 44 |
| Krk Island | 52-53 |
| Lanterna | 39, 44 |
| Losinj Island | 56-57 |
| Mali Losinj | 56 |
| Mareda | 38 |
| Martinscica | 56 |
| Medulin | 48, 50 |
| Nerezine | 57 |
| Novalja | 57 |
| Novigrad | 38-39 |
| Omis | 61 |
| Orebic | 63 |
| Otok Pag | 57-58 |
| Paklenica | 59 |
| Porec | 39-41, 44, 46 |
| Porto Sole | 43 |
| Premantura | 50 |
| Primosten | 60 |
| Pula | 49-51 |
| Punat | 52-53 |
| Rapoca | 57 |
| Rovinj | 45, 47-49 |
| Savudrija | 37 |
| Seget Donji | 61 |
| Selce | 52 |
| Simuni | 58 |
| Umag | 36-38 |
| Valkanela | 42 |
| Vrsar | 42-44, 46 |
| Zadar | 58 |
| Zagreb | 52 |
| Zelena Laguna | 41 |
| Zivogosce | 62 |

## Slovenia

| | |
|---|---|
| Ankaran | 71 |
| Bled | 67 |
| Bohinjska Bistrica | 68 |
| Bovec | 70 |
| Catez ob Savi | 75 |
| Gozd Martuljek | 67 |
| Izola | 71 |
| Kobarid | 69-70 |
| Lesce | 66 |
| Ljubljana | 72 |
| Mojstrana | 68 |
| Moravske Toplice | 75 |
| Postojna | 72 |
| Prebold | 73-74 |
| Ptuj | 76 |
| Recica ob Savinji | 74 |
| Smlednik | 73 |
| Soca | 69 |

## Romania

| | |
|---|---|
| Aurel Vlaicu | 80 |
| Baneasa - Bucuresti | 83 |
| Bran | 83 |
| Brasov | 83 |
| Carta | 81 |
| Gilau | 82 |
| Sovata | 82 |
| Timisoara | 81 |

## Hungary

| | |
|---|---|
| Abádszálok | 101 |
| Aggtelek | 97 |
| Aszófö | 90 |
| Baja | 103 |
| Balatonakali | 92 |
| Balatonalmádi | 89 |
| Balatonberény | 87 |
| Balatonfüred | 90 |
| Balatonszemes | 87 |
| Balatonszepezd | 91 |
| Borsodbóta | 98 |
| Budapest | 95-96 |
| Cserszegtomaj | 89 |
| Debrecen | 101 |
| Dömös | 93 |
| Dunafoldvar | 105 |
| Eger-Szarvaskö | 99 |
| Györszentivan-Kertváros | 93 |
| Keszthely | 86 |
| Kiskunmajsa | 102 |
| Lenti | 88 |
| Magyaregregy | 104 |
| Magyarhertelend | 103 |
| Martfü | 102 |
| Pannonhalma | 94 |
| Révfülöp | 91 |
| Sály-Lator Puszta | 98 |
| Simontornya | 104 |
| Siófok | 88 |
| Sopron | 92 |
| Szilvásvárad | 100 |
| Tiszaújváros | 99 |
| Tokaj | 100 |
| Törökbálint | 95 |
| Üröm | 97 |
| Vajta | 94 |
| Visegrad | 96 |
| Zalakaros | 89 |
| Zamardi | 88 |

## Slovakia

| | |
|---|---|
| Bratislava | 109 |
| Kosice | 112 |
| Levoca | 111 |
| Liptovsky Trnovec | 112 |
| Martin | 111 |
| Namestovo | 111 |
| Piestany | 108 |
| Trencin | 109 |
| Turany | 110 |
| Zvolen | 110 |

## Czech Republic

| | |
|---|---|
| Benesov | 133 |
| Benesov u Prahy | 123 |
| Bojkovice | 133 |
| Breznice | 123 |
| Cervená Recice | 131 |
| Ceské Budejovice | 130 |
| Chvalsiny | 127 |
| Dolni Brezany | 121 |
| Frantiskovy Lazne | 117 |
| Frymburk | 128 |
| Hluboka Nad Vltavou | 128 |
| Hluboke Masuvky | 135 |
| Janovice | 118 |
| Januv Dul | 125 |
| Jihlava | 134 |
| Kostelec n Orlici | 127 |
| Liberec | 126 |
| Lipova Lazne | 132 |
| Litomerice | 124 |
| Lodenice | 124 |
| Mariánské Lázne | 118 |
| Mohelnice | 131 |
| Nové Straseci | 122 |
| Nyrany | 117 |
| Opatov na Morave | 135 |
| Plzen | 118 |
| Praha | 119-122 |
| Protivin | 128 |
| Roznov pod Radhostem | 132 |

## Town and Village Index continued

| | | | | | | |
|---|---|---|---|---|---|---|
| Sobeslav | 130 | Sopot | 143, 144 | **Latvia** | |
| Trebon | 129 | Stegna | 145 | Broceni | 164 |
| Velká Hledsebe | 116 | Torun | 141 | Dzeni | 160 |
| Veverska Bityska | 134 | Ukta | 145-146 | Gauja | 161 |
| Vrchlabi | 126 | Warsaw | 141 | Jurmala | 162 |
| Zandov | 125 | Wroclaw | 140 | Perkone | 163 |
| Zdikov | 129 | Wygryny | 146 | Riga | 161 |
| | | Zakopane | 147 | Usma | 162 |
| **Poland** | | Zielona | 140 | Ventspils | 163 |
| Antonin | 142 | Zwyiec | 150 | | |
| Bielsko Biala | 150 | | | **Estonia** | |
| Czestochowa | 148 | **Lithuania** | | Haapsalu | 168 |
| Gaj | 149 | Neringa | 157 | Hiiumaa Island | 170 |
| Janowice Wielkie | 139 | Rudiskes | 154 | Laagri | 169 |
| Jelenia Góra | 138-139 | Seirijai | 155 | Pärnu | 167 |
| Katowice | 149 | Silutes reaj | 156 | Saaremaa Island | 169-170 |
| Krakow | 148 | Trakai | 154 | Toila | 168 |
| Leba | 142-143 | Tytuvenai | 156 | Vösu | 169 |
| Mikolajki | 144 | Vilkaviskio | 156 | | |
| Niedzica | 146 | Vistytis | 155 | | |
| Oswiecim | 147 | Zalvariai | 153 | | |
| Rydzewo | 144 | | | | |

# www.alanrogers.com

Around 500 of Europe's finest campsites, all bookable at the click of a mouse.

- View 'at-the-gate' prices and availability
- Book as many or as few nights as you like
- Book direct - no middleman fees or 'extras'
- 24-hour convenience
- Pitches and mobile homes
- Secure on-line payment

All campsites are inspected & selected by Alan Rogers.
**Just Click and Go!**

INSPECTED CAMPSITES & SELECTED

**UnityPlus CARD**

**Unique Discounts**
FOR CAMPERS AND CARAVANNERS

Full details at www.unity-plus.com Request your UnityPlus Card today!

# Campsite Index by Number

## Greece

| | | |
|---|---|---|
| ?GR8000 | Batis | 16 |
| GR8120 | Poseidon Beach | 17 |
| GR8125 | Comitsa | 17 |
| GR8130 | Delphini | 17 |
| GR8135 | Kouyoni | 18 |
| GR8140 | Lacara | 18 |
| GR8145 | Areti | 18 |
| GR8150 | Isa | 19 |
| GR8220 | Valtos | 19 |
| GR8225 | Enjoy-Lichnos | 19 |
| GR8235 | Kalami Beach | 20 |
| GR8255 | Vrachos Kastraki | 20 |
| GR8280 | Sikia | 21 |
| GR8285 | Hellas International | 21 |
| GR8300 | Dounis Beach | 22 |
| GR8320 | Olympia | 22 |
| GR8325 | Fournia Beach | 22 |
| GR8330 | Ionion Beach | 23 |
| GR8335 | Diana | 23 |
| GR8340 | Alphios | 24 |
| GR8370 | Dionysus | 31 |
| GR8375 | Karda Beach | 31 |
| GR8385 | Paleokastritsa | 31 |
| GR8420 | Poros Beach | 32 |
| GR8425 | Kariotes Beach | 32 |
| GR8450 | Milos | 25 |
| GR8470 | Rovies | 24 |
| GR8475 | Pefki | 24 |
| GR8520 | Delphi | 25 |
| GR8525 | Chrissa | 25 |
| GR8560 | Ramnous | 26 |
| GR8565 | Kokkino Limanaki | 26 |
| GR8580 | Bacchus | 26 |
| GR8590 | Athens | 27 |
| GR8595 | Nea Kifissia | 27 |
| GR8605 | Alkioni | 28 |
| GR8615 | Blue Dolphin | 28 |
| GR8625 | Bekas | 28 |
| GR8635 | New Triton | 29 |
| GR8640 | Kastraki | 29 |
| GR8685 | Gythion Bay | 29 |
| GR8690 | Anemomilos | 30 |
| GR8695 | Finikes | 30 |
| GR8700 | Erodios | 30 |

## Croatia

| | | |
|---|---|---|
| CR6600 | Plitvice | 52 |
| CR6710 | Kanegra (Naturist) | 36 |
| CR6711 | Pineta | 37 |
| CR6712 | Stella Maris | 37 |
| CR6713 | Mareda | 38 |
| CR6714 | Finida | 38 |
| CR6715 | Park Umag | 39 |
| CR6716 | Lanternacamp | 39 |
| CR6718 | Solaris (Naturist) | 44 |
| CR6719 | Puntica | 46 |
| CR6720 | Ulika (Naturist) | 40 |
| CR6722 | Zelena Laguna | 40 |
| CR6724 | Bijela Uvala | 41 |
| CR6725 | Porto Sole | 43 |
| CR6726 | Istra (Naturist) | 42 |
| CR6727 | Valkanela | 42 |
| CR6728 | Orsera | 46 |
| CR6729 | Koversada (Naturist) | 44 |
| CR6730 | Amarin | 48 |
| CR6731 | Valalta (Naturist) | 47 |
| CR6732 | Polari | 47 |
| CR6733 | Vestar | 45 |
| CR6734 | Medulin | 50 |
| CR6735 | Kazela (Naturist) | 48 |
| CR6736 | Valdaliso | 49 |
| CR6737 | Stupice | 50 |
| CR6739 | Indije | 49 |
| CR6742 | Stoja | 51 |
| CR6745 | Bi-Village | 51 |
| CR6750 | Autocamp Selce | 52 |
| CR6755 | Pila | 52 |
| CR6756 | Konobe (Naturist) | 53 |
| CR6760 | Bunculuka (Naturist) | 53 |
| CR6761 | Zablace | 54 |
| CR6765 | Kovacine | 54 |
| CR6768 | Slatina | 56 |
| CR6772 | Poljana | 56 |
| CR6773 | Rapoca | 57 |
| CR6776 | Strasko | 57 |
| CR6778 | Simuni | 58 |
| CR6782 | Zaton | 58 |
| CR6830 | Paklenica | 59 |
| CR6833 | Rio | 59 |
| CR6840 | Jezera Lovisca | 60 |
| CR6845 | Adriatic | 60 |
| CR6850 | Camp Seget | 61 |
| CR6860 | Autocamp Galeb | 61 |
| CR6865 | Vira | 62 |
| CR6870 | Kamp Dole | 62 |
| CR6874 | Kalac-Korcula | 63 |
| CR6875 | Nevio | 63 |
| CR6890 | Solitudo | 63 |

## Slovenia

| | | |
|---|---|---|
| SV4100 | Spik | 67 |
| SV4150 | Kamne | 68 |
| SV4200 | Bled | 67 |
| SV4210 | Sobec | 66 |
| SV4235 | Klin | 69 |
| SV4250 | Danica Bohinj | 68 |
| SV4265 | Lazar | 69 |
| SV4270 | Koren | 70 |
| SV4280 | Polovnik | 70 |
| SV4300 | Belvedere | 71 |
| SV4310 | Adria | 71 |
| SV4330 | Pivka Jama | 72 |
| SV4340 | Ljubljana Resort | 72 |
| SV4360 | Smlednik | 73 |
| SV4400 | Dolina Prebold | 73 |
| SV4402 | Plevcak-Povse | 74 |
| SV4405 | Menina | 74 |
| SV4410 | Moravke Toplice | 75 |
| SV4415 | Terme Catez | 75 |
| SV4440 | Terme Ptuj | 76 |

## Romania

| | | |
|---|---|---|
| RO7040 | International | 81 |
| RO7070 | Aurel Vlaicu | 80 |
| RO7090 | De Oude Wilg | 81 |
| RO7130 | Eldorado | 82 |
| RO7150 | Vasskert | 82 |
| RO7160 | Vampire | 83 |
| RO7170 | Darste | 83 |
| RO7190 | Casa Alba | 83 |

## Hungary

| | | |
|---|---|---|
| HU5000 | Vadvirág | 87 |
| HU5020 | Balatonbereny (Naturist) | 87 |
| HU5024 | Lentri | 88 |
| HU5025 | Zalatour | 89 |
| HU5030 | Panoráma | 89 |
| HU5035 | Keszthely | 86 |
| HU5040 | Autós | 88 |
| HU5060 | Aranypart | 88 |
| HU5070 | Kristof | 89 |
| HU5080 | Diana | 90 |

## Campsite Index by Number continued

| | | |
|---|---|---|
| HU5090 | Füred | 90 |
| HU5100 | Ozon | 92 |
| HU5110 | Dömös | 93 |
| HU5120 | Pihenö | 93 |
| HU5130 | Panorama | 94 |
| HU5135 | Aucost | 94 |
| HU5150 | Fortuna | 95 |
| HU5155 | Római | 95 |
| HU5165 | Zugligeti Niche | 96 |
| HU5175 | Kek Duna (Visegrad) | 96 |
| HU5180 | Jumbo | 97 |
| HU5185 | Baradla | 97 |
| HU5187 | Amedi | 98 |
| HU5190 | Farm Lator | 98 |
| HU5197 | Termál (Tiszaujvaros) | 99 |
| HU5205 | Öko-Park | 99 |
| HU5210 | Diófaház | 100 |
| HU5220 | Tiszavirág | 100 |
| HU5240 | Dorcas | 101 |
| HU5245 | Füzes | 101 |
| HU5255 | Martfü | 102 |
| HU5260 | Jonathermál | 102 |
| HU5290 | Nap a Szívemben | 104 |
| HU5300 | Kek-Duna (Dunafoldvar) | 105 |
| HU5310 | Sugovica | 103 |
| HU5315 | Forras | 103 |
| HU5320 | Máré Vára | 104 |
| HU5370 | Napfeny | 91 |
| HU5380 | Venus | 91 |
| HU5385 | Levendula (Naturist) | 92 |

### Slovakia

| | | |
|---|---|---|
| SK4900 | Trusalová | 110 |
| SK4905 | Stara Hora | 111 |
| SK4910 | Turiec | 111 |
| SK4915 | Liptovsky Trnovec | 112 |
| SK4920 | Trencin | 109 |
| SK4925 | Lodenica | 108 |
| SK4940 | Neresnica | 110 |
| SK4950 | Zlaté Piesky | 109 |
| SK4980 | Levocská Dolina | 111 |
| SK4990 | Salas Barca | 112 |

### Czech Republic

| | | |
|---|---|---|
| CZ4590 | Lisci Farma | 126 |
| CZ4640 | Areal Jadran | 117 |
| CZ4650 | Luxor | 116 |
| CZ4655 | Stanowitz Stanoviste | 118 |
| CZ4685 | Litomerice | 124 |
| CZ4690 | Slunce | 125 |
| CZ4695 | 2000 | 125 |
| CZ4700 | Jaroslav Kohoutek | 126 |
| CZ4710 | Chvalsiny | 127 |
| CZ4720 | Frymburk | 128 |
| CZ4730 | Kostelec | 128 |
| CZ4735 | Blanice | 128 |
| CZ4740 | Hracholusky | 117 |
| CZ4745 | U Dvou Orechu | 118 |
| CZ4750 | Bilá Hora | 118 |
| CZ4760 | Mlécna Dráha (Naturist) | 129 |
| CZ4765 | Trebon | 129 |
| CZ4770 | Dlouhá Louka | 130 |
| CZ4775 | Karvánky | 130 |
| CZ4778 | Kovarna | 131 |
| CZ4780 | Konopiste | 123 |
| CZ4785 | Drusus | 119 |
| CZ4795 | Cisarska Louka | 120 |
| CZ4800 | Caravancamp | 119 |
| CZ4805 | Dzban Praha | 120 |
| CZ4815 | Triocamp | 121 |
| CZ4820 | Valek | 124 |
| CZ4825 | Bucek | 122 |
| CZ4830 | Horjany | 123 |
| CZ4840 | Oase | 121 |
| CZ4845 | Busek Praha | 122 |
| CZ4860 | Orlice | 127 |
| CZ4870 | AutoMorava | 131 |
| CZ4880 | Roznov | 132 |
| CZ4885 | Bobrovnik | 132 |
| CZ4890 | Bojkovice | 133 |
| CZ4892 | Bongerd | 133 |
| CZ4894 | Pavov | 134 |
| CZ4895 | Hana | 134 |
| CZ4896 | Country | 135 |
| CZ4898 | Vidlak | 135 |

### Poland

| | | |
|---|---|---|
| PL3000 | Stoneczna Polana | 139 |
| PL3002 | Camping Park Nr. 130 | 138 |
| PL3003 | Boduwico | 139 |
| PL3006 | Olimpijski 117 | 140 |
| PL3010 | Lesny | 140 |
| PL3035 | Lido | 142 |
| PL3050 | Tramp | 141 |
| PL3070 | Morski | 142 |
| PL3080 | Intercamp | 143 |
| PL3090 | Kamienny Potok | 143 |
| PL3100 | Przy Plazy | 144 |
| PL3110 | Stegna | 145 |
| PL3155 | KamA | 144 |
| PL3160 | Echo | 144 |
| PL3170 | Galindia Mazurski Eden | 145 |
| PL3175 | Stanica Wodna | 146 |
| PL3190 | Horst Kruska | 146 |
| PL3210 | Astur | 141 |
| PL3230 | Olenka | 148 |
| PL3250 | Auto | 149 |
| PL3280 | Korona | 149 |
| PL3300 | Polana Sosny | 146 |
| PL3310 | Ustup | 147 |
| PL3320 | Auschwitz Centre | 147 |
| PL3330 | Ondraszek | 150 |
| PL3335 | C'est la Vie | 150 |
| PL3340 | Smok | 148 |

### Lithuania

| | | |
|---|---|---|
| LI2010 | Apple Island | 153 |
| LI2030 | Slenyje | 154 |
| LI2035 | Harmonie | 154 |
| LI2050 | Vitruna | 155 |
| LI2060 | Viktorija | 155 |
| LI2065 | Pusele | 156 |
| LI2090 | Sedula | 156 |
| LI2120 | Ventaine | 156 |
| LI2130 | Nida | 157 |

### Latvia

| | | |
|---|---|---|
| LA1020 | Meleku Licis | 160 |
| LA1030 | Gauja | 161 |
| LA1040 | Riga City | 161 |
| LA1060 | Nemo | 162 |
| LA1080 | Usma | 162 |
| LA1100 | Piejuras | 163 |
| LA1130 | Verbelnieki | 163 |
| LA1150 | Radi | 164 |

### Estonia

| | | |
|---|---|---|
| ET0010 | Konse | 167 |
| ET0015 | Pikseke | 168 |
| ET0020 | Peoleo | 169 |
| ET0040 | Eesti | 169 |
| ET0050 | Toila Spa | 168 |
| ET0100 | Tehumardi | 170 |
| ET0105 | Mandjala | 169 |
| ET0120 | Randmäe | 170 |

# Campsite Index by Country and Name

## Greece
| | | |
|---|---|---|
| GR8605 | Alkioni | 28 |
| GR8340 | Alphios | 24 |
| GR8690 | Anemomilos | 30 |
| GR8145 | Areti | 18 |
| GR8590 | Athens | 27 |
| GR8580 | Bacchus | 26 |
| GR8000 | Batis | 16 |
| GR8625 | Bekas | 28 |
| GR8615 | Blue Dolphin | 28 |
| GR8525 | Chrissa | 25 |
| GR8125 | Comitsa | 17 |
| GR8520 | Delphi | 25 |
| GR8130 | Delphini | 17 |
| GR8335 | Diana | 23 |
| GR8370 | Dionysus | 31 |
| GR8300 | Dounis Beach | 22 |
| GR8225 | Enjoy-Lichnos | 19 |
| GR8700 | Erodios | 30 |
| GR8695 | Finikes | 30 |
| GR8325 | Fournia Beach | 22 |
| GR8685 | Gythion Bay | 29 |
| GR8285 | Hellas International | 21 |
| GR8330 | Ionion Beach | 23 |
| GR8150 | Isa | 19 |
| GR8235 | Kalami Beach | 20 |
| GR8375 | Karda Beach | 31 |
| GR8425 | Kariotes Beach | 32 |
| GR8640 | Kastraki | 29 |
| GR8565 | Kokkino Limanaki | 26 |
| GR8135 | Kouyoni | 18 |
| GR8140 | Lacara | 18 |
| GR8450 | Milos | 25 |
| GR8595 | Nea Kifissia | 27 |
| GR8635 | New Triton | 29 |
| GR8320 | Olympia | 22 |
| GR8385 | Paleokastritsa | 31 |
| GR8475 | Pefki | 24 |
| GR8420 | Poros Beach | 32 |
| GR8120 | Poseidon Beach | 17 |
| GR8560 | Ramnous | 26 |
| GR8470 | Rovies | 24 |
| GR8280 | Sikia | 21 |
| GR8220 | Valtos | 19 |
| GR8255 | Vrachos Kastraki | 20 |

## Croatia
| | | |
|---|---|---|
| CR6845 | Adriatic | 60 |
| CR6730 | Amarin | 48 |
| CR6860 | Autocamp Galeb | 61 |
| CR6750 | Autocamp Selce | 52 |
| CR6724 | Bijela Uvala | 41 |
| CR6745 | Bi-Village | 51 |
| CR6760 | Bunculuka (Naturist) | 53 |
| CR6850 | Camp Seget | 61 |
| CR6714 | Finida | 38 |
| CR6739 | Indije | 49 |
| CR6726 | Istra (Naturist) | 42 |
| CR6840 | Jezera Loviscan | 60 |
| CR6874 | Kalac-Korcula | 63 |
| CR6870 | Kamp Dole | 62 |
| CR6710 | Kanegra (Naturist) | 36 |
| CR6735 | Kazela (Naturist) | 48 |
| CR6756 | Konobe (Naturist) | 53 |
| CR6765 | Kovacine | 54 |
| CR6729 | Koversada (Naturist) | 44 |
| CR6716 | Lanternacamp | 39 |
| CR6713 | Mareda | 38 |
| CR6734 | Medulin | 50 |
| CR6875 | Nevio | 63 |
| CR6728 | Orsera | 46 |
| CR6830 | Paklenica | 59 |
| CR6715 | Park Umag | 39 |
| CR6755 | Pila | 52 |
| CR6711 | Pineta | 37 |
| CR6600 | Plitvice | 52 |
| CR6732 | Polari | 47 |
| CR6772 | Poljana | 56 |
| CR6725 | Porto Sole | 43 |
| CR6719 | Puntica | 46 |
| CR6773 | Rapoca | 57 |
| CR6833 | Rio | 59 |
| CR6778 | Simuni | 58 |
| CR6768 | Slatina | 56 |
| CR6718 | Solaris (Naturist) | 44 |
| CR6890 | Solitudo | 63 |
| CR6712 | Stella Maris | 37 |
| CR6742 | Stoja | 51 |
| CR6776 | Strasko | 57 |
| CR6737 | Stupice | 50 |
| CR6720 | Ulika (Naturist) | 40 |
| CR6731 | Valalta (Naturist) | 47 |
| CR6736 | Valdaliso | 49 |
| CR6727 | Valkanela | 42 |
| CR6733 | Vestar | 45 |
| CR6865 | Vira | 62 |
| CR6761 | Zablace | 54 |
| CR6782 | Zaton | 58 |
| CR6722 | Zelena Laguna | 40 |

## Slovenia
| | | |
|---|---|---|
| SV4310 | Adria | 71 |
| SV4300 | Belvedere | 71 |
| SV4200 | Bled | 67 |
| SV4250 | Danica Bohinj | 68 |
| SV4400 | Dolina Prebold | 73 |
| SV4150 | Kamne | 68 |
| SV4235 | Klin | 69 |
| SV4270 | Koren | 70 |
| SV4265 | Lazar | 69 |
| SV4340 | Ljubljana Resort | 72 |
| SV4405 | Menina | 74 |
| SV4410 | Moravke Toplice | 75 |
| SV4330 | Pivka Jama | 72 |
| SV4402 | Plevcak-Povse | 74 |
| SV4280 | Polovnik | 70 |
| SV4360 | Smlednik | 73 |
| SV4210 | Sobec | 66 |
| SV4100 | Spik | 67 |
| SV4415 | Terme Catez | 75 |
| SV4440 | Terme Ptuj | 76 |

## Romania
| | | |
|---|---|---|
| RO7070 | Aurel Vlaicu | 80 |
| RO7190 | Casa Alba | 83 |
| RO7170 | Darste | 83 |
| RO7090 | De Oude Wilg | 81 |
| RO7130 | Eldorado | 82 |
| RO7040 | International | 81 |
| RO7160 | Vampire | 83 |
| RO7150 | Vasskert | 82 |

## Hungary
| | | |
|---|---|---|
| HU5187 | Amedi | 98 |
| HU5060 | Aranypart | 88 |
| HU5135 | Aucost | 94 |
| HU5040 | Autós | 88 |
| HU5020 | Balatonbereny (Naturist) | 87 |
| HU5185 | Baradla | 97 |
| HU5080 | Diana | 90 |
| HU5210 | Diófaház | 100 |
| HU5110 | Dömös | 93 |

205

## Campsite Index by Country and Name continued

| | | | | | | |
|---|---|---|---|---|---|---|
| HU5240 | Dorcas | 101 | | CZ4650 | Luxor | 116 |
| HU5190 | Farm Lator | 98 | | CZ4760 | Mlécna Dráha (Naturist) | 129 |
| HU5315 | Forras | 103 | | CZ4840 | Oase | 121 |
| HU5150 | Fortuna | 95 | | CZ4860 | Orlice | 127 |
| HU5090 | Füred | 90 | | CZ4894 | Pavov | 134 |
| HU5245 | Füzes | 101 | | CZ4880 | Roznov | 132 |
| HU5260 | Jonathermál | 102 | | CZ4690 | Slunce | 125 |
| HU5180 | Jumbo | 97 | | CZ4655 | Stanowitz Stanoviste | 118 |
| HU5175 | Kek Duna (Visegrad) | 96 | | CZ4765 | Trebon | 129 |
| HU5300 | Kek-Duna (Dunafoldvar) | 105 | | CZ4815 | Triocamp | 121 |
| HU5035 | Keszthely | 86 | | CZ4745 | U Dvou Orechu | 118 |
| HU5070 | Kristof | 89 | | CZ4820 | Valek | 124 |
| HU5024 | Lentri | 88 | | CZ4898 | Vidlak | 135 |
| HU5385 | Levendula (Naturist) | 92 | | | | |
| HU5320 | Máré Vára | 104 | | **Poland** | | |
| HU5255 | Martfü | 102 | | PL3210 | Astur | 141 |
| HU5290 | Nap a Szívemben | 104 | | PL3320 | Auschwitz Centre | 147 |
| HU5370 | Napfeny | 91 | | PL3250 | Auto | 149 |
| HU5205 | Öko-Park | 99 | | PL3003 | Boduwico | 139 |
| HU5100 | Ozon | 92 | | PL3335 | C'est la Vie | 150 |
| HU5130 | Panorama | 94 | | PL3002 | Camping Park Nr. 130 | 138 |
| HU5030 | Panoráma | 89 | | PL3160 | Echo | 144 |
| HU5120 | Pihenö | 93 | | PL3170 | Galindia Mazurski Eden | 145 |
| HU5155 | Római | 95 | | PL3190 | Horst Kruska | 146 |
| HU5310 | Sugovica | 103 | | PL3080 | Intercamp | 143 |
| HU5197 | Termál (Tiszaujvaros) | 99 | | PL3155 | KamA | 144 |
| HU5220 | Tiszavirág | 100 | | PL3090 | Kamienny Potok | 143 |
| HU5000 | Vadvirág | 87 | | PL3280 | Korona | 149 |
| HU5380 | Venus | 91 | | PL3010 | Lesny | 140 |
| HU5025 | Zalatour | 89 | | PL3035 | Lido | 142 |
| HU5165 | Zugligeti Niche | 96 | | PL3070 | Morski | 142 |
| | | | | PL3230 | Olenka | 148 |
| **Slovakia** | | | | PL3006 | Olimpijski 117 | 140 |
| SK4980 | Levocská Dolina | 111 | | PL3330 | Ondraszek | 150 |
| SK4915 | Liptovsky Trnovec | 112 | | PL3300 | Polana Sosny | 146 |
| SK4925 | Lodenica | 108 | | PL3100 | Przy Plazy | 144 |
| SK4940 | Neresnica | 110 | | PL3340 | Smok | 148 |
| SK4990 | Salas Barca | 112 | | PL3175 | Stanica Wodna | 146 |
| SK4905 | Stara Hora | 111 | | PL3110 | Stegna | 145 |
| SK4920 | Trencin | 109 | | PL3000 | Stoneczna Polana | 139 |
| SK4900 | Trusalová | 110 | | PL3050 | Tramp | 141 |
| SK4910 | Turiec | 111 | | PL3310 | Ustup | 147 |
| SK4950 | Zlaté Piesky | 109 | | | | |
| | | | | **Lithuania** | | |
| **Czech Republic** | | | | LI2010 | Apple Island | 153 |
| CZ4695 | 2000 | 125 | | LI2035 | Harmonie | 154 |
| CZ4640 | Areal Jadran | 117 | | LI2130 | Nida | 157 |
| CZ4870 | AutoMorava | 131 | | LI2065 | Pusele | 156 |
| CZ4750 | Bilá Hora | 118 | | LI2090 | Sedula | 156 |
| CZ4735 | Blanice | 128 | | LI2030 | Slenyje | 154 |
| CZ4885 | Bobrovnik | 132 | | LI2120 | Ventaine | 156 |
| CZ4890 | Bojkovice | 133 | | LI2060 | Viktorija | 155 |
| CZ4892 | Bongerd | 133 | | LI2050 | Vitruna | 155 |
| CZ4825 | Bucek | 122 | | | | |
| CZ4845 | Busek Praha | 122 | | **Latvia** | | |
| CZ4800 | Caravancamp | 119 | | LA1030 | Gauja | 161 |
| CZ4710 | Chvalsiny | 127 | | LA1020 | Meleku Licis | 160 |
| CZ4795 | Cisarska Louka | 120 | | LA1060 | Nemo | 162 |
| CZ4896 | Country | 135 | | LA1100 | Piejuras | 163 |
| CZ4770 | Dlouhá Louka | 130 | | LA1150 | Radi | 164 |
| CZ4785 | Drusus | 119 | | LA1040 | Riga City | 161 |
| CZ4805 | Dzban Praha | 120 | | LA1080 | Usma | 162 |
| CZ4720 | Frymburk | 128 | | LA1130 | Verbelnieki | 163 |
| CZ4895 | Hana | 134 | | | | |
| CZ4830 | Horjany | 123 | | **Estonia** | | |
| CZ4740 | Hracholusky | 117 | | ET0040 | Eesti | 169 |
| CZ4700 | Jaroslav Kohoutek | 126 | | ET0010 | Konse | 167 |
| CZ4775 | Karvánky | 130 | | ET0105 | Mandjala | 169 |
| CZ4780 | Konopiste | 123 | | ET0020 | Peoleo | 169 |
| CZ4730 | Kostelec | 128 | | ET0015 | Pikseke | 168 |
| CZ4778 | Kovarna | 131 | | ET0120 | Randmäe | 170 |
| CZ4590 | Lisci Farma | 126 | | ET0100 | Tehumardi | 170 |
| CZ4685 | Litomerice | 124 | | ET0050 | Toila Spa | 168 |

# Tell Us About the Alan Rogers Guides!

We're keen to constantly improve our service to you and the key to this is information. If we don't know what makes our readers 'tick' then it's difficult to offer you more of what you want.

**WIN A COMPLETE SET OF ALAN ROGERS GUIDES**
Return this completed questionnaire and you could win a complete set of 2008 Alan Rogers Guides. Why not complete an on-line version of this? Go to www.alanrogers.com/feedback

## About the Alan Rogers Guides

1. **For how many years have you used the Alan Rogers Guides?**
   Never    1-2 yrs    3-6 yrs    7-10 yrs    Over 10 yrs

2. **How frequently do you refer to it?**
   Never    Each year    Every 2 yrs    Every 3 yrs

3. **How frequently do you buy a new copy?**
   Never    Each year    Every 2 yrs    Every 3 yrs

4. **If you lend it to friends, how many others might refer to it?**
   1    2    3    4    Over 4

5. **Please rate the Alan Rogers Guides on a scale of 1–10 where 10 is excellent and 1 is extremely poor**
   1    2    3    4    5    6    7    8    9    10

6. **Do you have any comments about the Alan Rogers Guides?**

7. **What do you consider to be the best thing about the guides?**
   Independent reviews    Honest descriptions    Accurate information    Range of sites    Depth of information

   Other

8. **What do you consider to be the worst thing about the guides?**

9. **How many sites featured in the guides have you visited in the past?** *(best estimate)*

10. **Can you comment on any other campsite guides?**
    Title    Your opinion

## About Your Holidays

11. **a) Do you own any of the following?**
    Caravan    Motorhome    Trailer Tent    Tent

    Other *(please specify)*

    **b) How many times a year do you use it?**
    1    2-3    4-6    7-10    More than 10

12. **When on holiday, do you participate in any of the following?**
    Fishing    Golf    Cycling    Sailing/Boating    Walking    Bird Watching

    Other *(please specify)*

13. **How many years have you been camping / caravanning?**
    3 yrs or less    4 – 7 yrs    8 – 12 yrs    13 – 15 yrs    16 – 20 yrs    Over 20 yrs

**WIN A COMPLETE SET OF ALAN ROGERS GUIDES**

**WIN A COMPLETE SET OF ALAN ROGERS GUIDES**

## About You

Mr/Mrs/Ms, etc.　　　　Initial　　　　　　Surname

Address

　　　　　　　　　　　　　　　　　　　　　Post code

e-mail address　　　　　　　@　　　　　Telephone

14　**Your age**　　30 and under　　　　31-50　　　　51-65　　　　Over 65

15　**Do you have children – if so, how old is the youngest?**
　　　　　　　　　　　　6 and under　　　　7-12　　　　Over 12

16　**Do you work (full or part time)?**　　　　　　Yes　　　　No

17　**Are you retired?**　　　　　　　　　　　　　　Yes　　　　No

## About Your Leisure Time

18　**Are you a member of any caravan/motorhome clubs?**
　　　The Caravan Club　　The Camping & Caravanning Club　　The Motor Caravanners Club

　　　Other *(please specify)*

19　**Are you a member of the following?**
　　　　　National Trust　　English Heritage　　RSPB　　CSMA　　Ramblers

20　**Which (if any) camping/caravanning magazines do you read regularly?**
　　　　MMM　　Practical Motorhome　　Practical Caravan　　Caravan Life　　Which Motorcaravan　　Motor-caravan　　Caravan

21　**Which other magazines do you read regularly?**

22　**Which newspapers do you read regularly?**
　　　Express　　Mail　　Telegraph　　Times　　Guardian　　Observer　　Sun

　　　Other (please specify)

23　**Do you enjoy any particular hobbies?** *(please specify)*

24　**Do you have regular access to the internet?**　　　Yes　　　No

　　　If yes, which camping/caravanning websites do you visit regularly?

## And Finally

25　**Do you have any useful camping/caravanning tips?**

26　**If you could change one thing about camping/caravanning holidays what would it be?**

*We may wish to publish your comments, please tick this box if you would prefer us not to.*

Might you be interested in becoming an Alan Rogers site inspector?
If so, please tick the box and we will send you further information ☐

*Camping Cheque and Alan Rogers may use this data to send you information and Special Offers. Please tick here if you do not wish to receive such information*

**Thank you very much for your time and trouble in completing this questionnaire
Please return to: Alan Rogers Travel Service, FREEPOST NAT17734, Cranbrook, TN17 1BR**